Prentice Hall
Word and Information Processing
on Microcomputers Series

Dennis P. Curtin, Series Editor

Curtin, Information Processing: Concepts and Applications
Curtin, WordPerfect® 5.1 Procedures Manual
Curtin, Microsoft® Word 5.5 Procedures Manual
Custer, Skill Building Word Processing Exercises
Muehlman, Word Processing Applications and Exercises
Muehlman, Legal Word Processing Exercises

Original books in Series:

Curtin, Word Processing on Microcomputers: Systems and Procedures
Curtin, WordPerfect® 4.2 and 5.0 Procedures Manuals
Curtin, WordStar® 4 Procedures Manual
Curtin, Microsoft® Word 4 Procedures Manual
Curtin, DisplayWrite® Procedures Manual
Curtin, Multimate Advantage® II Procedures Manual
Deitel/Curtin, Microsoft® Word 4 Procedures Manual for the Macintosh™
Lee, WordStar® 5.5 Procedures Manual
Muehlman, Word Processing on Microcomputers: Applications and Exercises
Muehlman, Word Processing on Microcomputers: Applications and Exercises, Alternate Edition

Also by Dennis P. Curtin:

Compass Series (Computer Application Software Series)

Application Software: With WordPerfect®, Lotus® 1-2-3®, dBASE®
dBASE® IV: A Short Course
DOS: A Short Course
DOS 4: A Complete Course
Lotus® 1-2-3®: A Short Course
Lotus® 1-2-3®: A Complete Course
WordPerfect® 5.0: A Short Course
WordPerfect® 5.0: A Complete Course
WordPerfect® 5.1: A Short Course
Telecommunications with Procomm®: A Short Course

Information Processing
Concepts and Applications

DENNIS P. CURTIN

PRENTICE HALL CAREER & TECHNOLOGY, Englewood Cliffs, New Jersey 07632

Library of Congress Cataloging-in-Publication Data

Curtin, Dennis P.
　　Information processing : concepts & applications / Dennis P. Curtin.
　　　　p.　　cm.
　　Includes index.
　　ISBN 0-13-463696-1
　　1. Electronic data processing.　2. Microcomputers—Programming. 3. Computer software.　I. Title.
QA76.C885　　1991　　　　　　　　　　　　　　　　　　91-207
004.16—dc20　　　　　　　　　　　　　　　　　　　　　　CIP

This book is dedicated to Emily. Her progress while I was writing this book far exceeded my own. This was only partly due to her distracting me at every possible opportunity.

Editorial/production supervision: Nancy Benjamin
Cover and interior design: Linda J. Den Heyer Rosa
Manufacturing buyer: Ed O'Dougherty
Prepress buyer: Ilene Levy
Acquisitions editor: Liz Kendall

©1991 by Prentice Hall Career & Technology
Prentice-Hall, Inc.
A Paramount Communications Company
Englewood Cliffs, New Jersey 07632

All rights reserved. No part of this book may be
reproduced, in any form or by any means,
without permission in writing from the publisher.

Printed in the United States of America
10　9　8　7　6　5　4　3　2

ISBN 0-13-463696-1

Prentice-Hall International (UK) Limited, *London*
Prentice-Hall of Australia Pty. Limited, *Sydney*
Prentice-Hall Canada Inc., *Toronto*
Prentice-Hall Hispanoamericana, S.A., *Mexico*
Prentice-Hall of India Private Limited, *New Delhi*
Prentice-Hall of Japan, Inc., *Tokyo*
Simon & Schuster Asia Pte. Ltd., *Singapore*
Editora Prentice-Hall do Brasil, Ltda., *Rio de Janeiro*

Contents

PREFACE   x

CHAPTER 1   Computer Systems   1

System 2   Hardware 2   Software 3

1-1 INFORMATION PROCESSING IN THE MODERN OFFICE   4

What Is Information Processing? 4   How Is Information Processed? 5   The Information Processing Cycle 7   Computers in Business 7   Exercise 1-1A Listing Activities That Are Affected by Computers 8   Exercise 1-1B Locating Library Resources 9

1-2 THE DIGITAL REVOLUTION   10

Paul Revere's Ride — The First Digital Revolution? 11   The Telegraph — The First Digital Code 11   The Transistor — The Computer's Digital Device 13   Exercise 1-2A Converting Bytes, Kilobytes, and Megabytes 16

1-3 THE COMPUTER   17

The Central Processing Unit 19   Memory 20   Ports 22   Expansion Slots and Boards 23   Caring for Your Computer 24   Exercise 1-3A Investigating Types of Computers 25   Exercise 1-3B Describing Computers in the Lab 26   Exercise 1-3C Identifying Your Computer's Ports 26

1-4 INPUT DEVICES   28

Keyboards 28   Scanners 31   Voice Input Devices 33   Exercise 1-4A Identifying Keys on the Keyboard 35   Exercise 1-4B Identifying Keyboard Indicators 35

1-5 OUTPUT DEVICES — THE DISPLAY   37

Cathode Ray Tubes (CRTs) 37   Flat-Panel Displays 37   Color 38   The Screen Display 39   Exercise 1-5A Investigating Display Screens 41   Exercise 1-5B Identifying the Display Screen's Controls 42   Exercise 1-5C Exploring Flat-Panel Displays 42

1-6 OUTPUT DEVICES — THE PRINTER   43

How Characters Are Formed 43   How Characters Are Transferred to Paper 45   Printer Accessories 48   Using a Printer 49   Exercise 1-6A Determining How Printers Print 53   Exercise 1-6B Describing Printers in the Lab 53   Exercise 1-6C Identifying the Printer's Controls 54

1-7 INTRODUCTION TO APPLICATIONS PROGRAMS 55

Word Processing and Desktop Publishing Programs 55   Spreadsheet Programs 56   Database Programs 57   Graphics Programs 58   Communications Programs 58   Integrated Programs 59   Program Updates 60   Exercise 1-7A Read a Review 60   Exercise 1-7B Matching Tasks and Applications Programs 60

CHAPTER 2 Disks, Disk Drives, and Operating Systems 62

2-1 EXTERNAL STORAGE DEVICES 63

Floppy Disks and Disk Drives 63   Hard Disk Drives 66   Optical Disks 66   Protecting and Caring for Your Files and Disks 68   Exercise 2-1A Identify Parts of a Floppy Disk 71

2-2 INTRODUCTION TO THE OPERATING SYSTEM 72

The Functions of an Operating System 72   MS-DOS and PC-DOS 74   Graphical Operating System Environments 75   Exercise 2-2A View a Video 76

2-3 LOADING AND QUITTING THE OPERATING SYSTEM 77

The Command Prompt and the DOS Shell 78   Quitting DOS 280   Exercise 2-3A Booting Your System 81

2-4 UNDERSTANDING FILENAMES AND DRIVES 82

Assigning Filenames 82   The Default and Other Drives 83   Exercise 2-4A Assigning Filenames 85

2-5 USING DOS TO MANAGE YOUR DISKS AND FILES 87

Using Operating System Functions from Within Applications Programs 96   Exercise 2-5A Matching DOS Commands and Functions 97   Exercise 2-5B Specify Your System's Disks 97

2-6 WORKING WITH HARD DISKS 99

Changing Directories and Specifying Paths 99   Making and Removing Directories 103   Listing Directories and Files 104   Exercise 2-6A Creating Directories 105

2-7 SPECIAL DOS FILES 106

CONFIG.SYS Files 106   AUTOEXEC Files 106   Creating or Editing AUTOEXEC.BAT and CONFIG.SYS Files 108   Exercise 2-7A Exploring Your CONFIG.SYS and AUTOEXEC.BAT Files 109

CHAPTER 3 Word Processing and Desktop Publishing Applications 110

3-1 WORD PROCESSING PROCEDURES— AN OVERVIEW 112

Step 1 Load the Program 112   Step 2 Open a New Document (Or Edit an Existing One) 112   Step 3 Enter the Document 113   Step 4 Edit and Revise the Document 113   Step 5 Format the Document 114   Step 6 Save the Document 115   Step 7 Print the Document 115   Step 8 Continue or Quit 115   Exercise 3-1A Complete the Simulation on Screen 116

3-2 TYPICAL WORD PROCESSING PROGRAMS 117

WordPerfect 118   Microsoft Word 119   Word for Windows 120   Microsoft Works 121   Exercise 3-2A Complete the Simulation on Screen 122   Exercise 3-2B Identifying Screen Elements 122

3-3 LOADING AND QUITTING APPLICATIONS PROGRAMS 123

Loading Programs 123   Quitting the Program 124   Exercise 3-3A Loading Programs on Your System 125

3-4 EXECUTING COMMANDS 126

Getting Help 126   Using Function Keys and Typing Commands 126   Using Menus 128   Responding to Prompts and Dialog Boxes 129   Using a Mouse 131   Exercise 3-4A Preparing a Quick Reference Card 133

3-5 ENTERING DOCUMENTS 134

Keyboarding 134   Word Wrap 135   Carriage Returns 135   Correcting Mistakes 136   Tab Stops 136   Tables 138   Indents 139   Glossaries 139   Exercise 3-5A Indenting Text 140   Exercise 3-5B Setting Tab Stops 140

3-6 SAVING AND RETRIEVING FILES 142

Saving Files 142   Retrieving Files 142   File Types 143   File Exchange 146   Exercise 3-6A Saving a File 147   Exercise 3-6B Retrieving a File 148

3-7 EDITING DOCUMENTS 149

Moving the Cursor and Scrolling the Screen 149   Inserting or Replacing Text 151   Displaying Hidden Characters and Codes 151   Deleting Text 152   Undoing Mistakes 152   Joining Lines of Text Separated by Carriage Returns 152   Paragraph Realigning and Repagination 153   Working with Blocks 155   Search and Replace 158   Spelling Checkers 160   Thesauruses 160   Document Compare 160   Redlining and Strikeout 161   Exercise 3-7A Cursor Movement Commands 161   Exercise 3-7B Delete Commands 162   Exercise 3-7C Block Commands 162

3-8 FORMATTING DOCUMENTS 164

Page Breaks 166   Page Numbers 168   Text Alignment 168   Hyphenation 170   Text Emphasis 170   Horizontal Layout 171   Vertical Layout 172   Headers and Footers 173   Footnotes and Endnotes 175   Exercise 3-8A Formatting Documents 176

3-9 MERGE PRINTING 178

The Primary Document 179   The Secondary Document 179   Merge Printing 180   Exercise 3-9A Plan a Secondary Document 181   Exercise 3-9B Merge Print a Document 182

3-10 DESKTOP PUBLISHING 183

Fonts 184   Graphic Images 188   Style Sheets 189   Special Characters 190   Adding Lines and Boxes 190   Printing in Columns 192   Automatically Generated Lists 193   Exercise 3-10A Desktop Publishing Commands 194

CHAPTER 4 Spreadsheet Applications 196

4-1 SPREADSHEET PROCEDURES—AN OVERVIEW 198

Step 1 Load the Program 199   Step 2 Enter Labels 199   Step 3 Enter Numbers 199   Step 4 Enter Formulas 200   Step 5 Enter a Function 200   Step 6 Explore What-Ifs 201   Step 7 Print the Model 202   Step 8 Save the Model 203   Step 9 Quit or Clear the Screen 203   Exercise 4-1A Complete the Simulation on Screen 203

4-2 TYPICAL SPREADSHEET PROGRAMS 205

The Spreadsheet Screen Display 205   Getting Around a Spreadsheet 206   Typical Programs 207   Exercise 4-2A Complete the Simulation on Screen 211   Exercise 4-2B Identifying Cursor Movement Keys 211

Indicates core concepts.

4-3 ENTERING LABELS AND NUMBERS   213

Entering Labels 213   Entering Numbers 214   Exercise 4-3A Entering Labels 215   Exercise 4-3B Turning Protection On and Off 215

4-4 UNDERSTANDING RANGES   216

Global Commands 216   Range Commands 216   Naming Ranges 217   Exercise 4-4A Specifying Ranges 218

4-5 EDITING MODELS   219

Editing Cell Contents 219   Inserting and Deleting Rows and Columns 220   Exercise 4-5A Editing Cell Contents 221   Exercise 4-5B Inserting a Column 221

4-6 FORMULAS   222

Operators—The Basic Building Blocks 222   The Order of Operations 223   Constants and Variables 224   Ways to Enter Formulas 225   Exercise 4-6A Pointing to Enter Formulas 226

4-7 FUNCTIONS   227

Financial Functions 228   Statistical Functions 228   Numeric and Mathematical Functions 229   Date and Time Functions 229   Exercise 4-7A Functions That Sum and Average 231

4-8 CHANGING A MODEL'S APPEARANCE   232

Column Widths 232   Formatting Text 232   Formatting Values 232   Exercise 4-8A Changing Column Widths 233   Exercise 4-8B Formatting Numbers 233

4-9 COPYING AND MOVING DATA   234

Copying Data 234   Moving Data 234   Relative and Absolute Cell References 236   Exercise 4-9A Copying Data 239   Exercise 4-9B Moving Data 239

4-10 BUSINESS GRAPHICS   241

Creating Graphs 241   Types of Business Graphs 243   Exercise 4-10A Identifying Graph Options 246   Exercise 4-10B Selecting Graph Types 246

4-11 AUTOMATING WITH MACROS   248

Recording Macros 248   Macro Languages 248   User-Defined Menus 249   Exercise 4-11A Creating a Graph 250

CHAPTER 5   Database Management Applications   251

5-1 DATABASE MANAGEMENT PROCEDURES—AN OVERVIEW   253

Step 1 Planning the Database 253   Step 2 Defining the Database 253   Step 3 Entering Data 254   Step 4 Updating the Database 255   Step 5 Querying the Database 256   Step 6 Printing Reports 256   Exercise 5-1A Complete the Simulation on Screen 257

5-2 TYPICAL RECORD AND DATABASE MANAGEMENT PROGRAMS   258

Record Management Programs 258   Database Management Programs 258   dBASE 261   Spreadsheets 261   WordPerfect 262   Microsoft Works 262   Exercise 5-2A Complete the Simulation on Screen 263

5-3 DEFINING A DATABASE FILE   264

The Organization of a Database 264   Planning Your Database Files 265   Defining a Database File 265   Exercise 5-3A Planning a Database for Names and Addresses 268   Exercise 5-3B Planning a Database for Records or CDs 268

5-4 ENTERING AND UPDATING RECORDS   269

Updating Records 270   Exercise 5-4A Adding Records 272

5-5 DISPLAYING RECORDS   273

Query Languages 273   Using Criteria to Display Records 273   Exercise 5-5A Querying a Database 277

5-6 SORTING AND INDEXING RECORDS 278

Sorting Files 278 Indexing Files 280
Exercise 5-6A Sorting a Database 283

5-7 PRINTING REPORTS 284

Exercise 5-7A Printing a Report 285

5-8 MAKING NEW DATABASES FROM EXISTING FILES 287

Exercise 5-8A Creating a New Database 288

CHAPTER 6 Communications Applications 289

6-1 LOCAL AREA NETWORKS 291

Centralized Information Processing 291
Decentralized Information Processing 292
Local Area Networks 292 Users and Administrators 295 Exercise 6-1A Complete the Simulation on Screen 296

6-2 WIDE AREA NETWORKS 297

Calling Other Computers 297 Calling Information Services 298 Calling Electronic Mail Services 298 Calling Bulletin Boards 299 Packet-Switching Networks 300 Exercise 6-2A Complete the Simulation on Screen 300

6-3 TELECOMMUNICATIONS EQUIPMENT 302

Modems 302 Types of Modems 302
Exercise 6-3A Read a Review 304

6-4 COMMUNICATIONS PROGRAMS 305

Introduction to Communications Programs 305 Typical Communications Programs 306 Exercise 6-4A Complete the Simulation on Screen 308

6-5 TRANSFERRING FILES 309

ASCII Files 309 Binary Files 309
Displaying ASCII Files on the Screen 309
Uploading and Downloading ASCII and Binary Files 310

6-6 OTHER CONNECTIONS 312

Facsimile Machines 312 Voice Mail 313
Exercise 6-6A Read a Review 313

CHAPTER 7 Computers and Careers 314

7-1 ERGONOMICS AND HEALTH 315

Exercise 7-1A Completing an Ergonomics Checklist 317 Exercise 7-1B Organizing a Work Area 317

7-2 ETHICS AND MORALITY 318

Security 318 Theft of Software 319
Viruses 319 Exercise 7-2A License Agreements 321

7-3 CAREERS IN INFORMATION PROCESSING 322

Originator Positions 322 Processor Positions 322 Specialist Positions 323
Career Paths 323 Exercise 7-3A Locating Jobs That Require Computer Knowledge 324

7-4 COMPUTERS IN THE WORKPLACE 325

Professional Word Processing 325
Information Management for an Entire Department 327 Increased Productivity for Independent Professionals 328

INDEX 331

Preface

A revolution in information processing is going on in offices, factories, and schools at this very moment. Not too many years ago, most information was processed on machines that were primarily mechanical. Words were processed on typewriters, numbers on adding machines, lists on index cards, and graphics on drafting tables. Only large companies owned computers, and they used them only for the most important corporate-level tasks, like order processing and payroll. Operating these large and complicated computers was too costly to use them to solve problems and increase productivity at the individual employee or departmental levels. All this is changing with the growing popularity of microcomputers, also called personal or desktop computers, and a large variety of easy-to-use applications programs. Computers are now accessible to almost everyone in large corporations, small businesses, professional offices, schools, homes, and wherever else people think, create, organize, or plan.

The microcomputer's popularity comes not just from its low cost but also from its flexibility. You can use a microcomputer to prepare a financial analysis; then use it to write, edit, and illustrate a report on the results of that analysis; and finally use it to send the final document to an office halfway around the world over telephone lines. Because of this power and flexibility, the microcomputer is becoming as familiar to everyone in business as the telephone, typewriter, and calculator.

What does this revolution mean for you, one of the people who will be using this new breed of computer? For one thing, it means you will be able to do certain tasks faster and better. It also means you can do work now that you could not have done before the arrival of the microcomputer.

- You can use word processing programs to create memos, letters, term papers, and reports, then revise them so that the results are perfect without having to retype them. You can even make a document look as though it were prepared by a professional printer by using the desktop publishing features built into the latest word processing programs or available in separate desktop publishing programs. You can also merge names and addresses stored in the computer into form letters and send out customized copies by the hundreds or thousands — and each will be personalized. You can even print the envelopes or mailing labels for them, all automatically.

- You can use spreadsheet programs to create dynamic financial models. If you change one number, the program automatically changes the results so you can instantly see the effects of a change. For example, you could explore the effects of various discounts on your profits. You can then use a spreadsheet's integrated graphics program to create graphs, not by drafting them on a board in the traditional way but by creating them almost instantly on a microcomputer. Graphs come alive; they no longer have to show only the final results but can enhance the analysis of numbers to show trends and relationships you never saw before.
- You can use record management or database programs for tasks as simple as keeping a phone list or as complicated as controlling inventory.
- You can use communications programs to connect your computer to other computers so that you can have instant access to the information stored in them.

This text is designed to help you understand the concepts behind and the applications of computers—in other words, to make you computer literate. It can get you started on the right foot. Full understanding, however, requires some hands-on experience with a computer. After all, a computer is nothing but a sophisticated machine—it is easier to understand what the computer does while it's doing it. Trying to understand computers without practice is like trying to learn how to drive or ski by reading books. Books can give you some principles and ideas, but it's only when you first get behind the wheel, or stand at the top of the hill, that you realize there is more to it than what you read.

If you are anxious about this course, don't worry. Anxiety is a common feeling among people when they are introduced to computers. This anxiety will shortly pass and you will then be wondering why you felt it in the first place. When beginning, avoid worrying about the many unfamiliar details you have to learn. Just keep in mind that all these details boil down to a few basic steps when you are working at a computer. After you grasp these basic steps, you can increase your understanding through further study and practice.

A NOTE TO THE INSTRUCTOR

This text is designed for the introductory course on computers. It assumes the student has no previous computer experience, and can be used successfully in a course with or without a lab section. The goal of the text is to stress the basic principles that underlie computers and their applications. Its focus is on microcomputers because that is what most people in business now use, but mainframes and minicomputers are also discussed. The text also discusses the major types of applications programs: word processing, spreadsheets and graphics, databases, and communications. Rather than focusing on specific products, this text uses a generic approach. This gives students a grasp of the basic concepts behind computers so that when they are faced with new or different products they will adjust more easily. Texts organized around specific products inevitably limit their discussion to the features contained in those programs.

The Structure of the Text

The text is organized into seven chapters:

Chapter 1, Computer Systems, discusses the hardware that makes up a computer system and introduces applications software programs.

Chapter 2, Disks, Disk Drives, and Operating Systems, discusses external storage devices and the operating system.

Chapter 3, Word Processing and Desktop Publishing Applications, discusses the programs that are used to prepare documents. Desktop publishing features, which include fonts, graphics, and columns, are discussed in the context of both word processing and desktop publishing, because they are now widely available on both types of programs.

Chapter 4, Spreadsheet Applications, discusses spreadsheets and how to use them to analyze numbers. It includes discussions on graphics and macros.

Chapter 5, Database Management Applications, discusses both record management and database management programs.

Chapter 6, Communications Applications, discusses how computers communicate in local and wide area networks.

Chapter 7, Computers and Careers, discusses issues related to health, ethics, and morality. It ends with a discussion of the many types of careers that are available to people with computer experience.

Core Concepts

Chapters 1, 2, and 7 contain core concepts that apply to all areas of computing. There are other core concepts, however, that also apply regardless of the program being used. Because these subjects are so basic to running a computer, they are discussed in this text where it seems most appropriate. For example, loading and quitting programs, executing commands, saving and retrieving files, and desktop publishing are discussed in the chapter on word processing, even though these concepts also apply to all other program areas. Typical core concepts include:

- Loading and quitting applications programs, executing commands, and saving and retrieving files are all discussed in the chapter on word processing because it is the first chapter on applications software. The same concepts apply, of course, to all programs.
- Desktop publishing is discussed in the chapter on word processing, but you can also desktop publish data with the latest spreadsheet or database programs.
- Formulas are discussed in the chapter on spreadsheets, but you also use formulas to make calculations in word processing math procedures and in database reports.
- Macros are discussed in the chapter on spreadsheets, but almost all programs allow you to create macros to automate your work.
- Displaying records is discussed in the chapter on databases, but it also discusses relational and logical operators, which are also used in word processing macros, mail merge, and spreadsheet functions.
- Sorting records is discussed in the chapter on databases, but you use the same principles to sort lines or paragraphs in word processing and rows in a spreadsheet.

Core topics have been identified in the table of contents with the logo shown below. You can cover these core concepts at any time if you feel the sequence should be changed. For example, should you want to discuss sorting in spreadsheets, you can assign the section on relational and logical operators at that time.

Key Features

Many features make this text a better teaching and learning tool.

- The text focuses on the most important concepts of computers. This ensures that students who master the text will be capable of mastering existing hardware and software, and also prepares them to adapt to the rapid changes in this field.
- Over 300 illustrations and accompanying captions make it easier for students to grasp the principles behind microcomputer applications.
- The presentation of word processing includes a detailed discussion of desktop publishing. These two fields have been integrated because the trend in this area is to incorporate almost all desktop publishing features into standard word processing programs.
- Hundreds of questions test students' understanding of the material presented in each section.
- The margins of the text contain glossary definitions of words highlighted in the text.
- Keystroke summary boxes provide the basic keystrokes you need to use to complete many procedures when working with DOS. Students can use these as a quick reference when they begin to work on a computer.
- Many exercises can be completed using disk-based simulations of leading software programs such as Windows, WordPerfect, Lotus 1-2-3, dBASE, and ProComm. These simulations require no computer experience and can help students understand the applications of computers and see how programs differ from one another.

Supplements

In addition to this text, other supplemental materials and services are available to support your efforts in the classroom:

Information Processing Lab Manual. This manual contains hands-on tutorials on WordPerfect 5.1, Lotus 1-2-3, dBASE III Plus, and ProComm Plus.

Instructor's Manual with Tests. The manual contains lecture outlines, helpful teaching tips, and a test bank of over 1,000 items, and answers to the test questions.

Information Processing Software Sampler. The disk contains disk-based simulations of 13 leading applications programs available in 3½" or 5¼" disk format.

Software Videos. These tutorial videos guide students through popular applications packages such as DOS, WordPerfect, Word, Lotus 1-2-3, dBASE III Plus, and Ventura. They are free on adoption for qualifying quantities.

Acknowledgments

Special thanks are due to those who helped turn the manuscript into a finished book. Peggy Curtin did all the picture research and handled all contacts with the computer companies that gave so much assistance. Nancy Benjamin handled all aspects of production to turn a large pile of manuscript and illustrations into the finished text.

During the development of this text many teachers were kind enough to share their opinions and suggestions with the author. I would like to thank all of the following for their guidance: Eleanor Davidson and Elaine Schmittke of Nassau Community College; Jean J. Smith of Chabot College; Linda L. Dowell of St. Johns River Community College; Susan Mazzola of Barclay College, Fresno; Janice Pattison of Stark Technical College; Andrea Weeks of The Fashion Institute of Design and Merchandising; and Craig Winston of CareerCom School of Business.

Note

The author and publisher of this series want to ensure that it meets your needs, and we would appreciate your comments. If you have any suggestions for improvements or new titles to be added to the series, please write to:

Dennis P. Curtin
c/o Editor of Introductory Computing
College Division
Prentice-Hall, Inc.
Englewood Cliffs, NJ 07632

Dennis P. Curtin
Marblehead, MA

CHAPTER 1

Computer Systems

OBJECTIVES

After finishing this chapter, you will be able to:

- Define the term *system*, and explain how a computer system contains both hardware and software
- Describe business information processing and the information processing cycle
- Explain what the term *digital* means and describe how the concept is the basis of modern information processing
- Explain how computers function, and describe how their various components work
- Describe typical devices, such as keyboards and scanners, that you use to enter data into the computer
- Describe typical devices, such as display screens and printers, that you use to view information processed by the computer
- Briefly list and describe the main types of applications programs that you run on a computer

System. Any collection of elements designed to work together to perform a task.

Hardware. The physical equipment that makes up a computer system.

Computer. A device that makes calculations.

Peripheral. Any stand-alone device like a printer or modem, connected to a computer by cables.

Computers are widely used to process information. To use them for this purpose, you should understand the concepts behind the computer and the other components that make up a computer system. Understanding these concepts makes your work on a computer easier and prepares you to understand and cope with future changes in technology.

SYSTEM

Although most users would say they do their work on a computer, they actually do their work on a computer system. A *system* is a set of related parts that operate together to perform a specific function. You encounter systems every day. For example, your circulatory system moves blood through your body. This system contains your heart, lungs, and blood vessels that work together to distribute energy throughout your body. Your stereo is also a system. Its amplifier, CD player, and speakers all work together so that you can hear music. A computer system, like these other systems, comprises several interacting parts that work together to perform tasks. These parts are classified as either hardware or software.

HARDWARE

Hardware (Figure 1-1) is the physical equipment in the system. A *computer* is the hardware component at the center of the system, and it performs all the processing of information. Other hardware components, called *peripherals*, connect to the computer. The most common peripherals are the keyboard, display screen, and printer. You use these peripherals to feed information into the computer and get the results back to view, file, or distribute.

Distribution devices, like **modems** and **networks**, allow you to exchange information with other users of other computers.

Output devices like a **display screen** or **printer**, get data out of a computer so you can examine, edit analyze, file or distribute it to others.

The **microcomputer** performs all calculations and processes all data.

External storage devices, like **disk drives**, store programs and data that you are not currently processing with the computer.

Input devices, like the **keyboard**, enter data into the computer so it can be processed.

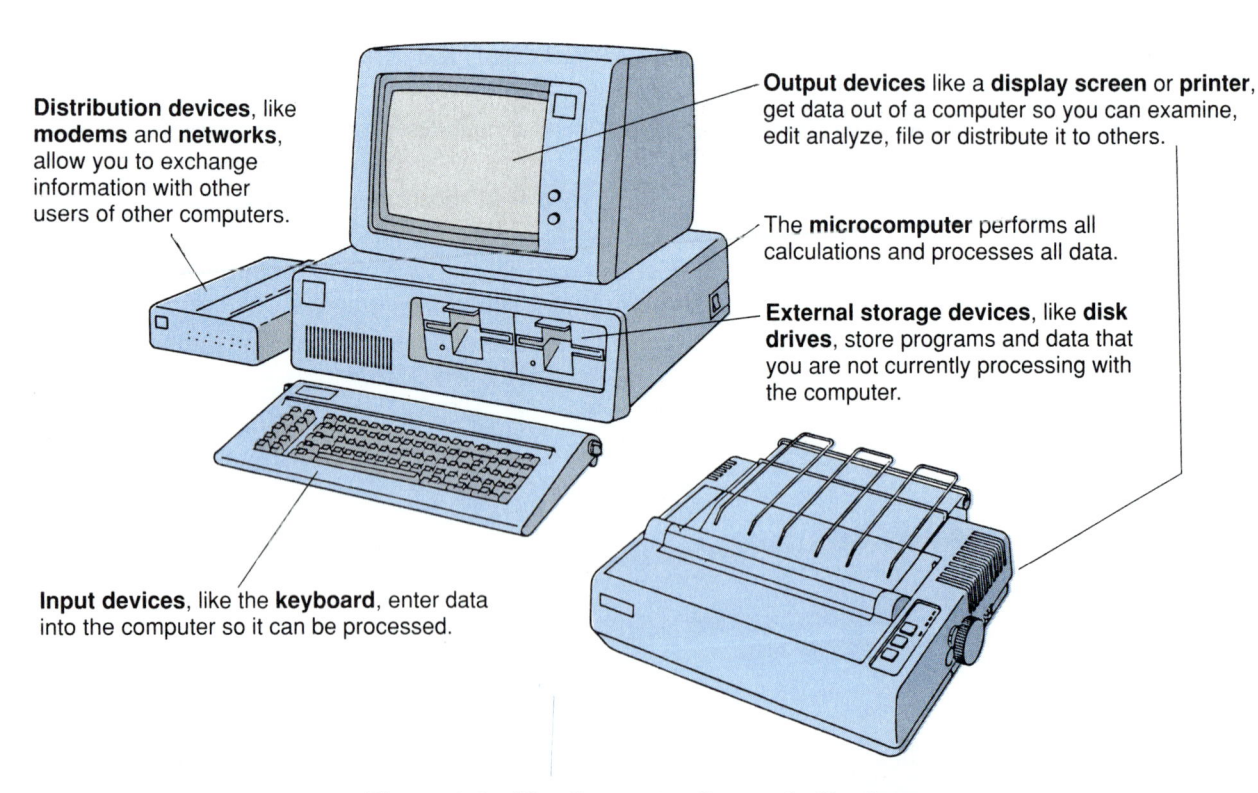

Figure 1-1 The Computer System's Hardware
A typical computer system contains these hardware components.

Software. A general term that refers to programs saved onto a magnetic medium.

Program (n). A set of instructions that tells the computer what to do and when to do it. Programs are subdivided into systems programs, like the operating system, and applications programs used for word processing, spreadsheets, or graphics.

Program (v). To write a set of instructions that will run on a computer.

SOFTWARE

Computers are versatile machines with many capabilities. You determine their specific applications by the software you use. This is what distinguishes computers from machines such as typewriters or calculators that can perform only a single function. *Software* is the set of instructions, called a ***program***, that tells the computer what to do and when to do it. These programs are written by professionals and then stored on disks and sold just like records or books.

The computer is like an actor, and the software is like a script. When the actor changes scripts, he or she then performs a different role. By changing the software, you can make your computer perform different functions (Figure 1-2). For example, if you want to use your computer for word processing, you load a word processing program into the computer's memory from the disk it is stored on. If you want to use your computer for financial analysis, you load a spreadsheet program. You do not have to learn programming to make the computer a valuable tool. Instead, you learn how to effectively use these widely available software programs.

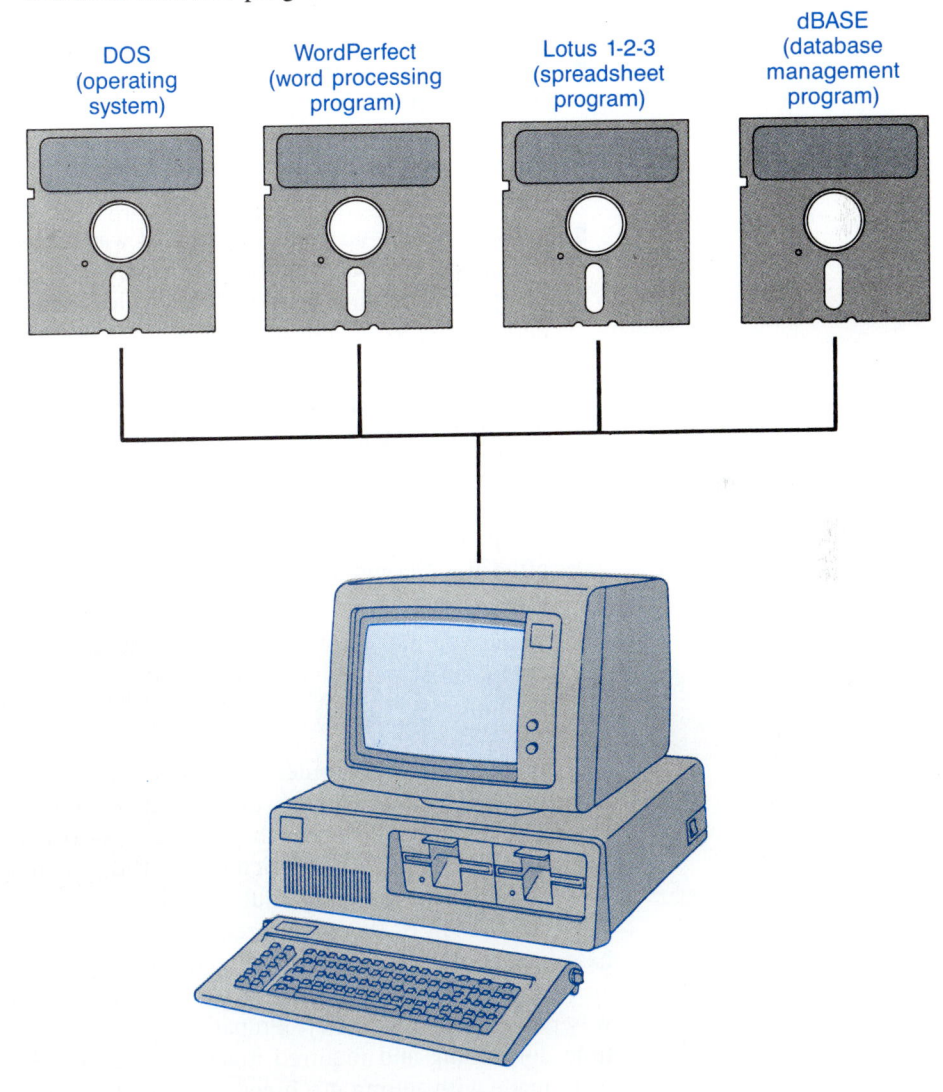

Figure 1-2 The Computer System's Software
Computers allow you to load a variety of software, called programs, into memory so that you can change their applications. You can use the same piece of equipment to process words, numbers, and graphics.

1-1 INFORMATION PROCESSING IN THE MODERN OFFICE

Information processing. The processing of words, numbers, and graphics with a computer.

Graphics. Images such as line drawings and photographs that are comprised of more than text characters.

Information is the lifeblood of modern business. It is used to make decisions, convey actions, evaluate results, and exchange ideas. But to be useful, information must be processed.

WHAT IS INFORMATION PROCESSING?

Information processing refers to the use of computers to create, file, distribute, and store words, numbers, *graphics*, and even sounds that communicate facts or ideas. The field of information processing is so vast that you encounter computerized information processing systems almost every day.

- When you call to make an airline reservation, an agent enters your request into a computer. The computer then displays all the flights available, the time they depart and arrive, and their fares. If you make a reservation, your request is entered into the computer, and a seat is reserved for you.
- When you pick up your paycheck, it was probably printed by a computer. The same computer probably charged the amount of the check to the company's accounting records and calculated withholding taxes and other deductions.
- When you drive your car to the store, its computers monitor and control some aspects of the car's performance—for example, its ignition, brakes, dashboard display, and stereo. More than 60 million cars with computers built into them were sold between 1982 and 1988.
- When you open your mail, you are likely to find personalized letters automatically generated by computers. Magazines and other businesses often use "computer mail" to try to sell you something. The computer inserts your name at selected points to make the letter seem personal.
- When you make a withdrawal from a bank's automatic teller machine, a computer dispenses the money and charges the withdrawal against your account.

The influence of the computer in our lives has become widespread within a very short period. In 1946, there was only one operational computer in the United States. Since then, the growth has been explosive. In 1980, there was one computer for every 160 Americans. By 1985, there was one for every ten, by 1990, almost one for every four.

As a result of this widespread use of computers, information processing has changed dramatically during your lifetime. Your parents, if they worked in an office, used equipment that was primarily mechanical, although some of it was powered by electricity. Preparing written documents on a typewriter was time consuming and required much skill to get the best results. Calculations were made with adding machines or calculators. If errors were discovered, or if circumstances changed, the entire process had to be redone from scratch. Names and addresses and other important data were stored on cards or sheets of paper that were manually arranged into some order and then stored in filing cabinets. Graphics were prepared on drafting tables. Communications with people at a distance were limited to the phone, mail, or telegrams. Although

Data. Any alphanumeric input or output from the computer. It also refers to any collection of information stored in the computer's memory.

Data processing. The processing of company data with a computer.

Word processing. Entering, editing, storing, distributing, and printing words with a computer.

these manual processes are still widely used, the computer is changing the way many people work.

HOW IS INFORMATION PROCESSED?

All information processed on computers falls into three broad classes: data, words, and graphics (Figure 1-3). Let's look more closely at what these terms mean.

INFORMATION PROCESSING		
Words	**Data**	**Graphics**
Memos Letters Reports Articles Books Plays Poems	Accounting Science Engineering Statistics Reservations	Illustrations Designs Charts and graphs Organization charts

Figure 1-3 Information Processing
Information processed on computers falls into three main classes: data, words, and graphics.

Data Processing

The term *data* refers to any information used to record, discuss, or decide something. When computers were first developed, their primary function was to process highly structured data. Large computers in company data processing departments are still used largely for this purpose. They process payrolls and keep track of inventory and sales. These tasks require the computer to calculate numbers, sort entries into a specified order, and find a specific record when needed. Programmers write programs for each of these tasks. Often these programs display a form on the screen that is filled in by an operator to feed information into the computer. If the form does not have a space to enter a comment, you cannot enter one. Because the purpose of the computer is to process this highly structured data, the general term *data processing* is used to describe the procedure.

Word Processing

As the information processing field matured, specialty areas emerged. *Word processing* programs were developed that made it possible to work with words so that correspondence could be written, edited to improve its content, and formatted to control its final appearance. These programs allow much more flexibility than data processing programs. Instead of just entering predefined data, you can enter any kind of information and then manipulate it on the screen. For example, you can enter a paragraph and then copy, move, delete, or format it.

1-1

Graphics processing.
The ability to create and manipulate graphic images.

Graphics Processing

Later in the evolution of information processing, it became possible to create and manipulate images with the computer. *Graphics processing* programs have been developed that read images into the computer, let you draw them on the screen, or create graphs of numeric data. These graphics can then be manipulated, stored, printed, and distributed just like data and words.

Information Processing

The specialized areas of information processing overlap (Figure 1-4). For example, a document prepared with a word processing program can also include the date or other numbers, graphic symbols such as bullets (■ and ▶), lines, and even graphic images such as line drawings, maps, or photographs. A graphic image prepared with a graphics program can include numbers and words. For example, you can create an outline map of the United States, label each location where your company has a branch office, and show the sales achieved by each office. Because of this overlap, data processing, word processing, and graphics processing obviously do not refer to the content as much as to how the data are handled by the computer and the intent of the operator. When processing data, people focus on having the computer compile and organize data so that they can be analyzed and used for decision-making purposes. When processing words, people focus on preparing written information. When processing graphics, people are interested in generating graphic information.

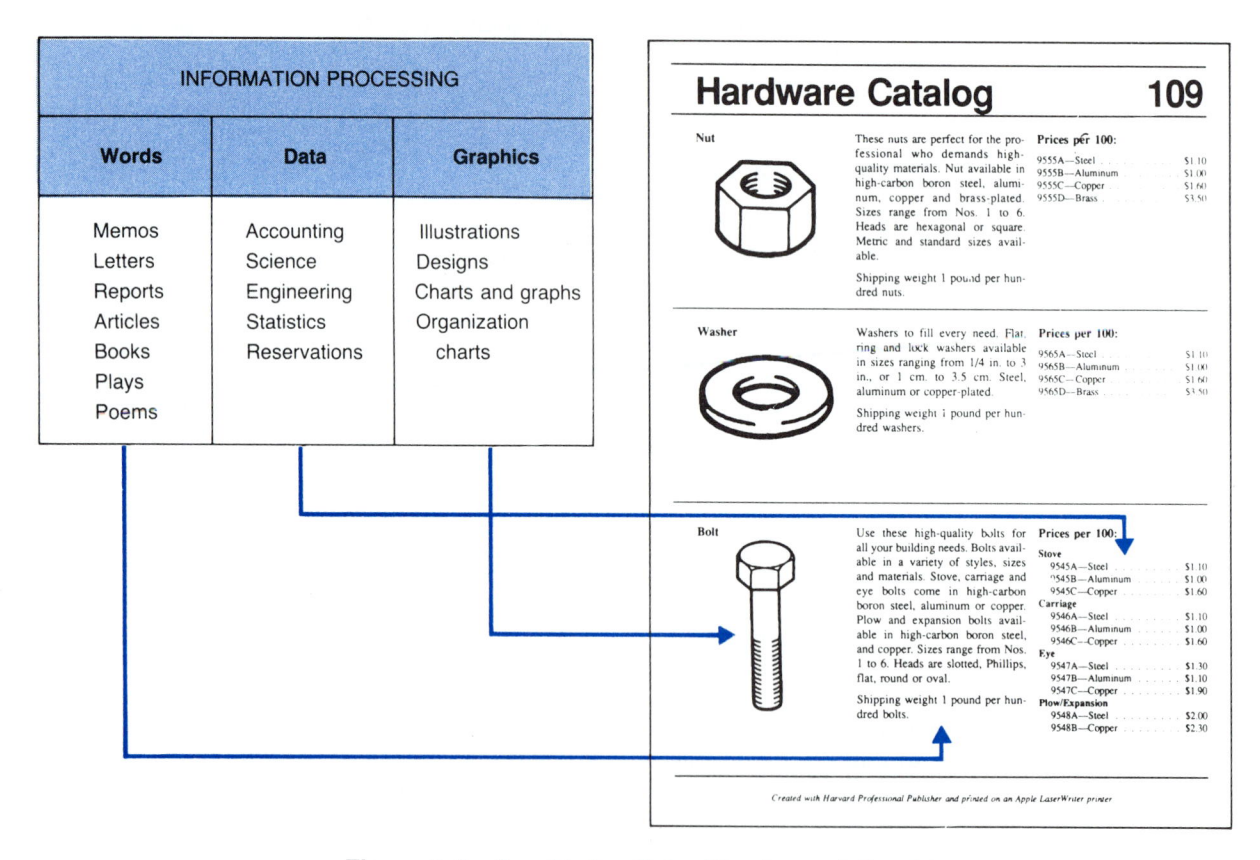

INFORMATION PROCESSING		
Words	Data	Graphics
Memos	Accounting	Illustrations
Letters	Science	Designs
Reports	Engineering	Charts and graphs
Articles	Statistics	Organization
Books	Reservations	charts
Plays		
Poems		

Figure 1-4 Combining Data, Words, and Graphics
Information processing includes words, data, and graphics. When you combine them, you can create documents or other files that describe, illustrate, and calculate.
Courtesy of Software Publishing Corporation

Information processing cycle. The five stages in processing words, graphics, and data; input, processing, output, storage and retrieval, and distribution and communications.

Output. The information in a computer that is displayed on the screen or printed out on paper.

Print. To send a document that is in the computer's memory to a printer to be printed out.

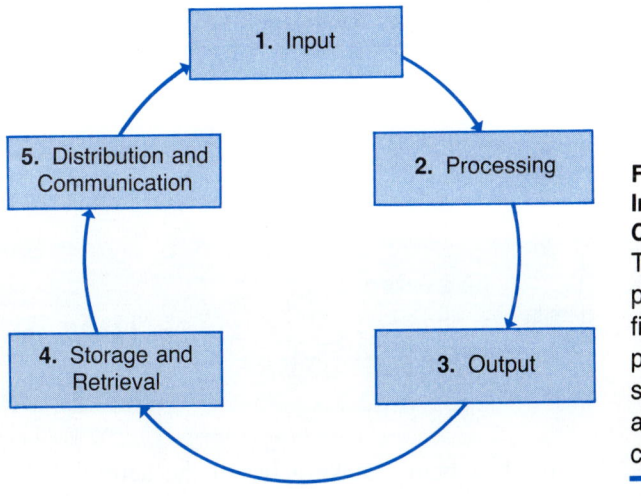

THE INFORMATION PROCESSING CYCLE

Information processing has a cycle of steps that usually follow each other in a specific order. The *information processing cycle* generally contains the following five steps (Figure 1-5):

Step 1   Input.   During the input stage, you enter information into the computer. You can either type it at the keyboard or use one of the other available input devices, such as a scanner.

Step 2   Processing.   Once information is in the computer, you can process it. For example, with a word processing program you can edit and format text. With a spreadsheet program you can calculate numbers and perform financial analysis.

Step 3   Output.   Once information is processed you have to be able to see it. This displayed information is called *output*. There are two ways to see this output. While you are entering and processing data, it is constantly being displayed on the screen. After the information is processed, you can **print** it out.

Step 4   Storage and Retrieval.   You can file copies so that you can easily locate and retrieve them if needed. You can file printed copies manually or store the information in the computer onto magnetic or optical media.

Step 5   Distribution and Communication.   You can distribute copies of the information to the intended recipients. You can send printed copies or send the data electronically to other computers over cables or telephone lines.

Figure 1-5 The Information Processing Cycle
The information processing cycle has five steps: input, processing, output, storage and retrieval, and distribution and communication.

COMPUTERS IN BUSINESS

The applications of computers in large and small firms are generally the same. Let's look at a few of them.

- All departments use computers routinely to create and print correspondence and interoffice memos, and to design, illustrate, and publish forms, brochures, catalogs, and reports.

INFORMATION PROCESSING IN THE MODERN OFFICE

1-1

Application. A specific task to which a computer is put, for example, word processing, financial analysis, and record management.

Applications program. A program designed to turn the computer into a tool for a specific task, such as word processing.

- Sales and marketing departments use computers to analyze sales and maintain mailing lists of their customers.
- Production and manufacturing departments use them to analyze costs, design products or components, and control manufacturing equipment.
- Finance and accounting departments use them for financial analysis and to computerize the accounting process.
- Administration and management use them for many purposes. They analyze performance, prepare correspondence, maintain lists of phone numbers, and prepare reports.
- Design departments use them to create designs for products, exhibits, advertisements, and publications.

Each of these groups performs many tasks or *applications*. As you have seen, the computer is a general-purpose machine. You adapt it for specific tasks by loading an *applications program* into its memory. The applications program used depends on the task. Table 1-1 lists some typical tasks and the applications programs used to implement them.

Table 1-1
TASKS AND APPLICATIONS PROGRAMS

Task	Applications Program	Example Program
Memos, letters, and reports	Word processing	WordPerfect
Publications	Desktop publishing	Ventura
Planning and budgeting	Spreadsheets	Lotus 1-2-3
List management	Database	dBASE
Charts and graphs	Graphics	Lotus 1-2-3
Electronic mail	Telecommunications	ProComm
Bookkeeping and accounting	Accounting	DAC Easy

EXERCISES

Exercise 1-1A
LISTING ACTIVITIES THAT ARE AFFECTED BY COMPUTERS

In the box below make a list of the activities in your life where you think computers do and do not have an influence. Exchange your list with another student, and then challenge each other's responses.

Activities Affected	Activities Not Affected

Exercise 1-1B
LOCATING LIBRARY RESOURCES

One source of computer resources is the library. Visit the library and list the computer magazines and periodicals to which your library subscribes. You should read some of the articles and ads in these magazines to become familiar with computer terms and applications.

- ☐ *PC World*
- ☐ *MacWorld*
- ☐ *PC Week*
- ☐ *PC Magazine*
- ☐ *BYTE*
- ☐ *InfoWorld*
- ☐ _____
- ☐ _____
- ☐ _____

QUESTIONS

1. List as many places that computers are being used that you can think of. What information are they used to process?
2. Describe the primary application of data processing.
3. What is the function of the data processing department?
4. Describe the primary application of word processing.
5. Describe the primary purpose of graphics processing.
6. Describe information processing.
7. List the five steps in the information processing cycle, and briefly describe what is done at each stage.
8. List some examples of how computers are being used in business.

1-2 THE DIGITAL REVOLUTION

Digital processing. Processing digital data in a computer.

Digital. Representing data with the digits 0 and 1.

Decimal system. A math system based on the number 10.

Binary system. A number system that presents all numbers as combinations of 0s and 1s.

A single concept behind the computer, and almost all other modern electronic equipment, is revolutionizing the field of information processing. It is the concept of *digital processing*. You may have heard this term used in connection with the music industry, where music is stored on compact discs in *digital* form. Digital processing simply refers to a way information, be it music or documents, is stored so that it can be processed.

The term *digital* comes from the word *digit*, which means a single number. When you write a check or count your change, you use the digits 0 through 9 to convey numbers. The digits 1 and 9 can convey $1 or $9, or they can be combined to convey $19, $91, $19.19, and so on. This numbering system, which uses the ten digits from 0 to 9, is called the *decimal system*. You use this system when you dial the phone, look up pages in the index of a book, or address a letter to a specific street address.

Computers and other digital equipment use a simpler numbering system, the *binary system*. The binary system uses only two numbers, 0 and 1, to convey all other numbers. Any number can be conveyed with these two digits (see Table 1-2).

Table 1-2
DECIMAL AND BINARY EQUIVALENTS

Decimal Number	Binary Equivalent
0	0
1	1
2	10
3	11
4	100
5	101
6	110
7	111
8	1000
9	1001
10	1010
11	1011

Because binary numbers comprise only 0s and 1s, their major advantage is that they can be processed in several ways with a variety of devices:

- If you have a device that can be turned on and off, you can have on represent 1 and off represent 0.
- If you have a device that can emit high or low voltages, you can have the high voltage represent 1 and the low voltage represent 0.
- If you can align magnetic particles on a surface so that they point in opposite directions, you can have one direction represent 1 and the other direction represent 0.
- If you can have dots on a display screen be either illuminated or dark, you can have 1 illuminate a dot and 0 leave a dot dark.

Code. An agreed-upon meaning assigned to signals or symbols so that they can be interpreted and understood by others.

Digital signal. A signal that is transmitted via electrical pulses. In a computer, the digital 0s and 1s are transmitted as low and high voltages.

▌If you can have a printer that prints dots on a sheet of paper, you can have 1 tell it to print a dot and 0 to leave a white space.

All these techniques are used in computers to store, process, and display information. To take it one step further, you can convey information with these numbers if you have an agreed-upon *code*. We now see how various digital devices and codes can be used to convey information.

PAUL REVERE'S RIDE — THE FIRST DIGITAL REVOLUTION?

You may have heard or read Longfellow's poem *Paul Revere's Ride*. Here are a few stanzas of the poem:

> Listen, my children, and you shall hear
> Of the midnight ride of Paul Revere,
> On the eighteenth of April, in Seventy-five;
> Hardly a man is now alive
> Who remembers that famous day and year.
>
> He said to his friend, "If the British march
> By land or sea from the town tonight,
> Hang a lantern aloft in the belfry arch
> Of the North Church as a signal light,
> One, if by land, and two, if by sea;
> And I on the opposite shore will be,
> Ready to ride and spread the alarm
> Through every Middlesex village and farm,
> For the country folk to be up and to arm."

This was a digital message. When America was a colony of England, Paul Revere was assigned the job of notifying the Minutemen who lived in the countryside if the British left Boston to attack them. He and his friend Robert Newman, the sexton of Old North Church, decided that Revere would wait on the other side of the harbor so that he had a head start should the British troops begin to move. Newman would remain in Boston to watch for any troop movements. Because Revere would be miles away, they needed a way for Newman to let him know the route the British were taking if they left Boston to attack. They decided that Newman would light one lantern in the belfry of Old North Church if the British were leaving Boston by land, and two lanterns if they were going by sea. This simple *digital signal* (Figure 1-6) sent Paul Revere on his famous ride that resulted in "the shot heard round the world" at the bridge in Concord.

THE TELEGRAPH — THE FIRST DIGITAL CODE

Lanterns have their limits when it comes to sending information. It is hard to spell out messages. For example, if the British had been able to take an unexpected route, Paul Revere's prearranged code would not have been able to convey the message. This problem was solved by Samuel Morse when he invented the telegraph in the early 1800s.

With the telegraph (Figure 1-7), a sender taps on a key to send pulses of electricity down a wire to a distant listener. At the listener's end, a device called a sounder clicks when each pulse arrives. Like the lanterns in the tower, this is a digital process. Random clicks, however, do not convey information, so Morse had to develop a code. He based the code on the pauses between the clicks,

When one lamp was on (1) and the other was off (0), it meant the British were moving by land.

When both lamps were on (1), it meant the British were moving by sea.

Figure 1-6   The First Digital Revolution
Two lanterns were used to signal Paul Revere which way the British were heading.

A.

Letters					
A	.—	Q	——.—	7	——...
B	—...	R	.—.	8	———..
C	—.—.	S	...	9	————.
D	—..	T	—	0	—————
E	.	U	..—		
F	..—.	V	...—	Punctuation	
G	——.	W	.——		
H	....	X	—..—	.	......
I	..	Y	—.——	;	—.—.—
J	.———	Z	——..	:	.—...
K	—.—	Numbers		?	..——..
L	.—..	1	.————	!	——..——
M	——	2	..———	Formats	
N	—.	3	...——	Underline ..——.—	
O	———	4	....—	Return —..—	
P	.——.	5	.....		
		6	—....		

B.

Figure 1-7   The First Digital Code
The telegraph (A) was used to send short dots and longer dashes down a wire to the recipient. These dots and dashes communicated information because they followed a code (B).
Courtesy of The Bettman Archive, Inc.

Transistor. One of the components of an integrated circuit.

Chip. A small piece of silicon on which numerous electronic components and an electronic circuit are etched. Chips are used in computers as microprocessors and as internal memory.

Integrated circuit (IC). A solid-state circuit containing electronic devices like transistors.

Bit. The smallest unit of data stored in (or communicated) to a computer. A bit is a digital signal consisting of two possible states, 0 and 1. *Bit* is a contraction of the words *bi*nary and digi*t*.

Binary digit. See Bit.

Byte. A unit usually containing 8 bits. Each byte contains the information necessary for identifying a single character.

using a short pause and a long pause. (When printed, these were represented as dots and dashes.) An experimental telegraph line was run between Baltimore and Washington, and on May 24, 1844, a series of short and long pauses between clicks sent the historic message "What hath God wrought" down this first telegraph line.

THE TRANSISTOR—THE COMPUTER'S DIGITAL DEVICE

Like these early message systems, computers need a device that can send, process, and store information and a code that gives the information meaning. Instead of lanterns or a key to send electrical pulses in a wire, modern computers use *transistors*. These transistors are created on silicon wafers (four-inch mirrorlike disks of pure silicon made from sand) and then cut apart (Figure 1-8). Each *chip* contains thousands of transistors arranged in circuits called *integrated circuits*.

Like lanterns, transistors have only two possible states: on and off. Instead of using a code of short and long pauses, as Morse did, a computer uses the transistor's on and off states. The code is based on bits and groups of bits called bytes.

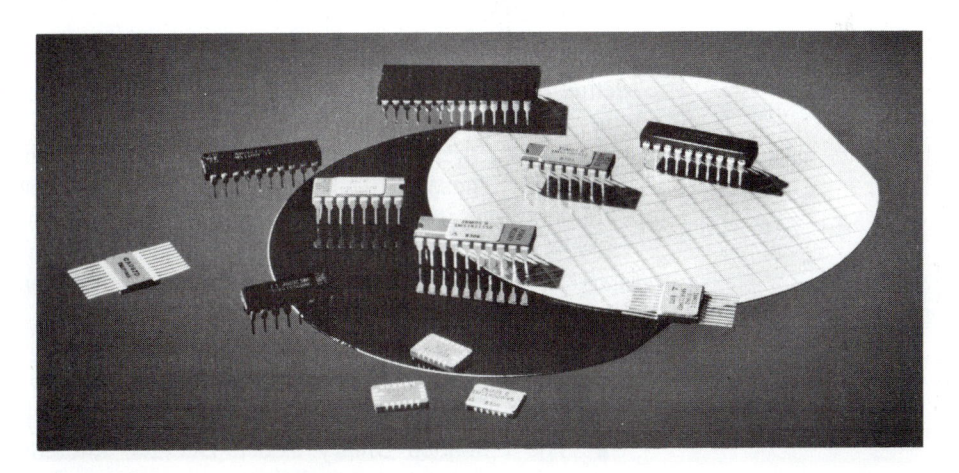

Figure 1-8 The Transistor
In computers, thousands of transistors are created on a silicon wafer. This wafer is then cut apart and the sections are mounted in protective cases with places to connect wires. These "chips" are the reason modern computers are so small.
Courtesy of the Computer Museum and Inmos Corporation

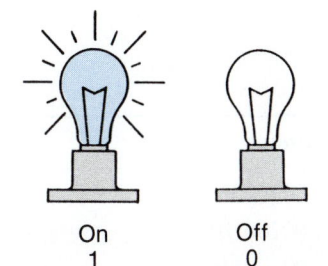

On 1   Off 0

Figure 1-9 A Bit
A bit is like a light bulb—it is either on to indicate 1, or off to indicate 0.

Bits

The smallest unit of information is the *bit*, a contraction of the more descriptive phrase *binary digit*. A bit is a single element in the computer that is set to 1 or 0 (Figure 1-9). In the computer, on (1) is represented by a high voltage, and off (0) is represented by a low voltage.

Bytes

Because bits are small units and can convey only two possible states, they can be organized into larger units to convey more information. This larger unit is a *byte*, and it is the basic unit of information in a computer system. It usually

ASCII. Acronym for American Standard Code for Information Interchange. This group sets standards for the codes that represent characters in the computer field.

EBCDIC. A code that assigns characters to specific binary numbers. Used primarily on large main-frame computers.

ANSI. Acronym for American National Standards Institute.

Off	On	Off	Off	Off	Off	Off	On
0	1	0	0	0	0	0	1

Figure 1-10   A Byte
To understand a byte, imagine using eight light bulbs instead of one. Each letter in the alphabet could easily be assigned a pattern of lights. For example, this pattern could represent the letter A.

contains 8 bits. Because each bit has two states and there are 8 bits in a byte, the total amount of information that can be conveyed is 2^8 (2 raised to the 8th power), or 256 possible combinations. These combinations can represent characters, numbers, or symbols. For example, an A, a, +, −, &, or 5 can each be communicated in 1 byte. To better understand this concept, imagine using eight light bulbs instead of one to represent the letter A (Figure 1-10). Inside the computer, the letter A is represented by the binary number 01000001.

Characters

By themselves, bytes are meaningless. To have meaning, they must be assigned definitions that form a code (Table 1-3). With 8 bits that can be either on (meaning 1) or off (meaning 0), there are 256 possible combinations. If all the bits are off, the byte reads 00000000. If all the bits are on, the byte reads 11111111. These two numbers, and any in between such as 10000000 or 11000000, can stand for anything the computer's designer wants them to. They can represent characters, numbers, symbols, or commands to the computer. To standardize the meaning of these number combinations, the computer industry uses several codes, including

- The American Standard Code for Information Interchange, or *ASCII* (pronounced ''as-key''), the code used most often on microcomputers
- The Extended Binary Coded Decimal Interchange Code, or *EBCDIC* (pronounced ''eb-see-dick''), the code used most often on mainframe computers
- The American National Standards Institute, or *ANSI* code (pronounced ''an-see''), is used by some programs, like Microsoft's Windows, Excel, and Word for Windows.

Table 1-3
ASCII CHARACTERS

Letters				Numbers and Symbols			
A	01000001	a	01100001	0	00110000	!	00100001
B	01000010	b	01100010	1	00110001	%	00100101
C	01000011	c	01100011	2	00110010	&	00100110
D	01000100	d	01100100	.	.		.
E	01000101	e	01100101	.	.		.
.	.	.	.	.	.		.
.	.	.	.	.	.		.
Z	01011010	z	01111010	9	00111001	+	00101011

The characters you see on your screen are determined by which code your computer uses. The first 128 characters are almost the same. You'll learn more about these characters in Chapter 3 on desktop publishing.

Shorthand

Most references to a computer's digital memory, processing, storage, and communication use the byte as a unit of measurement. The number of bytes is usually given in shorthand. For example, you can say a computer's internal memory is 128,000 bytes or 128KB. The KB (for kilobyte) indicates a magnitude of 1,000. As memory increases, the KB is replaced by an MB (for megabyte), which indicates a magnitude of 1,000,000. For example, you can say the computer's memory is 1,000,000 bytes, 1,000 kilobytes, or 1 megabyte. As computer capacity expands, you'll begin to encounter the next levels of magnitude: the gigabyte (1 billion bytes) and the terabyte (1 trillion bytes).

When referring to bytes in this way, the numbers are rounded so that you do not have to remember odd numbers. Bytes are calculated by raising the number 2 to various powers. The number 2 is used because digital devices have two states, for example, on and off. The number 2 raised to the 10th power is 1,024. This is usually rounded off to 1,000 (or 1KB). Table 1-4 shows the number 2 raised to powers between 0 and 30, the actual bytes that result, and how these bytes are expressed in shorthand as kilobytes, megabytes, or gigabytes.

Table 1-4
BYTES, KILOBYTES, MEGABYTES, AND GIGABYTES

Power	Actual	Shorthand
2^0	1	1 byte
.	.	.
.	.	.
2^{10}	1,024	1KB (kilobyte)
.	.	.
.	.	.
2^{17}	131,072	128KB
2^{18}	262,144	256KB
2^{19}	524,288	524KB
2^{20}	1,048,576	1MB (megabyte)
.	.	.
.	.	.
2^{30}	1,073,741,824	1GB (gigabyte)

EXERCISE

Exercise 1-2A
CONVERTING BYTES, KILOBYTES, AND MEGABYTES

Memory and other devices are frequently described in terms of bytes, kilobytes, and megabytes. In the table below, bytes are listed in the first column. In the next two columns, indicate the same bytes in kilobytes and then megabytes. Round off where necessary.

BYTES, KILOBYTES, AND MEGABYTES

Bytes	Kilobytes	Megabytes
1,024	_____	_____
524,288	_____	_____
1,048,576	_____	_____
2,097,152	_____	_____
16,777,216	_____	_____

QUESTIONS

1. What is the binary number system? How is it used in computers?
2. What is the name of the digital device used inside a computer to store and process information? When thousands of these are put together, what is the device called?
3. Many digital devices can store, communicate, or process a digital signal because they have only two states, on or off. List at least two other things that have only two states, so they can also be considered digital.
4. What is the difference between a bit and a byte?
5. What is the name of the code used to assign characters to numbers or bytes on most microcomputers?

1-3 THE COMPUTER

Computers come in many designs but one way to classify them is according to their size and portability (Figure 1-11).

- Mainframe computers are room-sized and require a special staff.
- Minicomputers are anywhere from refrigerator-sized to desktop-sized and are frequently used by small companies or by departments within large corporations.
- Desktop computers, those used by individuals, are relatively large, at least too large to carry easily.
- Portable computers are smaller than desktop computers so that they can be carried, but you wouldn't want to carry one with you on a subway or a long walk through an airport terminal.
- Laptop computers can be carried like a small attaché case or packed in a suitcase. They are designed so that they can run on rechargeable battery packs.
- Notebook computers are designed to be easily carried in a briefcase. In that sense, they are almost as convenient as a pocket calculator. However, they are working computers that can run programs and exchange information with other, larger computers.
- Handheld computers have very small keyboards so they cannot be easily used for word processing or other applications that require you to enter a

Figure 1-11 Computers
Computers come in all sizes, from the very largest mainframes to the smallest handhelds.

Mainframe Computers. Mainframe computers are room-sized computers operated by a centralized staff. *Courtesy of IBM Corporation*

Figure 1-11 Computers, continued

Minicomputers. Minicomputers are less powerful than mainframe computers and are usually used in departments within a company. *Courtesy of IBM Corporation*

Desktop Computers. Desktop computers, the most common microcomputer design, are relatively large units designed to be permanently positioned on a desk. *Courtesy of IBM Corporation*

Figure 1-11 Computers, continued

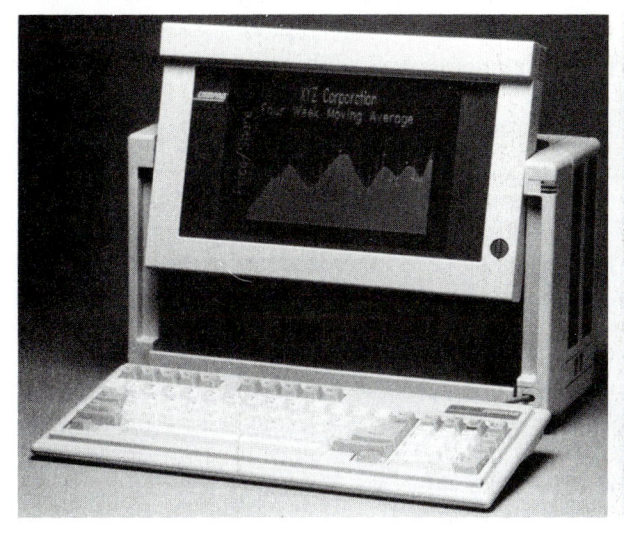

Portable Computers. Portable computers are smaller than desktop computers and they can be easily moved from one location to another. *Courtesy of Compaq*

Laptop Computers. Laptop computers are small enough to fit on your lap on an airplane or to be packed in a larger suitcase when traveling. *Courtesy of Toshiba*

Notebook Computers. Notebook computers are the smallest microcomputers with usable keyboards. They are small enough to be carried in a briefcase. *Courtesy of Toshiba*

Handheld Computers. Handheld computers are the smallest microcomputers, but their extremely small keyboards make them difficult to use except in special applications. *Courtesy of Poqet Computer Corp.*

Central processing unit (CPU). The CPU is the heart of the microcomputer and is composed of integrated circuits etched into a silicon chip.

Microprocessor. A chip containing thousands of circuits that allow it to process data. Used as the central processing unit in a microcomputer.

lot of data. However, their small size makes them useful in many special applications. For example, sales people use them to record customers' inventories, and others use them to maintain appointment schedules and phone numbers and addresses.

THE CENTRAL PROCESSING UNIT

The heart of a computer is the *central processing unit* (*CPU*). The CPU in a microcomputer is a *microprocessor*—the device that made microcomputers possible in the first place. The CPU performs three key functions:

THE COMPUTER **19**

1-3

Internal memory. That part of the computer that stores data while the computer is in use. Generally divided into random-access memory (RAM) and read-only memory (ROM).

Read-only memory (ROM). ROM holds the instructions that the computer needs in order to function when it is first turned on. The information in ROM is not lost when the power is turned off.

Nonvolatile memory. Memory that does not lose data when the power is turned off.

▮ In conjunction with the operating system (discussed in Chapter 2), it coordinates all the computer's activities. It controls retrieving files from the disk, interprets data and commands you enter from the keyboard, and sends data to the printer.

▮ It performs arithmetic calculations such as addition and subtraction using the system of binary arithmetic. For example, if you enter a list of numbers in a document, many programs allow you automatically to calculate a total.

▮ It performs logical operations using equal to, greater than, and less than comparisons. For example, it can be programmed to determine if your grades are higher or lower than those of other students in the same course and to print a list that ranks everyone in descending order by grade.

Although powerful, microprocessors are extremely small. Figure 1-12 shows one of the latest and most powerful microprocessors. New microprocessors are periodically introduced because advances in technology allow them to be improved. Table 1-5 lists the Intel microprocessor chips used in various IBM and compatible computers. (The latter three are commonly referred to as the 286, 386™, and i486™.)

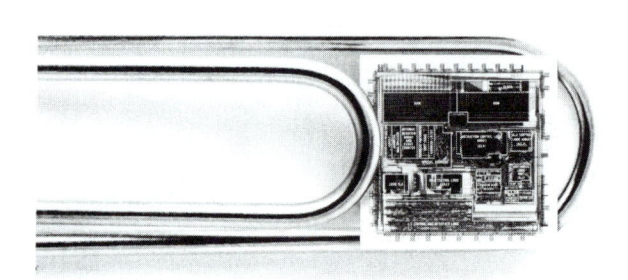

Figure 1-12 The Microprocessor
The microprocessor is an extremely small but powerful device that is used as the central processing unit (CPU) in the latest generation of microcomputers. *Courtesy of AT&T Bell Labs*

Table 1-5
IBM MICROPROCESSOR CHIPS

Microprocessor	Date	Models Used in
8086 or 8088	1981	Original PC and XT
80286	1984	AT
80386	1986	PS/2
80486	1989	PS/2

MEMORY

When you work on a computer it must store programs and data where the microprocessor can quickly find it. The place where it is stored is the computer's *internal memory*. Internal memory is divided into two parts: read-only memory (ROM) and random-access memory (RAM). Figure 1-13 shows how the Scrabble® brand crossword game is analogous to a computer's memory.

Read-Only Memory (ROM)

Read-only memory (ROM) is static, unchanging—sometimes called **nonvolatile**—memory. Your computer can read data stored in ROM, but you cannot enter data into ROM or change the data already there. The data in ROM are

20 COMPUTER SYSTEMS

Random-access memory (RAM). That part of memory that holds the programs and data currently in use. Also called main, primary, or user memory.

Volatile memory. Memory that will be lost if the power fails. RAM, for instance, is usually volatile.

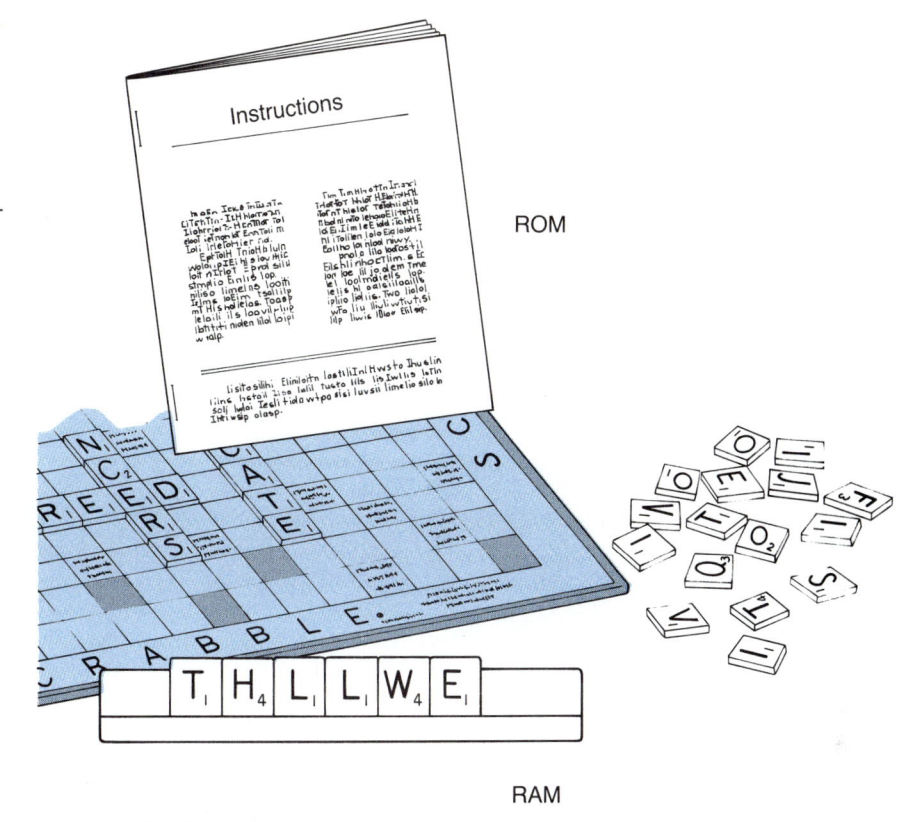

Figure 1-13 Read-Only Memory.
The Scrabble® brand crossword game is like a computer's memory. The instruction booklet is like ROM—you can read it, but you cannot change it. The board is like RAM—you can add, remove, or move information around on it.

permanently recorded on memory chips by the computer's manufacturer. Neither turning the computer off nor electrical power failure affect it; the data will still be there when you resume. ROM is generally used to store programs and instructions that the computer frequently needs. For example, it contains the instructions the computer follows to start up when you first turn it on.

Random-Access Memory (RAM)

When you load a program into the computer or create a word processing document or spreadsheet model, the program and the data you enter using the keyboard is stored in *random-access memory* (*RAM*) (also called *main*, *primary*, or *user* memory). Usually, if you turn off the computer, any programs or data stored in this memory are lost; thus RAM is said to be *volatile* memory.

The expression *random-access* comes from the way the data in memory can be located or accessed by the computer. One way to visualize random-access is to think of the differences between a tape player and compact disc player. If you want to play the third song on a tape, you must first advance the tape past the first two songs. This is called sequential access because you must got through each song in sequence. On a compact disc player, you can advance the laser directly to the track on the CD disc where the third song begins. This is called random-access because you can go directly to a song anywhere on the disc without first advancing through songs that precede it.

THE COMPUTER   21

Port. An electrical connection on the computer into which a cable can be plugged so the computer can communicate with another device such as a printer or modem.

Serial port. A port that transmits information one bit at a time, as opposed to a parallel port that transmits several bits of data at a time. Also known as RS-232-C.

Parallel port. A port that carries data 8 bits at a time on parallel paths. Frequently used for printers and connections to networks. Also known as a centronics interface.

1-3

PORTS

A computer system includes many types of peripherals, including the printer, display screen, modem, keyboard, digitizing tablet, and mouse. You connect these peripherals using cables that plug into *ports*, sockets mounted on the computer's cabinet through which information enters and leaves the computer. Ports are generally located on the back of computers (Figure 1-14) and are either serial or parallel.

Figure 1-14 Ports
Ports are where information enters and leaves the computer.

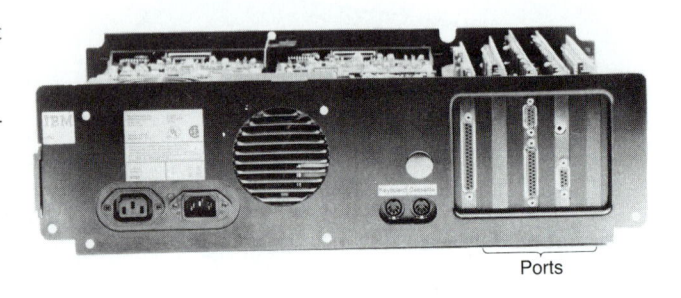

Ports are mounted on the back of the computer.
Courtesy of IBM Corporation

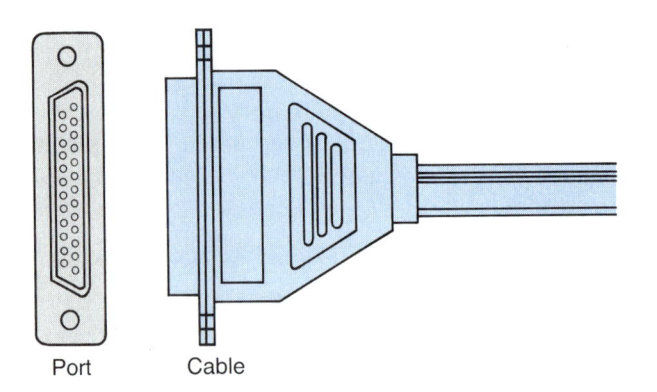

You plug cables into ports to connect peripherals such as printers or modems.

Port   Cable

Serial Ports

Serial ports (sometimes called *RS-232-C ports*) are where you attach modems—devices used to communicate with other computers—and some types of printers. When data are sent out a serial port, they are sent 1 bit at a time (Figure 1-15). Because the data are processed inside the computer 8, 16, or even 32 bits at a time, a serial port is like a narrowing on a highway at a tunnel. Data slow down, just as the highway traffic does, so that they can funnel out of the computer in single file. Serial ports provide slower communications and are therefore not ideal for printer connections. But when used with modems, serial ports are essential, because the telephone lines that most modems are connected to are also serial.

Parallel Ports

Parallel ports (sometimes called *centronics interfaces*) carry data 8 bits at a time on parallel paths (Figure 1-16). Because they can transmit data 8 bits or 1 byte at a time, they are a faster way for the computer to communicate with input and output devices. There is less narrowing than on a serial port, so traffic moves faster. Parallel ports are usually used to plug in printers.

22 COMPUTER SYSTEMS

Expansion slot. An electrical connection inside the computer's cabinet into which you can plug add-on boards or boards and peripherals and thereby expand the computer's functions.

Add-on boards. Boards containing electronic circuits that are inserted into the computer's expansion slots to expand its capacity or improve its performance. Also referred to as cards, boards, or expansion boards.

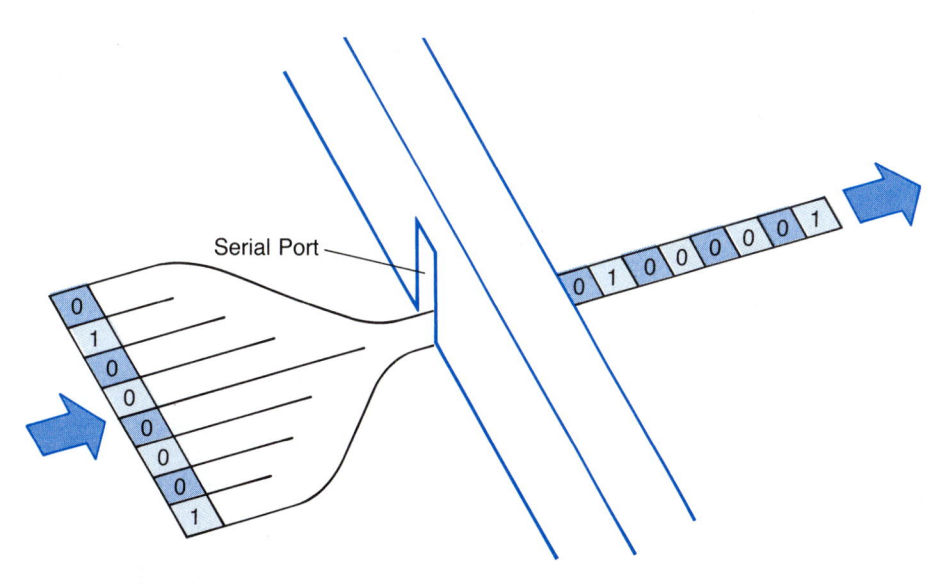

Figure 1-15 Serial Ports
Serial ports are like a single-lane tunnel. Information fed to it has to squeeze through the port a single bit at a time. Here, the ASCII code for the letter A is sent 1 bit at a time through the port.

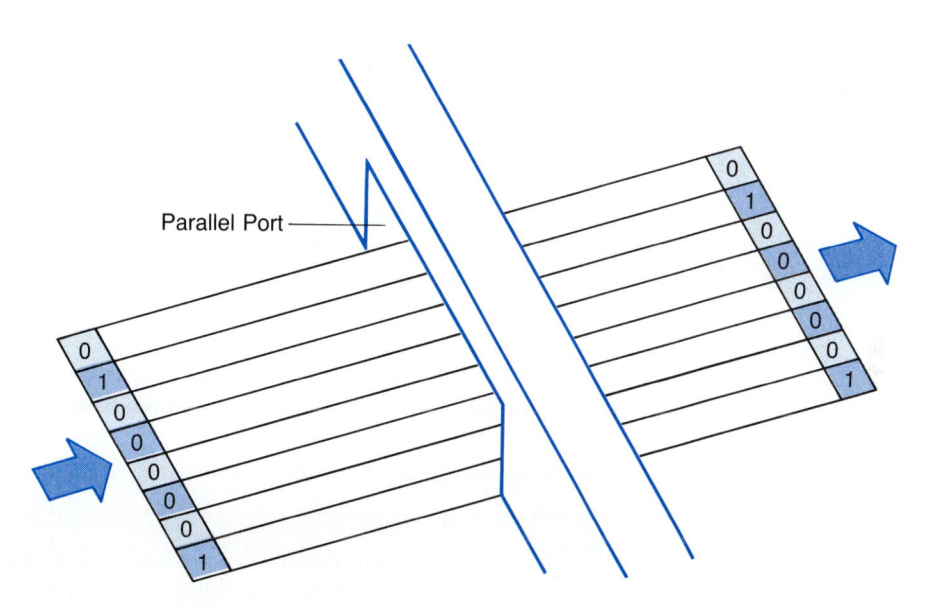

Figure 1-16 Parallel Ports
Parallel ports are like tunnels with the same number of lanes as the highway that feeds them. Information flows through faster as there is little or no constriction.

EXPANSION SLOTS AND BOARDS

Many users like to customize or update their computers to better serve their needs. To make this possible, most computers have *expansion slots* inside the cabinet into which you can plug *add-on boards* (also called *add-in boards* or *cards*) that contain electronic components (Figure 1-17). Boards plugged into these slots perform just as if they were built into the computer. Add-on boards

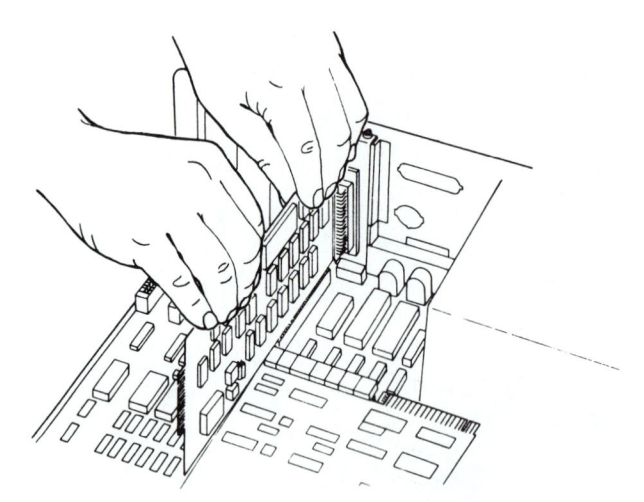

**Figure 1-17
Expansion Slots and
Add-On Boards**
Expansion slots inside the computer allow you to plug in add-on boards that expand the computer's capabilities.
Courtesy of IBM Corporation

can serve any one of many functions. Boards can be added to expand the computer's memory, allow the computer to display colors or graphics, allow you to send and receive FAXes, or call up other computers. Still others connect peripherals or are the peripherals themselves. For example, you can plug in a board that controls a hard disk drive located elsewhere in the system, or you can plug in a board that contains the hard disk drive itself.

1-3 THE DEVELOPMENT OF THE COMPUTER

The first electronic digital computer built in the United States, ENIAC, was unveiled at the University of Pennsylvania in 1946. It weighed 30 tons, filled the space of a two-car garage, and contained 18,000 vacuum tubes, which failed on average at the rate of one every seven minutes. It cost half a million dollars at 1946 prices.

Today, the same amount of computing power is contained in a pea-sized silicon chip. Almost any home computer costing as little as $100 can outperform ENIAC. Put another way, if the automobile and airplane businesses had developed like the computer business, a Rolls Royce would cost $2.75 and run for 3 million miles on one gallon of gas. And a Boeing 767 would cost just $500 and circle the globe in twenty minutes on five gallons of gas.

Tom Forester, ed., *The Information Technology Revolution* (Cambridge, Mass.: The MIT Press, 1985).

CARING FOR YOUR COMPUTER

Computers are rugged and will provide good service with minimal maintenance if you treat them properly. Here are a few important dos and don'ts that will ensure you get the maximum life out of your equipment.

DO turn down the screen intensity if you will be away from the computer awhile so that an image is not burned into its phosphor surface.

DO use a surge protector, a device that you plug into an outlet and then plug the computer into. This device protects the computer from any surges that might come down the power line. Surges occur when the power company restores service after it has been lost or when a nearby line is struck by lightning. A surge temporarily increases the current in the line, much like a wave of water is created if you suddenly remove a dam from a river. This surge, or wave, of current can damage a computer.

DON'T get it wet.

DON'T use it during lightning storms. Better yet, to be completely safe, unplug it when it is lightning.

DON'T drop it.

DON'T smoke around it.

DON'T leave it where it is exposed to direct sunlight.

DON'T turn the computer on and off more than is necessary. Computers, like other electronic equipment, are harmed more by the surge of power that runs through them when you first turn them on than they are by being left on all the time. Many users never turn their computers off; others just turn them off at the end of the day or on weekends.

DON'T use an ultrasonic humidifier without a mineral filter nearby the computer. These units break the water and the minerals it contains into small particles that are then distributed throughout the room. When the particles land on a computer, the water evaporates, leaving behind a powder that can damage sensitive equipment.

EXERCISES

Exercise 1-3A
INVESTIGATING TYPES OF COMPUTERS

Read a review in a computer magazine on one of the following kinds of computers:

A. A desktop computer
B. A portable computer
C. A laptop computer

List the following if they are mentioned:

A. Size of internal memory
B. Kind of microprocessor

Exercise 1-3B
DESCRIBING COMPUTERS IN THE LAB

List and describe in the table below the computers in your lab. Because some of the information is not noted on the computer, you may have to ask your instructor or refer to the computer's manual.

A. Who is the manufacturer of each? Typical manufacturers are IBM and Apple. If the computer is not one of these brands, does it act as if it were; for example, is it compatible with IBM's products?

B. What models are the computers? For example, they might be IBM PCs, XTs, ATs, or PS/2s.

C. How much random-access memory (RAM) does each computer have?

D. What kind of microprocessor (chip) does each use?

E. How many expansion slots does each have?

COMPUTERS IN THE LAB

Manufacturer	Model	RAM	Chip	Number of Slots

Exercise 1-3C
IDENTIFYING YOUR COMPUTER'S PORTS

Using Figure 1-14 as a guide, sketch one of the computers in the lab, and then label the ports to which the peripherals are attached. They are probably not labeled on the computer, so you may have to ask. Try to identify the following ports, and then list what is attached to them:

A. Parallel port
B. Serial port
C. Keyboard port

QUESTIONS

1. List three types of computers in descending order of their size.
2. List three functions performed by the computer's central processing unit (CPU).
3. What kind of device is used for the CPU in a microcomputer?
4. Describe the differences between RAM and ROM.
5. What is the function of a port? List the two kinds of ports on a computer, and describe the basic difference between them.
6. What is the purpose of the expansion slots inside a computer? What can they be used for?
7. What are some typical functions performed by add-on boards?
8. List four things you should never do with your computer.
9. List two things you should always do with your computer.
10. Match the items in column A with their descriptions in column B.

A	B
___ Central processing unit (CPU)	A. Storage for documents and programs
___ Expansion slots and boards	B. Used to attach peripherals like printers
___ Memory	C. Processes data and controls computer operations
___ Ports	D. Used to expand the computer's capabilities

1-4 INPUT DEVICES

Input device. Any device used to enter information into the computer.

Keyboard. The input device from which you type information into the computer.

Directional arrow keys. The four arrow keys on the keyboard that move the cursor around the screen a character or line at a time.

Programmer. A person who writes computer programs, including those you use to process words and information.

Alphabetic keys. The keys on the computer's keyboard that are usually arranged just as they are on a typewriter keyboard.

QWERTY keyboard. The standard arrangement of keys on the keyboard. Named after the arrangement of the first six keys on the top row.

Dvorak keyboard. A layout of alphabetic keys on the keyboard designed for greater speed and efficiency.

Autorepeat feature. Any key that, when held down, will continue to enter the character or function until it is released.

Caps Lock key. The key that switches the alphabetic keys between entering uppercase or lowercase letters.

Num Lock key. The key that activates the number keys (which also double as cursor movement keys) on the numeric keypad.

Toggle. Many computer commands toggle, that is, they turn a mode either on or off or switch back and forth between two states.

Input devices are used to enter data into the computer where they can be processed. All computers come equipped with a keyboard, but several other input devices are also available that can enter data into your computer for processing. For example, you can scan text or images into your computer, or you can give it verbal instructions in special applications. As you enter data, they are fed to the CPU and then either executed (if a command) or stored in memory (if data).

KEYBOARDS

Keyboards vary in design and layout from computer to computer, but all have essentially the same types of keys. For example, Figure 1-18 shows the original IBM PC keyboard and the enhanced keyboard introduced with the IBM AT. The main differences between the old and new keyboards are the locations of the function keys and the *directional arrow keys*. A person writing a software program (called a *programmer*) can assign any function he or she chooses to each of the keys on the keyboard. Thus, the actual function that each key performs varies from program to program. But in general, the following points apply to all keyboards.

- The most common layout of the *alphabetic keys* is identical to the layout on a typewriter. This layout is called a *QWERTY keyboard* because those are the first six keys on the upper row of letter keys. There are also several other arrangements, such as the *Dvorak keyboard*, named after its developer, Dr. August Dvorak. This keyboard was designed to be much faster than the QWERTY keyboard and numerous tests have shown it to be so.

- Many keys have an *autorepeat feature*; that is, if you hold them down, they continue entering the key's character or repeating its function until you release the key.

- The **Caps Lock**, **Num Lock**, and **Scroll Lock** keys *toggle*. The term toggle comes from light switches, where you can toggle a light on or off. On the computer, toggling means that if one of these keys is not engaged when you press it, it becomes engaged. If it is engaged when you press it, it becomes disengaged. As these three keys can be engaged or disengaged, most keyboards and applications programs display indicators that indicate their current status.

- Alphabetic keys are arranged on the keyboard just as they are on a typewriter. When you press them, they enter lowercase letters. If you hold down the **Shift** key when you press the letter keys, or if you engage the **Caps Lock** key, you enter uppercase (capital) letters. If you engage **Caps Lock** and then hold down **Shift** while typing, you enter lowercase letters.

- Numeric keys are located above the alphabetic keys and are labeled with both numbers and symbols. When you press these keys, you enter either the indicated numbers or, if you hold down **Shift**, the indicated symbols.

  On many computers, you can also enter numbers using the *numeric keypad* at the right of the keyboard. If some of the keys on the numeric

28 COMPUTER SYSTEMS

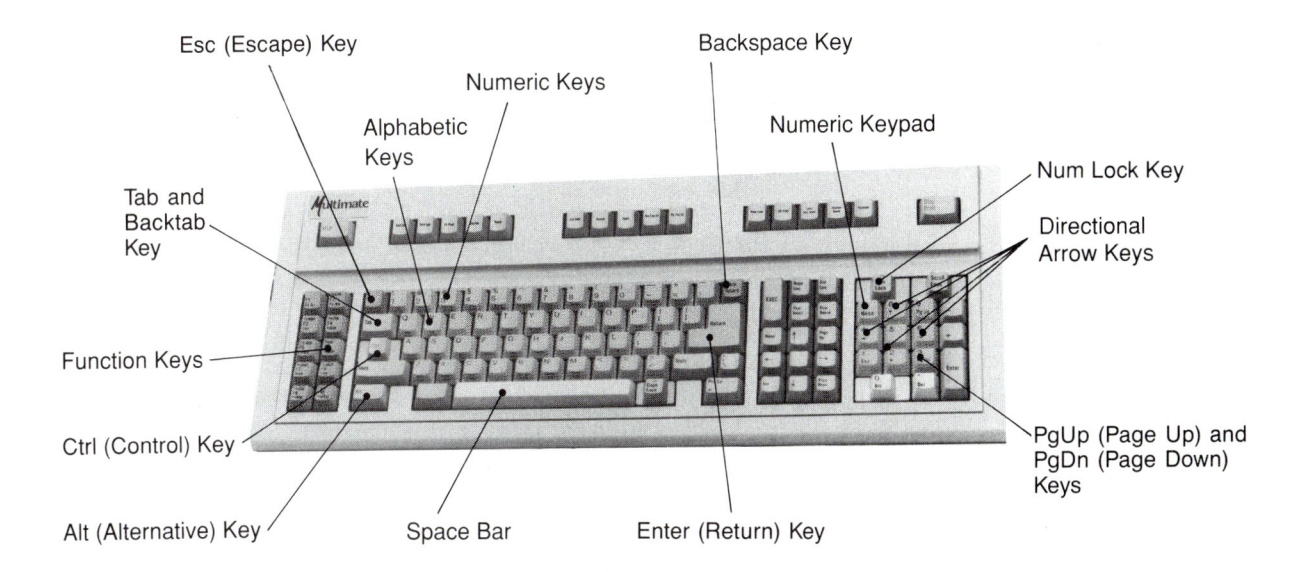

Figure 1-18 Typical Keyboards
On most computers, the keyboard will be either an original or enhanced keyboard.
Courtesy of IBM Corporation

Numeric keypad. Number keys arranged like those on a calculator.

Enter key. Frequently the final keystroke; for example, used when entering data into spreadsheet cells, ending paragraphs in documents, or executing commands. Also known as the **Return** key.

keypad also move the cursor, you must press **Num Lock** to switch back and forth between entering numbers and moving the cursor. When engaged, the keys enter numbers. When not engaged, they move the cursor.

- If you are an experienced typist and are used to typing a lowercase **L** for 1 or an uppercase **O** for 0 (zero), do not do this on your computer. The computer treats numbers and letters differently, and although you usually won't have problems, you could run into difficulties by disregarding this distinction.

- The **Enter** key (also called the **Return** key) is often pressed as the final keystroke. (This key is labelled ↵ on many keyboards.) It is used:
  - when sending commands to the computer. You often have to type a command, or highlight one on a menu and then press **Enter** to send the command to the CPU.

INPUT DEVICES   **29**

Cursor movement keys. The specified keys on the keyboard, including the four directional arrow keys, used to move the cursor.

Cursor. A bright underscore character, one-character-wide highlight, or one-cell-wide reverse video highlight that you move with cursor movement keys to enter, delete, or select text in a document or spreadsheet.

PgUp key. A key that scrolls the screen up one full screen or one page.

PgDn key. A key that scrolls the screen down one full screen or one page.

Spacebar. Inserts spaces when in insert mode and erases characters in typeover mode.

Backspace key. The key used most frequently to correct errors. The **Backspace** key moves the cursor to the left and deletes characters as it moves back through the line of characters.

Destructive backspace. Describes a **Backspace** key that deletes characters to its left when pressed.

Esc key. A key frequently used to cancel commands.

Function key. Any of several specific keys on the keyboard that makes the computer execute a particular function. The specific function one of these keys performs is generally assigned by the programmer who develops the program. For example, on the IBM PC, the **F1** key will frequently display a help screen if you are running an applications program.

Ctrl key. A key you use to enter commands. You hold the **Ctrl** key down while you press other keys.

Alt key. A special-purpose key that is usually held down while pressing another key to execute a command.

- when ending paragraphs or lines of text on a word processing program before they reach the right margin. But, unlike a typewriter, you don't have to press it to end lines within a paragraph.
- when entering data into spreadsheet cells. You type the data, and then press **Enter**.

▌ *Cursor movement keys* move the *cursor*, a reverse video (a dark character against a light background or vice versa) or underline character, around the screen. You use the cursor to point to where you want to enter or edit data on the screen. Because keyboards vary and program designers can change their functions, the keys used to move the cursor also vary. Generally, the directional arrow keys (Figure 1-19) move the cursor one line or character at a time in the direction of the arrow. On most programs, the **PgUp** and **PgDn** keys move the cursor a screen or page at a time.

▌ The **Spacebar** enters spaces. On a typewriter, pressing **Spacebar** moves the print element over existing text, but on a computer, pressing **Spacebar** often pushes the next characters, if any, to the right.

▌ The **Backspace** key backs the cursor up. If the program assigns this key the ability to delete characters you back it over, it is called a *destructive backspace*. This lets you quickly back over and delete characters when you discover a mistake while entering text.

▌ The **Esc** (Escape) key (or other designated key) is often used to cancel a command in progress if you change your mind before completing the command.

▌ Computer manufacturers recognize the need for special keys to which software designers can assign frequently used tasks. They have therefore added special keys that can be used for this purpose. These *function keys* (often designated **F1**, **F2**, **F3**, and so on) perform functions assigned to them by the programmer. For example, on a word processing program, function keys are often assigned to select, copy, move, or delete text. On some keyboards, the function keys are grouped at the side of the keyboard. On other computers, they are the top row of keys.

▌ Many keys are assigned more than one function. For instance, pressing the right directional arrow key may move the cursor one column or character at a time, but pressing the right directional arrow key while holding down the **Ctrl** (Control) key may move the cursor several columns or characters at a time. Pressing the letter **B** enters the letter alone, but pressing **B** while holding down the **Alt** (Alternate) key might enter a code that tells the printer to begin boldfacing text. Neither **Ctrl** nor **Alt** sends characters to the computer; they change what is sent when you press other

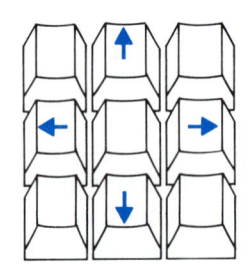

All computers have directional arrow keys on the numeric keypad that only work when **Num Lock** is not engaged.

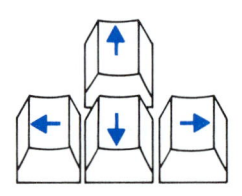

Newer computers also have a separate set of directional arrow keys that work at any time.

**Figure 1-19
Directional Arrow Keys**
Almost all computer keyboards have directional arrow keys.

30 COMPUTER SYSTEMS

Tab key. The key that moves the cursor from left to right between tab stops. See also **Backtab** key.

Backtab key. The key that moves the cursor from right to left between tab stops. Usually the same as the **Tab** key but pressed while holding down **Shift**. Also see **Tab key**.

Bar codes. The universal product codes on packages that can be scanned and fed to a computer.

Scanner. An input device that reads information from hard copy and transmits it to the computer in digital form. There are currently three kinds of scanners: character recognition scanners, bar-code readers, and bit-image converters (digitizers).

Optical character recognition (OCR). The process of converting printed characters to computer data with a scanning device.

keys. Using combinations of keys in this way lets the software designers assign many more functions to the keyboard than there are keys available. This is much like the standard typewriter, which uses **Shift** to type uppercase letters. Using this approach, fifty-two characters (twenty-six uppercase and twenty-six lowercase letters) can be generated by only twenty-six keys.

When you use these modifier keys, you hold them down first, and then press the other key. The sequence in which you press the keys is important — so follow these procedures:

1. Hold down the **Alt**, **Shift**, or **Ctrl** key. These keys do not repeat or send commands to the computer, so you can hold them down as long as you want.
2. Press the function key just as if you were typing a character, then release both keys. If you hold the second key down, the command will repeat until you release it, and the computer will start beeping. This can create problems.

▎ The **Tab** key moves the cursor to the next tab stop. The **Backtab** key does the same thing but moves the cursor in the opposite direction. **Backtab** is usually the same key as **Tab** but you press it while holding down **Shift**.

SCANNERS

You do not have to type everything into a computer. Scanners allow you to enter text and graphics from hard copy such as printed or typed documents, photographs, or line drawings. You have seen scanners at work whenever you visit the supermarket. At the checkout counter, a clerk runs a handheld wand over a product or passes the product over a slot in the counter. These devices read the *bar code* on the product and display its price on the register. They also record the sale and make adjustments in inventory so the store knows when to reorder. In most offices there are two basic types of scanners, text scanners and graphics scanners.

Text Scanners

When you type text into a computer and then print it out on a printer, you are actually converting the text from a digital form (the form used by the computer) to a printed form. Until recently, this conversion process had been like a one-way street. It was not easily possible to convert printed copy into an electronic form that could be processed by a computer or word processing program. For example, if a document has already been typed and printed but not saved in a digital form, it is time consuming to rekeyboard it back into the computer. To make the conversion from printed text to electronic text more efficient, *scanners* have been developed. Because documents may be typed or printed using many different typefaces, the conversion process is done with *optical character recognition* (*OCR*) devices (Figure 1-20).

    The scanner reads the pattern of dark characters against a light background and converts each character to its digital ASCII number. This ASCII number is then stored in the computer's memory or on a disk. Because the text is converted into its ASCII numbers, it can be stored, displayed, printed, and otherwise manipulated just as if it had been entered into the computer with the keyboard. Text you enter with one of these devices can be edited by word processors and processed by other programs that accept ASCII input.

INPUT DEVICES   **31**

Graphics scanner. A scanner that converts images on paper into a digital form that can be displayed and processed by a computer. Also called an image digitizer.

Desktop publishing. The process of preparing high-quality printed documents with a microcomputer and laser printer.

Pixel. A dot on the screen illuminated to create an image.

Gray scale. A range of tones from pure white to pure black in a series of steps, each of which is increasingly darker.

Figure 1-20   OCR Scanner
An OCR scanner scans documents into the computer a character at a time so that the text can be manipulated just as if it had been entered through the keyboard.
Courtesy of Dest

Graphics Scanners

To scan graphic images such as photographs, line drawings, charts, and maps into the computer, **graphics scanners** (also called *image digitizers*) convert the printed image into digital form. Instead of converting the image into characters, graphics scanners take a digital picture of it, much as a copy machine does. The difference, of course, is that the copy is stored in the computer in digital form. Graphics scanners (Figure 1-21) are becoming more and more useful now that **desktop publishing** programs allow you to combine text and graphics in documents. The scanner works by breaking the image up into small spots, called **pixels** (for picture elements). It then assigns a numeric value to each pixel and stores it in memory or on the disk. The image can then be incorporated into a word-processed or desktop published document or manipulated with a program designed to work with images of this kind.

Graphics scanners are available in both inexpensive 1-bit and more expensive 8-bit versions. Scanners that use 1 bit to store an image can scan only black-and-white images, because with 1 bit you can specify only if a pixel is either black or white. Many images, such as photographs, have intermediate gray tones, and more information is needed to scan these accurately. The spectrum of tones in these images is called a **gray scale**. When arranged from darkest to lightest, they look like Figure 1-22. Eight-bit scanners can store up to 256 tones ($2^8 = 256$), so they can be used to scan images of this kind. They can also scan color images and assign any one of 256 colors to each pixel.

32   COMPUTER SYSTEMS

File compression. The process of shrinking a file so it takes up less room on the disk. A compressed file can also be transmitted more quickly.

Figure 1-21 Graphics Scanners
Graphics scanners scan images, converting each point or pixel on the document into electronic signals that are sent to the computer. Unlike text scanners, the electronic signals do not indicate characters.
Courtesy of Dest

The number of bytes required to store a graphic image depends on the number of bits assigned to each pixel. For example, an 8½-by-11-inch image printed 300 dots to the inch has over 8 million pixels. To store a graphic image of this size, a 1-bit scanner requires almost 1MB of memory. An 8-bit scanner requires almost 8MB. Because these file sizes would create serious storage problems, scanners use a special procedure called *file compression* to store the files in much less space on the disk. This does not change the image at all, it just stores it in less space on the disk.

VOICE INPUT DEVICES

Despite the incredibly fast processing speed of the computer, it is slowed down by the keyboard. To process information, you must first enter it into the com-

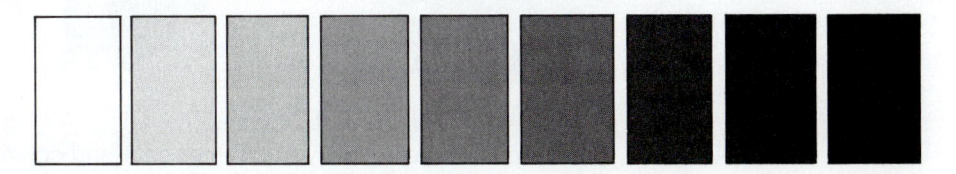

Figure 1-22 Gray Scale
Eight-bit graphics scanners can store up to 256 values to reproduce images, like photographs, that have many tones. The arrangement of tones from light to dark is called a gray scale.

INPUT DEVICES 33

Voice input device. An input device that recognizes the human voice and converts it into computer code.

Voice template. An electronic pattern for individual spoken words that allows a computer to recognize speech.

puter, and people can type only so fast. Ideally, people should be able to talk to the computer as they talk to friends and co-workers. This would not only make the process faster but would also make the computer accessible to those who do not know how or are unable to type. It is not yet possible to converse with your computer, but *voice input devices* have been developed that, though limited, do convert the human voice into a signal the computer can understand (Figure 1-23). This is not a simple task. A recent article in *The Economist* uses the following two sentences to illustrate the difficulty:

> *This new display can recognize speech.*
> *This nudist play can wreck a nice beach.*

Read each sentence aloud. To tell the difference between them requires very good hearing. Even then you probably could not tell the difference unless the words were pronounced very carefully. Imagine how difficult it is to program a computer so that it can tell the difference!

Advances are slowly being made, and systems have been developed that can understand up to 20,000 words. To use one of these systems, you must first "train" the computer to make it familiar with the way you pronounce each word. To do so, each word in the program's vocabulary is displayed on the screen, and you speak each aloud into a microphone. The computer then stores your pronunciation, along with the matching word displayed on the screen. This computerized match is called a *voice template*. The next time you speak to the computer, it quickly matches the pattern of your voice against the voice templates stored in its memory. If it finds a match, it can display the word or execute the command.

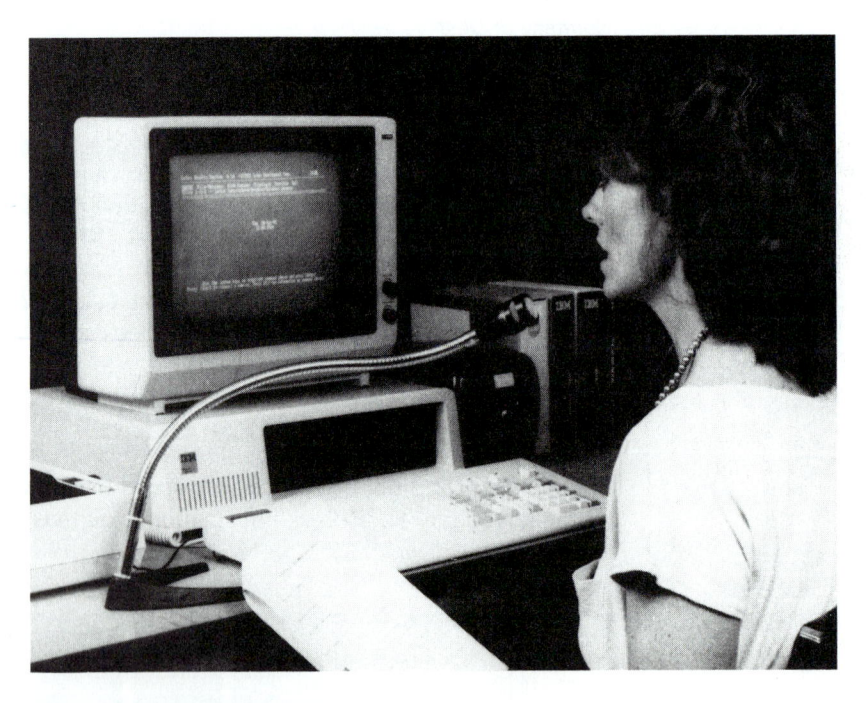

Figure 1-23   Voice Input Devices
Voice input devices allow you to enter data and commands with your voice by converting speech into electronic signals.
Courtesy of The Voice Connection

EXERCISES

Exercise 1-4A
IDENTIFYING KEYS ON THE KEYBOARD

Sketch the keyboard of a computer in the lab, and then determine if it is a standard or enhanced keyboard. Identify the location of the following keys:

A. Alphabetic keys
B. Numeric keys
C. Numeric keypad
D. **Enter (Return)** key
E. Directional arrow keys
F. **Spacebar**
G. **Backspace** key
H. **Escape** key
I. **Shift** keys
J. **Control** key
K. Function keys
L. **Num Lock** key
M. **Caps Lock** key

Exercise 1-4B
IDENTIFYING KEYBOARD INDICATORS

If one of the keyboards in the lab has indicator lights built into it, sketch the lights, and then label each of them as follows:

A. On/off indicator
B. **Num Lock** indicator
C. **Caps Lock** indicator
D. **Scroll Lock** indicator

INPUT DEVICES

QUESTIONS

1. What does it mean when you say a key autorepeats? How do you make it do so? How do you stop it?
2. What does it mean when you say a key toggles?
3. What is the purpose of a numeric keypad?
4. What are cursor movement keys?
5. Match the keys in column A with their functions in column B.

A	B
___Spacebar	A. Enters uppercase letters when engaged
___Backspace	B. Cancels commands
___Caps Lock	C. Toggles the numeric keypad between entering numbers and moving the cursor
___Shift	
___Num Lock	D. Enter commands
___Enter	E. Deletes characters
___Esc	F. Enters spaces
	G. Enters uppercase letters when held down

6. What are function keys, and what are they used for?
7. What is the purpose of a scanner? What two types are there and what is each used for?
8. What is the first step you must complete when using most voice input systems?

1-5
OUTPUT DEVICES—THE DISPLAY

Output device. Any device used to get information from a computer. Typical output devices are the display screen, printers, plotters, and modems.

Display screen. The computer's screen. The screen gives you instant feedback by displaying whatever input you have entered. Known also as a monitor.

Cathode ray tube (CRT). A display tube used in many desktop computer displays to create the image you see on the screen.

Flat-panel display. A display screen that is thin so it can be easily carried. Usually found on portable computers.

When working at a computer, you want to be able to see what you are working on. The devices that you use to do this are called *output devices* because they display information stored in the computer. One of the most common output devices is the *display screen* (also called a *video display* or *display monitor*) attached to your computer. This screen is a window into your computer's memory. As you type data on the keyboard, they are entered into memory and displayed on the screen so that you can see what you have entered. Because you spend most of your time looking at the display screen, its quality and capabilities are important. Display screens are available in many styles that fall into two main categories: cathode ray tubes and flat-panel displays.

CATHODE RAY TUBES (CRTS)

Most computer displays are equipped with a *cathode ray tube* (*CRT*) similar to the one in your TV set because these displays create the best image (Figure 1-24). Many CRTs display twenty-four or twenty-five lines of eighty characters each, but some display up to sixty-six lines, enough to show a full 8½-by-11-inch page of text (Figure 1-25). Displays capable of showing the full page, or even two facing pages, are highly desirable but still quite expensive. With the increasing popularity of desktop publishing, however, these full-page displays will inevitably become more popular and less expensive.

FLAT-PANEL DISPLAYS

CRTs are bulky, so portable computers must use *flat-panel displays* (Figure 1-26). On these displays, the image is created using various technologies, all of which offer advantages and disadvantages, with the trade-offs usually being made between readability, power consumption, and cost. Because these screens are most often used in portable computers, power consumption is a major concern. If a display requires too much power, the battery life between recharges is very short, perhaps as short as one hour. Lower power consumption can increase a battery's life to six or more hours.

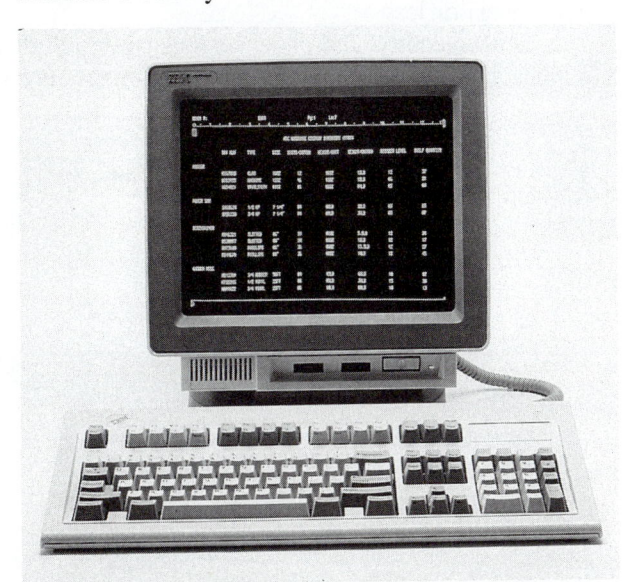

FIGURE 1-24 CRT Displays
CRT displays are the most common display screen. They provide a very sharp and readable image.
Courtesy of IBM Corporation

FIGURE 1-25 Full-Page Displays
Full-page display screens are ideal for many applications, such as word processing. They are especially useful when formatting pages with a desktop publishing program. Some models can be turned horizontally so they can display two facing pages.
Courtesy of IBM Corporation

Pitch. The spacing of illuminated dots or stripes on the screen that determines a screen's resolution.

COLOR

Displays are also classified as either monochrome or color. Monochrome screens display a single color, usually white, green, or amber characters against a black background. On some of these screens, you can reverse the display so that dark characters are displayed against a light background.

Color displays have become increasingly popular. To generate colors, three dots or thin stripes of phosphor (red, green, and blue) must be illuminated to create a single dot from which characters are created. The size, or *pitch*, of the dots (or stripes) determines how sharp a character displayed on the screen will appear. High-quality monitors have a pitch of 0.31 mm (about 1/3 of a millimeter) or less.

Until recently, flat-panel screens could not display color. However, new screens can display 256 colors and the images are sharp and the colors vivid.

**FIGURE 1-26
Flat-Panel Displays**
Flat-panel displays are light and use little power so they are ideal for use in portable computers.
Courtesy of IBM Corporation

Character set. The characters that are permanently stored in the computer's memory.

Character display. A display screen that can display only characters and not graphics. See also Graphics display.

Graphic display. The process by which each dot (pixel) on the display screen is given a corresponding bit in the computer's memory. Also known as bit-mapped displays.

THE SCREEN DISPLAY

The display that you see on the screen is either a character display or a graphic display. The differences are startling, and graphic displays are becoming increasingly more common.

Character Displays

When computers were first developed, all display screens displayed just the characters A through Z, numbers 1 through 10, and a very limited set of other special characters like ¶, ■, and Φ. Altogether, 256 characters, called the *character set*, can be displayed. Because only this fixed set of characters can be displayed, these displays are called *character displays* (Figure 1-27).

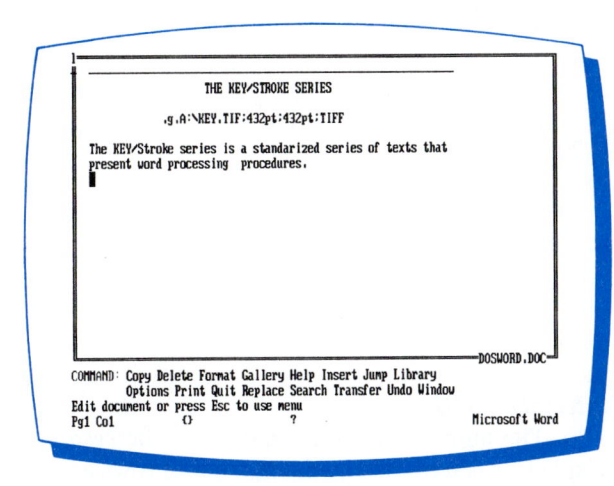

Figure 1-27 A Character Display Until recently, character displays were the most common display. Here, Microsoft Word, a typical character-based program, is shown.

ADVANTAGES AND DISADVANTAGES OF CHARACTER DISPLAYS

- Character displays require little memory.
- Character displays operate very quickly.
- Character displays display only the characters in the computer's character set.
- Character displays can display only simple graphics using the graphic characters in the character set. For example, the IBM character set has ruled lines and corners so that you can create boxes. But you cannot create circles because these are not stored in the character set.
- Characters must occupy a fixed position on the screen; they cannot be offset half a line or half a column. This prevents you from seeing on the screen the effects of proportional spacing, different type sizes, subscripts, and superscripts.
- A character display cannot display italic type, photographs, or line drawings and all text characters are the same size.

Graphic Displays

Because character displays can display only a specified set of characters, they cannot display graphics. To overcome this limitation, *graphic displays* (also called *bit-mapped displays*) have been developed and are now widely used (Figure 1-28).

OUTPUT DEVICES – THE DISPLAY

Graphic user interface (GUI). A screen display that can show graphic images as well as text characters.

Resolution. An indication of the sharpness of characters or images on a printout or the display screen.

Color graphics adapter (CGA). An early standard that allows graphics to be displayed on a computer screen when an add-on card and display screen using the standard are added to the computer.

Enhanced color graphics adapter (EGA). A graphics add-in card that permits the display of graphics on the screen.

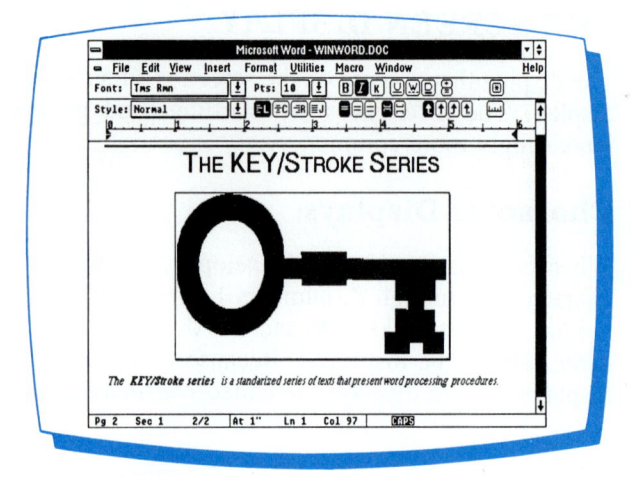

Figure 1-28 A Graphic Display
Graphic displays are becoming increasingly popular. Here, the same document as the one shown in Figure 1-27 is shown on a graphic-based word processing program.

On a graphic display, the screen is divided into a grid, as shown in Figure 1-29. The grid divides the screen into small boxes or dots called picture elements, or pixels. When an image is displayed on the screen, some of the pixels are illuminated and some are left dark. On a color monitor, the colors of each pixel can also be set to one of many colors. The patterns of illuminated or colored pixels form characters and other images on the screen. This flexibility allows text and illustrations to be displayed on the screen. For this reason, graphic displays, and programs that take advantage of them, are becoming increasingly common. These programs have what is called a *graphic user interface (GUI)*.

The number of pixels, and hence the *resolution* (sharpness) of a graphic display, is determined by the number of rows and columns the screen is divided into (Figure 1-30). The number of pixels displayed horizontally on the screen by the number displayed vertically indicates the resolution. For example, a resolution of 640-by-480 pixels indicates the screen has 640 pixels horizontally and 480 vertically. Resolution is determined by which of the three most widely used standards your system is using. In ascending order of sharpness, *Color graphics adapters* (*CGA*) display 320-by-200 resolution in four colors, *Enhanced color graphics adapters* (*EGA*) display 640-by-350 resolution in

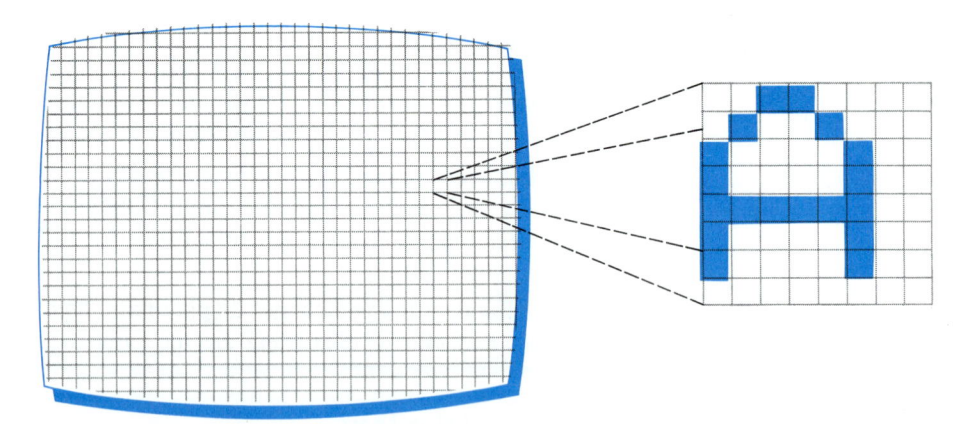

Figure 1-29 Pixels
Picture elements, or pixels, are small dots into which the screen is divided. By illuminating selected pixels, the computer can display text and other images.

Video graphics array (VGA). A high-resolution graphics standard for display screens.

High Resolution

Low Resolution

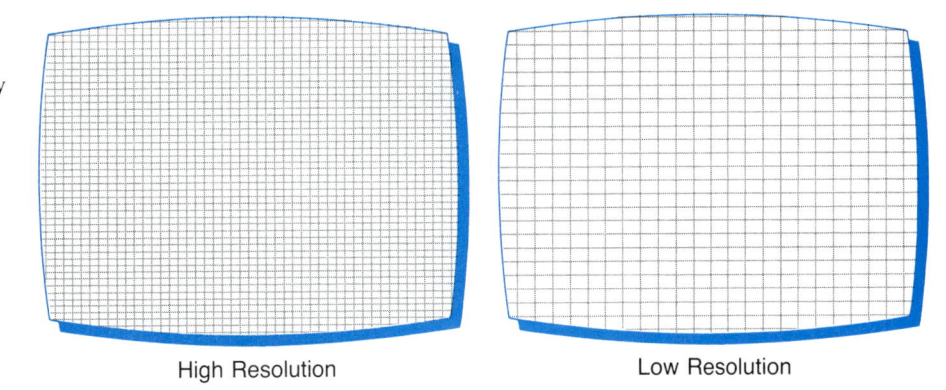

Figure 1-30 Resolution
High-resolution displays divide the screen into more pixels than a low-resolution screen does. The result is a sharper image because each character is formed from more dots.

sixteen colors and *Video graphics array* (*VGA*) displays 640-by-480 resolution in sixteen colors and 320-by-200 resolution in 256 colors. The standard your system uses is determined by the video display that is built in or added by inserting an add-on board.

ADVANTAGES AND DISADVANTAGES OF GRAPHIC DISPLAYS

- Graphic displays can display different fonts, type sizes, and enhancements, such as italics and proportional spacing.
- Both text and graphics can be displayed on the screen at the same time, which is especially important in desktop publishing applications.
- Graphic displays require a lot of memory.
- Graphic displays operate slowly.

EXERCISES

Exercise 1-5A
INVESTIGATING DISPLAY SCREENS

Read a review of a display in one of the computer magazines in the library, and then list the following features if they are mentioned:

A. The resolution
B. The number of colors
C. Text or graphic capabilities

Decide whether you would pay extra for these features if you were writing college term papers or composing a graphic layout.

Exercise 1-5B
IDENTIFYING THE DISPLAY SCREEN'S CONTROLS

Sketch and label the controls on one of the display screens in the lab. Briefly describe the purpose of each control listed below.

THE DISPLAY'S CONTROLS

Control	Description
On/off switch	
Contrast	
Brightness	
Horizontal hold	
Vertical hold	
Other	

Exercise 1-5C
EXPLORING FLAT PANEL DISPLAYS

Visit a local computer store and ask to see a portable computer. Ask what type of display it uses. Look carefully at the display from all angles. Is it easy to read?

QUESTIONS

1. Describe the two basic types of display screens.
2. What do the terms *low resolution* and *high resolution* refer to?
3. What is the difference between a graphic display and a character display? What are their advantages and disadvantages?
4. What is the primary difference among CGA, EGA, and VGA?
5. List two advantages and two disadvantages of character displays.
6. List two advantages and two disadvantages of graphic displays.

1-6
OUTPUT DEVICES — THE PRINTER

Fully formed character printer. A printer that creates characters on the paper by striking a metal or plastic character against an inked ribbon, much as a typewriter does.

Print wheel. A type element. See Daisy wheel printer.

Daisy-wheel printer. A fully formed character printer whose print element is shaped like the head of a daisy with each character on a petal.

Thimble. A type element used in some fully-formed character printers.

After the display screen, the most widely used output device is the printer. Having a printer is essential if the data you process with your computer are to be filed or physically distributed to others. Hundreds of printers are available, and nearly all of them have unique features. There are, however, at least two ways to categorize printers: by how they form characters and by how they transfer them to the paper.

HOW CHARACTERS ARE FORMED

Printers use one of two approaches when they form letters (Figure 1-31). Characters are printed fully formed, similar to the way a typewriter prints, or they are created by arranging a series of dots on the paper, much as characters are displayed on the screen.

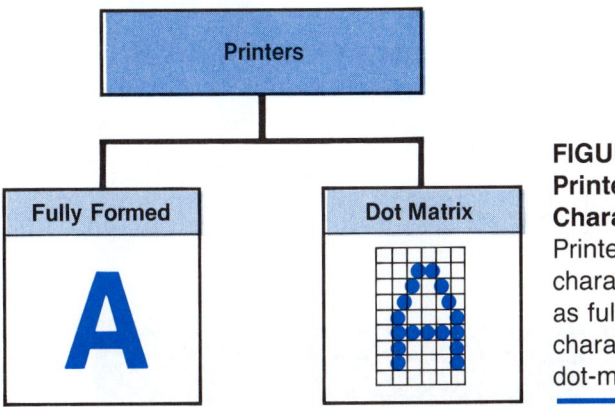

FIGURE 1-31 How Printers Form Characters Printers can form characters in two ways: as fully formed characters or as dot-matrix characters.

Fully Formed Character Printers

Fully formed character printers print solid characters using a type element with raised characters like those on a typewriter. The two basic type elements these printers use are print wheels and thimbles. Printers using **print wheels** are commonly called daisy-wheel printers. The term *daisy wheel* comes from the way individual characters are arranged on flexible "petals" radiating from the center of the type element (Figure 1-32). *Thimbles* also have raised characters, but they are arranged on an inverted thimble.

ADVANTAGES AND DISADVANTAGES OF FULLY FORMED CHARACTER PRINTERS

- Fully formed character printers transfer sharp, crisp characters onto the paper.
- Fully formed character printers are relatively slow.
- Fully formed character printers cannot print graphics.
- Typefaces and type sizes can be changed only by changing the type element. To do this, you have to stop the printer. This is so time consuming that most users use the same typestyle and type size for the entire document.

FIGURE 1-32 Daisy Wheels and Thimbles Letter-quality impact printers use type elements with raised characters.

A daisy wheel is named after its shape. Petals with raised characters radiate from the center.
Courtesy of Qume Corporation, San Jose, Calif.

Thimbles work just like daisy wheels, but the characters are on petals that take the shape of a thimble.
Courtesy of NEC Technologies

Dot-matrix printer. A printer that creates characters or images from a pattern of dots. Some dot-matrix printers use a type element with pins arranged in a matrix; others use heat, a laser, or diodes to create the images. A dot-matrix printer is more flexible than a fully formed character printer, and offers a wider range of typestyles.

Dot-Matrix Printers

Dot-matrix printers form characters using an array of dots. The spacing of the dots affects the resolution and density, or quality, of the characters. Characters will appear more like those printed on a fully formed character printer if the dots are closer together (Figure 1-33).

Dot-matrix printers can also print graphics. Because graphics are displayed on a screen, and stored in memory, in a similar grid, it's a simple matter to transfer images from memory to paper. Whenever the value stored in memory is a 1, the dot is printed in the corresponding position on the paper. Whenever the value in memory is a 0, the corresponding position on the paper is left blank. By controlling the position dots are printed in, an illusion of brightness can be conveyed. The ability to convey brightness allows dot-matrix printers to print realistic, almost photographic, images (Figure 1-34).

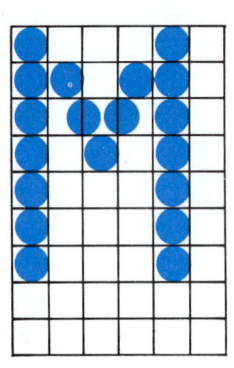

FIGURE 1-33 Print Quality
The quality of the character is determined by the spacing of the dots. This enlargement of a dot-matrix character shows that the closer the dots are, the more like letter quality the character is.

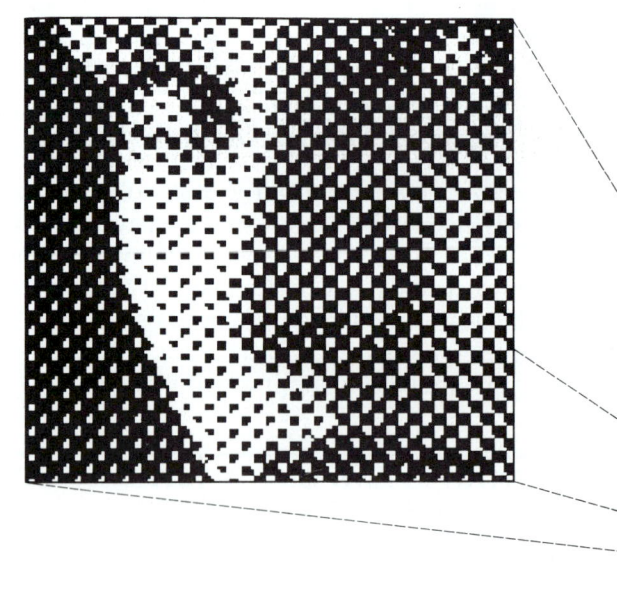

FIGURE 1-34 Dot-Matrix Graphics
Graphic images such as photographs are printed with dots. Here, an enlargement of a small area of the illustration clearly shows how the image is formed from dots.

44 COMPUTER SYSTEMS

Impact printer. A printer that transfers characters to paper by striking an inked ribbon against the paper.

ADVANTAGES AND DISADVANTAGES OF DOT-MATRIX PRINTERS

▌ Dot-matrix printers can print any image on the paper. The image does not have to be available on a print element, as it does on a fully formed character printer. Any image that can be created in memory or displayed on the screen can be printed on a dot-matrix printer.

▌ You can use a wide range of fonts (typestyles and type sizes) within the same document. The ease with which you can do this depends on the program you are using.

▌ Dot-matrix printers can print graphics because they can print dots anywhere on the page. By varying the spacing between the dots, an illusion of brightness can be created.

▌ The less expensive models do not print characters as clearly as fully formed character printers or more expensive dot-matrix printers.

HOW CHARACTERS ARE TRANSFERRED TO PAPER

Printers can also be categorized by how they transfer the characters to paper. The two methods of transfer are impact and nonimpact (Figure 1-35).

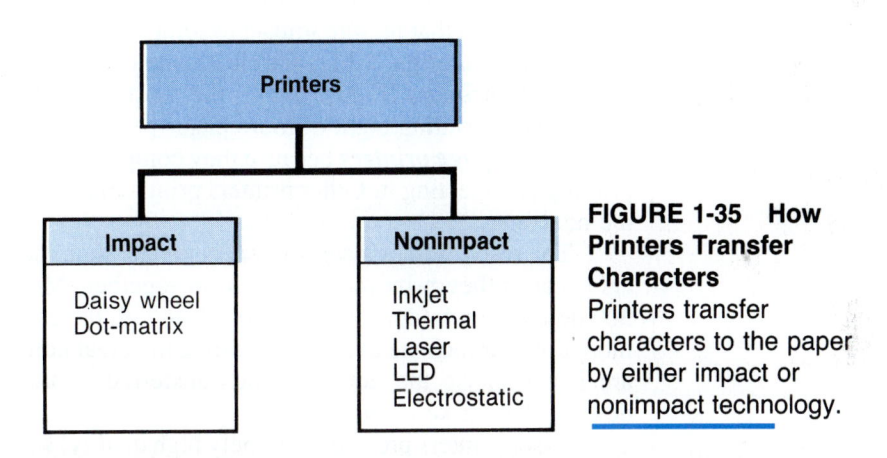

```
                    Printers
                   /        \
              Impact        Nonimpact
            Daisy wheel      Inkjet
            Dot-matrix       Thermal
                             Laser
                             LED
                             Electrostatic
```

FIGURE 1-35 How Printers Transfer Characters Printers transfer characters to the paper by either impact or nonimpact technology.

Impact Printers

Impact printers create an image on paper using a mechanical printhead that strikes an inked ribbon against the surface of the paper. There are two types of impact printers: fully formed character printers and dot-matrix impact printers.

Fully formed character printers use a type element with raised, fully formed characters, much like the type element used on electric typewriters. A character on this type element is struck against an inked ribbon to transfer the character to the paper.

Dot-matrix impact printers use a printhead containing pins, or wires, arranged in a column to print characters. As the printhead passes across the paper (Figure 1-36), the computer tells it which pins in the printhead are to be fired to form a particular character. As the pins are fired, they strike an inked ribbon against the paper. The number of wires and dots determines the character's resolution. Older, less expensive printers usually use nine pins to create characters. The latest, and more expensive, printers have eighteen or twenty-four wires in their printheads.

Nonimpact printer.
Printers that form characters without striking an inked ribbon against paper.

Laser printer. A dot-matrix printer that uses a laser beam and revolving drum to create high-resolution printed pages.

Page printer. A printer, such as a laser printer, that forms an entire page in its memory before it begins printing it.

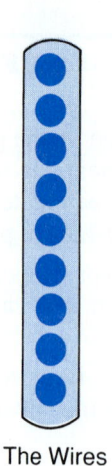

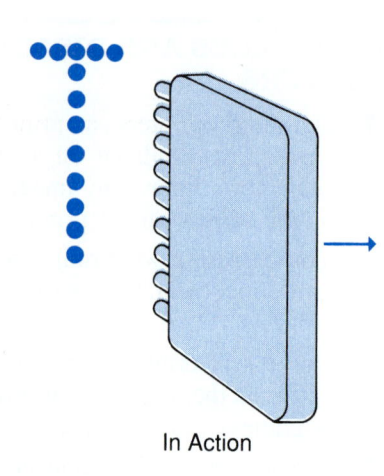

The Wires   In Action

FIGURE 1-36 Dot-Matrix Impact Printers Dot-matrix impact printers have a printhead that contains pins. The pins are fired against the paper, and the ribbon between the printhead and paper creates an inked image on the paper.

Nonimpact Printers

Nonimpact printers do not use an inked ribbon. Characters are transferred to the paper using electrostatic charges and toner, sprayed ink, or heat. All nonimpact printers, however, form characters with patterns, much like those in a dot-matrix impact printer. These printers have replaced impact printers as the most popular type of printer. Nonimpact printers offer many advantages, including their speed and quietness. Their one drawback is they cannot print multipart forms that require impact to print the image through the carbon paper. Laser, ink-jet, thermal, LED, and electrostatic printers are all nonimpact printers.

Laser printers (Figure 1-37), the most popular type of printer, are very fast, usually printing eight or more pages per minute. Unlike most other printers, they are *page printers* because they compose a page in their memory before printing and ejecting it. Other printers print a line and then advance the paper to the next line.

The resolution of laser printers is greater than most other dot-matrix printers because they print more dots closer together. Most laser printers can print 300 dots per inch (dpi), although printers with the capability of printing 400 or more dots per inch are available. Despite the great number of dots, laser printers are fast because the dots are not transferred to the paper with mechanical devices that strike a ribbon.

Laser printers provide extremely high quality. Figure 1-38 shows a sample (text and graphics) of laser printing. The technology of laser printers is similar to that of office copiers (Figure 1-39). Current laser printers can print in only

FIGURE 1-37 Laser Printer
Laser printers are usually sheet fed and print only on 8½-by-11-inch paper. They are quiet and give good results.
Courtesy of Hewlett-Packard Company

Duplex printing. Printing on both sides of a sheet of paper.

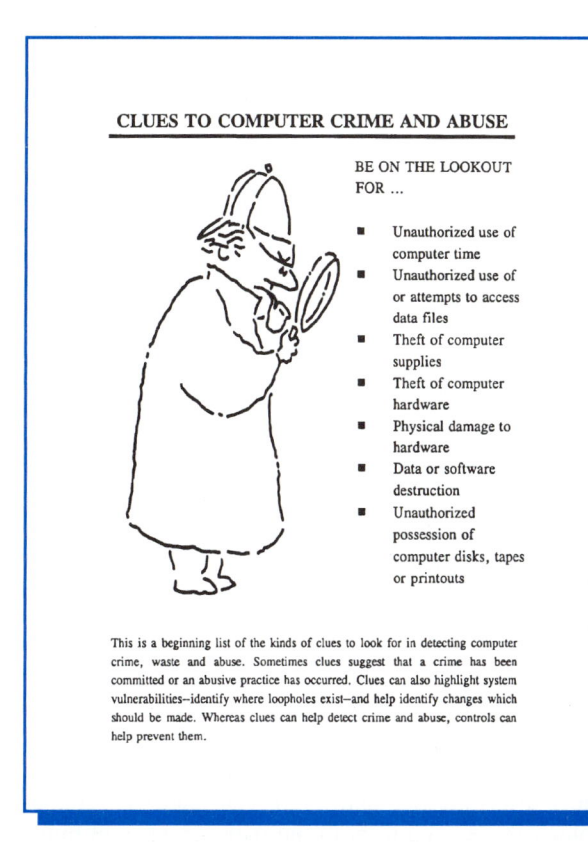

FIGURE 1-38 Laser Printer Output
Laser printers can print both text and graphics and are very close to letter quality. The dots making up the image are so closely spaced that they look like characters typed on a typewriter.

FIGURE 1-39 How Laser Printers Work
Laser printers first focus a laser beam onto a moving drum using a mirror. The moving drum is charged with electricity. As the drum revolves, it is scanned by the laser, and the image is "painted" onto the drum. The intensity of the laser beam is varied, and at selected points it removes the electrical charge from the drum to form invisible characters with a neutral charge. Charged toner is then electrostatically attracted to these characters. This toner is transferred to the paper and fused to it by heat and pressure as it is pressed against the revolving drum.

one color, but strides are being made in the development of color laser printers. Moreover, laser printers are now available that print on both sides of a sheet of paper at the same time. This process is called *duplex printing*.

LED printers have many of the same performance characteristics as laser printers, but instead of using a laser to create the image, they use an array of light-emitting diodes.

Electrostatic printers use a dot-matrix printhead to apply electrostatic charges to the surface of the paper. When the paper is passed through toner, the toner adheres to the charged areas, making the image visible. This process is similar to that used in copy machines.

Ink-jet printers use moving nozzles to focus a stream of ink onto the paper. Color ink-jet printers use three separate jets, one for each of the primary colors (red, green, and blue).

Thermal printers use a dot-matrix printhead and heat-sensitive paper to create images. Recent models, however, no longer require heat-sensitive paper

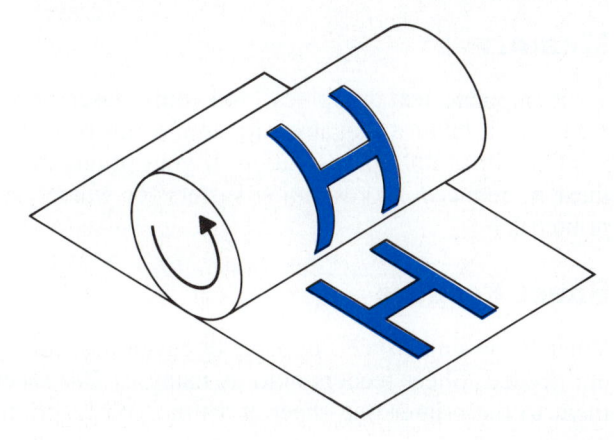

OUTPUT DEVICES—THE PRINTER

Continuous form paper. Individual sheets of paper connected together, usually with perforations between them. Also called fan-fold.

Tractor feed. An accessory device used on many printers to feed continuous form paper to the printer.

Pin feed. The pins built into a printer to engage the holes in continuous form paper.

Toner. The chemical in a laser printer that is fused to paper to create an image.

Font. A complete set of characters in one typeface, style, and size, for example, Courier, bold, 12 point.

Sheet feeder. A mechanical device that automatically feeds cut sheets of paper to a printer. Also called a bin.

but can print on any paper. The printhead of a thermal printer comprises a grid of wires. When an electric current is applied to any pair of wires, heat is generated where they intersect, leaving a dot on the paper.

PRINTER SPEED

Printer speeds vary widely, based on their design and the document that is being printed. Generally speaking, dot-matrix printers are faster than fully formed character printers. Laser printers, which print a page at a time, are the fastest. When printing graphics, all printers slow down; if there are many graphics on the same page, or if the graphics are large, each page can take a long time to print. Heavily formatted text also prints more slowly than straight text.

PRINTER ACCESSORIES

Printers require supplies and accessories for specific purposes.

Paper

Most printers accept both single sheets of paper and **continuous form paper** (also called *fan-fold*), which has perforated margins with holes. These holes are engaged by a **tractor feed** or **pin feed** to pull the paper through the printer one sheet after another and keep it aligned. After the printout is completed, the holes can be used to hold the paper in special binders, or they can be torn off. Continuous form paper is available as single sheets or as multipart carbon forms. It can also be preprinted with specially designed forms or company letterheads on each sheet.

Ribbons or Toner

Inked ribbons for dot-matrix printers or *toner* for laser printers, are needed to transfer the characters to the paper. Both cloth and film ribbons are available. Cloth ribbons are more economical, but film ribbons produce sharper characters on the paper.

Fonts

Many newer printers can print type in various styles, or *fonts*. Some fonts may be permanently stored in the printer's memory (ROM). Others are available on cartridges or stored on disks. We describe fonts in detail in Chapter 3 but two typical fonts are shown in Figure 1-40.

Memory

To manipulate text, graphics, and fonts, laser printers need a great deal of memory. It takes a megabyte to store a full-page graphic image that is to be printed with a 300-dpi resolution. If your printer has less memory, the graphic must be reduced, or resolution suffers (or worse yet, the entire image is not printed).

Sheet Feeders

When using single sheets of paper or envelopes, **sheet feeders** (also called *bins*) are needed. Sheet feeders hold as many as 500 sheets of stationery and feed them to the printer one sheet at a time. When printing letterhead, two sheet

1-6

> Times Roman
> Helvetica

Figure 1-40 Fonts
This figure shows two typical fonts, Times Roman and Helvetica.

48 COMPUTER SYSTEMS

Buffer. A part of the computer's memory where keystrokes or sections of deleted text are stored temporarily. The deleted text stored there can be copied back into the document. Also known as a clipboard, scrapbook, or scrap.

feeders are needed. One holds the letterhead used for the first sheet, and the other holds the nonletterhead paper used for subsequent sheets.

USING A PRINTER

When you want to send a file to the printer, you first load the printer with paper and turn the printer on. The way you load paper varies, depending on the type of printer and paper you are using. If you are using single sheets, you usually stack them in a paper tray or bin. If you are using continuous form paper, you feed it into the printer as shown in Figure 1-41.

Figure 1-41 Loading Continuous Form Paper
Loading continuous form paper into a printer is quite simple.
Courtesy of Epson

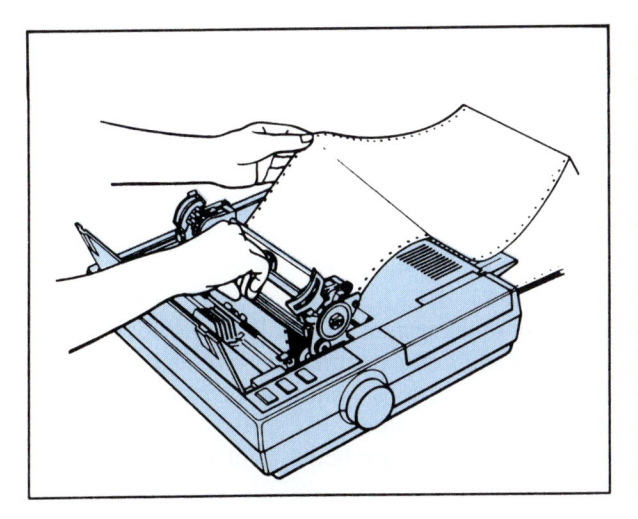

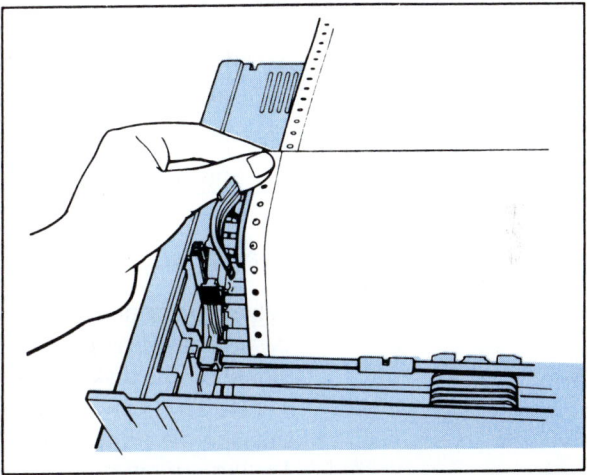

1. You feed it through a slot, around the platen, and back out of the printer.

2. As you do so, you engage the holes in the perforated, tear off margins with the tractor or pin feed mechanism.

The settings you can make on the printer vary. Many have some or all of the following switches:

- **On/Off** turns the power to the printer on and off. Knowing when to use this switch is important.
  - If you turn the printer off while it is operating, all data in its *buffer* will be lost. When you turn the printer back on, your document may resume printing, but a large block will have been missed.
  - If you have canceled a print job and want to start over, turning the computer off and back on is a good way to ensure that text from the previous job does not remain in the buffer.
  - If, after you turn the printer off, you turn it back on, it resets the top of the form so that the printer considers the line that the print element is resting on the top line of the sheet of paper. It uses this line as the starting point when calculating top margins and page length. This is useful as you can adjust your paper in the printer, and just turn it off and then back on to set the top of the form.

- **Off-Line/On-Line** connects the printer to and disconnects it from the computer. The printer must be on line to print documents, but it must be off line to use some of the other switches on the printer, such as Form Feed and Line Feed.

Print queue. One or more files waiting to be printed.

- **Form Feed** (FF) advances a sheet of paper out of the printer. If the printer has an automatic sheet feeder or tractor feed, it inserts a new sheet. For this switch to work, the printer must be off line.

- **Line Feed** (LF) advances paper in the printer by one line. This is useful when making fine adjustments to the paper's position in the printer. For this switch to work, the printer must be off line.

- **Letter Quality/Draft Quality** switches the printer between its high-quality but slower letter-quality setting and its lower-quality but faster draft-quality setting.

- **Font** changes the default font so that the entire document is printed in that font unless you specified otherwise by entering font change codes within the document.

EJECTING PAPER

To advance a printed page out of your printer
1. press the printer's on-line switch to take it off line.
2. press the printer's form-feed switch to advance or eject the page.
3. press the printer's on-line switch to put it back on line.

Managing a Print Queue

When you print a document, it is sent to the printer. If, while the first document is still being printed, you specify that additional documents be printed, they are stored on the disk in a *print queue*, a line of jobs waiting to be printed (Figure 1-42). The jobs appear in the queue in the order you specify. But you can manage the print queue, including the current job being printed, with the following options:

- *Change position* moves a print job higher or lower in the queue waiting to be printed. If you expedite a print job, the program may ask if you want to interrupt the document that is printing. If you indicate that you do, the printer finishes the current page, prints the expedited document, and then resumes printing the original document.

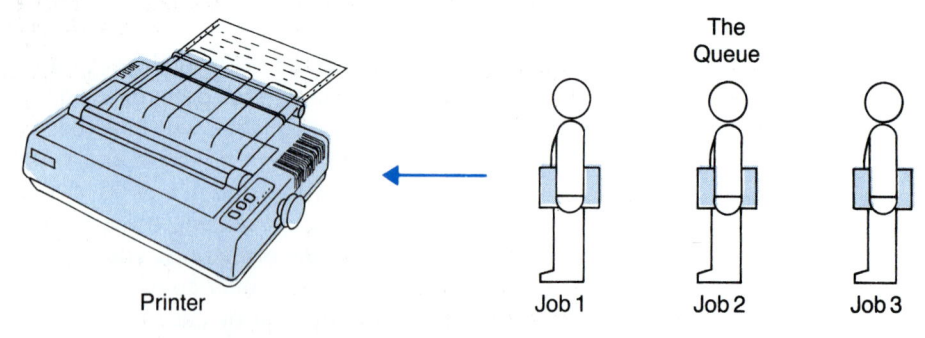

Figure 1-42 Print Queue
A print queue contains the current job being printed and all other print jobs you have requested that have yet to be done.

Bin selection. A printing option, offered by some programs, that gives you a choice of paper to print on. For example, you can store letterhead paper in one bin and plain paper in another bin. The program then uses the letterhead paper for the first page of each letter and the plain paper for the second and subsequent pages.

Collation. Arranging printed pages in sequential order.

- *Pause* temporarily stops the printer so that you can later continue printing exactly where you left off. You can use this command to pause the printer while you change paper or load more paper.
- *Resume* restarts a printer after you have made it pause. The printer resumes printing the document from where it stopped.
- *Stop* stops the printer so that you can start over from the beginning or return to another task. Unlike *Pause*, you cannot resume printing; you must repeat the *Print* commands to begin again. This is helpful when you notice something is wrong, for example, when the paper is improperly inserted or the margins incorrectly set.
- *Cancel* deletes a specified job from the print queue so that it is not printed.

Printing Options

Most applications programs provide several options you can use when printing documents.

- *Printer selection* allows you to specify the printer you want the job printed on. This is useful when you have a special printer for draft copies and another for final copies or when you have a local printer nearby and a remote one located elsewhere on a network.
- *Pages to be printed* can usually be specified. This is helpful when you are making corrections to individual pages. Certain pages can be reprinted without reprinting the entire document. The pages you specify are called a range. For example, you can print from the beginning of the document to a specific page, all pages between two specified pages, or from a specified page to the end of the document. Some programs allow you to specify individual pages and ranges of pages together. For example, the command to print pages 1–6,9,11,15–20 would print pages 1 through 6, pages 9 and 11, and then pages 15 through 20.
- *To printer or disk* can be specified. If you select the printer, a copy is printed on the printer. If you select the disk, a copy is printed to the disk, just as if it had been sent to the printer. All format commands are interpreted; for example, all margins are set as you request, and page numbers, headers, and footers, if any, are printed.
- *Number of copies* can be specified so that you can avoid having to photocopy your documents after printing.
- *Draft* is used to print documents more quickly by causing the printer to ignore commands, like boldfacing, that slow it down. This command must be supported by the printer and can sometimes be set on the printer rather than the program.
- **Bin selection** specifies the bin that the paper for the job is stored in. Some programs allow you to print on paper stored in two or more bins. For example, when you are printing business correspondence, the first page is printed on letterhead paper, which is stored in one bin, and the second and subsequent pages are printed on plain paper, which is stored in another bin.
- *Document Preview* displays a page on the screen the same way it will look when printed (Figure 1-43). Though you cannot edit the document when it is displayed with this command, you can see where improvements might be made before you print it out.
- *Collation* specifies if multiple copies are to be collated or not. If documents are collated, each copy prints in sequence, page 1, then 2, then 3

Figure 1-43 Document Preview
A document preview command lets you see exactly what the document will look like when printed.

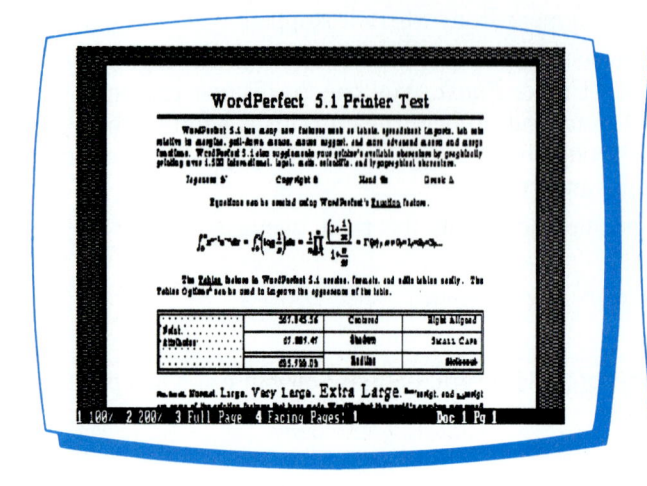

Here a document is displayed by WordPerfect at 100% of its printed size.

Here the document has been enlarged to 200% to check some details more closely.

Install. The process of preparing an applications program disk so that it can communicate with the hardware. Also includes changing any system default settings such as margins, drives or directories, and so on.

Installation program. The program that is used to install an applications program. Also called a setup program.

Driver. A small program that runs between an applications program and the hardware, so that they will work together.

and so on. When the first copy is completed, the next one starts. If copies are not collated, multiple copies are printed on page 1, then page 2 and so on.

INSTALLING PROGRAMS

Before you actually use a new applications program, you must *install* it. The installation process copies the files to your working disk and tells the program what printer and screen are attached to your system. You may find that these steps already have been done for you by the time you get a program. It's unlikely that you will have to do them until you are working on your own, with your own programs. To install a program, software companies include an ***installation program*** (also called a *setup program*).

Installing a program is generally a one-time task unless you change equipment, for example, when you add a new printer. The program may then have to be reinstalled. When you run the installation program, it displays prompts or lists of choices on the screen. You answer the prompts or select choices from the lists to tell the program what type of display screen, printer, and other peripherals you are using. You can also specify default drives for program and data files and, sometimes, change the way files are formatted on the screen.

Based on the information you supply about your screen and printer, the program then knows what ***drivers*** to use. Drivers are small programs that translate the programmer's generic instructions into instructions for a specific piece of hardware. Programs using drivers do not have to be revised by the software companies when new devices become available because the program addresses only the drivers, not the device itself. As new components become available, software companies just add new drivers.

Applications programs generally have a library of drivers, one for each specific hardware item. There may be a driver for a specific model of dot-matrix impact printer and another for a specific model of laser printer. If you tell the installation program what printer you are using, it knows to use that driver.

If you have a piece of hardware that the program does not include a driver for, you may be unable to use it with the program. Using a printer or display

52   COMPUTER SYSTEMS

Emulate. To act the same as or be like something else.

INSTALLING PROGRAMS, CONTINUED

"Your hardware doesn't like your software and they both despise your printer!"

Reprinted from INFOSYSTEMS, May 1985, (c) Hitchcock Publishing Company

screen without the correct driver can give totally unexpected results. Type that you expected to appear small may be large, headers and footers may not print, or margins may be incorrect. When buying applications programs, always be sure they contain the drivers needed to work with your equipment.

When installing a program, if drivers are not supplied for your equipment, you can specify a different device if your equipment has the ability to *emulate* (act like) it. For example, many laser printers can emulate the Hewlett-Packard LaserJet, and many display screens can emulate IBM's enhanced graphics adapter (EGA) or video graphics array (VGA). If your program does not list the drivers for your printer or screen, but your printer or screen can emulate another, you can select their drivers and the program will run correctly.

EXERCISES

Exercise 1-6A
DETERMINING HOW PRINTERS PRINT

Read a review of a printer in one of the computer magazines in the library, or check out one of the printers in the lab. Describe the following:

A. The way characters are formed

B. The way characters are transferred to the paper

Exercise 1-6B
DESCRIBING PRINTERS IN THE LAB

List the kinds of printers in your lab. How does each form characters? How does each transfer the characters to paper?

Exercise 1-6C
IDENTIFYING THE PRINTER'S CONTROLS

Sketch and label the controls on one of the printers in the lab. Briefly describe the purpose of each control listed below, and indicate the procedures you follow to use the control. For some of this information, you may have to ask your instructor or refer to the printer's manual.

THE PRINTER'S CONTROLS

Control	Description
On/off switch	
On line	
Form feed	
Line feed	
Fonts	
Other	

QUESTIONS

1. What are the two methods used by printers to form images? What are the advantages and disadvantages of each?
2. What are the two methods used by printers to transfer characters to paper? List some examples of each.
3. Of printers that form characters from dots, what determines the sharpness or resolution of the characters?
4. What are fonts?
5. What are printer sheet feeders used for?
6. What does it mean to say a printer is on line or off line? What switch on the printer do you use to take the printer off line and then put it back on line?
7. What switch on the printer do you press to advance the paper to the top of the next sheet?
8. What happens when you turn a printer off and then back on while a job is printing?
9. Why would you want to print to the disk instead of to the printer?
10. What is a print queue?
11. List some typical printer options, and describe them.
12. Why do you install a program the first time you use it? When do you have to reinstall the program?
13. What is the purpose of a driver? What happens when you use a program that does not have a driver for your printer?
14. What does it mean when you say a printer emulates another printer?

1-7 INTRODUCTION TO APPLICATIONS PROGRAMS

Word processing program. An applications program designed specifically to handle the creation of written documents such as memos, letters, reports, articles and books.

Desktop publishing program. A program that is used in desktop publishing.

The final part of the computer system, and the one you will become most familiar with, is the software. Let's look briefly at some of the most popular types of applications programs before we discuss these programs in greater detail in Chapters 3 through 6 of this text.

WORD PROCESSING AND DESKTOP PUBLISHING PROGRAMS

Word processing programs are used to enter and edit text. They are typically used to prepare memos, letters, reports, manuscripts, contracts, and other types of documents. In addition to entering and editing, these programs allow you to format documents to control how they look when printed. For example, you can set margins and tab stops, boldface headings, and automatically print personalized copies of form letters (Figure 1-44).

Since the introduction of the laser printer, new formatting procedures have become available. For example, you can print in different type sizes and typestyles, and you can combine graphics with text. To take advantage of these new possibilities a new class of *desktop publishing programs* was introduced. These programs offer a wide selection of typestyles, make it easy to organize type into columns, add ruled lines, and combine text with graphics on the same

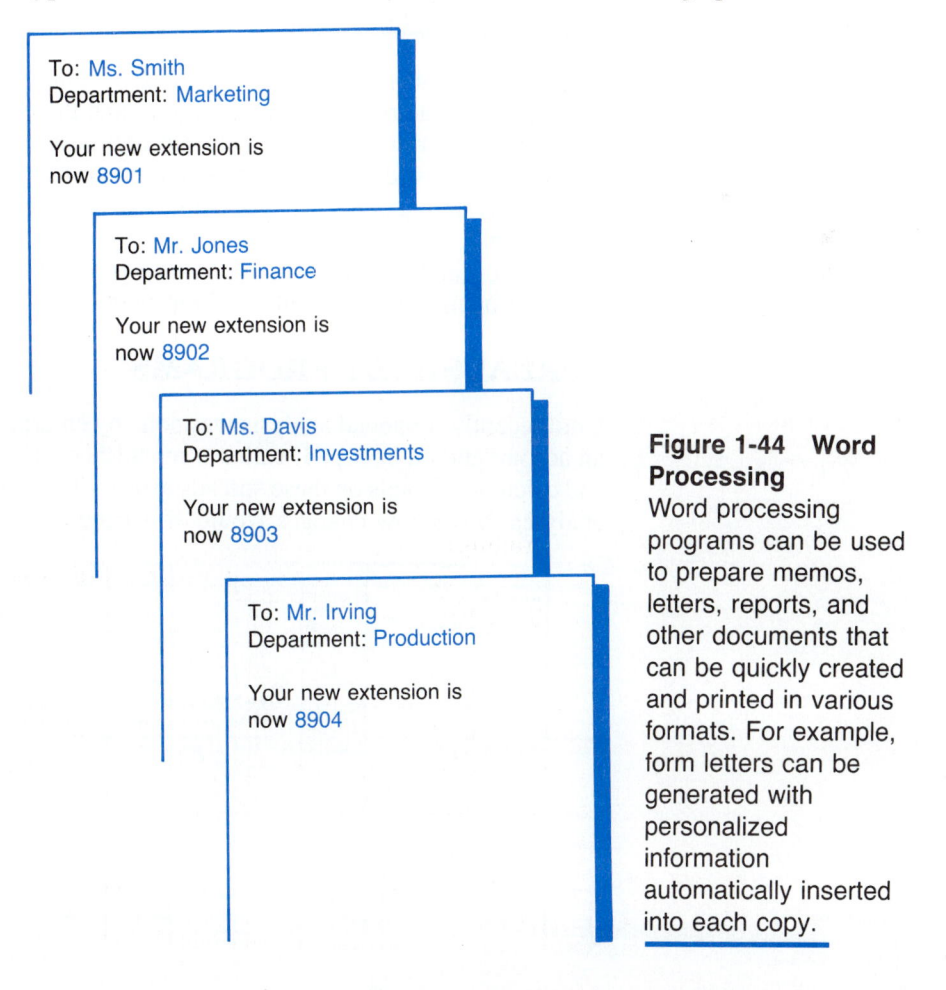

To: Ms. Smith
Department: Marketing

Your new extension is now 8901

To: Mr. Jones
Department: Finance

Your new extension is now 8902

To: Ms. Davis
Department: Investments

Your new extension is now 8903

To: Mr. Irving
Department: Production

Your new extension is now 8904

Figure 1-44 Word Processing
Word processing programs can be used to prepare memos, letters, reports, and other documents that can be quickly created and printed in various formats. For example, form letters can be generated with personalized information automatically inserted into each copy.

INTRODUCTION TO APPLICATIONS PROGRAMS 55

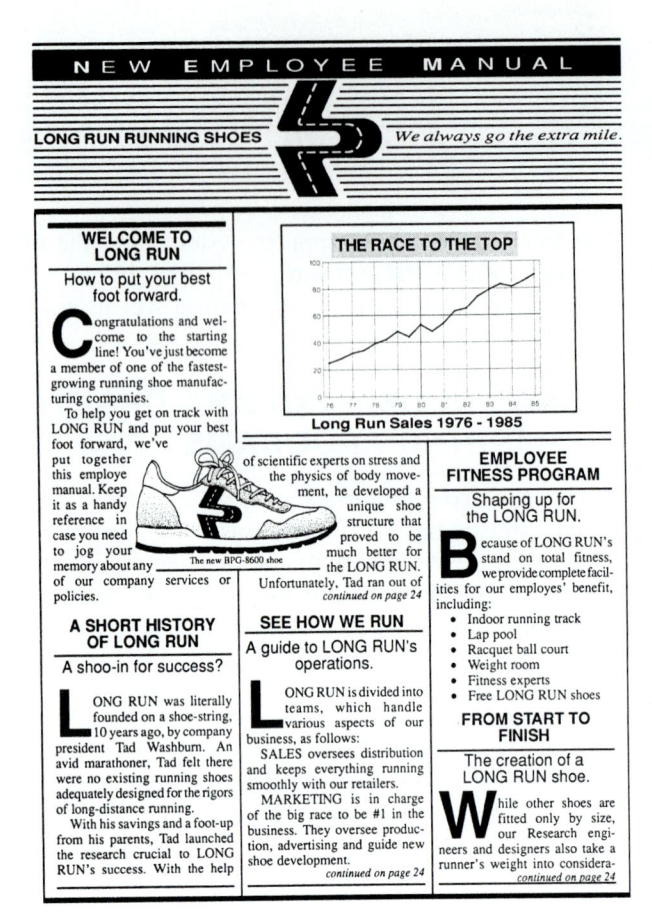

Figure 1-45 Desktop Publishing Programs
Desktop publishing allows you to combine text and graphics, print in multiple columns, and change formats so that type is printed in different sizes and styles where desired. You can then print the finished document on a high-quality laser printer. Desktop publishing opens up a whole new world of opportunities. You can now inexpensively generate typeset-quality copy for newsletters, catalogs, advertising brochures, reports, articles, and books. *Courtesy of Software Publishing Corporation*

page (Figure 1-45). To use one of these programs you first enter and edit a document on a word processing program, and then you transfer it to a desktop publishing program where you lay out and design the final document. Until very recently, word processing programs were better at editing than at formatting, and desktop publishing programs were better at formatting than at editing. Increasingly, however, the features offered by desktop publishing programs are being incorporated into word processing programs and word processing features are being integrated into desktop publishing programs.

SPREADSHEET PROGRAMS

Until recently, financial analysis was done by entering numbers on the pages of an accountant's ledger pad, called a spreadsheet (Figure 1-46). Gathering data and calculating totals on these spreadsheets took a long time. And doing what-if analyses to see how changes would affect the outcome was laborious.

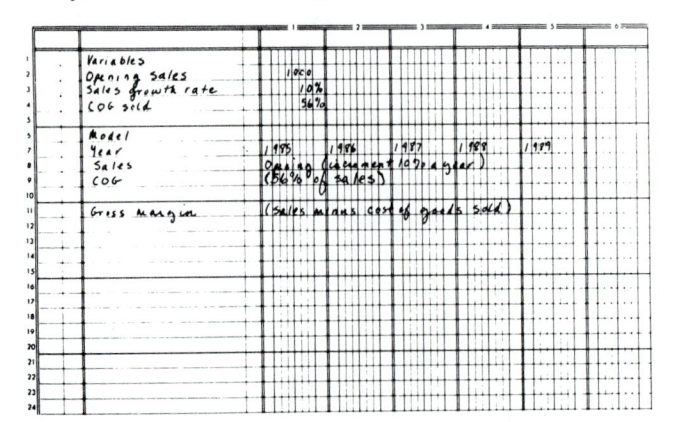

Figure 1-46 Ledger Pads
An accountant's ledger pad has ruled lines into which labels and numbers are written to keep financial records or do financial analysis.

1-7

56   COMPUTER SYSTEMS

Spreadsheet program.
A program that allows you to enter labels, numbers, formulas, and functions into cells to calculate and organize information. Also called an electronic spreadsheet.

Database management program. A program that organizes, manipulates, and retrieves information from one or more database files. Also called record or file management programs.

Database. Information stored in one or more files and organized into fields and records.

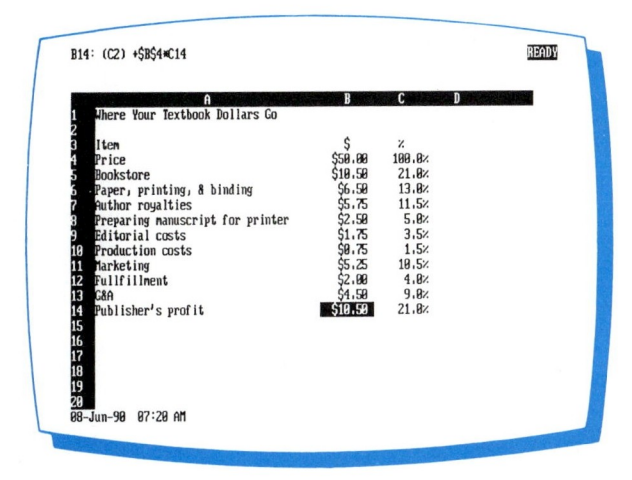

Figure 1-47 Spreadsheet
A spreadsheet program is an electronic ledger pad. You can enter labels, numbers, or formulas in each of the cells. The formulas can refer to numbers in other cells so that if you change the numbers, the formula instantly calculates a new result.

Spreadsheet programs (also called *electronic spreadsheets*) have taken the drudgery out of working with numbers. On a spreadsheet, you quickly create a model of a situation by entering labels, numbers, and formulas (Figure 1-47). You use the program's built-in functions to perform complicated calculations, such as the monthly payments due on a loan. You then use the completed model to explore what-if questions. For example, when you change the interest rate for the loan, the spreadsheet instantly recalculates your new monthly payment.

DATABASE PROGRAMS

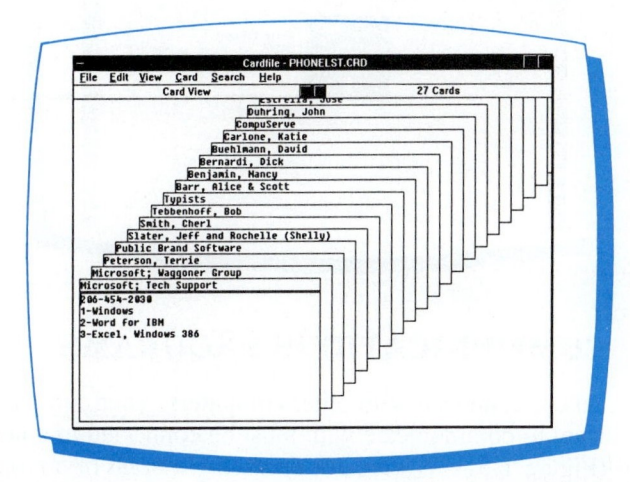

You use *database management programs* (sometimes called *record* or *file management programs*) for tasks as simple as keeping a phone list or as complicated as controlling inventory. A *database* is any logically connected collection of data. The concept behind database management programs is simple: They allow you to store information in an organized way so that you can retrieve or update it when you need to (Figure 1-48).

These programs do the same things you can do with a set of index cards, but they let you do it faster and more easily. You can store large amounts of information, such as mailing lists, inventory records, or billing and collection information, in lists stored as files. You can then sort, edit, add to, or delete from the information in these files. Database management programs are often used to maintain mailing lists, which are then used automatically to print names and addresses on letters, envelopes, and mailing labels. They are also frequent-

Figure 1-48 Database Management Programs
Database management programs allow you to enter information by filling out a form on the computer screen. The information is then stored in tables in the computer's memory. Here, Window's Cardfile program is used to store names and addresses.

INTRODUCTION TO APPLICATIONS PROGRAMS   57

Graphics program. A program that allows you to create or manipulate graphic images in a computer.

Business graphics programs. Programs that create graphs of business data for analysis or presentation.

Interactive graphics programs. Graphics programs whose images can be directly manipulated on the screen. Also called a paint or draw program.

Network operating system. A program that allows computers to communicate with each other over wires.

Communications programs. Programs that allow communication between computers over telephone lines.

ly integrated into other applications programs, such as word processing and spreadsheet programs.

GRAPHICS PROGRAMS

The saying "a picture is worth a thousand words" applies to computer graphics. In a glance, graphics can convey information that would be difficult to put into words. You can easily use your microcomputer to generate graphics. Two kinds of *graphics programs* are business graphics programs and interactive graphics programs.

Business graphics programs, which are often integrated into spreadsheet programs, create charts and graphs that represent numeric data (Figure 1-49). *Interactive graphics programs* (also called *paint programs*) generate original, free-form art and designs (Figure 1-50). These programs are called interactive because you create, edit, and manipulate the images directly on the screen. Business and interactive graphics programs are being used more and more to create images that are then incorporated into word-processed or desktop-published documents.

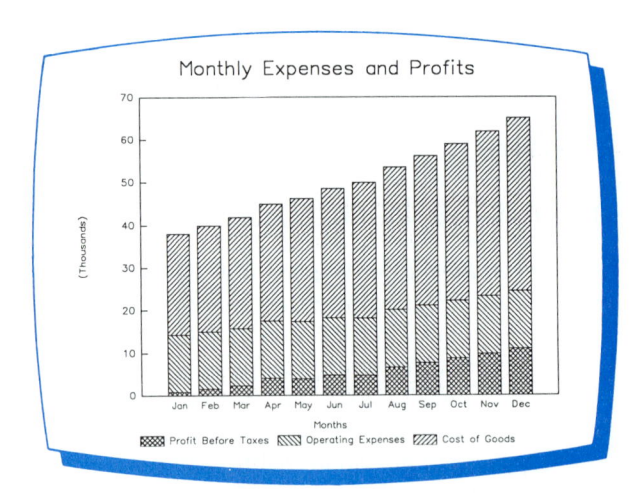

Figure 1-49 Business Graphs
A business graph can convey a great deal of information in a single picture. Here, a stacked bar graph represents profits and expenses for a 12-month period.

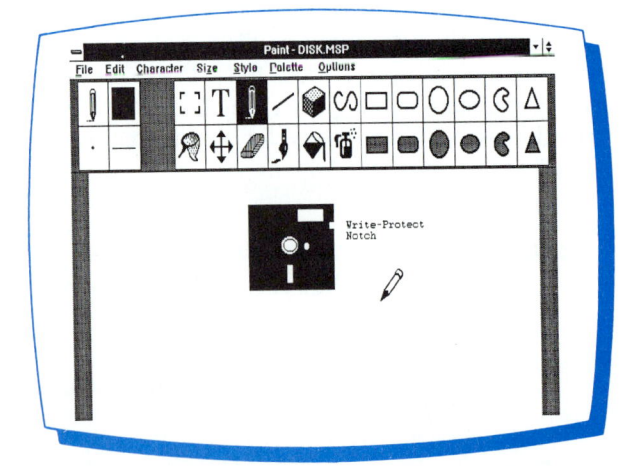

Figure 1-50 Line Drawings
Interactive graphics programs allow you to draw and manipulate an illustration on the screen. Graphics programs can be used to prepare art or create and polish graphs for presentations.
Courtesy of Xerox Corporation

COMMUNICATIONS PROGRAMS

To communicate with other computers, your computer and the computers you want to communicate with must be connected to a network or a telephone line (Figure 1-51). A *network operating system* or a *communications program* is

58   COMPUTER SYSTEMS

Standalone programs.
Programs that are designed for a single function, such as word processing.

Integrated program. A program that includes several applications, such as word processing, spreadsheet, and graphics, so that you can switch quickly back and forth between them and transfer data.

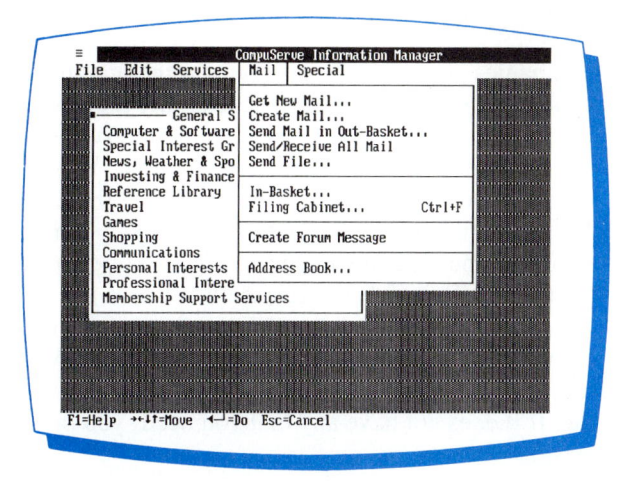

**Figure 1-51
Communications Programs**
Here, the CompuServe Information Manager program is being used to check on E-mail.

then used so that the computers can communicate and exchange data. One application of these programs is to send and receive electronic mail (E-mail). You can use a communications program to send a message to another user's computer in the same building, on the same campus, or anywhere in the world that can be reached with a telephone call. The recipient checks his or her "electronic mailbox" to find the message.

INTEGRATED PROGRAMS

Most programs do one task and thus are called *standalone programs*. But several programs are available that combine two or more of the five basic types of applications programs—word processing, database management, spreadsheets, graphics, and communications (Figure 1-52). These *integrated programs* try to meet the following standards:

- Use common commands or command structures in all functions
- Allow data to be shared by all functions
- Have sufficiently powerful functions so that standalone programs are not needed

Generally, a program designed to integrate many functions must make some compromises, and it is unlikely that any integrated program will ever contain the best program for all five functions. Many integrated programs stress ease of use. Though these programs are not as powerful as some of the early integrated programs, they meet most of the needs that many users have.

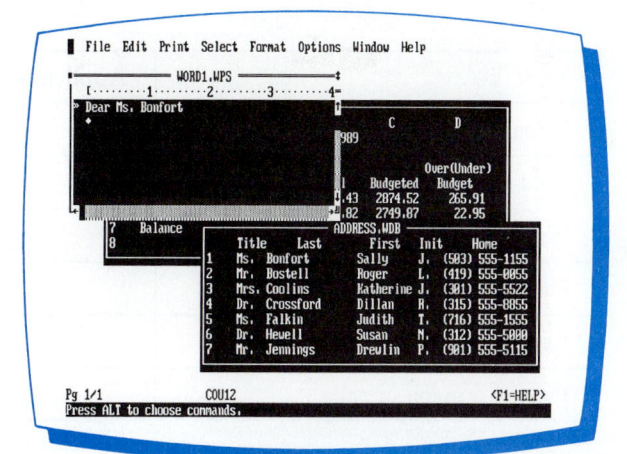

**Figure 1-52
Integrated Programs**
Microsoft Works is a popular integrated program. It has a word processor, spreadsheet, database, and communications program all in the same package. You can display the various programs on the screen in windows.

INTRODUCTION TO APPLICATIONS PROGRAMS   59

Updates. New releases of existing programs that correct problems in the previous version or that contain improvements. Also called upgrades.

PROGRAM UPDATES

Companies that publish programs generally update them every year or so. *Updates* (also called *upgrades*) generally include corrected old features as well as new features that improve the program. To identify new versions, version or release numbers are changed. For example, WordPerfect revised their program several times and called it release 4.2, 5.0, 5.1, and so on. Changes in the decimal number usually indicate relatively minor changes. Changes in the whole number indicate major revisions. For example, release 5.1 is only slightly different from 5.0 but release 5.0 was a big change from release 4.2.

New versions usually add new features. If these just build on the previous version, you need only learn the new features. When faced with a new version, you should be an informed consumer. Find out what features the new program has. If it does not have any that you need, you probably should not buy the new version.

EXERCISES

Exercise 1-7A
READ A REVIEW

Obtain a copy of a recent computer magazine and read a review of any new program. List its main applications and briefly describe some of the features that the reviewer thought important.

Exercise 1-7B
MATCHING TASKS AND APPLICATIONS PROGRAMS

The box below lists some typical business tasks that lend themselves to microcomputer solutions. Indicate the type of applications program you would use to automate each task.

Task	Applications Program
Prepare a budget	
Send an electronic message	
Write a letter	
Publish a newsletter	
Keep a list of customers	
Prepare a graph of sales	

QUESTIONS

1. What are word processing programs used for?
2. What are desktop publishing programs? How do they differ from a word processing program?
3. What is a spreadsheet program used for?
4. What similarities are there between an accountant's ledger pad and a spreadsheet program?
5. What is a database management program used for?
6. What two kinds of graphics programs are widely used in business?
7. What is a communications program used for?
8. What is an integrated program? What are the five most commonly integrated applications?
9. What are program updates?

CHAPTER 2

Disks, Disk Drives, and Operating Systems

OBJECTIVES

After finishing this chapter, you will be able to:

- Explain the purpose of external storage and describe the different types of media used to store data
- Explain the basic functions of the operating system and describe some of the more popular types, including DOS
- Load and quit the operating system
- Describe filenames and explain the difference between the default and other drives
- Describe the DOS commands that you use to manage your files
- Explain how hard disks can be organized, and describe the commands you use with a hard disk drive
- Know the two special files your computer looks for when you boot it up

Disk. The magnetic medium on which the computer records information. Disks represent the most common form of computer storage.

Command. Any instruction that you give to the computer to tell it what to do.

Interface. The point at which two different elements meet; for example, the connection between a computer and a modem, a user and a computer, or a computer and a printer.

Most new computer users are eager to get to the fun and productive part, working with applications programs. If you have someone who sets up all of your *disks* for you, you can do so. But to do serious work on the computer, you have to understand external storage devices and how the operating system can make your work more productive and efficient. Until recently, operating systems were somewhat difficult to learn because you had to type *commands*, which weren't always easy to remember. Gradually, however, these difficult to learn operating systems are being replaced with menu driven *interfaces* that you can learn in a few minutes and that list commands in a way that prevents your ever forgetting them. In this chapter, we introduce you to both types, the command prompt operating systems still used on most computers, and the newer operating systems with graphical user interfaces that will be standard for most computers in the near future.

2-1 EXTERNAL STORAGE DEVICES

File. Associated data in the computer's memory or saved onto a disk. This may be a program, data for a database, a spreadsheet model, or a letter that you create with your word processor.

External storage. Information that is stored outside of the computer's memory (RAM). Also called auxiliary or secondary storage.

Floppy disk. A round disk covered by a magnetic material and enclosed in a square plastic cover. Used to store program and data files.

When you work on a computer, the programs and *files* you work on are stored internally in the computer's random-access memory. This memory is a limited resource, yet it must serve many uses. Not only do you load different applications programs, you also create files for your own work. The computer's memory is not large enough to store all the programs and files that you work on. Moreover, most memory will lose its data when you turn the computer off.

For these reasons, *external storage* (also called *auxiliary* or *secondary storage*) is provided (Figure 2-1). This storage is used to store programs and data that you are not using at the moment. Once data are stored externally, you can reload them into the computer's internal memory without having to rekeyboard them.

Computers usually use magnetic disks to store programs and files externally. Magnetic disks, and the devices used to store and retrieve data on them, fall into two major classes: *floppy disks* and disk drives, and hard disk drives.

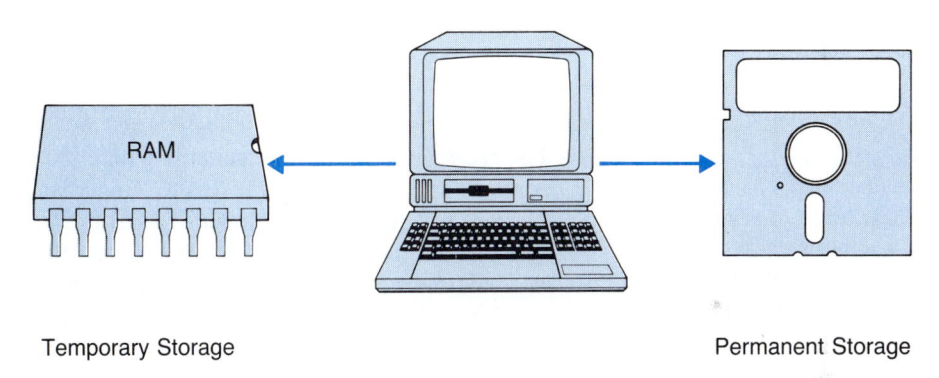

Temporary Storage   Permanent Storage

Figure 2-1 External Storage
When you are finished working on a file on the screen, you store it on an external storage device, which is a more permanent form of storage than the computer's memory. When you need the file later, you retrieve it from the external storage device and transfer it to the computer's memory.

FLOPPY DISKS AND DISK DRIVES

Floppy disks for microcomputers come in two sizes: 5¼ and 3½ inches. Each size works only with drives specifically designed to accept it. Though they vary in size, they have certain features in common (Figure 2-2):

1. A storage envelope protects 5¼-inch disks from scratches, dust, and fingerprints. Some envelopes are treated to eliminate the static buildup that attracts abrasive grit. These envelopes are not used on the better-protected 3½-inch disks.

2. A plastic outer covering protects the disk itself while allowing it to spin smoothly inside the jacket. 5¼-inch disks are protected by flexible plastic jackets, whereas 3½-inch disks are mounted in a rigid plastic housing. The jacket or housing is permanently sealed and contains lubricants and cleaning agents that prolong the life of the disk.

2-1

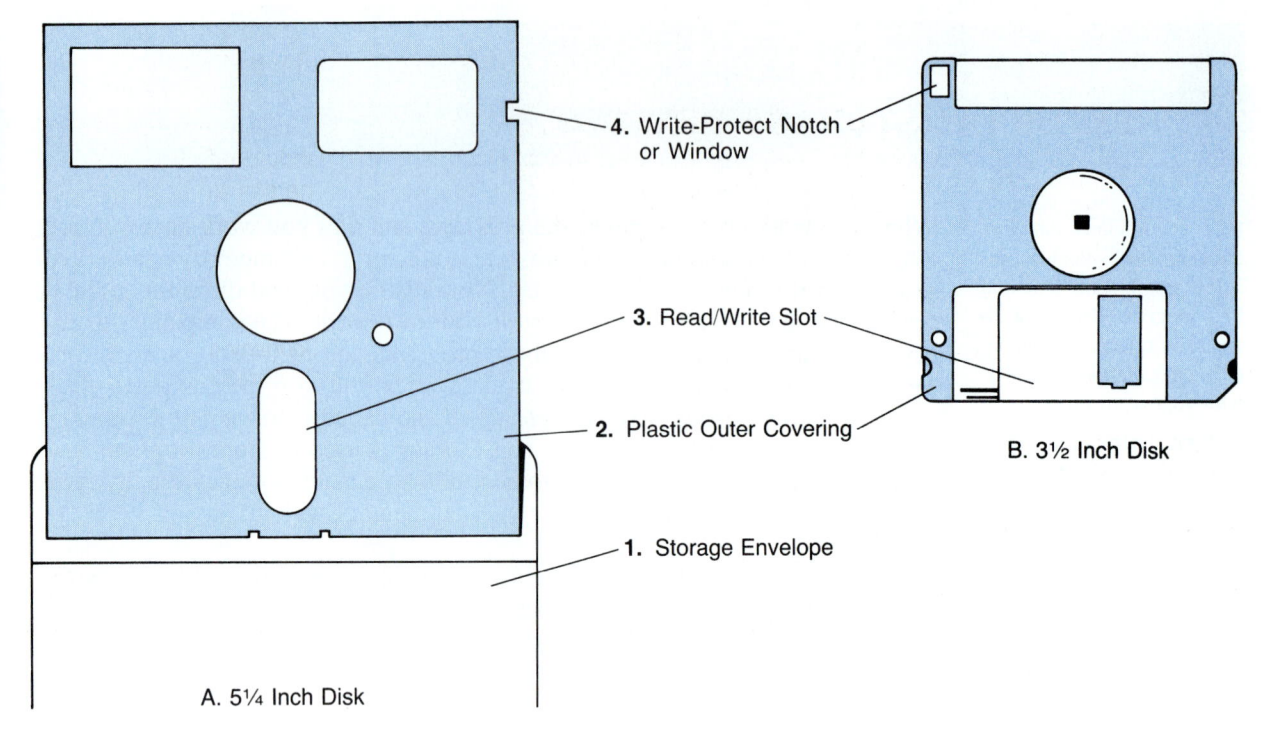

Figure 2-2 Floppy Disk Characteristics
(A) 5¼-inch and (B) 3½-inch disks have many features in common.

Read/write slot. The oblong opening in the outer plastic jacket of a floppy disk through which the drive's read/write head comes in contact with the magnetic disk.

Shutter. The sliding metal cover on a 3½-inch disk that protects the surface of the disk.

Write-protect notch. The notch on a floppy disk that allows you to store, erase, and rename files on the disk when it is uncovered, but prevents you from doing so when it is covered.

Write-protect window. The window on a 3½-inch disk that can be opened to write-protect the disk.

Write-protected. A 5¼-inch disk on which the write-protect notch has been covered, or a 3½-inch disk where the window has been opened to prevent files from being stored on it or erased from it.

3. The *read/write slot* in the jacket is where the disk drive's read/write head contacts the surface of the disk. This read/write head stores data on (writes) and retrieves data from (reads) the surface of the disk as the disk spins inside the drive. On 3½-inch disks, the read/write slot is protected by a sliding metal cover called the **shutter**. When you insert the disk into the drive, this shutter is automatically pushed aside so that the read/write slot is exposed, and the drive can come in contact with the floppy disk within.

4. The *write-protect notch* or *write-protect window* allows you to store files on and erase them from a disk when it is not **write-protected** and prevents you from doing so when it is (see the section ''Write-Protect Your Disks''). A switch or photoelectric circuit inside the disk drive determines if the disk is write-protected. If it finds that it is, the switch disables the drive's ability to write information onto the disk.

The *floppy disk drive* is the device that the floppy disk is inserted into so that you can store data to and retrieve data from it. The floppy disk drive has two parts you should be familiar with: the slot and the light (Figure 2-3).

1. The slot is where you insert a floppy disk into the drive (see the box ''Inserting Floppy Disks'').

2. The light on the front of the drive goes on when the drive is operating. When the light is on, you should not open the door or eject a disk. Doing so can damage the disk and cause you to lose data. If you make a mistake and the drive spins when the door is open or without a disk inserted, do not close the door or insert a disk. In a few moments, a message will usually appear telling you the drive's door is open or no disk is in the drive. When the light goes out, close the door or insert a disk, and then follow the instructions displayed on the screen.

Floppy disk drive. A disk drive that saves files to and retrieves them from floppy disks.

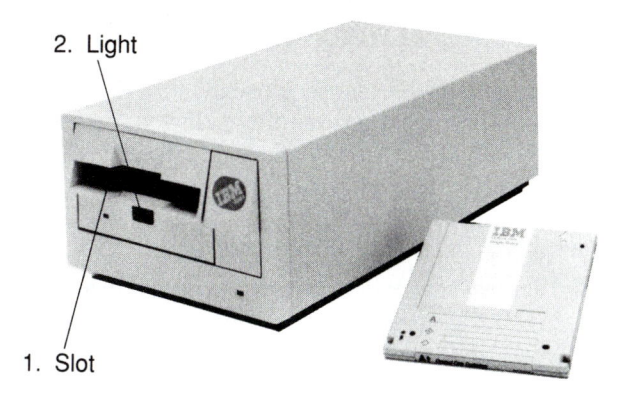

2. Light

1. Slot

Figure 2-3 The Floppy Disk Drive
The floppy disk drive has two parts that you should be familiar with: the slot and the light. Here, they are shown on a standalone drive, but most disk drives are built into the computer.
Courtesy of IBM Corporation

INSERTING FLOPPY DISKS

The way you insert floppy disks depends on the type of system you are using. Most floppy disk systems have two drives, A and B. When loading a program from a floppy disk, you insert it into drive A, the startup drive. To save your work onto a floppy disk, you insert it into drive B on a floppy disk computer and into drive A on a computer with a hard disk. The arrangements of floppy disk drives vary.

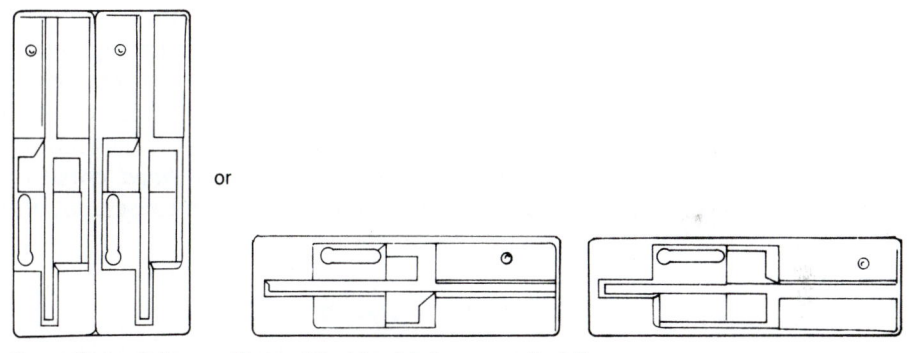

or

If your floppy disks are side by side, drive A is the one on the left.

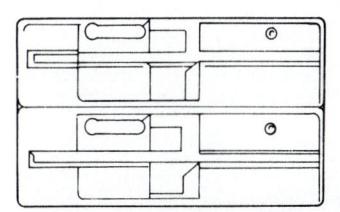

If one drive is above the other, drive A is the one on the top.

■ **To insert a 5¼-inch disk**, open the door to the disk drive. Hold the disk with the label facing up to insert it into a horizontal drive. Hold it with the label facing to the left and with the write-protect notch up to insert it into a vertical drive.

Point the oblong read/write slot toward the slot in the drive, and insert the disk into the slot. (On some systems, it "clicks" into place.) Never push hard because a 5¼-inch disk will buckle if it gets caught on an obstruction. Carefully jiggle the disk to make sure it is inserted all the way into

EXTERNAL STORAGE DEVICES

2-1

Hard disk drive. A disk drive that contains a hard, magnetic disk on which data is stored. A hard disk can store much more data than a floppy disk.

Head crash. A damaging collision of the hard disk's read/write head with the spinning disk. Head crashes occur because of power failures when the disk is operating, or other malfunctions.

Optical disk. An external storage device that can store vast amounts of data. A laser is used to read the data.

INSERTING FLOPPY DISKS, CONTINUED

the disk drive. Gently close the disk drive's door, or press the button that locks the disk into the drive. If you encounter any resistance, jiggle the disk and then close the door or press the button again. To remove the disk, open the door and pull the disk out. On some drives, gently pushing the disk in and then quickly releasing the pressure pops it out of the drive; on others, you have to press a button.

▪ **To insert a 3½-inch disk**, hold it so that the arrow embossed on the case is facing up or to the left and pointing toward the drive's slot. Insert the disk gently into the drive, and press until it clicks into place. To remove the disk, press the disk eject button just above or below the drive's slot.

HARD DISK DRIVES

Hard disk drives (also called *fixed disks* or *Winchester disk drives*) (Figure 2-4) use rigid metal platters that allow them to store data more densely than on floppy disk drives. This increased density and the number of platters greatly increase their storage capacity. Hard disk drives generally provide 20, 40, 80, or more megabytes of storage capacity, much more than a floppy disk. In addition, a hard disk drive spins at 3,600 rpm, about ten times faster than a floppy disk drive, allowing data to be stored and retrieved faster.

In a floppy disk drive, the read/write heads are in contact with the disk. In a hard disk drive, they fly over its surface on a cushion of air smaller than a piece of dust separating the head from the rapidly spinning disk. To imagine the small tolerances involved, picture an airplane flying at high speed ½ inch above the ground without making contact. With the high speeds and small spaces involved, even a tiny particle can cause the read/write head to come in contact with the disk's surface, creating a **head crash** (Figure 2-5). With the disk spinning at almost 60 mph, this can cause a lot of damage to the disk and the data stored on it.

OPTICAL DISKS

One of the most recent and far-reaching developments in the microcomputer field is the new technology of **optical disks** (Figure 2-6). Data are stored on and

Figure 2-4   Hard Disk Drives
Hard disk drives use metal platters instead of plastic disks to store data.
Photo courtesy of Seagate

66   DISKS, DISK DRIVES, AND OPERATING SYSTEMS

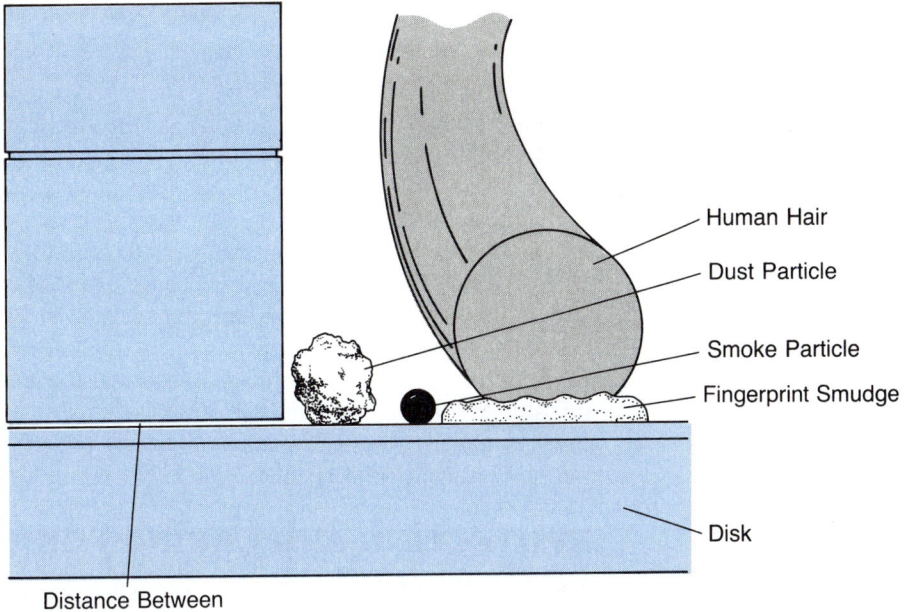

Figure 2-5 Hard Disk Tolerances
Hard disks have very small tolerances. When the read/write head is flying over the surface of the disk, the two are so close that smoke, a dust particle, a hair, or even a fingerprint could cause the head to crash.

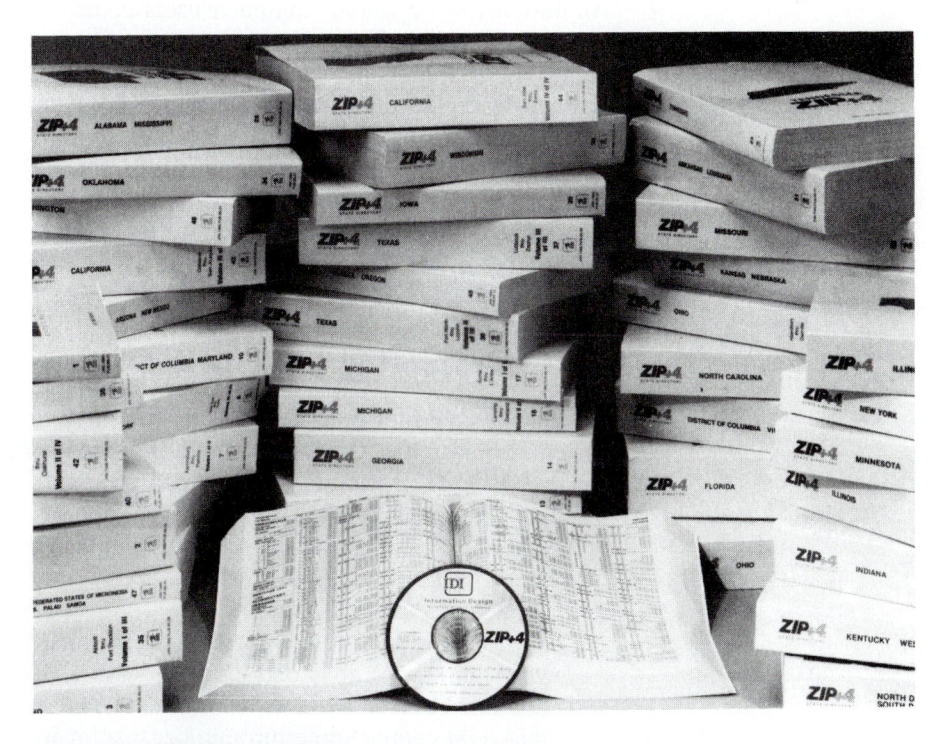

Figure 2-6 Optical Disks
One CD-ROM disk contains all forty-seven volumes of the U.S. Postal Service ZIP + 4 Code information on a single disk. These nine-digit ZIP codes identify areas of cities, including apartment buildings, office suites, and floor numbers in commercial buildings. Software included with the disk can check a new address as it is being entered and display the full address and ZIP code for approval.

EXTERNAL STORAGE DEVICES 67

2-1   **CD-ROM disk.** Information stored on a laser disk and read into the computer from a CD-ROM disk drive.

retrieved from these disks with a laser. One of the most popular kinds of optical disks is called a **CD-ROM disk**. These disks are similar in concept to the compact disks (CDs) now popular in the music industry. A small 4¾-inch CD-ROM disk can store up to 600MB (megabytes) of data. This is equivalent to about 250,000 pages of text or 40,000 images.

These disks are changing the way information is stored, distributed, and accessed. One of the first optical disks to be published was *Microsoft's Bookshelf CD-ROM Reference Library*. This CD-ROM disk contains ten of the most widely used reference works, including *The World Almanac and Book of Facts*, *Bartlett's Familiar Quotations*, *The Chicago Manual of Style*, and the *U.S. ZIP Code Directory*. It also includes search and retrieve software, which makes it possible to look for information while working on another program. With just a few keystrokes, you can find information in any of these references and insert it into a document on the screen.

PROTECTING AND CARING FOR YOUR FILES AND DISKS

When you enter data into the computer, they are not stored permanently until you save them onto disks. But even then the data are not protected from loss or damage. However, there are several ways you can protect your disks and files.

Labeling Your Disks

An unwritten rule among computer users is that an unlabeled disk contains no valuable files. People often do not take the time to check what files, if any, an unlabeled disk contains. Thus, the first step when you use a disk is to label it. Always write the disk title, your name, the date, and the operating system version that you are using on the labels.

If you are using 5¼-inch floppy disks, also be sure to fill out labels before you affix them to the disks. If you write on a label that is already on a disk, you can damage the disk if you press down too hard. If you must write on a label that is already on a disk, use a felt-tip pen, and write very gently. Do not apply pressure.

Write-Protecting Your Disks

When you save files onto a disk, format a disk to prepare it for use on your system, or erase files from a disk; you can damage files if you make a mistake. If a disk is write-protected, you can read files on the disk, but you cannot save files on it, format it, or erase files from it. When you have an important disk that you want to protect the files on, write-protect it so that you do not inadvertently damage or delete files (Figure 2-7).

- When the write-protect notch on a 5¼-inch floppy disk is not covered, you can save, copy, and erase files on a disk. When the write-protect notch is covered by tape, you cannot. You must use a write-protect tape that light cannot shine through because many drives use a light to determine if the notch is covered or not. If you use a transparent tape, the light will shine through the notch just as if it were not covered, and the drive will assume it is not write-protected.

- 3½-inch floppy disks have a sliding tab that you press to open or close the write-protect window. When the window is closed, you can save, copy, and erase files on a disk. When the window is open, you cannot.

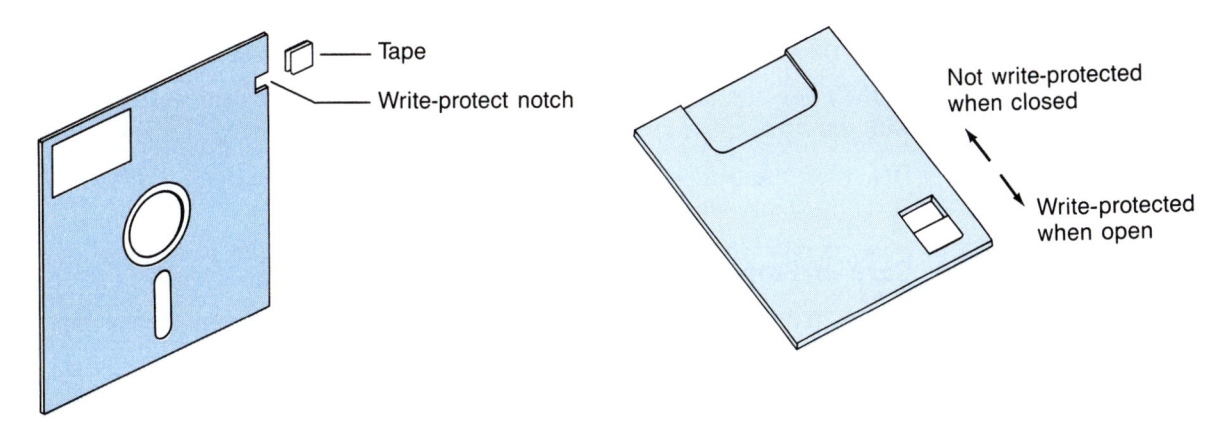

Figure 2-7 Write-Protect Your Disks
You write-protect your disks by taping over the write-protect notch on a 5¼-inch disk or opening the write-protect window on a 3½-inch disk.

> **Backup copy.** A duplicate of a file saved onto a separate disk in case the original disk is damaged.
>
> **Park program.** A utility program that moves a hard disk drive head to an unused area of the disk so that banging or moving the computer does not damage data.

Making Backup Copies

Always make *backup copies* of your important files and disks, and store them a safe distance from your working area. Make sure the same accident cannot happen to both the original disk and its backup copy. The information on the disk is usually worth much more than the disk itself, so don't take chances. You can back up floppy disks using the COPY or DISKCOPY commands described in this chapter, and hard disks using the BACKUP command described in the DOS manual. No one ever heeds this advice until they lose important information and have to spend hours or days recreating it. Don't be like everyone else; follow these recommendations before you lose data.

If you are using a hard disk drive, you might need a tape backup unit to back up your files. Backing up large hard disks onto floppy disks can be very time consuming. It takes so much work and time that most people don't do it and place their work at risk. Most hard disk users have tape backup units that store data on a tape similar to those used to store music. Tape backup units make backing up files an easy job because all of the data can be automatically stored on one tape.

Caring for Your Disks

Disks, both hard and floppy, are very reliable storage media. However, the data they contain can be lost or damaged if you do not take a few precautions. Floppy disks are relatively durable under ordinary conditions and have a useful life of about forty hours' spinning time. But that life can be shortened or abruptly ended by improper handling. Proper care ensures that disks will accurately store and play back the data you need.

Care of Hard Disk Drives

DON'T drop or jar them. They are very sensitive.

DO use the *park program* (found on a disk that comes with your computer) to park the read/write head before moving your computer. This program moves the read/write head to a section of the disk that has no data. This prevents the head from damaging data on the disk should it move. Even slightly jarring your computer may damage your files.

Care of Floppy Disk Drives

DON'T use commercial cleaning kits too often. Overuse can cause problems with the drive.

DO insert the cardboard protectors that come with 5¼-inch disk drives, and close the doors when moving the computer.

Care of Floppy Disks

DO keep disks in their protective storage envelopes. These envelopes reduce static buildup, which can attract dust that might scratch the disk.

DO keep disks dry, away from sneezes, coffee, or anything wet. A wet disk is a ruined disk.

DO prevent disks from getting too hot or too cold. They should be stored at temperatures of 50°–150°F (10°–52°C). Extremes of temperature can destroy a disk's sensitivity, so treat them the same way you treat photographic film; that is, keep them out of direct sunlight, do not leave them in a car exposed to temperature extremes, and so forth.

DO keep disks at least two feet away from magnets. The magnets found in copy stands, telephones, radio or stereo speakers, vacuum cleaners, televisions, air conditioners, novelty items, electric motors, or even some cabinet latches can ruin a disk's data.

DON'T touch a disk's recording surface. Handle them only by their protective covers.

DON'T use a hard-tipped pen to write on a disk label that is affixed to the disk. This can crease the disk inside the protective cover and cause you to lose data. Write on the label before affixing it to the disk, or use a felt-tip pen with very light pressure.

DON'T leave a disk in a nonoperating disk drive with the door closed for long periods. Open the drive door to lift the read/write head from the surface of the disk.

DON'T insert or remove a disk from the drive when the disk drive is running (that is, when the drive's light is on).

DON'T bend, curl, or fold disks.

DON'T use paper clips to attach a floppy disk to a file folder or copy of a printout. Special folders are available that let you keep disks and printed documents together.

DON'T expose disks to static electricity. In dry climates or in heated buildings, static builds up when you walk on carpeted and some other kinds of floors. If you experience shocks when you touch metal objects, you are discharging the static that has built up. If you touch a disk when still charged with this static, you can damage the data. To prevent this, increase the humidity in the air, use static-proof carpets, or touch something like a typewriter to discharge the static before you pick up a disk.

Even with the best of care, floppy disks can last only so long. Close to the end of their useful life, they show their own form of senility by losing information or giving invalid commands. These are signs that it is time to replace the disk, which ideally you have already made another backup copy of.

EXERCISE

Exercise 2-1A
IDENTIFY PARTS OF A FLOPPY DISK

Sketch a 5¼- or 3½-inch floppy disk, and then label each of its parts.

QUESTIONS

1. List and briefly describe the two main types of external storage media and devices.
2. Describe the purpose of the light on the front of a disk drive.
3. What is a hard disk drive? What other names are used for the same device?
4. List at least two advantages a hard disk drive has over floppy disks and disk drives.
5. How are data stored on optical disks? What does search and retrieve software allow you to do when combined with optical disks?
6. What would you do if you found an unlabeled disk in the computer lab? Would you use it for your own files or try to find out whose it is?
7. Why should you write out a label before you stick it onto a 5¼-inch disk?
8. What is the purpose of the write-protect notch or window on a floppy disk? What can you do when the disk is write-protected, and what can you not do? What can you do when it is not write-protected?
9. Why would you not use a piece of clear tape to cover the write-protect notch on a 5¼-inch disk?
10. Why should you make backup copies of important disks?
11. When you are going to move a microcomputer, what preventive step should you take to protect the hard disk drive?
12. List three things you should do to protect floppy disks and three things you should not do.

2-2 INTRODUCTION TO THE OPERATING SYSTEM

Operating system. The program that controls the computer's hardware.

Although you do your computer work on applications programs such as WordPerfect or 1-2-3, the heart of the computer's software is the *operating system*. The operating system coordinates activity between you and the computer (Figure 2-8). Through the operating system, you tell the computer to run your word processing program, save a document, or print a file, and so forth.

Because the operating system coordinates activity between any applications program you run and the computer hardware, you must load the operating system into the computer's memory before you load an applications program. Most applications programs that you buy do not contain the operating system. To use these programs, you must first load the operating system from another disk, or copy the appropriate operating system files to the applications program disk or hard disk.

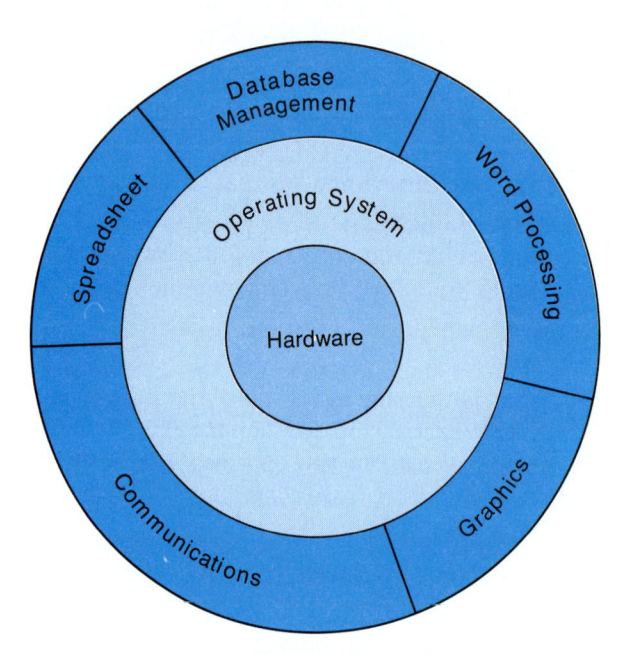

Figure 2-8 The Operating System and Applications Programs
The operating system communicates between applications programs and the hardware. The operating system must always be loaded into the computer's memory before any applications are loaded.

THE FUNCTIONS OF AN OPERATING SYSTEM

The primary function of the operating system is to coordinate the activities of the computer. The operating system controls your computer without your involvement or awareness. In this respect, it is like your body's respiratory system, which keeps you breathing and your heart beating even though you are hardly aware of it. The operating system decides where programs and data are stored in the computer's memory and handles communications among the computer's components, the applications programs, and you, the user.

Picture a busy intersection at rush hour with no traffic lights and no police officer (Figure 2-9). No one approaching the intersection knows what to do or when to do it. The traffic backs up and tempers flare. The solution is the installation of traffic lights or a police officer to tell people when to stop and go. In your computer, this function is handled by the operating system's input/output manager and command processor.

Input/output (I/O) manager. The part of DOS that controls the exchange of information between the computer and peripherals such as the keyboard, printers, and display screens.

Command processor. The component of an operating system that interprets commands entered on the keyboard and converted to signals understandable to the microprocessor.

Figure 2-9 The Operating System Coordinates Traffic
Intersections without traffic control are confusing. Those with traffic control are more efficient. Everyone knows when to stop and when to go. The operating system performs traffic control functions within the computer.

Input/Output Management

The *input/output (I/O) manager* coordinates the computer's communications with all peripheral devices. For example, it coordinates the flow of data to the display screen and to other output devices such as printers and modems. It also controls the flow of data to and from the disk drives.

Command Processing

The *command processor* interprets what you enter using the keyboard or other input devices. In this respect, it is rather like an interpreter (Figure 2-10). If you spoke only English and tried to carry on a discussion with someone who spoke only French, you both would need an interpreter to translate what was being said so that you could understand each other. The same is true of a computer. For example, on one program, you might save the file that you are working on by pressing **/FS** and then pressing **Enter**; on another, you might press the function key **F10** and then press **Enter**. The operating system interprets these commands and instructs the disk drive to spin while it copies the file to the disk from the computer's internal memory.

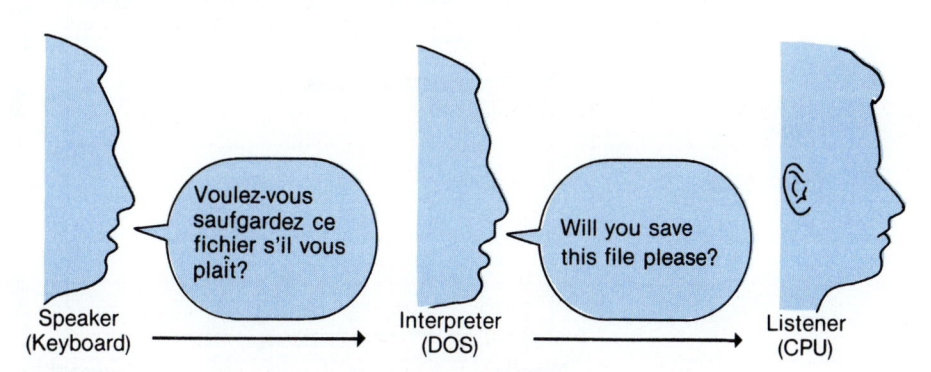

Speaker (Keyboard) — Voulez-vous saufgardez ce fichier s'il vous plaît?
Interpreter (DOS) — Will you save this file please?
Listener (CPU)

Figure 2-10 The Operating System Interprets
Command processing is a form of interpreting. The commands you enter on the keyboard are interpreted by the operating system and sent to the central processing unit.

2-2

MS-DOS. Abbreviation for the Microsoft disk operating system. This operating system, a variation of PC-DOS, is generally required on IBM PC compatible computers.

PC-DOS. A version of the MS-DOS operating system that runs on IBM PCs and compatible computers.

Disk operating system. (DOS). DOS is the interface between you and your personal computer. All applications programs require that you first load the disk operating system before you load the programs. DOS also includes several utility programs that you use to format disks, copy, delete, and rename files and so on.

Command prompt. The prompt that is displayed on the screen when the operating system is running, the shell is not displayed, and no applications programs have been loaded.

Shell. A menu-driven, user-friendly interface that makes operating system commands easier to use.

MS-DOS AND PC-DOS

When IBM developed the IBM PC, they asked Microsoft to develop an operating system called *MS-DOS* (Microsoft Disk Operating System) or *DOS* for short. The IBM PC version of this program was named *PC-DOS*. (Throughout the remainder of this text, we refer to both versions as DOS.) The PC-DOS version usually runs on IBM PC computers, and the MS-DOS version usually runs on compatibles made by manufacturers other than IBM. These two versions of the operating system are almost identical in the way they work and the commands you use to operate them; usually, they are interchangeable.

When you load DOS, versions before DOS 4 always display a *command prompt* (Figure 2-11). At this prompt you type commands, and then press **Enter** to execute them.

Because many DOS commands are hard to remember, several programs, called *shells*, have been developed (Figure 2-12). You load one of these shells into the computer's memory after you load DOS, and it displays menus and lists of files. Using the menus, you can execute many of the most frequently used DOS commands without having to remember how to type them. With the introduction of DOS 4, a shell with pull-down menus was built into the operating system.

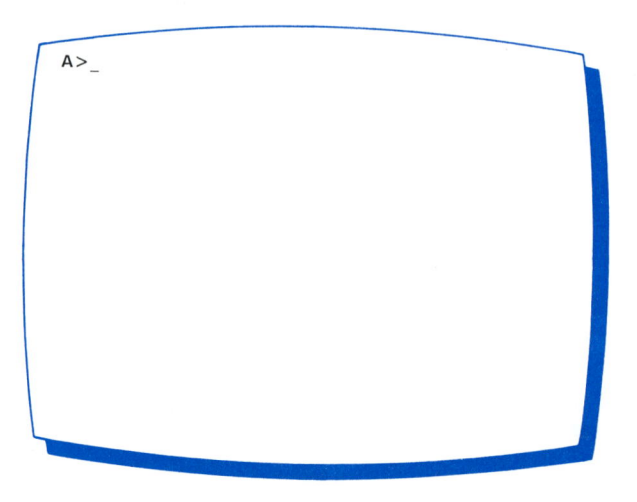

Figure 2-11 The DOS Screen Display
All versions of DOS can display the command prompt. From this prompt, you load applications programs and execute DOS commands.

Figure 2-12 The DOS 4 Shell
When you load DOS 4 and later versions, the Shell is displayed if your startup disk is set up to do so. (Your screen may look slightly different if you do not have a graphic display or a mouse.)

74 DISKS, DISK DRIVES, AND OPERATING SYSTEMS

Graphical operating system environment.
A more sophisticated version of an operating system that allows more than one program to be run, more than one file to be displayed on the screen, and allows the user to execute most commands from menus.

GRAPHICAL OPERATING SYSTEM ENVIRONMENTS

Graphical operating system environments (also called *graphical user interfaces* or *GUIs*) like Microsoft's Windows (Figure 2-13) make using the computer easier and more efficient. For example, Windows incorporates a graphic display that allows you to choose commands from pull-down menus and to divide the screen into windows in which multiple applications programs can be displayed and run at the same time. It gives a common look to most programs that are developed to take advantage of its features. For example, it allows you to operate the computer using standardized commands to load programs; call up

Figure 2-13 Microsoft Windows
Microsoft Windows, a typical operating system environment, allows you to load more than one program into memory so that you can quickly switch between them. It also allows you to perform many operating system functions, such as copying files, without having to learn the commands usually required.

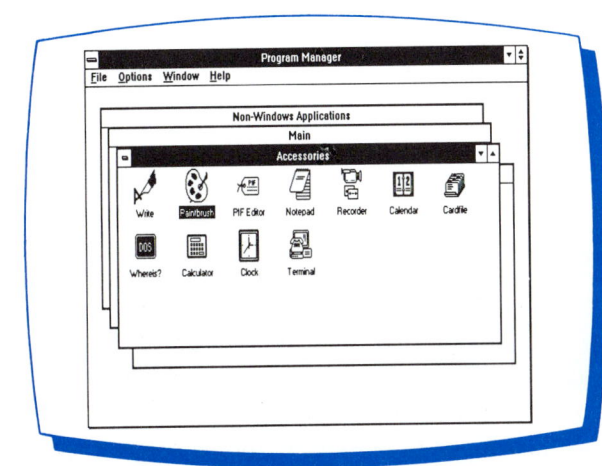

1. The Windows screen lists some of the programs that can be run. To run a program, you just point to it and double click one of the buttons on a mouse.

2. By clicking on a drive's icon, you can see how the disk is organized. This is called a tree.

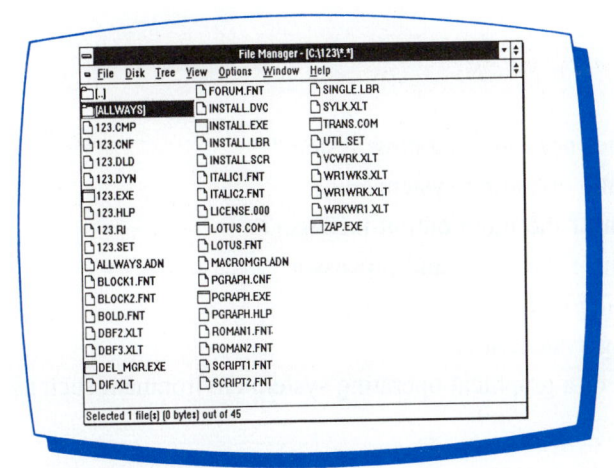

3. By clicking on any part of the tree, you can list the files on the disk or in the directory.

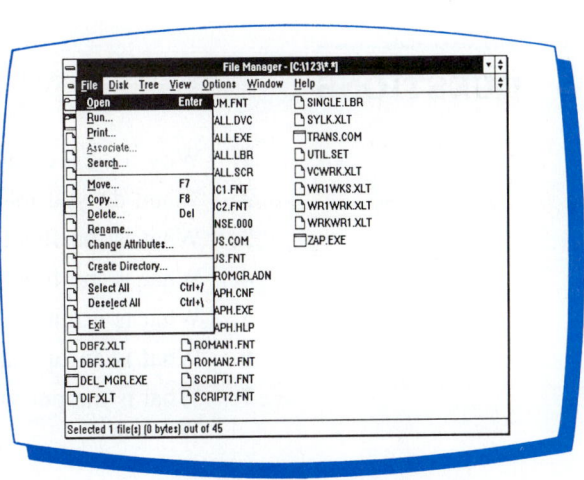

4. To run programs or manage files, you just pull down the File menu and choose a command.

INTRODUCTION TO THE OPERATING SYSTEM

Multitasking. The computer's ability to run more than one program at the same time.

Window. The area on a screen that displays different parts of the same file (or different files).

Foreground. The program currently being used when two or more programs are being run on the computer simultaneously. See also Background.

Background. The program not currently being used when two or more programs are simultaneously being run on the computer.

Cut. To move part of a file you are working on to a buffer.

help; cancel commands; format disks; copy, rename, and erase files; and quit to return to the operating system.

Operating system environments also let you *multitask* by displaying *windows* on the screen. You can run more than one program at a time and switch between or among the programs currently in memory. For example, you can run your favorite spreadsheet in one window and your favorite word processor in another. The program you are currently working on is in the *foreground*. The other programs, which you are not currently working on, are in the *background*.

With Windows you can also copy data between applications. You first select the part of the text that you want to copy or move. You then select Window's Copy or *Cut* command to copy the selected text to the clipboard. You then switch to the other program, and use the Paste command to move the text from the clipboard to this program.

EXERCISE

Exercise 2-2A
VIEW A VIDEO

Many videocassettes have been developed to introduce users to specific operating systems. Visit your library, learning center, or computer lab to see if any are available for you to view. If so, view it, and then summarize its key points.

QUESTIONS

1. Why does a computer need an operating system?
2. When do you load the operating system?
3. What is the function of the input/output manager?
4. What is the function of the command processor?
5. What is a multitasking operating system?
6. What is an operating system shell?
7. What is the purpose of a graphical operating system environment such as Windows?

2-3
LOADING AND QUITTING THE OPERATING SYSTEM

Boot. To load a program into the computer's memory.

Cold boot. Starting the computer by turning it on.

Warm boot. Restarting the computer by pressing designated keys instead of turning it off and back on. On the IBM PC, you warm boot by pressing **Ctrl-Alt-Del**.

Startup drive. The drive to which the computer looks for programs when you first turn it on. The startup drive is drive A on a floppy disk system and drive C on a hard disk system.

Because the operating system coordinates activity between any applications program you run and the computer hardware, you must load the operating system into the computer's memory before you load an applications program. This is called *booting* the system. The term comes from the expression "pulling one's self up by the bootstraps." When you boot the system by turning it on, it is called a *cold boot* (see the box "Warm Booting a Computer"). Once the operating system is loaded, you can load your applications programs or use the operating system's commands to manage your files.

WARM BOOTING A COMPUTER

You can warm boot a computer if it is already on. To *warm boot* the system, you hold down **Ctrl** and **Alt** while pressing **Del**, or press the computer's Reset button. This command clears all data from the computer's memory and has almost the same effect as turning the computer off and then back on again. Use this command with restraint. You normally use this procedure only when you encounter a problem with your system, or when you have changed some system settings that take affect only when you reboot the computer. You should not warm boot on a regular basis. It doesn't cause harm but it is a bad habit because you might lose data if you do it at the wrong time.

If your system is off, you load the operating system by turning it on. When you do so, the computer automatically looks to the *startup drive* for the operating system files that it needs to start up.

- On a floppy disk system, the startup drive is drive A, so you have to insert a disk that contains the operating system files into that drive.
- On a hard disk system, the startup drive is drive C but the computer still looks to drive A first. Therefore, before you turn on a hard disk system, be sure to open the door to drive A or eject the disk so that the program does not try to load the operating system from that drive (see the box "Error Messages").

ERROR MESSAGES

When you boot an IBM computer system, you may see the message *Non-bootable disk* or *Non-System disk or disk error* (or a similar message on compatible computers). One of these error messages appears when you turn on the computer with a disk in drive A that does not contain the operating system files that the computer needs.

- On a floppy disk system, insert the DOS disk into drive A, and then press any key to continue.
- On a hard disk system, open drive A's door or eject the disk in that drive, and then press any key to continue.

With the drives set, you turn on the computer. The position of the on/off switch varies from computer to computer. Frequently, it is on the front or on the right side toward the back. On many systems, you have to turn on the display screen using its own switch. When you turn on the computer, it pauses for a few moments. During this pause, the computer is very busy.

1. The computer first executes a small diagnostic program that is permanently stored in its read-only memory (ROM). This program checks the computer's memory to make certain it is operating correctly. If the computer finds a problem, it displays a message on the screen indicating where the problem is located and then stops.

2. If the diagnostic program finds no problems, the program in ROM executes two operating system programs on the disk in the startup drive (named IBMBIO.COM and IBMDOS.COM on IBM versions of DOS). If the disk does not have the two system files (which are put on the disk when it is formatted), the computer displays an error message and stops. If there is no disk in drive A and there is no hard disk, some systems automatically load BASIC, a programming language. (If this happens to you—the screen indicates that you are in the BASIC program—type **SYSTEM** and then press **Enter**.)

3. Once the two operating system programs are executed, the computer looks for a program called COMMAND.COM, which contains the most frequently used internal operating system commands. Executing this program loads a copy of it into RAM, where it remains as long as the computer has power.

If your system's clock is not set automatically, you are prompted to enter the date and time each time you turn it on. If you are prompted to do so, see the box "Entering Dates and Times."

The loading process is now complete. The screen display, and the way the system operates, are determined by the version of the operating system that you are using and the way your system has been set up.

You have to load the operating system only once during a session. If you are already running an applications program, you do not have to boot the system to return to the operating system, as it is already in memory. You just use the applications program's Quit or Exit command, and that returns you to the operating system.

THE COMMAND PROMPT AND THE DOS 4 SHELL

When you load DOS, either the command prompt or the DOS 4 Shell is displayed. Which appears depends on the version of DOS that you are using and how your system has been set up.

The Command Prompt

On some systems, the command prompt appears on the screen when you boot the system (see Figure 2-11). It will normally be *A>* or *A:\>* if you loaded from a floppy disk or *C:\>* if you loaded from a hard disk drive. However, the command prompt can be customized, so it may be different on your system.

The command prompt tells you that you are in DOS and that the default, or active, disk drive is drive A or C. From this command prompt, you can execute all DOS commands or start applications programs like WordPerfect, 1-2-3, or dBASE.

ENTERING DATES AND TIMES

When you first turn on some computers, you are prompted to enter the date and time. Entering the correct date and time is important because the computer's clock date and time mark files that you save. The clock is also used by some programs to enter dates and times into files and to display them on the screen.

You enter the date and time as described below, and then press **Enter** (⏎ on IBM and compatible keyboards). If you enter either incorrectly, an error message is displayed, and you are prompted to reenter them.

Entering Dates
Enter dates in the format MM-DD-YY.

- MM (month) is a number from 1 to 12.
- DD (day) is a number from 1 to 31.
- YY (year) is a number from 80 to 99 or from 1980 to 1999.

You can use hyphens (-), slashes (/), or periods (.) to separate the day, month, and year. For example, to enter the date January 10, 1992, enter it as 1-10-92, 1/10/92, or 1.10.92.

If you fail to enter a date, the system's clock remains set to 1-01-80, and all files that you save are marked with that date. You cannot enter a date earlier than 1/1/1980. To enter a date later than 12/31/1999, you must enter all four digits for the year. For example, to enter January 1, 2001, type `1/1/2001`.

Entering Times
Enter times in the format HH:MM.

- HH (hours) is a number between 0 and 23.
- MM (minutes) is a number between 0 and 59.

Separate the hours and minutes with colons (:) or periods (.).
You can use military time or, if you are using DOS 4, standard time.

- Military time is based on a 24-hour day. For example, to set the clock to 1:30 P.M., enter `13:30`.
- Standard time is based on a 12-hour period. To specify the time when using DOS 4, you enter a `p` or an `a` after the last time unit. For example, to set the clock to 1:30 P.M., enter `1:30p`. To set it to 10:30 A.M., enter `10:30a`. Do not enter spaces between the time and the letters.

The DOS 4 Shell

If you are using DOS 4, and your system has been set up to do so, the DOS 4 Shell appears on the screen when you boot the system. The first screen displayed is the Start Programs screen (see Figure 2-12). The menu-operated Shell makes it easy to execute commands without remembering cryptic keystrokes. All you have to know is how to use the Shell's menus.

Although you might want to use the Shell for most of your work, some advanced procedures can be completed only from the command prompt. Also, when the command prompt is displayed, the system works just like earlier versions of DOS. You can quickly switch back and forth between the Shell and the command prompt whenever you want to.

LOADING AND QUITTING THE OPERATING SYSTEM

- To display the Shell from the command prompt, type **DOSSHELL** and then press **Enter**.
- To display the command prompt when the Shell is on the screen, press **F3** from Start Programs to remove the Shell from memory. (You first have to press **F3** if you are in the File System, or **Esc** if you are in the DOS Utilities' subgroup, to return to Start Programs.)

QUITTING DOS

When you are done for the day, you should always exit the program you are using to return to the operating system, and then:

- Open the floppy disk drive doors or eject the disks in the drives so that the disk drives' read/write heads don't leave indentations in the disks' surfaces.
- Remove your disks from the disk drives to prevent their loss, increase security, and ensure that no one mistakenly erases them.
- Turn off the computer or use the display monitor's controls to dim the screen so that an image will not be "burned" into its phosphor surface.

PRINTING THE SCREEN DISPLAY

When working with DOS commands, you can make printouts of the information that appears on the screen.

- To print a snapshot of the screen, hold down **Shift** and press **PrtSc** (or just press **Print Screen** on an enhanced keyboard).
- If you want to have a running, printed record of what you are doing while working from the command prompt, hold down **Ctrl** and press **PrtSc** to send screen text to the printer. From then on, a copy of whatever the computer sends to the screen will also be sent to the printer. After executing this command, you can turn it off by holding down **Ctrl** and pressing **PrtSc** again.

EXERCISE

Exercise 2-3A
BOOTING YOUR SYSTEM

The way you boot a system varies, depending on how your system has been set up. If your system is on a network, or for some other reason your startup does not follow the same rules described in this section, enter your startup procedures here.

1. _____
   _____
   _____

2. _____
   _____
   _____

3. _____
   _____
   _____

4. _____
   _____
   _____

QUESTIONS

1. What does booting a computer mean?
2. What is the difference between a warm and a cold boot? How do you do each?
3. What does the *A>* prompt mean? The *C:\>* prompt?
4. When entering a date on your computer, what characters can you use to separate day, month, and year?
5. If you fail to enter a date when you start your computer, what happens?
6. What characters do you use to separate hours and minutes when entering the time?
7. What command captures a still picture of the screen? A moving picture of the screen?

2-4 UNDERSTANDING FILENAMES AND DRIVES

Filename. The name you assign to a file when you save it onto a disk so that you can retrieve it later. The computer's operating system determines the length of the filename, as well as the characters you can use in it.

Legal characters. Characters that are acceptable to the computer for specific purposes.

Batch file. A file that contains commands, for example, the names of programs to be executed, to accomplish a specific task.

Overwrite. When you save a file, any other file by the same name is erased, and the new one replaces it.

To work with an operating system, or any applications program, it is important that you understand *filenames* and how files are directed to the drive you want to save or manage them on.

ASSIGNING FILENAMES

The files for the programs you use have already been assigned names. When you use these programs to create and save your own work, you must assign names to your files. The number and type of characters that you can use in a file's name are determined by the operating system you are using. For example, with DOS or OS/2, you can create filenames that have up to eight characters and an optional three-character extension separated from the filename by a period (Figure 2-14). The characters that are allowed are called *legal characters*, and they are listed in Table 2-1. Using any other character results in a name the computer will not accept. If you specify an illegal filename, the program normally does not accept it and prompts you to enter a correct filename.

Table 2-1
CHARACTERS THAT CAN BE USED IN FILENAMES

Characters	Examples
Letters	A through Z (uppercase or lowercase)
Numbers	0 through 9
Characters	! @ # $ % ^ & ( ) — _ { } ~ ` '

You can type filenames in uppercase letters, lowercase letters, or a combination of uppercase and lowercase. If you do not use uppercase letters, the computer automatically converts your characters into uppercase.

Extensions are made up of a period (.) followed by up to three of the same characters that can be used for filenames. Often you do not enter the extension; the applications program you use enters it for you. As you use different programs, you will discover that many employ their own extension to identify files that they create. The extension is also reserved for special uses. For instance, .EXE and .COM are used for program files, and .BAT is used for *batch files*.

Each filename you use must be unique. If you assign the same name and extension as one already assigned to a file on the disk, the new file will *overwrite* the previous file and erase it. You can assign the same name only under the following circumstances:

- When you save the files onto different disks
- When you save the files in different directories on a hard disk drive

However, you can use the same filename with different extensions, for example, LETTER.DOC and LETTER.BAK. You can also use the same extension with different filenames.

FILENAME.EXT
↑   ↑
Filename Extension

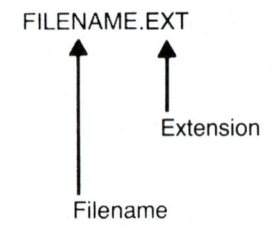

Figure 2-14
Filenames
Filenames usually have two parts, the filename and an extension.

Wildcard. A character used in search and replace operations to stand for one or more characters in the same position in the string. For example, DIR FILE?.* would list any file that began with FILE followed by any single character and any extension.

Address (v). When one component sends a signal to another component that tells the component that it wants its attention. For example, "The computer will address drive A."

Default drive. The drive that the computer will automatically look to when a command is issued, unless a different drive is specified in the command.

USING WILDCARDS

In many DOS commands, you specify the name of a single file. Frequently, however, you will want to work with groups of files. For example, when making a backup disk, you might want to copy all the files from one disk to another. Instead of copying one file at a time, you can copy several files at once using wildcards. A *wildcard* is simply a character that stands for one or more other characters, much like a wildcard in a card game. MS-DOS and PC-DOS wildcards are the question mark (?) and the asterisk (*).

The question mark can be used to substitute for any single character:

- BOO? will stand for BOOT, BOOK, or any other four-letter word beginning with BOO.
- BO?? will stand for BOOT, BOOK, BORE, or any four-letter word beginning with BO.
- B??? will stand for BOOT, BOOK, BORE, BLOT, or any other four-letter word beginning with B.

The asterisk is more powerful; it represents any number of characters:

- *.* will stand for any file with any extension.
- B* will stand for BOOT, BOTTLE, or any word of any length beginning with B.
- *.DOC will stand for any file with an extension .DOC.
- LETTER.* will stand for any file named LETTER with any extension.

THE DEFAULT AND OTHER DRIVES

Because most computers have two or more disk drives, you must often tell the computer which drive to use, or to *address*. For example, you do this when you run a program or copy, save, or retrieve files. When addressing the drive, the operating system spins the disk in the drive so that it can read information from, or write information to, the disk.

When you first turn on your computer and load the operating system, drive A spins. If a disk in that drive contains the necessary operating system files, the operating system is loaded. Drive A operates because the computer's designers have placed a program in the computer's ROM telling it that it should address this drive when first turned on. Because it addresses drive A automatically, drive A is the *default drive*. The DOS command prompt indicating that drive A is the default drive is *A>*.

Although you cannot change the default drive that the computer addresses when you first turn it on, you can, and often do, copy, rename, delete, and save files from a drive other than the default drive. There are two ways to do this: You can change the default drive, or you can specify the other drive in the command.

Changing the Default Drive

Whenever the operating system is on the screen, you can quickly change the default drive (Figure 2-15). To do so with the command prompt on the screen, type the letter of the drive, a colon (**:**), and then press **Enter**. For example, to change the default drive from A to B, type **B:** and then press **Enter**. The command prompt changes from *A>* to *B>*.

UNDERSTANDING FILENAMES AND DRIVES **83**

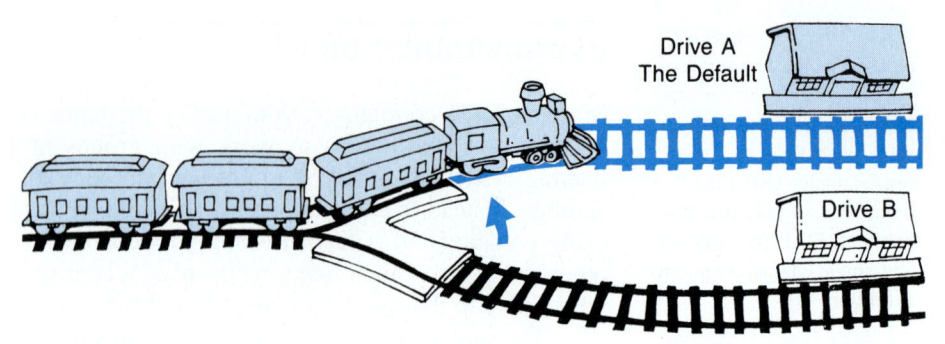

The default drive is the drive that the computer automatically addresses when you execute commands or copy files. It's like a model railroad set where you can set a switch to send a train down either one track or another.

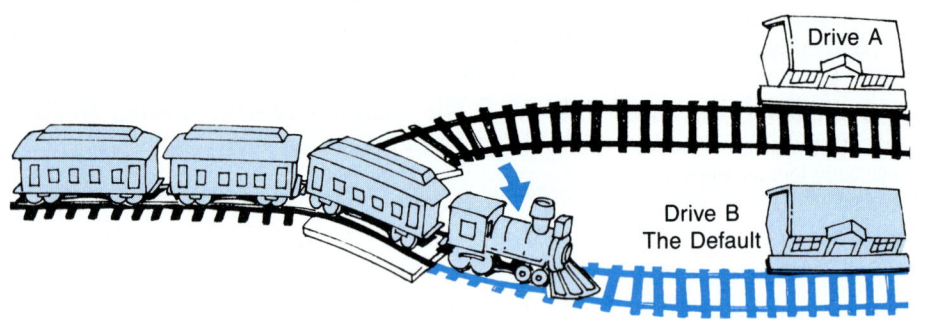

You can change the default drive so that the program automatically addresses it rather than the original default drive. It's like changing the position of the switch on a model railroad to send the train down another track.

Figure 2-15   The Default Drive
When working with files, you may have to change the default drive.

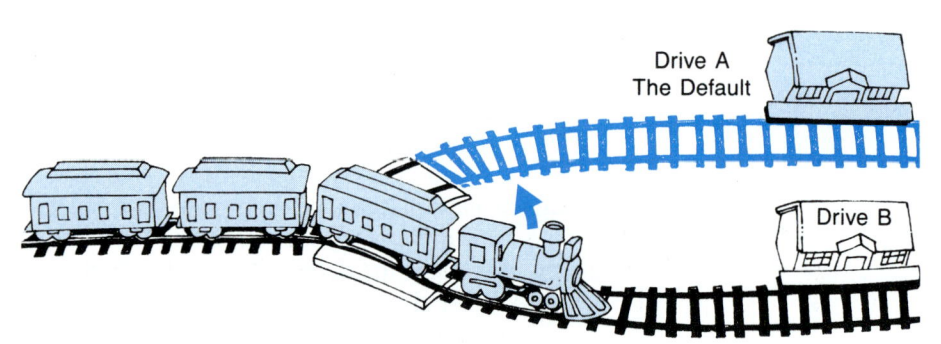

You can leave the default drive unchanged and specify another drive when you save or retrieve a file. This ignores the setting for the default drive and sends the file to or retrieves it from the drive that you specify. It's like sending a model train down a specified track regardless of how the switch is set.

Figure 2-16   Specifying the Other Drive
You can leave the default drive unchanged and specify another drive in your commands.

84   DISKS, DISK DRIVES, AND OPERATING SYSTEMS

Specifying the Other Drive

To copy a file to a drive other than the default drive, or to delete or rename a file on such a drive, you must specify the drive in the command (Figure 2-16). For example, if the default drive is set to A, and you want to copy a file named LETTER on drive A to drive B, you would type either `COPY A:LETTER B:` or `COPY LETTER B:`. In the first command, you specified both drives, so the command reads "copy the file named LETTER in drive A to drive B." In the second command, you did not specify drive A. You do not have to because drive A is the default drive, and you never need to specify the default drive except as a precaution. This command reads "copy the file named LETTER in the default drive to drive B."

EXERCISE

Exercise 2-4A
ASSIGNING FILENAMES

You have been assigned the task of preparing four letters and sending the disk to someone else to print. Using the recipient's name, company, and date sent, assign eight-letter filenames to each file. Give a list of your filenames to a fellow student, and see if they can tell which file contains which letter. The letters were sent to the following people:

Alice Barr at Exxon on January 1
Liz Kendall at IBM on January 2
Susan Willig at AT&T on January 1
Nancy Benjamin at Prentice Hall on January 2

QUESTIONS

1. Why do you have to give a file a name?
2. What are the two parts of a filename called? How many characters are allowed for each part? What are the parts separated with?
3. Indicate whether the filenames listed below are legal or illegal on a PC-DOS or MS-DOS system.

Filename		
FILENAME.DOC	____ Legal	____ Illegal
FILE/DOC	____ Legal	____ Illegal
LETTER.DOCUMENT	____ Legal	____ Illegal
DOCUMENTS.DOC	____ Legal	____ Illegal
MEMO JOHN.DOC	____ Legal	____ Illegal
MEMO^5.DOC	____ Legal	____ Illegal
99999.999	____ Legal	____ Illegal
2	____ Legal	____ Illegal
2_2	____ Legal	____ Illegal

4. What are wildcards used for? What are the advantages of using wildcards? What are the potential disadvantages?
5. What two wildcards are used with DOS? Describe what each does.
6. What is the default drive?
7. Using DOS, how do you change the default drive?
8. If you want to direct a file to a drive other than the default drive, how do you do so?

2-4

2-5

2-5
USING DOS TO MANAGE YOUR DISKS AND FILES

Internal commands.
DOS commands that are automatically loaded into the computer along with the operating system. You can use these commands whenever the command prompt is displayed on the screen.

External commands.
DOS commands that are not automatically loaded into memory along with the operating system. To use external commands, their files must be on a disk in one of the disk drives.

FORMAT command.
The command you use to prepare new disks for use on your computer. The format command magnetically divides a disk into tracks and sectors used by the computer to find information stored on the disk.

Formatting. The process of putting a series of 0s and 1s onto a blank disk with the operating system's FORMAT command so that it can receive digital information.

System disk. A disk that contains the operating system so that the operating system can be loaded from it. Also called a "self-booting" disk.

FORMAT/S command.
The DOS command that formats a disk and transfers to it the operating system files the computer needs to start up.

Normally, the operating system handles its functions without your direct involvement. However, all operating systems include several utility programs that you use to manage your files. To use these utilities from the command prompt, you type the name of the utility program that performs the desired function. You use these utilities to prepare disks for use on the computer and to copy, rename, erase, and otherwise manage files you have saved on your disks. The utilities available on DOS fall into two classes: internal commands and external commands. (Table 2-2 lists some of the most frequently used DOS commands.)

- *Internal commands* are available whenever the command prompt is on the screen. Internal commands are automatically loaded into the computer's memory whenever you load DOS because they are included in the COMMAND.COM file that is loaded automatically whenever you turn on the system.

- *External commands* are stored on the DOS disk or hard disk until you need them. These commands are used less often than internal commands. Not loading external commands into memory until they are needed leaves room for other programs and data.

If you enter an external command and its program is not on the disk in the drive, the computer tells you it cannot find the command. When this occurs, check to see what commands are on the disk and if you specified the correct command. External commands are little more than small programs that are loaded into the computer's memory and then executed when you type their name and then press **Enter**. Thus, if you use an external command frequently, copying the appropriate program file from the DOS disk onto an applications program disk may be helpful.

Formatting Disks (an external command)

When you open a box of new floppy disks, they will usually not run on your computer because they have been designed to work with a variety of computer systems. To customize them so that they will run with the equipment you are using, you format the disks with the ***FORMAT command***. *Formatting* checks the disk surface for unusable spots, divides the disk into tracks and sectors (see the box "Selecting Floppy Disks for Your System"), and creates a directory.

When you want to load a program without first having to load DOS from another disk, you format it as a *system disk* with the ***FORMAT/S command***. This command does the same thing as the regular FORMAT command, but the /S (called a *parameter*) copies the necessary operating system files onto the disk. This allows you to load DOS directly from the new disk and use all the internal DOS commands.

The FORMAT command completely erases any data on a disk. You therefore have to be careful with this command. You should never format a previously used disk unless you are sure you will not need any of the files on it. Also, you should never format a hard disk drive unless you are willing to lose every file on the disk.

Table 2-2
SUMMARY OF DOS COMMAND PROMPT COMMANDS

Command	Description	Type
Basic Commands		
`VER`	Displays DOS version number	Internal
`DATE`	Displays system date and changes it	Internal
`TIME`	Displays system time and changes it	Internal
`PROMPT`	Changes the command prompt	Internal
`CLS`	Clears the screen	Internal
Displaying Lists of Files		
`DIR A:`	Lists the files on drive A	Internal
`DIR B:`	Lists the files on drive B	Internal
`DIR B:*.DOC`	Lists all files on drive B with a DOC extension	Internal
Changing Default Drives		
`A:`	Makes drive A the default drive	Internal
`B:`	Makes drive B the default drive	Internal
`C:`	Makes drive C the default drive	Internal
Formatting Disks		
`FORMAT`	Formats a data disk	External
`FORMAT/S`	Formats a system disk	External
Copying Files		
`COPY`	Copies individual files	Internal
`COPY A:*.* B`	Copies all files from A to B	Internal
Duplicating and Comparing Disks		
`DISKCOPY`	Duplicates a disk	External
`DISKCOMP`	Compares duplicated disks	External
Renaming and Erasing Files		
`RENAME` or `REN`	Renames files	Internal
`ERASE` or `DEL`	Deletes files from disk	Internal
Checking Disks		
`CHKDSK *.*`	Gives status of memory, disk space, and any noncontiguous blocks	External
`CHKDSK/V`	Displays each filename as it is checked	External
`CHKDSK/F`	Displays a prompt that asks you if you want to correct errors	External
Making and Changing Directories		
`MD`	Creates a new directory	Internal
`CD`	Changes the default directory	Internal
`RD`	Removes a directory	Internal
`CD\`	Returns to the root directory	Internal
`CD ..`	Returns to one level up	Internal
`TREE`	Displays a list of directories	External
`TREE/F`	Displays a list of directories and files	External
ASCII File Displaying and Printing Commands		
`TYPE`	Displays ASCII text file on screen (**Ctrl-S** freezes scrolling screen display)	Internal
`PRINT`	Prints ASCII text file	External
`PRINT/T`	Stops a printing ASCII text file	External
Batch File Commands		
`COPY CON`	Copies from console (keyboard) to disk file	Internal
`F6`	Ends a COPY CON command	Internal

Tracks. The concentric paths around a disk on which data are stored.

Sector. A portion of the floppy or hard disk that data are written to, or read from. The space on a formatted disk is divided into tracks and sectors so that data can be located easily.

Formatted disk. A disk that has been coded with 0s and 1s with the operating system's format command so it can store digital data from the computer.

Tracks per inch (TPI). The number of tracks per inch on a disk determines disk density. The higher the TPI, the more data the disk can store.

Density. Determines the amount of data that can be stored on a disk.

Single-sided disk. A magnetic disk on which data are stored on only one side.

Double-sided disk. A disk on which both sides have been certified for storing data.

Single-density disk. A floppy disk on which data are stored on forty-eight tracks.

Double-density disk. A disk that has forty-eight tracks per inch.

High-density disks. Disks that store data on 96 TPI. Also called high-capacity or quad-density disks.

SELECTING FLOPPY DISKS FOR YOUR SYSTEM

When you format a floppy disk, the operating system divides it into *tracks* and *sectors*, an invisible magnetic pattern something like a dartboard.

On a *formatted disk*, tracks run in circles around the disk. The number of *tracks per inch* (*TPI*) determines the *density* of the disk and the amount of data that can be stored on it. A high-density disk has more tracks per inch than a low-density disk and can therefore store more data.

Because tracks can store a great deal of data, the computer needs to divide them into sectors, which makes it easier to find a location on the disk. These sectors are like pie-shaped wedges that divide each track into the same number of sectors.

A formatted disk looks something like a dartboard; it has circular and pie-shaped sections

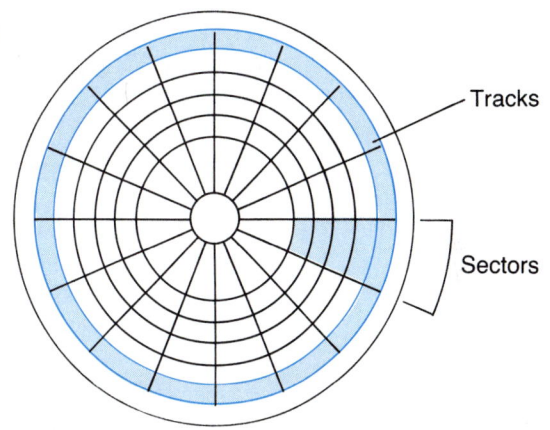

Because there are slight variations in the way computers assign tracks and sectors, the disks you use must be appropriate for your system. Disks are rated as single or double sided. *Single-sided disks* can store data on only one side of the disk. *Double-sided disks* can store data on both sides of the disk if your system's disk drive is capable of writing to both sides.

To store more data, the tracks on the disk are placed closer together. The spacing of these tracks is measured as tracks per inch (TPI). The maximum density that can be used to store data on a disk is indicated on the disk label and box. For example, on 5¼-inch disks:

- *Single-density disks* can store data on 24 TPI or up to 180 KB (KB stands for kilobytes)
- *Double-density disks* can store data on 48 TPI or up to 360KB
- *High-density disks* (also called *high-capacity* or *quad-density disks*) can store data on 96 TPI or up to 1.2 MB (MB stands for megabytes)

3½-inch floppy disks can store 720KB or 1.44MB. These smaller disks can store more data than the larger 5¼-inch disks because they can store data on 135 TPI. You can tell the two types of disks apart as follows:

- A 720KB disk is labeled "1.0MB" or "2HC" and has a single square cutout.
- A 1.44MB disk is labeled "2.0MB" or "HD" and has two square cutouts.

> **KEY/Strokes**
>
> **FORMATTING DATA DISKS**
>
> 1. • On a floppy disk system, insert the DOS disk into drive A. Then, type `A:` and press **Enter** to make drive A the default drive
>   • On a hard disk drive, type `C:` and then press **Enter** to make drive C the default drive
> 2. Type `FORMAT B:` (on a floppy disk system) or `FORMAT A:` (on a hard disk system), and then press **Enter**. The prompt asks you to insert a disk into drive B or A
> 3. Insert the disk to be formatted into drive B (on a floppy disk system) or drive A (on a hard disk system)
> 4. Press the key suggested on the screen (some versions of DOS ask you to press **Enter**; others ask you to press any key)

DIR command. The DOS command that displays a list of the files on a disk.

Listing Files (an internal command)

Because a disk has the potential for holding many files, it is often necessary to find out what files are on a particular disk. The names of the files on a disk are held in a directory, and the ***DIR command*** is used to display the contents of that directory. Besides listing the filenames, the DIR command also displays

- The size of each file in bytes
- The date and time the file was last saved (useful only if you set the date and time each time you turn on the computer)
- The number of files and how much free space is left on the disk

In its simplest form, this command asks for a listing of the directory of the disk in the default drive. For example, with the *A>* command prompt on the screen

- To list the files in drive A, type `DIR` or `DIR A:` and press **Enter**.
- To see the files in drive B, type `DIR B:` and press **Enter**.

If a list of files is too long to be displayed on the screen, some of the filenames will quickly scroll up and off the screen. Adding two parameters to the commands prevents this. Type `DIR A:/P` or `DIR B:/P` and press **Enter**. The /P parameter tells the DIR command to display files until the screen is full. To display additional files, simply press any key. To display the files horizontally instead of vertically, type `/W` following the DIR command. This command drops the file size, date, and time information to make room for a horizontal listing of filenames.

> **KEY/Strokes**
>
> **LISTING THE FILES ON DISKS**
>
> 1. Insert the disk with the files that you want to list into drive A or B
> 2. Type `DIR A:` or `DIR B:` to list all of the files on the disk

COPY command. The command used to duplicate text or files.

Source disk. The disk that holds data destined to be transferred to a target disk.

Target disk. The disk that receives data transferred from the source disk.

Access. The process of locating information stored in memory or on a disk.

Copying Files (an internal command)

When you want a duplicate copy of one or more files, you use the *COPY command*. This command copies one or more specified files from a disk in one drive or directory to a disk in another drive. The COPY command is often used to make backup copies of important files. It is also used with wildcards to copy more than one file. For example, with the operating system *A>* prompt on the screen, the disk that files are being copied from in drive A, and the disk that files are being copied to in drive B:

- To copy a file named FILENAME.EXT, type `COPY A:FILENAME.EXT B:` and then press **Enter**.
- To copy all files, type `COPY A:*.* B:` and then press **Enter**.
- To copy all files named with the extension .EXT, type `COPY A:*.EXT B:` and then press **Enter**.
- To rename a file while copying it, specify the new name. For example, type `COPY A:OLDNAME.EXT B:NEWNAME.EXT`.

SOURCE AND TARGET DRIVES

When managing your files, you should understand the source and target drives. The source is the drive containing the disk that you want the action performed on. The target is the drive containing the disk that you want to be affected by the source. For example, when you copy files from one disk to another, the disk you copy from is the *source disk*, and the disk you copy to is the *target disk*. When you place these disks into the drives, the drives become the source drive and target drive.

If you have only one floppy disk drive, specify the source drive as drive A and the target drive as drive B. The operating system will then prompt you to swap disks whenever it needs *access* to the source or target disk and it is not in the drive.

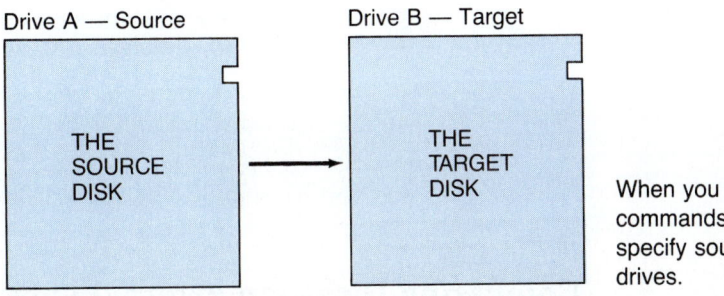

Drive A — Source   Drive B — Target

THE SOURCE DISK → THE TARGET DISK

When you use DOS commands, you frequently specify source and target drives.

- To copy a file from drive A to drive B, you use the command `COPY A:FILENAME.EXT B:`. The A: specifies the source drive that contains the file to be copied, and the B: specifies the target drive that you want the file copied to.
- To duplicate a disk in drive A onto a disk in drive B, you use the command `DISKCOPY A: B:`. The A: specifies the source drive that contains the original disk, and the B: specifies the target drive that you want it duplicated to.

USING DOS TO MANAGE YOUR DISKS AND FILES

> ### KEY/Strokes
> **COPYING FILES**
>
> 1. • On a floppy disk system, insert the source disk into drive A and the target disk into drive B
>   • On a hard disk system, insert the source disk into drive A. You will be prompted to swap disks periodically
> 2. Either type `COPY A:*.* B:` and then press **Enter** to copy all files
>   Or type `COPY A:`*filename.ext* `B:` and then press **Enter** to copy a single file

DISKCOPY command. A DOS command that makes an exact copy of a disk.

DISKCOMP command. A DOS command that compares two disks to see if they are the same.

Duplicating Disks (an external command)

As you have already seen, you can use the COPY command with wildcards to copy all the files from one disk to another to make a backup copy. The *DISKCOPY command* also lets you make a backup copy of a disk. Why are there two commands to do the same thing? For one thing, the DISKCOPY command does not require you to format the disk you are copying the files to. The DISKCOPY command automatically formats the disk before it begins to copy the files. For another, the COPY command does not make an exact copy of a disk. It copies the files, but not their exact location on the disk.

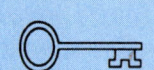

> ### KEY/Strokes
> **DUPLICATING DISKS**
>
> 1. On a floppy disk system, insert the DOS disk into drive A
>   On a hard disk system, change the default drive to C
> 2. Type `DISKCOPY A: B:` and then press **Enter**. You are prompted to insert the source and target disks
> 3. Either on a floppy disk system, insert the source disk into drive A and the target disk into drive B
>   Or on a hard disk system, insert the source disk into drive A. You will be prompted to swap disks periodically

Comparing Disks (an external command)

After you duplicate a disk, you can use the *DISKCOMP command* to check that the disks are identical. If they aren't you can make another copy. (This command does not compare disks copied with the COPY command.)

> ### KEY/Strokes
> ### COMPARING DISKS
>
> 1. • On a floppy disk system, insert the DOS disk into drive A, then type **A:** and press **Enter** to make drive A the default
>   • On a hard disk system, type **C:** and then press **Enter** to make drive C the default
> 2. Type **DISKCOMP A: B:** and then press **Enter**
> 3. Follow the prompts that appear on the screen (on a system with a single floppy disk drive, you will be periodically prompted to swap disks)

ERASE command. A DOS command that deletes files from a disk.

File recovery program. A utility program that allows you to recover programs that you have deleted with the DOS ERASE or DELETE command.

Erasing Files (an internal command)

It is important that you monitor the amount of free space on a disk because many applications programs misbehave when you ask them to save files on a full disk, or the program creates temporary files that take up a lot of space. Most people tend to keep files around long after they are useful. It is good practice occasionally to use the DIR command to list the files on a disk and then the ***ERASE*** (or the identical DEL) ***command*** to delete any no longer needed.

You can use wildcards with the ERASE command, but it is dangerous to do so. Miscalculating even slightly the effects that wildcards have can cause the wrong files to be deleted. One trick is to use the planned wildcards in the DIR command. If only the files you want to delete are listed, the same wildcards will be safe to use with the ERASE command. For example, if you plan on deleting all files with the extension .BAK, type **DIR *.BAK** first to see which files will be affected.

> ### KEY/Strokes
> ### ERASING FILES
>
> 1. Insert the disk with the files that you want to erase into drive A or drive B
> 2. Type **ERASE A:***filename.ext* or **ERASE B:***filename.ext* to erase a file from the disk

RECOVERING ERASED FILES

The ERASE command does not actually erase a file from the disk. It merely changes the first letter of its name in the file directory to a special character. All programs that access the directory know that if a filename begins with this character, the file has been deleted, and new files can be saved in the space previously reserved for the deleted file. If you save another file on this disk, it might be saved on top of, and thus erase, the file you ''erased'' with the ERASE command. If you ever erase a file by mistake, do not save any files on the disk because ***file recovery programs*** are available that you can use to put its name back in the directory so that you can retrieve it from the disk.

USING DOS TO MANAGE YOUR DISKS AND FILES

RENAME command. A DOS command that changes the name of a file.

Renaming Files (an internal command)

There are times when you want to change the name of a file after it has been saved. To do this, you use the *RENAME* (or the identical REN) *command*.

KEY/Strokes

RENAMING FILES

1. Insert the disk with the files that you want to rename into drive A or drive B
2. Type `REN A:`*oldname.ext newname.ext* or `REN B:`*oldname.ext newname.ext* to rename a file on the disk

---

Cluster. Two or more allocation units assigned to a file when it is saved.

CHKDSK command. The DOS command that you use to find out if all of the files stored on a disk are in contiguous sectors. This command also tells you how much total memory there is in the computer and on a disk and how much remains unused and available for other programs, documents, or other files

Checking Disks and Files (an external command)

When you save a file on a new disk, it is stored neatly on adjacent sectors around adjacent tracks on the disk. After the disk begins to fill up and some files have been erased, however, the disk drive has to work harder to store a file. It tends to store different parts of the file wherever it can find free sectors. After awhile, a file may end up scattered all over the disk. Files stored this way take longer to save and retrieve because the drive's read/write head has to keep moving over the disk's surface to reach parts of the file. Files like this can also end up with lost sections, called *clusters*, because the drive can't find all the sections.

You can check your disks with the **CHKDSK command** to see if any files are scattered. The CHKDSK command is an external command, so insert the DOS disk in drive A. Then, to check the files on a disk in drive B, type `CHKDSK B:*.*` and press **Enter**. In a moment or so, the screen will tell you if all files are contiguous or show you the files that are not (Figure 2-17). Contiguous means the files are stored in adjacent sectors, as they should be (Figure 2-18). If any files are noncontiguous, they are scattered. To save the files so that they are contiguous, copy all the files to a new formatted disk with the COPY *.* command. The DISKCOPY command will copy the noncontiguous files exactly as they are, so nothing is gained.

If sectors of a file become scattered, the operating system may not be able to find clusters. The CHKDSK command occasionally displays a message tell-

```
A>CHKDSK B:*.*

322560 bytes total disk space
217088 bytes in 29 user files
105472 bytes available on disk

524288 bytes total memory
492112 bytes free

B:\PART1.DOC
Contains 3 non-contiguous blocks
B:\PART2.DOC
Contains 2 non-contiguous blocks

A>
```

Figure 2-17 The CHKDSK Screen Display
If the CHKDSK *.* command finds that files have been fragmented, the screen tells you there are noncontiguous sectors. If your disk has these, you should copy the files to a new disk.

94 DISKS, DISK DRIVES, AND OPERATING SYSTEMS

TYPE command. The DOS command that displays ASCII files on the screen.

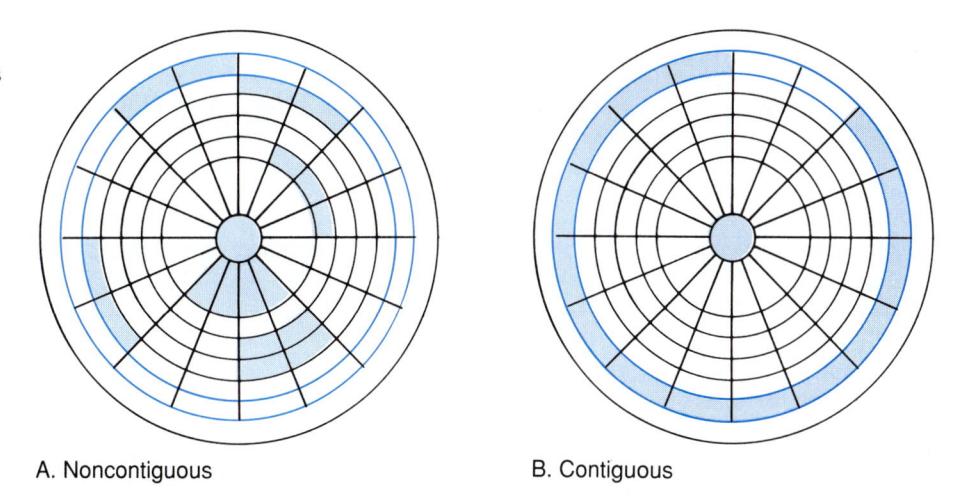

A. Noncontiguous

B. Contiguous

Figure 2-18 Contiguous and Noncontiguous Sectors
A disk with noncontiguous sectors (A) has a file stored in sectors that are not adjacent to each other. A disk with contiguous sectors (B) stores the file in adjacent sectors.

ing you the disk has lost clusters and asks if you want them fixed. To do so, there are two other versions of the CHKDSK command you should be familiar with:

- To have a series of messages displayed as the disk is checked, type `CHKDSK B:/V` (or `CHKDSK B:*.*/V`) and press **Enter**.
- To correct any errors discovered by the CHKDSK command, type `CHKDSK B:/F` (or `CHKDSK B:*.*/F`) and press **Enter**. This stores lost clusters in a file named FILE0000.CHK, FILE0001.CHK, or a similarly numbered file that you can then retrieve with many word processing programs to recover the lost material.

KEY/Strokes

CHECKING DISKS

1. • On a floppy disk system, insert the DOS disk into drive A, then type `A:` and press **Enter** to make drive A the default
   • On a hard disk system, type `C:` and then press **Enter** to make drive C the default
2. Insert the disk to be checked into drive A (on a hard disk system) or drive B (on a floppy disk system)
3. Type `CHKDSK A:` (on a hard disk system), or `CHKDSK B:` (on a floppy disk system) and then press **Enter**

Displaying ASCII Files on the Screen (an internal command)

If you have ASCII text files on the disk, you can display them on the screen with the *TYPE command*. If a file displayed with this command is longer than the screen, it will scroll by too fast to read. You can freeze the screen at any point by holding down the **Ctrl** key while you press the letter **S**. To resume scrolling, just press any other key.

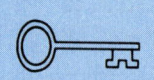

> ### KEY/Strokes
>
> **DISPLAYING ASCII TEXT FILES**
>
> 1. Insert the disk with the ASCII files that you want to display into drive A or drive B
> 2. Type **TYPE A:**_filename.ext_ or **TYPE B:**_filename.ext_ to display the file

PRINT command. A DOS command that sends a text or print file to the printer.

Printing ASCII or Print Files (an external command)

You can also print ASCII files or files that you previously printed to the disk. The command to do this is the **PRINT command**. When you use this command the first time in a session, a prompt asks you for the name of the print device and suggests LPT1 (the normal printer port). If your printer is attached to that port, you just press **Enter** to print the file. If the printer is attached to a different port, for example, LPT2, COM1, or COM2, you type the name of the port and press **Enter**. To stop a file that is currently being printed with this command, type **PRINT/T** and then press **Enter**.

> ### KEY/Strokes
>
> **PRINTING ASCII TEXT FILES**
>
> 1. • On a floppy disk system, insert the DOS disk into drive A and the disk with the ASCII text file into drive B
>   • On a hard disk system, insert the disk with the ASCII text file into drive A and change the default drive to C
> 2. Type **PRINT B:**_filename.ext_ (on a floppy disk system) or **PRINT A:**_filename.ext_ (on a hard disk system) and then press **Enter**
>
>   The prompt may read _Name of list device [PRN]:_ If this happens, press **Enter** to answer the prompt for the name of the list device. The message then reads _Resident part of PRINT installed, B:filename.ext is currently being printed._

USING OPERATING SYSTEM FUNCTIONS FROM WITHIN APPLICATIONS PROGRAMS

There are times when you want to use DOS commands while working on an applications program. But to quit the program, return to DOS, perform the tasks, and then reload the program is time consuming. Therefore, most applications programs let you execute DOS commands without quitting. There are two approaches.

- The program has commands that perform the most common operating system commands. For example, you use the applications program's commands to copy or rename a file instead of the operating system's commands.

■ The program allows you to access the operating system to perform these tasks without actually leaving the applications program. There is not standard name for this command. For example, Windows calls it DOS Prompt, WordPerfect calls it Go to DOS, 1-2-3 calls it System. When you use this command, the command prompt appears on the screen. You can then use any of the standard operating system's commands. When finished, you type a command, usually **EXIT**, and then press **Enter**. This returns you to where you were before you accessed the operating system.

■ EXERCISES

Exercise 2-5A
MATCHING DOS COMMANDS AND FUNCTIONS

Using Table 2-2 as a guide, match the DOS commands in column A with the function they perform in column B.

A	B
__FORMAT	A. Displays an ASCII text file on the screen
__COPY	B. Displays a list of files on the disk
__DISKCOPY	C. Compares two disks
__DISKCOMP	D. Copies two or more files
__TYPE	E. Prints an ASCII text file
__PRINT	F. Tells you if there are any noncontiguous sectors on a disk
__CHKDSK	G. Changes the name of a file
__DIR	H. Prepares a disk so that you can store data on it
__RENAME	I. Prepares a system disk from which you can load the operating system
__FORMAT/S	J. Makes an exact duplicate of a disk

Exercise 2-5B
SPECIFY YOUR SYSTEM'S DISKS

Identify, in detail, the type of disks you should use with one of the computers in the lab. List all the specifications, for example, the number of sides and density. To do so, refer to the manual that accompanies the computer. Look up "disks" or "disk drives" in the index and refer to the listed sections. If you cannot find the information in the manual, refer to the specifications printed on the box that the disks came in.

QUESTIONS

1. What is the basic difference between an internal and an external DOS command?
2. Why do you format a data disk? What command do you use? Why must you be careful when using the command?
3. What is the difference between a system disk and a data disk?
4. When you format a disk, what does DOS do to the disk?
5. Is the DIR command an internal or external command?
6. What information does the DIR command give you in addition to a list of filenames?
7. If drive A is the default drive, what command do you use to display a list of files on the disk in that drive? What command lists the files on the disk in drive B?
8. What command do you use to display filenames horizontally across the screen? What command do you use to display filenames a page at a time?
9. What command do you use to copy files? Is the command an internal or external command?
10. When the default drive is set to A, and you want to copy a file named FILENAME.EXT from drive A to drive B, how do you enter the command?
11. When the default drive is set to A, and you want to copy a file named FILENAME.EXT from drive B to drive A, how do you enter the command?
12. What command do you use to duplicate disks? Is the command an internal or external command? When would you not want to use the command? What are the differences between this command and the COPY *.* command? Why is it preferable to use the COPY command when making a backup copy of files?
13. What command do you use to compare disks? Is the command an internal or external command? Can you use the command to compare disks you copied with the COPY command? What should you do if the command finds that your disks do not exactly match?
14. What command do you use to rename files on a disk? Is the command an internal or external command?
15. What commands do you use to erase files? Are these commands internal or external? Why must you be careful when using wildcards to erase files? When using wildcards to erase groups of files, how can you preview the names of the files to be deleted? Can you retrieve a file that you inadvertently erased? What should you do to salvage it?
16. What command do you use to check disks? Is the command an internal or external command? What happens to files, when the disk begins to get full, that makes the drive work harder and take longer to retrieve and save the files? If you get a message telling you your files have noncontiguous sectors, what does it mean? If a disk has noncontiguous sectors, how can you fix the files so that they are all in adjacent sectors on the disk? What is the difference between the CHKDSK and CHKDSK *.* commands?
17. What command do you use to display ASCII files on the screen? Is the command an internal or external command?

2-6
WORKING WITH HARD DISKS

Directory. A list of the files stored on a disk.

Subdirectory. One of several other directories you create from the main root directory. See also Root directory.

Root directory. The topmost directory on a disk that is created when the disk is first formatted. The root directory can be subdivided into additional subdirectories, so files can be organized more efficiently.

A hard or floppy disk can be divided into directories, which help you organize files. Imagine if you used a file drawer to store all of your memos, letters, and reports. Before long, the drawer would become so crowded that you could not find anything. But with a little organization and planning, the documents could be arranged in folders, making it easier to locate the needed document (Figure 2-19).

A hard disk is like an empty drawer in a new filing cabinet: It provides a lot of storage space but no organization (Figure 2-20). To make it easier to find items in the drawer, you can divide it into categories using hanging folders. You can file documents directly into the hanging folders, or you can divide them into finer categories with manila folders. A *directory* is like a hanging folder, and a *subdirectory* is like a manila folder within a hanging folder. A file is a letter, report, or other document within either a directory or a subdirectory.

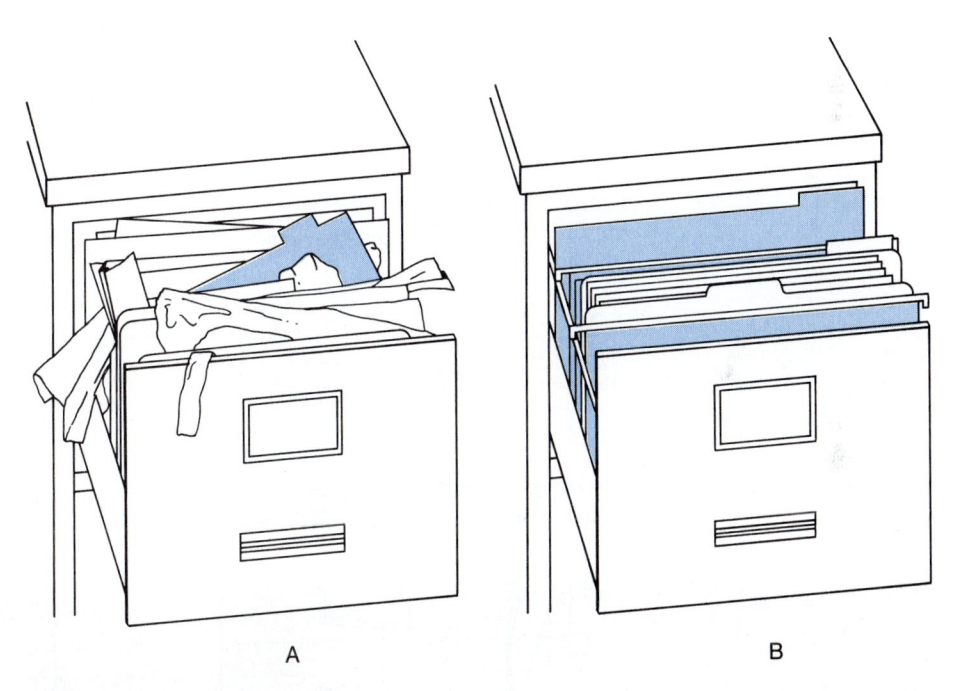

Figure 2-19 File Drawers
Unorganized file drawers make it difficult to find files when you need them (A). Organized file drawers make it easy to find the file you want (B).

CHANGING DIRECTORIES AND SPECIFYING PATHS

To work with directories, you have to know how to change the default directory or specify paths. Directories on a hard disk drive are organized in a hierarchy (Figure 2-21). The main directory, the one above all other directories, is called the *root directory*. Below the root directory, any number of other directories or subdirectories can be created.

Figure 2-20 Directories
When working on a hard disk system, you have to understand how the hard drive is organized into directories and subdirectories. One way to think of it is like a file cabinet.

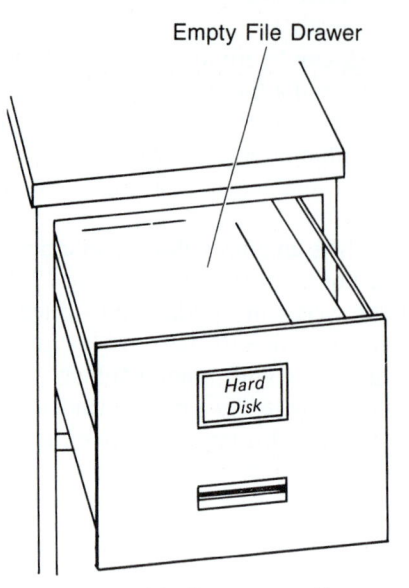

Empty File Drawer

A new hard disk is like an empty file drawer. It has lots of room for files but no organization.

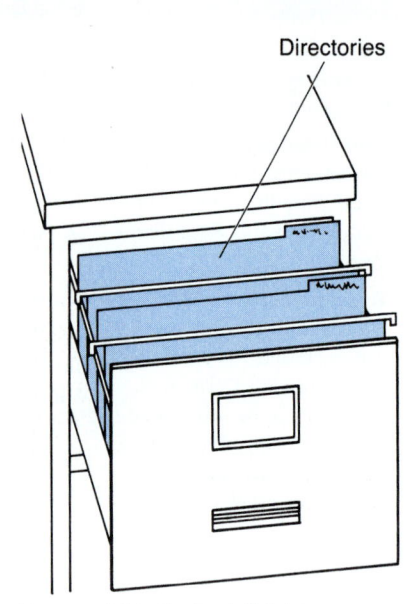

Directories

You can divide the hard disk into directories, which is like dividing the file drawer with hanging folders.

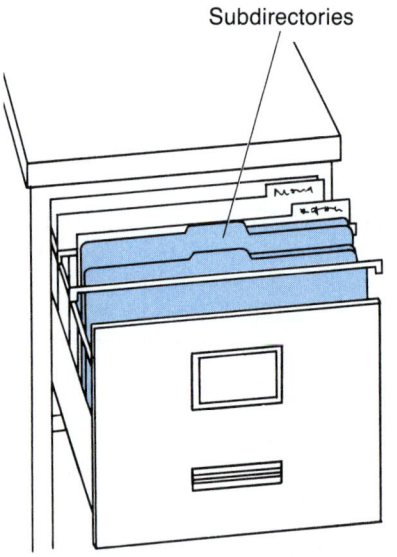

Subdirectories

If you want, you can then subdivide the directories into smaller subdirectories, which is like dividing the hanging folders with manila folders.

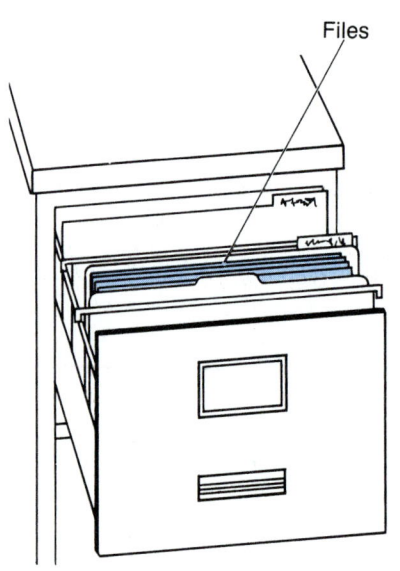

Files

You can save files in any of these directories or subdirectories the same way you would file a document in one of the hanging or manila folders.

Changing Directories

To change default directories, you use the CD (Change Directory) command. There are several versions of this command. For example, if you wanted to move through the directories shown in Figure 2-21, you could use the following commands:

100 DISKS, DISK DRIVES, AND OPERATING SYSTEMS

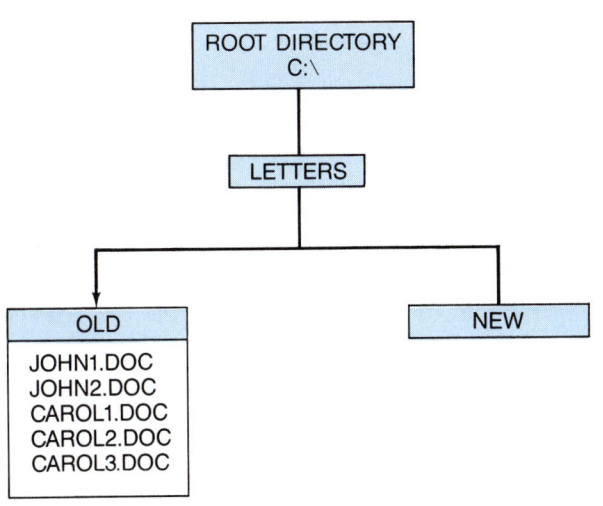

**Figure 2-21
Directories**
Directories and subdirectories on a disk are organized into a treelike hierarchy. The topmost directory is called the root directory. Directories below it are simply called directories. When directories are subdivided into additional directories, they are called subdirectories.

- To change the default directory, type **CD** and then the name of the drive and directory, and then press **Enter**. If you are changing more than one level, list the directories in order, separated by a backslash. For example, to make the subdirectory OLD the default directory, you type **CD\LETTERS\OLD** and then press **Enter**.
- To move up one level, type **CD..** and then press **Enter**. For example, to move from the OLD directory to LETTERS, you type **CD..** and then press **Enter**.
- To change to a subdirectory within the current directory, type **CD** and then the name of the directory, and then press **Enter**. For example, to move from LETTERS to OLD, type **CD OLD** and then press **Enter**.
- To return to the root directory, type **CD** and then press **Enter**. For example, to move from OLD to C:\, type **CD** and then press **Enter**.
- To display the default directory on the current drive, type **CD** and then press **Enter**. To display the current default directory on another drive, type **CD** followed by the drive identifier and then press **Enter**. For example, to display the current directory on drive C, type **CD C:** and then press **Enter**.

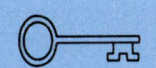

KEY/Strokes

CHANGING DIRECTORIES

- To move to the specified directory, type **CD\DIRECTORY**
- To return to the root directory, type **CD**
- To move up one level, type **CD..**
- To move down one level, type **CD DIRECTORY**
- To display the default directory on drive C, type **CD C:**

When changing directories, it is easy to get lost. It's claimed that in Maine, when someone from out of state asks directions, a native will respond, "If you don't know where you are, you don't belong here." The same is true of directories. If you type **PROMPT PG** and then press **Enter**, the prompt changes to indicate the default directory. For example, when OLD is the default directory, the prompt reads, *C:\LETTERS\OLD>*.

WORKING WITH HARD DISKS

Path. A way of specifying the location of a file on a hard disk drive when saving or retrieving. A path starts from the root directory and narrows down to the specific file you are looking for. For example, C:\LETTERS\1987 specifies that the file 1987 in the directory LETTERS on drive C.

Specifying Paths

When a disk is divided into directories, you not only must specify a drive, you also must specify a directory in many commands. Specifying the drive and directories is called specifying a *path*.

Paths are instructions to the program that tell it what subdirectory a file is located in or where it should be placed. It is like telling someone, "The letter to ACME Hardware is in the manila folder labeled ACME in the hanging folder labeled Hardware in the third file cabinet from the right." These precise instructions make it easy to locate the file. To specify a path, you must indicate:

1. The drive
2. The name(s) of the directory (directories)
3. The filename

When specifying paths from the command prompt, you frequently have to consider both the source and target directories.

- If the source directory is the default, you have to specify only the path to the target.
- If the target directory is the default, you have to specify only the path to the source.
- If neither the target nor the source directory is the default, you have to specify the path for both.

For example, if your directories looked like those in Figure 2-22, you would copy, display directories, and delete files as follows:

- When copying files from the command prompt, you have to specify a path only when the source or target directory is not the default.
  - When OLD is the default, the path you specify to copy FILE1 to the NEW directory is specified only for the target. For example, from the command prompt, you type **COPY FILE1 C:\NEW**
  - When NEW is the default, the path you specify to copy FILE1 to the NEW directory is specified only for the source. For example, from the command prompt, you type **COPY C:\OLD\FILE1**
  - When the root directory is the default, the paths you specify to copy FILE1 to the NEW directory are for both the source and the target. For example, from the command prompt, you type **COPY C:\OLD\FILE1 C:\OLD**

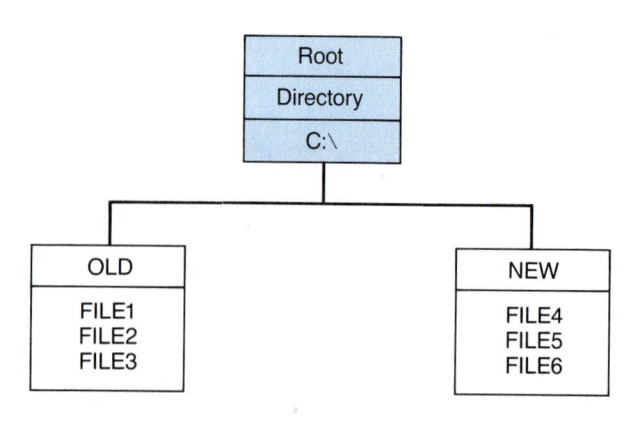

```
              Root
              Directory
              C:\
             /      \
          OLD        NEW
         FILE1      FILE4
         FILE2      FILE5
         FILE3      FILE6
```

Figure 2-22 Paths
When copying files, displaying directories, or deleting files from the command prompt, you have to specify a path when the source or target directory is not the default.

- When you want to display a directory, the same principles work.
  - When the root directory is the default, you can display its directory just by typing `DIR` and then pressing **Enter**.
  - To display the files in the OLD directory, you type `DIR C:\OLD` and then press **Enter**.
  - To display the files in the NEW directory, you type `DIR C:\NEW` and then press **Enter**.
- When you want to delete a file, the same principles work. For example, when OLD is the default directory:
  - To delete FILE1, you type `DEL ILE1` and then press **Enter**.
  - To delete FILE4, you type `DEL C:\NEW\FILE4` and then press **Enter**.

MAKING AND REMOVING DIRECTORIES

When you want to organize your work on a hard disk drive, you create directories. When they are no longer needed, you remove them (after first deleting all the files they contain).

Making Directories

To make a directory from the command prompt, you type `MKDIR` (or `MD`), followed by the name of the directory you are creating (Figure 2-23). If you are creating a directory more than one level down, you must specify the complete path starting at the root directory. For example:

- To create a directory named LETTERS off the root directory when the root directory is the current directory, type `MD C:\LETTERS` or `MD LETTERS` and then press **Enter**.
- To create a directory NEW under a directory named LETTERS, type `MD C:\LETTERS\NEW` from any directory.

If you wanted to create the directories shown in Figure 2-23, you would proceed as follows:

- To make the three directories off the root directory, you type
  `MD\LETTERS` and then press **Enter**
  `MD\MEMOS` and then press **Enter**
  `MD\REPORTS` and then press **Enter**
- To make the two subdirectories off the LETTERS directory, you type
  `MD\LETTERS\NEW` and then press **Enter**
  `MD\LETTERS\OLD` and then press **Enter**

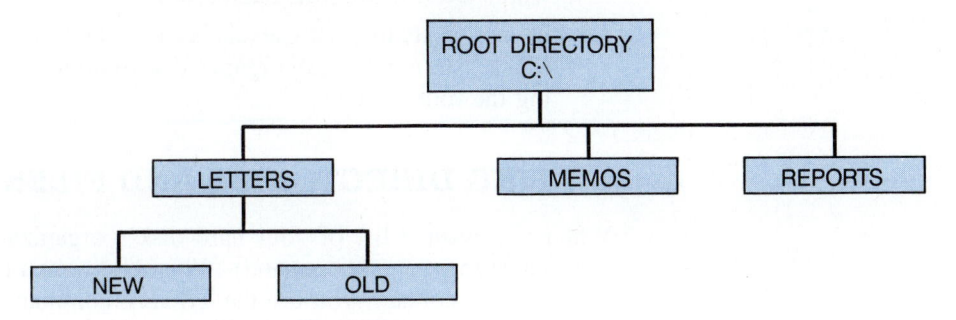

Figure 2-23 Making Directories
You make new directories with the MKDIR command.

WORKING WITH HARD DISKS 103

When creating directories, here are some rules to keep in mind:

- When you create directories, you assign them names. These names follow the same conventions that you use for filenames. However, you should not use a period and extension, or you might confuse directories with filenames at some later date. Files and subdirectories in one directory can have the same names as files and subdirectories in other directories.
- You can create as many directories and subdirectories as you want, but the path cannot exceed sixty-three characters.

Removing Directories

To remove a directory from the command prompt, you must first delete all the files that it contains. To do so, make the directory to be removed the default directory. Then type `DEL *.*`. A prompt asks *Are you sure (Y/N)?* Press `Y` to delete all the files. Next, you have to move to the directory above the one to be removed. To do so, type `CD..` and then press **Enter**. Now, type `RMDIR` (or `RD`), followed by the name of the directory you are removing.

When deleting directories, here are some rules to keep in mind:

- Before you can remove a directory, you must delete all the files it contains. If the directory contains subdirectories, you must first also delete the files they contain, and then delete the subdirectories.
- You cannot delete the current directory or the root directory.

ORGANIZING YOUR WORK IN DIRECTORIES

When creating directories, you should have some kind of a plan. It makes sense to follow these rules:

- Keep only essential files, like AUTOEXEC.BAT and CONFIG.SYS, in the root directory.
- Store all program files related to a program in their own directory. For example, you might want one directory for DOS, one for 1-2-3, one for WordPerfect, and one for dBASE..
- Do not store the data files that you create in the same directory as the program files. Keep all related data files in their own directories. For example, you might have separate directories for letters, reports, financial documents, and name and address lists. You might also create separate directories for the files you create with different programs. For example, you might have separate directories for WordPerfect documents, 1-2-3 worksheets, or dBASE database files.
- Do not create too many levels because it takes time to move around them. Most disks can be well organized with no more than three levels, including the root directory.

LISTING DIRECTORIES AND FILES

When you want a list of your hard disk's organization, you use the TREE command (an external command). When you want a list of the directories, and the files they contain, you use the TREE/F command. This command, unlike the DIR command, lists files in all directories, not just the one you specify.

EXERCISE

Exercise 2-6A
CREATING DIRECTORIES

Your boss gives you a new computer with a hard disk drive and asks you to set it up so all information is stored systematically. To do so, you have to create directories. After thinking about the problem, you decide to divide the disk into directories for the years 1991, 1992, and 1993, and then file documents for each year under the categories memos, letters, and reports. Make a sketch similar to Figure 2-22 that shows the organization of these directories.

QUESTIONS

1. What is the topmost directory on a hard disk called?
2. What command do you use to change directories? What command to move up one level?
3. In the following examples, you are given the name of a file and the drive and directory it is stored on. Write out the path you would specify to direct the file to the indicated drive and directory.

Filename	Drive	Directory	Path
LETTER1.DOC	C	LETTERS	_____
LETTER2.DOC	D	1987	_____
LETTER3.DOC	C	Root Directory	_____

4. What command do you use to make directories?
5. What command do you use to remove directories?
6. What must you do before you remove a directory from a hard disk?
7. What command do you use when you want to display the directories on a hard disk? When you want to display both the directories and the files?
8. You are working on a document named MEMO.DOC and want to save it on a disk or in a directory other than the default. For each of the following, specify the path and filename:

To Save the File on This		I Would Specify This Path
Drive	**Directory**	
B:	None	_____
A:	None	_____
C:	Root	_____
C:	LETTERS	_____
C:	LETTERS\1987	_____

9. Assume you are writing three term papers for each of your classes on a computer. List the filename you would assign to each paper so that you could later identify the course and the papers from them.

2-7
SPECIAL DOS FILES

CONFIG.SYS. A file that the computer looks for when you first start it up. The file contains commands that configure the system.

Configuration file. A file that a program looks to for special instructions when you first load it. Configuration files normally contain the default settings that the program uses.

AUTOEXEC.BAT file. A DOS batch file that automatically provides instructions to the computer when you first turn it on, for example, to set the clock and then load a program.

When you boot the computer, it always looks for two important files that you should be familiar with, CONFIG.SYS and AUTOEXEC.BAT.

CONFIG.SYS FILES

When you first turn on your computer, it looks for a file named *CONFIG.SYS* on the disk in the startup drive and executes the commands that are contained in this file. This file is called a *configuration file* because it stores commands that "configure," or set up, your system. By changing the commands stored in this file, you can change the way your system operates. For example, many applications programs work better and faster when there are BUFFERS and FILES statements in the CONFIG.SYS file. Table 2-3 describes these and other commands frequently used in CONFIG.SYS files.

Table 2-3
TYPICAL CONFIG.SYS FILES

Command	Description
BUFFERS	Sets the number of disk buffers used by the system (should normally read *BUFFERS=8*)
FILES	Sets the number of files that can be opened at one time (should normally read *FILES=20*)
LASTDRIVE	Sets the maximum number of drives that can be addressed; for example, *LASTDRIVE=B* means you can address only drives A and B
COUNTRY	Sets the country for keyboards and other country-dependent information, such as date formats
DEVICE	Specifies the name of a device driver file. For example, if you are using a mouse, your file will have the line *DEVICE=MOUSE.SYS*.

AUTOEXEC FILES

When you first turn on your computer, it also looks for a file named *AUTOEXEC.BAT* and executes any commands that it finds in that file. You use this file to store all commands that you want executed every time you turn on the computer. A typical AUTOEXEC file for a floppy program disk might include the commands shown in Figure 2-24.

A typical AUTOEXEC file on a hard disk system might contain the commands shown in Figure 2-25. You could enter these commands from the keyboard each time you turn on the computer, but that would require sixty-seven keystrokes. You can replace these keystrokes with a single AUTOEXEC file that automatically executes these commands when you turn on the computer. The file shown in Figure 2-25 contains the commands:

- The PATH command specifies the directories and subdirectories the computer looks into when you type a command that is not in the current default directory. If you want to be able to run programs from any directory, you enter a PATH command after loading the operating system. (Or enter it in the AUTOEXEC batch file so that it loads automatically when you boot the system.)

PATH command. The command in an AUTOEXEC.BAT file that lists the directories in which the computer should look for programs to execute when you type the command that loads a program.

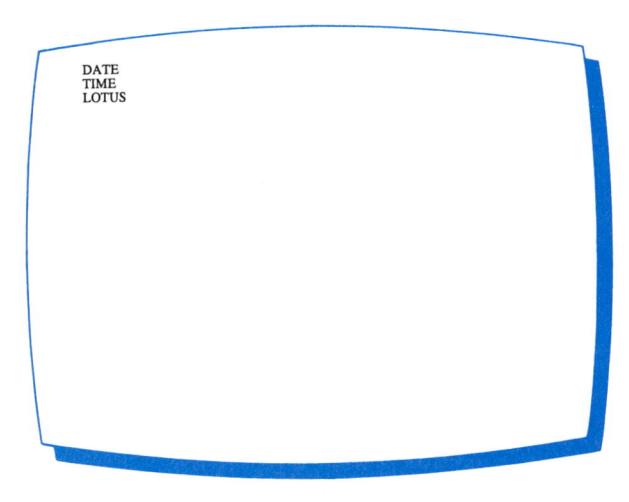

```
DATE
TIME
LOTUS
```

Figure 2-24 An AUTOEXEC.BAT File for a Floppy Program Disk When you insert a system disk into drive A and turn on the computer, you can have the program automatically loaded. For example, this batch file then loads the Lotus Access System.

```
PATH C:\;C:\DOS;C:\123;C:\WORD;C:\DBASE
PROMPT $P$G
CLS
DIR *.BAT
```

Figure 2-25 An AUTOEXEC.BAT File for a Hard Disk The AUTOEXEC file is read by the computer when you turn it on. Any commands stored in the file are automatically executed.

On a hard disk system, the *PATH command* is one of the most important commands to put in an AUTOEXEC file. Normally, you have to make a directory containing a program the default directory before you can execute the program. But the PATH command lets you load a program regardless of where you are in the disk's directories.

To enter the PATH command, type **PATH** followed by the directories the operating system should look in for the program files you want to execute. For example, to run programs from the root directory or the directories named DOS, WP5, 123, and dBASE, you type **PATH C:\; C:\DOS;C:\WP5;C:\123;C:\DBASE** and then press **Enter**.

When entering a PATH command like this, keep the following points in mind:
- You must separate the directory specifications with a semicolon.
- If you enter a command not in the current directory, the operating system searches for it in the directories in the order in which they are listed in the PATH command.
- The PATH command can be up to 128 characters long.

▌ The PROMPT PG command sets the prompt so that it displays the current directory.

▌ The CLS command clears the screen.

▌ The DIR *.BAT command displays a list of all batch files in the root directory. This is useful if you have several batch files that automatically load your programs.

COPY CON command.
The DOS command you can use to create batch files.

CREATING OR EDITING AUTOEXEC.BAT AND CONFIG.SYS FILES

If your system does not have an AUTOEXEC.BAT or CONFIG.SYS file, you can easily create them with any word processing program that allows you to save files as ASCII text files. You can also create them from the command prompt using the *COPY CON command*. This command has only very limited editing procedures so you can correct errors only on the current line. If you notice a mistake on a previous line you have to press **F6**, then **Enter** to close the file. Then, you can reenter the file correctly or edit it with an editing program.

These two files are so important, if they exist, you should not edit them unless you are sure of what you are doing. Before editing or revising either, you should make a backup copy of the original version so you can recover it if something goes wrong. A good way to back it up is to copy it and change its name to AUTOEXEC.OLD or CONFIG.OLD. If anything goes wrong with the new version, you can just rename the backup file so it has its original name.

KEY/Stroke

CREATING AN AUTOEXEC.BAT OR CONFIG.SYS FILE

1. Load the operating system so that the command prompt is displayed on the screen. (If you are creating the batch file on a floppy disk, insert the program disk you want to create a batch file on into drive A.) Make the drive on which you are creating the file the default drive

2. Type `COPY CON AUTOEXEC.BAT` or `COPY CON CONFIG.SYS` and then press **Enter**. You use these names because these are the files the computer looks for automatically whenever you turn it on

3. Type in the commands you want executed just as you would normally enter them from the keyboard. Press **Enter** after entering each command except the last

4. When you are finished entering commands, hold down **Ctrl** while you press the letter **Z**. (On an IBM PC, you can just press the **F6** function key.)

5. Press **Enter**. The drive spins, and in a moment, the command prompt reappears

6. You can now execute the batch file by typing its name and then pressing **Enter** or by turning on the computer with the disk on which it is stored in the startup drive. On the IBM PC and compatible computers, you can press **Ctrl-Alt-Del** to reboot the system

EXERCISE

> ### Exercise 2-7A
> ### EXPLORING YOUR CONFIG.SYS AND AUTOEXEC.BAT FILES

If you are using a system with a hard disk drive, display the commands in the CONFIG.SYS file if the computer has one. To do so:

1. Type `C:` and then press **Enter** to make drive C the default drive.
2. Type `C:\` and then press **Enter** to make the root directory the default directory.
3. Type `TYPE CONFIG.SYS` and then press **Enter** to display the contents of the file.

Hold down **Shift** and press **PrtSc** (or just **Print Screen** on an enhanced keyboard) to make a printout of the screen display or write down the commands in the file. Now, repeat steps 1 through 3 but type AUTOEXEC.BAT instead of CONFIG.SYS to see the contents of that file. Again make a printout or write down the commands. Identify the purpose of as many commands in the file as you can.

QUESTIONS

1. What does an AUTOEXEC.BAT file do?
2. What is the purpose of the PATH command?
3. When you enter the PATH command, what character do you use to separate different directories?
4. If you do not want to enter the PATH command each time you turn on the computer, what can you do?
5. What is the command you type to begin entering a batch file from the command prompt?
6. What key(s) do you press to end a batch file and save it to the disk?

CHAPTER 3

Word Processing and Desktop Publishing Applications

OBJECTIVES

After finishing this chapter, you will be able to:

- Describe the basic procedures that you can perform with any word processing program
- Describe some typical word processing programs and how they work
- Explain how you load and quit word processing and other applications programs
- Describe the way you execute commands when using an applications program
- Describe how to enter text with a word processing program
- Explain how you save and retrieve application program files
- Describe how to move the cursor through a document to make changes
- Describe how you format documents to improve their appearance
- Explain the purpose of merge printing and describe the files you create to use this feature
- Describe the key concepts in desktop publishing and explain what types of programs contain these features

Document (n). Any file containing text created on a word processor.

Format (word processors). The arrangement or layout of lines of text on a page and the typefaces and styles used to print them. Formats include page breaks, text alignment, margins, and boldfacing or underlining.

Word processing is probably the most common application of computers. The ease with which you can draft and revise memos, letters, reports, and other *documents* with a word processing program increases both the speed and quality of your writing. You can enter, edit, change, reorganize, *format*, and print text without having to retype all of it each time you make a change. This ease of use encourages you to revise and reorganize your material more frequently so that you can express your ideas more clearly or to prepare more professional-looking documents.

There are many word processing programs on the market. All of them allow you to accomplish the basic word processing functions, such as entering, editing, formatting, and printing text. They differ from one another in two major respects: the features they offer and the procedures you follow to obtain specific results.

The number of features offered by word processing programs increases almost daily. A few years ago, a program that allowed you to enter, edit, format, and print a document was considered sufficient. These functions alone were such an improvement over the typewriter that many people switched to microcomputer-based word processing systems. Newer programs, however, have added built-in spelling checkers and thesauruses and the ability to draw lines, make calculations, print in multiple columns, and so on. Gradually, features once considered exotic have become standard. Today, programs that lack these features are considered inferior or incomplete. The improvements are continuing. Features considered exotic today, such as those found in desktop publishing oriented programs, will be considered standard tomorrow.

The applications of word processing software are almost endless, ranging from the same tasks that can be done on a typewriter (for example, writing memos, letters, and reports) to entirely new kinds of tasks that aren't possible without the power of the computer. For example:

- Memos, letters, and reports can quickly be entered, edited, revised, saved, and printed in various formats.
- Form documents can be prepared and used over and over again, with just a name or phrase changed here and there. Contracts, sales letters, and collection notices are typical form documents.

Copy for printing can be prepared on a computer. Recent advances make it possible to lay out and illustrate text on your word processing system. The text can be sent to a high-quality laser printer that prints your material using a much wider variety of typestyles and type sizes than those found on a regular printer. This printed copy can then be distributed as is or used as camera-ready copy to make plates to print copies. This emerging technology opens up a new world of opportunities as you can now inexpensively generate typeset-quality copy for catalogs, advertising circulars, reports, articles, and books.

3-1 WORD PROCESSING PROCEDURES— AN OVERVIEW

Save. To copy a file from the computer's memory onto a disk.

In the first chapter, we introduced you to the five steps in the information processing cycle: input, processing, output, storage and retrieval, and distribution and communications. Let's now look at how a word processing program is used in this cycle, from loading the program to clearing the screen or quitting. Later in this chapter, we explain these procedures in detail and introduce you to the many variations that programs offer for each of these procedures.

STEP 1   LOAD THE PROGRAM

The first step in word processing is loading the program. To do so, you first load the computer's operating system and then the word processing program into the computer's memory from the disks they are stored on. If you are using a computer with floppy disk drives, you also insert a formatted data disk into drive B. If you are using a hard disk system, and want to save your work on a floppy disk, you insert the disk into drive A.

STEP 2   OPEN A NEW DOCUMENT (OR EDIT AN EXISTING ONE)

When you load the program, it usually displays a copyright notice and then does one of two things: It displays either the document screen (Figure 3-1) or a Main menu. If a Main menu appears, it lists choices you can select from, usually by typing a number preceding the desired choice. When you select the choice that opens a new document, the document screen appears. However you get there, once the document screen appears, you are ready to enter text.

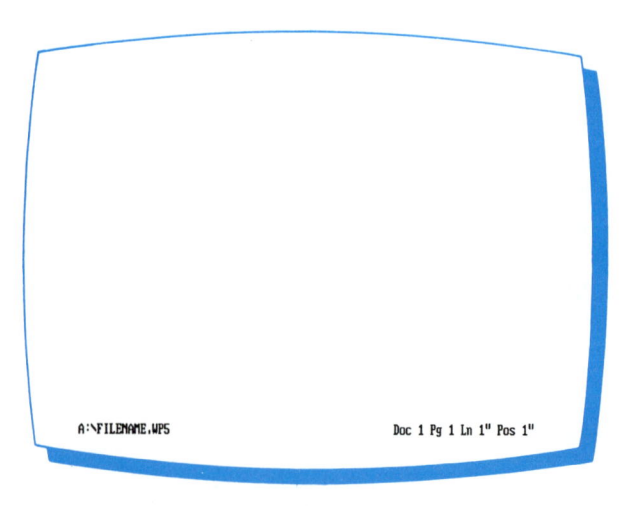

Figure 3-1   The Document Screen
The document screen always displays a cursor.

Naming Documents

Depending on the word processor you are using, you may have to name the document file before creating (typing and editing) it. However, most programs are designed so that you don't assign a name until you *save* the document.

112   WORD PROCESSING AND DESKTOP PUBLISHING APPLICATIONS

Retrieve. To transfer a file from a disk into the computer's memory.

Cursor. A bright highlight on the screen that you move with the cursor movement keys.

Reverse video. When text is highlighted on the screen by reversing the normal colors. For example, if the screen normally displays black characters against a white background, inverse video displays characters as white characters against a black background.

Delete. To erase or remove characters from a document and the computer's memory.

Retrieving Existing Documents

If you created the memo earlier and saved it onto a disk, you must first *retrieve* it from that disk. You retrieve existing documents for editing using the Edit Existing Document, Retrieve, or Load command and then specifying the filename assigned when it was created and saved. When you retrieve a file from the disk, it is "copied" into memory; the document file on the disk remains unchanged.

STEP 3   ENTER THE DOCUMENT

The document screen always displays a *cursor*, a one-characterwide underline or a box that is displayed in *reverse video* (the character highlighted by the cursor appears dark against a bright background). The cursor indicates where the next character you type will appear. When you type a character, it appears on the screen, and the cursor moves one space to the right. The text you enter is not only displayed on the screen (Figure 3-2), it is also stored in the computer's memory.

Entering text on a word processor is similar to entering it on a typewriter. The main difference is that you do not have to press **Enter** at the end of each line (as you have to press the carriage return on a typewriter); the program automatically does that for you. You have to press **Enter** only at the end of paragraphs and when you want a line to end before the right margin is reached or when you want to insert a blank line.

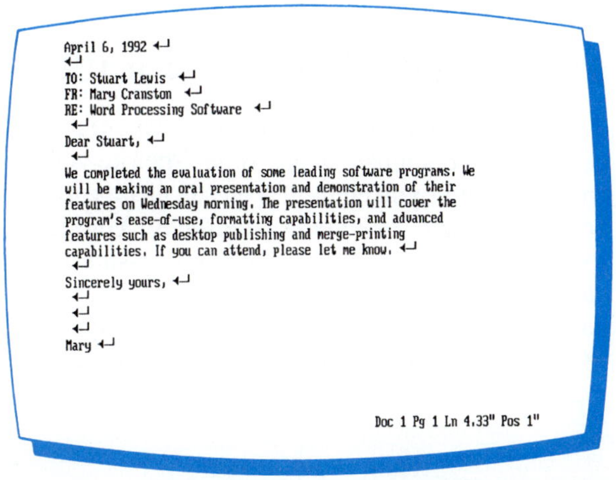

Figure 3-2   Entering the Document
You enter a document by typing, pressing **Enter** only at the end of lines and paragraphs (where indicated by the symbol ↵).

STEP 4   EDIT AND REVISE THE DOCUMENT

After you enter the document, you proofread it and correct any mistakes. Generally, it is easier to proofread a printout of a document (Figure 3-3) than to proofread the document on the screen. To edit a document on the screen after you have proofread it, you use the cursor movement keys to move the cursor through the text of the document. You can then *delete* or insert characters, words, or phrases, or you can select blocks—large sections of text—to copy, move, or delete in one step. You can also use advanced editing features, such as search and replace and spell checking, to speed up the editing.

WORD PROCESSING PROCEDURES–AN OVERVIEW   113

3-1

Indent. Any measurement in from the margin of a text. An indent often marks the beginning of a paragraph, column, or new subheading. See also Hanging indent.

Default format settings. The settings entered into a program by its designers with the expectation that they will satisfy most users most of the time. Examples are margin settings, page size, text alignment, and the number of lines printed per inch. Generally, the default settings can be changed by the user.

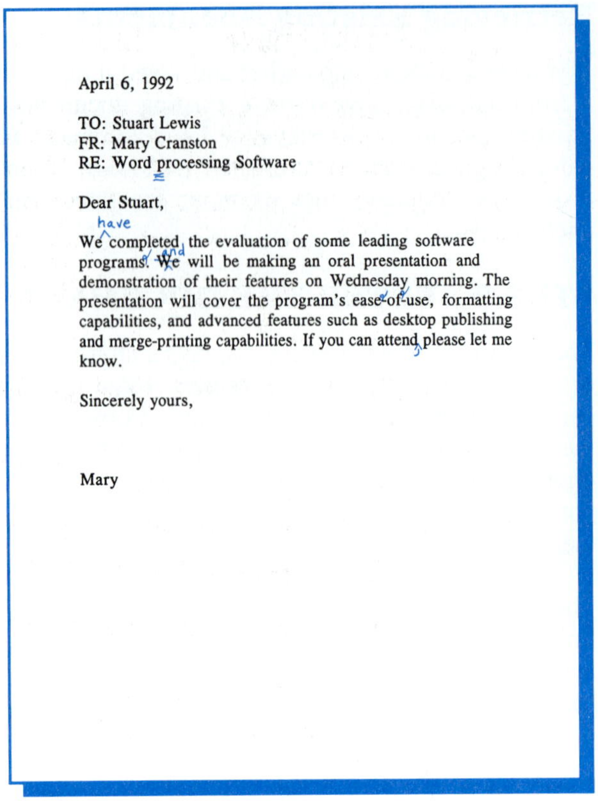

Figure 3-3 Editing the Document
Generally, you make a printout of a document so that you can carefully proofread it. You then edit the document on the screen by moving the cursor and inserting or deleting text.

STEP 5 FORMAT THE DOCUMENT

You format a document to control its layout and appearance (Figure 3-4). You can format a document at any time—before you enter the document, while you enter it, or after you enter it. You can change margins, emphasize key words by boldfacing them, or *indent* paragraphs. You do not need to know much about formatting when you begin word processing because nearly every program is already set to print a document single spaced on an 8½-by-11-inch sheet of paper. These *default format settings* anticipate the most frequent applications of word processing programs—the preparation of memos, letters, and reports.

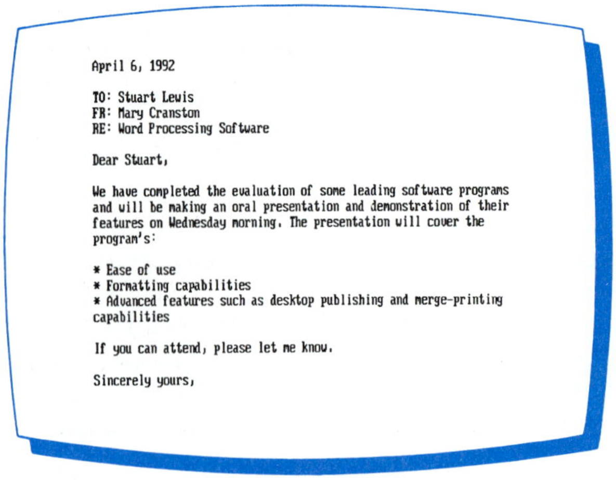

Figure 3-4 Formatting the Document
You can format a document to change its layout or appearance. Here, a paragraph was broken up into a bulleted list.

114   WORD PROCESSING AND DESKTOP PUBLISHING APPLICATIONS

Quit. To leave the program and return to the computer's operating system.

STEP 6 SAVE THE DOCUMENT

When you have completed the document, you save it before printing. To save the document, you use the program's Save command, and the document on the screen and in memory is copied to a file on the disk. If the document is long, you normally would have saved it several times while entering it so that it would not be lost if the power failed or something else went wrong. Most programs have two save commands.

- One command saves the file and leaves it on the screen so that you can continue working on it.
- The other command saves the file and returns you to the Main menu (if any) or clears the document from the screen so that you can create a new document or retrieve an existing one.

STEP 7 PRINT THE DOCUMENT

You make a printout using the program's Print command. This command sends the document to the printer, where it is printed using the formats you specified in Step 5 (Figure 3-5).

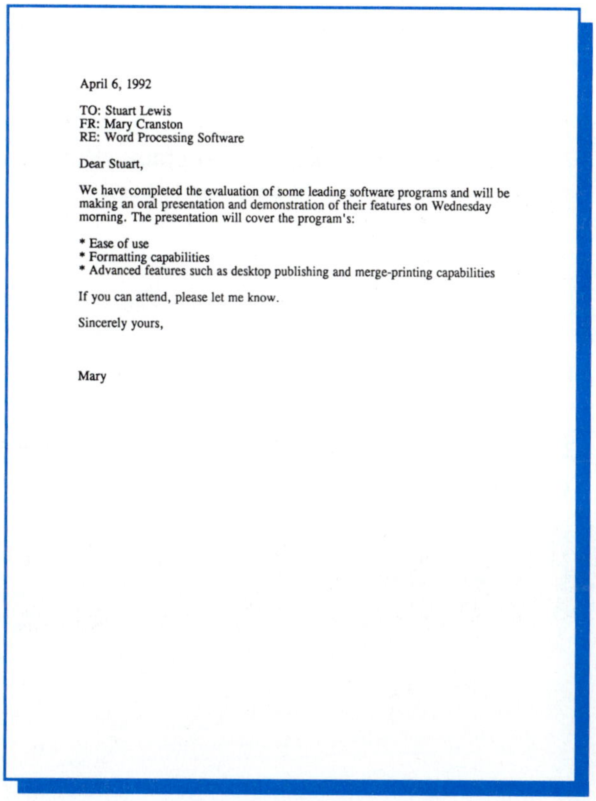

Figure 3-5 Printing the Document. Most programs are set so that documents are automatically printed on 8½-by-11-inch paper with 1-inch margins.

STEP 8 CONTINUE OR QUIT

When you have finished a document and saved it, you have three choices: open a new document, retrieve an existing document, or *quit* the program.

Open a New Document or Edit an Old One

If you want to open a new document or edit an old one, you first clear the existing document from the screen and the computer's memory. You then open a new document or retrieve an existing one just as you did in Step 2.

Quit the Program

If you are done for the day or want to run another program, you select the Quit command. This command removes the program and any document you are working on from the computer's memory and from the screen. In a moment, the operating system reappears. Because this command removes from memory the document and program you are working on, you must save the document before quitting or it is lost.

EXERCISE

Exercise 3-1A
COMPLETE THE SIMULATION ON SCREEN

The *Information Processing Software Sampler* contains an on-screen simulation of several word processing programs. Run the simulation of WordPerfect, and summarize the key features of a word processing program.

QUESTIONS

1. List the eight steps in the word processing cycle, and briefly describe each of them.
2. What does it mean to open a new document file?
3. What does it mean to format a document?

3-2 TYPICAL WORD PROCESSING PROGRAMS

Document screen. The screen display that appears on a word processing program when you enter or edit a document. Also called the edit screen.

Text area. The area of the screen where you enter your document. It always contains a cursor that indicates where the next character that you type will appear.

Status line. The line at the top or bottom of the screen that provides important information. For example, on a word processing program it may give the current page, line, and column in which the cursor is positioned. On spreadsheet programs the current cell, its contents, and its format are generally given.

Mode. Any of several states of operation that the computer adopts to perform certain functions. For example, on a word processing program you switch to insert mode when you want to insert characters into existing text, and to typeover mode when you want to type over and replace existing characters.

Menu. A list of choices displayed on the screen from which you can select a command.

Message. Text displayed on the screen informing you of the program's status.

Prompt. A screen request that asks you for more information before executing a command. Prompts are answered by typing a reply and pressing the **Enter** key.

Ruler line. A line at the top or bottom of the screen that displays margins and tab stops. Also called a tab ruler.

When you open a new document, the **document screen** (also called the *edit screen*) is blank, like a piece of blank writing paper. The document screen is a window into your computer's memory. It shows only part of a document, which can be many pages longer or wider than your screen. Document screen displays vary widely from program to program, but all have the elements shown in Figure 3-6.

A. The **text area** is where you enter text. The actual number of lines of text displayed varies according to the display screen you are using, and the number of lines occupied by a particular word processing program's menus, ruler lines, and so on.

B. The *cursor* moves as you enter text to indicate where the next character you type will appear. After you have entered text, you can move the cursor with the cursor movement keys or a mouse to point to places in the document where you want to insert, delete, format, copy, or move text.

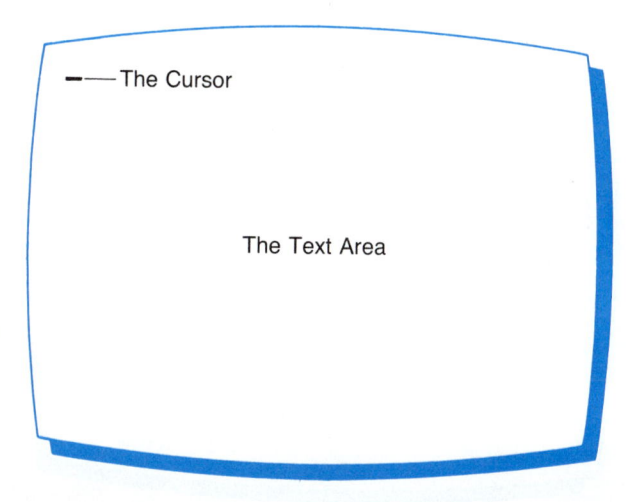

Figure 3-6 Typical Document Screen A typical document screen always contains a cursor and the text area where you enter the document.

Other items are also displayed on most word processing screen displays, although their location may vary.

- The **status line** indicates the position of the cursor by column, row, and page. Other information may also be displayed on this line. For example, indicators may note whether **Caps Lock**, **Num Lock**, or **Scroll Lock** are engaged or whether you are currently in insert or typeover **mode**.
- **Menus** that execute commands may be listed so that you can easily save or retrieve files, copy or move text, and so on.
- **Message** and **prompt** areas display text that guides you when you execute commands.
- The **ruler line** (also called a *tab ruler*), or a similar guide, shows where margins and tab stops are set. Frequently, you can turn these lines on and off.

Control keys. Keys that, when held down, change the effect of the next key that is pressed. Also called modifier keys.

Menu bar. A bar at the top of the screen listing menu names. When a menu name is selected, its menu descends.

WORDPERFECT

WordPerfect is one of the most popular word processing programs. When you load WordPerfect, the document screen appears automatically (Figure 3-7). The cursor is initially in the upper left-hand corner of the screen. It indicates where the next character that you type will appear. The status line at the bottom of the screen indicates the position of the cursor.

You execute most WordPerfect commands by pressing one of the ten function keys, **F1** through **F10**, on the keyboard. Each function key can perform any one of four tasks; for example, the **F2** key can perform four tasks. To change its function, you hold down another key while you press it. Using combinations of keys in this way makes it possible to execute many more tasks from the keyboard than there are keys. The other keys that you hold down are called *control keys* or *modifier keys* and include **Shift**, **Alt**, and **Ctrl**. These keys do not send characters or commands to the computer; rather, they change what is sent when you press other keys. For example, when using **F2**:

- Press **F2** by itself to search down through a document.
- Hold down **Shift** and then press **F2** to search toward the top of the document.
- Hold down **Alt** and then press **F2** to search and replace in the document.
- Hold down **Ctrl** and then press **F2** to spell check the document.

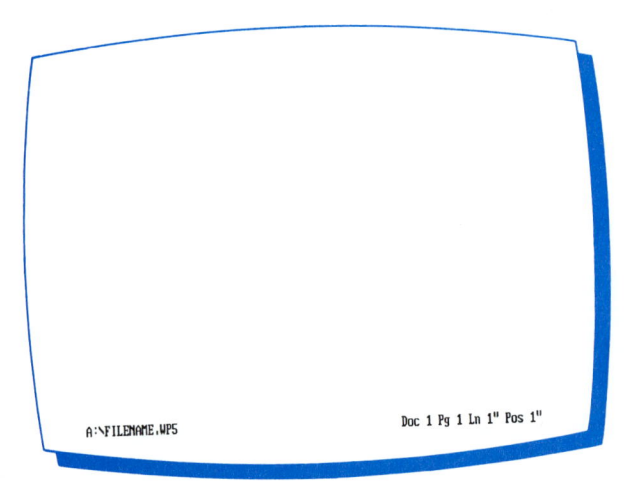

Figure 3-7 WordPerfect When you load WordPerfect, its document screen appears.

WordPerfect 5.1 added a new feature—pull-down menus. These menus make it easier to execute many commands because you choose them from a list instead of memorizing them. To display the pull-down *menu bar* at the top of the screen (Figure 3-8), press **Alt-=**. The menu bar lists the names of menus.

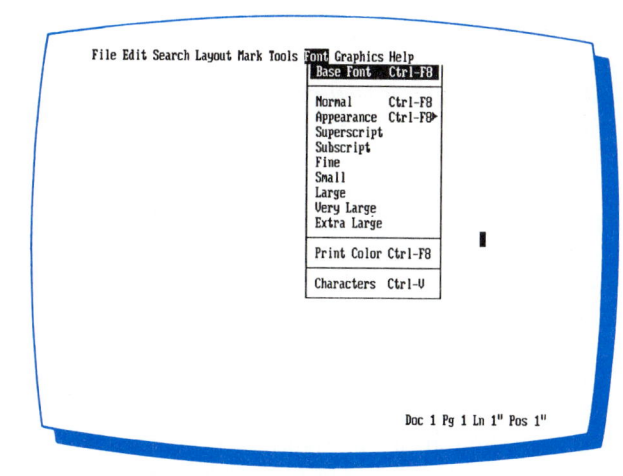

Figure 3-8 Pull-down Menus
Pull-down menus make WordPerfect easier to learn and use. The small dark rectangle is the mouse pointer that you can use to make menu choices.

MICROSOFT WORD

Microsoft Word (Figure 3-9) is a well-established program that has attracted more and more users because it is both powerful and easy to use. The program has pulldown menus that you can use from the keyboard or with a mouse. It also

Figure 3-9 Microsoft Word
Microsoft Word features menus and the ability to split the screen into windows.

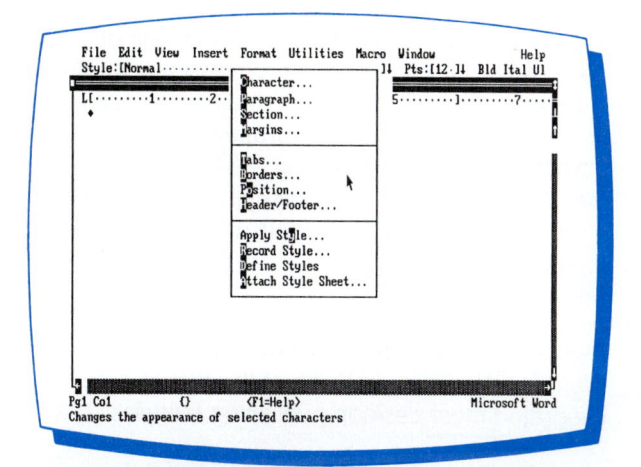

When you load Microsoft Word, its document screen is displayed. You can pull down menus to execute most commands.

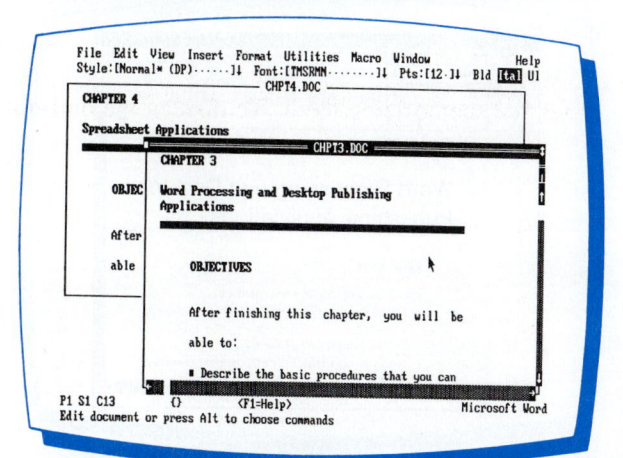

Word can display up to nine different windows, each with a different document, or different parts of the same document.

TYPICAL WORD PROCESSING PROGRAMS

WYSIWYG. The acronym for "what you see (*on the screen*) is what you get (*on the printout*)."

has a ribbon bar (just below the menu bar) from which you can make choices to change styles and fonts without having to use the menus. This feature is being introduced on many new programs because it can greatly speed up formatting documents.

If you are using a mouse, you pull down menus and make choices from them by pointing to the desired choice and then clicking the left mouse button. If you are using the keyboard, you hold down **Alt** and press the first letter in a menu's name to pull down that menu. For example, to pull down the Format menu, you press **Alt-F**. Once a menu is pulled down, you can execute the commands in two ways:

- Press the down and up arrow keys to move the highlight between choices on the menu. As you do so, the bottom line on the screen displays a description of the highlighted choice. When the desired choice is highlighted, press **Enter** to execute the command.
- Press the key that corresponds to the highlighted letter in the desired choice.

Word, like many new programs, allows you to display more than one window on the screen. You can use this feature to display either different parts of the same document or different documents. Windows make it easy to compare, copy, or move text within the same document or between two or more different documents.

WORD FOR WINDOWS

Word for Windows (Figure 3-10) was one of the first of the new generation of powerful word processing programs that combined sophisticated desktop publishing features. The most obvious difference between this and older programs is its **WYSIWYG** display (pronounced "whizzy-wig"). This simply means "what you see is what you get." The display on the screen looks very much like the printout you will get. Other programs, such as WordPerfect and Word, have a preview mode that lets you do the same thing, but you can't edit in that mode.

Figure 3-10 Word For Windows
Word for Windows was one of the first of a new generation of programs that integrated most desktop publishing features.

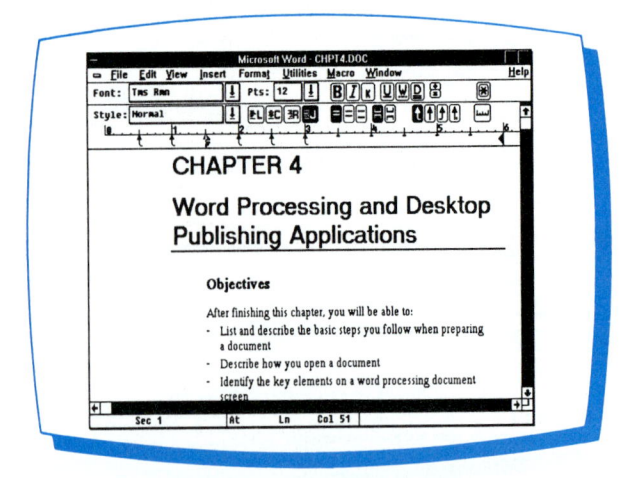

Word for Windows features a WYSIWYG display.

120   WORD PROCESSING AND DESKTOP PUBLISHING APPLICATIONS

Figure 3-10 Word For Windows, continued

The program can be easily operated using its pull-down menus.

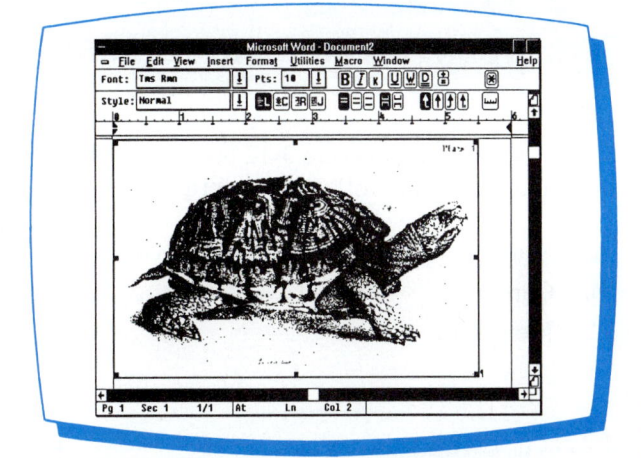

Graphics integrated into a document can be displayed on the screen.

In addition to its desktop publishing capabilities, Word for Windows, like many newer releases of older programs, can import spreadsheets and graphics, easily create tables with ruled lines and boxes, and save formats so you can automatically format new documents just like previous ones.

MICROSOFT WORKS

Besides the standalone word processing programs described here, word processors are included in almost all integrated programs. Figure 3-11 shows Microsoft Works' document screen, which displays a menu bar at the top.

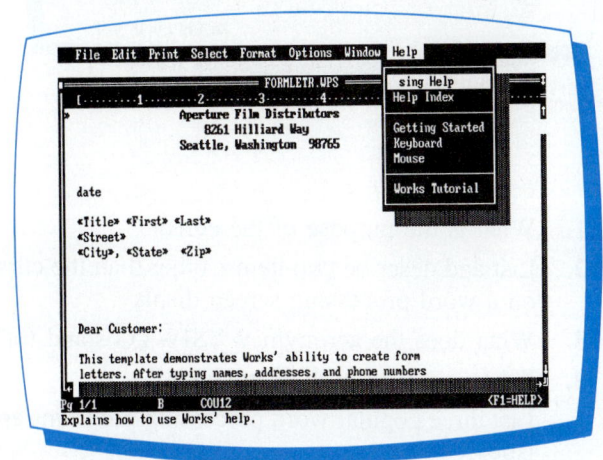

**Figure 3-11
Microsoft Works**
The word processing part of the program displays a menu bar at the top of the screen. When you press **Alt**, or click on one of the menu names, a menu listing commands is pulled down.

TYPICAL WORD PROCESSING PROGRAMS **121**

EXERCISES

3-2

Exercise 3-2A
COMPLETE THE SIMULATION ON SCREEN

The *Information Processing Software Sampler* contains a simulation of several word processing programs. Run the simulations for WordPerfect, Word for Windows, and Microsoft Works. Summarize the key differences among the programs.

3-3

Exercise 3-2B
IDENTIFYING SCREEN ELEMENTS

The screen shown in Figure 3-12 has some typical elements. Label the parts of the screen using the following descriptions.

A. Status line D. Pull-down menu
B. Cursor   E. Text area
C. Menu bar

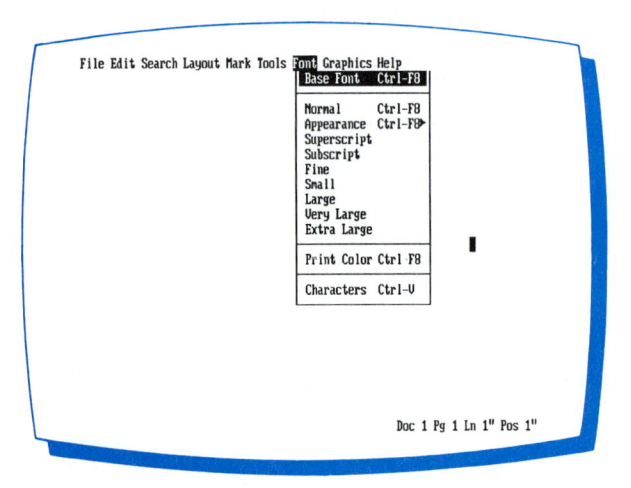

Figure 3-12 Typical Screen Display

QUESTIONS

1. What is the purpose of the cursor?
2. List and describe two items, other than the cursor, that may be displayed on a word processing screen display.
3. What does the acronym WYSIWYG stand for?
4. What is the purpose of windows?
5. List three popular word processing programs and some of their characteristics.

3-3
LOADING AND QUITTING APPLICATIONS PROGRAMS

Once the operating system is loaded, you can then load your applications program. When you are finished, you quit the program and return to the operating system.

LOADING PROGRAMS

To load a program from the operating system's command prompt, you simply type its name, or an abbreviation of its name, and then press **Enter**. For example, to load WordPerfect, you type `WP`, to load Lotus 1-2-3, you type `123`, and to load dBASE, you type `DBASE`. To load a program from a shell, or an environment like Windows, you double-click on the program's name or icon. On networks, menus on the screen usually list the programs that you can run, and you press a number to run one of them. However, to load a program, its files must be on a disk in one of the disk drives.

Loading Programs on a Floppy Disk System

On a floppy disk system, the program's files are on the program disk, so you insert that disk into drive A. To load programs from a floppy disk, you must know what disk or disks to insert into drive A. This depends on how the program disk has been set up. There are three basic variations:

- **The Disk Is Not Self-Booting**. If your program disk does not contain the operating system files needed to load it, you must first load the operating system from the operating system disk. When the operating system is loaded, you then remove the operating system disk and insert the program disk.
- **The Disk Is Self-Booting**. If the needed operating system files have already been copied to your program disk, the disk is a self-booting system disk. It is called self-booting because you can load both the operating system and the program from the same disk.
- **The Disk Contains an AUTOEXEC.BAT File**. If your program disk is self-booting and contains an AUTOEXEC.BAT file that lists the command to load the program, the operating system and program are loaded automatically when you boot the system with the disk in drive A.

Once the program is loaded, many programs require that you leave the program disk in drive A. In some cases, the program is not loaded entirely. Parts of the program are retrieved from the disk only when needed. In other cases, the program creates temporary files on the disk that it erases when you quit. If you remove the disk, you may get an error message when you execute a command.

Loading Programs on a Hard Disk System

On a hard disk system, the program's files are usually stored in a directory on a hard disk drive, normally drive C. To load the program, you may first make the directory with these files the default directory. However, you do not have to do so if your disk contains an AUTOEXEC.BAT file with the appropriate PATH command.

When you first turn on your computer, it looks for a file named AUTOEX-EC.BAT and executes any commands stored in that file just as if you typed them from the keyboard. You use this file to store the commands that you want executed every time you turn on the computer. If the AUTOEXEC.BAT file on your hard disk contains a *PATH command* that lists the directory in which the program files are stored, you can load the program by typing the program's name, and then pressing **Enter** from any directory. You do not have to change to the directory that contains that file before you load the program.

QUITTING THE PROGRAM

At the end of a session, you quit the program you are working on to load another program or turn the computer off. It is always advisable to quit a program using the commands or menu choices designed for this purpose. Although you can quit a program by simply turning off the computer, this is a bad habit to get into because some day you will do it without thinking and may lose files as a result.

Moreover, many programs create temporary files on the disk while you are working. The program then deletes these files when you quit the program. If you do not use the Quit command, these files remain on the disk, and your own files may be corrupted. For example, many applications programs print a file to the disk before sending it to the printer. It then automatically erases the file from the disk when it is no longer needed.

When you use the Quit command to leave a program, it returns you to the computer's operating system. Some programs check documents on the screen to see if any changes have been made that you have not yet saved. If documents like this are found, the program asks if you want to save them before quitting. After you indicate whether you want to save or abandon the documents, the operating system screen is displayed. You can now load another program, format disks or copy files, or turn off the computer to quit for the day.

If you are quitting for the day (or for any period longer than about an hour), you should do four things.

- Make a backup copy of any files you created so that you have at least the original and one copy.
- Turn off the display screen, or use its controls to dim the screen, so that an image will not be "burned" into its phosphor surface.
- Open the floppy disk drive doors to lift the disk drives' read/write head off the disks. This prevents the read/write heads from leaving an indentation in the disks' surface.
- Remove your disks from the disk drives. This prevents their loss, increases security, and ensures that no one mistakenly erases them.

EXERCISE

Exercise 3-3A
LOADING PROGRAMS ON YOUR SYSTEM

The way you load programs varies, depending on how your system has been set up. If your system is on a network, or for some other reason loading a program does not follow the same rules described in this section, enter your procedures here.

1. _____
2. _____
3. _____
4. _____

QUESTIONS

1. How do you load a program that does not have the operating system files on it?
2. List the steps you would follow to load a program from a floppy disk drive.
3. List the steps you would follow to load a program from a hard disk drive.
4. What two ways are there to quit a program when you are done? Which one should you use?
5. If you are quitting for the day, what steps should you take?

3-4
EXECUTING COMMANDS

Quick reference card. A card that comes with many programs and that summarizes all of their commands.

Help key. The function key you press to see explanations of your program's commands.

Context sensitive. A help system that displays help based on the command you are using at the moment.

One of the main differences among programs is the number of commands they contain and the way you execute them. However, help is readily available when learning new programs and the increasing use of menus makes learning new programs easier.

GETTING HELP

Most programs come with a *quick reference card* that lists many of the program's commands and briefly describes how you execute them. These cards are useful when you cannot remember a specific command. Until you are familiar with a program, you should always keep a quick reference card handy when working on the computer.

One function key on the keyboard (frequently **F1**) is usually designated by the program as the *help key*. If you need help at any time, pressing this key displays text that describes the program's commands and how to use them (Figure 3-13).

If the help screens are *context sensitive*, the help displayed may be directly related to what you are trying to do at the moment. For example, if you have begun the sequence of commands to save a file and cannot remember how to complete the sequence, pressing the help key displays help on saving files.

Most help screens also have a table of contents, an index, or a menu that lists all the topics for which help is available. By selecting a topic from this list, you can look up information on any topic at any time.

When you have finished with help, you press the key specified, or select *Quit* or *Resume* from the Help menu to return to where you were in your procedure before you asked for help.

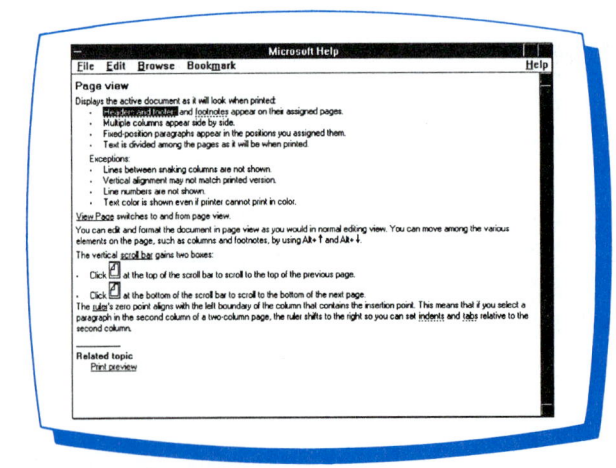

Figure 3-13 Help Screens
A help screen displays instructions on the screen. This illustration shows one of the Windows help screens.

USING FUNCTION KEYS AND TYPING COMMANDS

One way to execute commands is to press function keys, or other designated keys, and then type the commands. Typing commands is fast, especially for touch-typists. For example, if the program's command to save a file is to hold down the **Ctrl** key while you press the letters **K** and **S**, you can execute the command without looking at the keyboard or screen.

126   WORD PROCESSING AND DESKTOP PUBLISHING APPLICATIONS

Keyboard template. A plastic or cardboard card that fits on or over the keyboard to guide you when using a program.

Computer keyboards have several function keys whose sole purpose is to perform tasks assigned to them by the program's author. For example, on a word processing program, **F10** may be assigned the task of saving a document, whereas on a database program, the function key **F10** may be assigned the task of adding a record.

Many keys are assigned more than one task; for example, pressing the right arrow key may move the cursor one column or character at a time, but pressing the right arrow key while holding down **Ctrl** may move the cursor several columns or characters at a time. The **Ctrl** key does not send characters to the computer; rather, it changes what is sent when other keys are pressed. Using combinations of keys in this way allows software designers to assign many more tasks to the keyboard than there are keys.

When you use these control keys—usually the **Ctrl**, **Alt**, and **Shift** keys—the sequence you press them in is important. For example, to use the **Ctrl** and right arrow keys together, you press the **Ctrl** key and hold it down while you quickly press the right arrow key. On many commands, if you hold down both keys, the computer keeps repeating the command, causing unexpected results.

Programs that assign specific tasks to keys often supply a plastic or cardboard *keyboard template* (Figure 3-14) that fits over some of the keys (usually

Figure 3-14   Keyboard Template
A keyboard template provides a quick guide to a program's commands.
Courtesy of WordPerfect Corporation

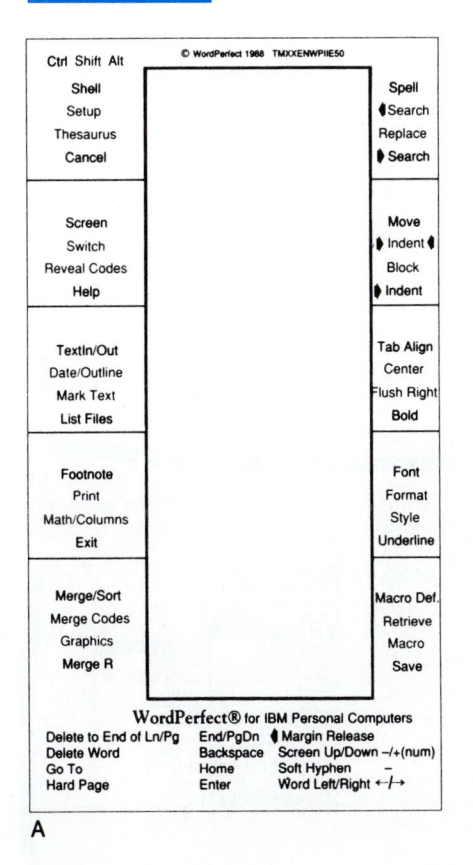

One type of template fits over the function keys at the left end of a regular keyboard.

Another type fits above the function keys on enhanced keyboards.

EXECUTING COMMANDS **127**

Menu pointer. A bright highlight moved by the directional arrow keys to point to or highlight a choice on the menu.

Multilevel menus. A way of arranging menu commands so that making a selection from a menu displays another menu. Each succeeding level of menus offers more specific choices. Known also as nested menus.

Submenus. A way of arranging menu commands so that making a selection from a menu displays another menu. Each succeeding level of menus offers more specific choices.

the function keys). These templates briefly describe the tasks assigned to each key so that you need not memorize them.

USING MENUS

Another way to execute commands is to use menus (Figure 3-15). Choosing commands from a menu is easy because you need not memorize commands. Menus are like those you get in a restaurant—they list available choices. To execute commands listed on a menu, you usually have three options.

- Use designated keys to highlight a selection with a ***menu pointer***, and you then press **Enter** to execute the highlighted command.
- Type the number preceding the command or the highlighted character in the command's name. On some programs, you must press **Enter** after doing this.
- Point to the menu choice with a mouse pointer, and then click one of the buttons on the mouse to execute the command.

Many menu-driven programs use more than one level of menu. Choosing many of the commands listed on one of these ***multilevel menus*** just displays another menu on the screen. Getting to the actual command you want to execute occasionally means you must select a series of commands from the displayed ***submenus*** (Figure 3-16).

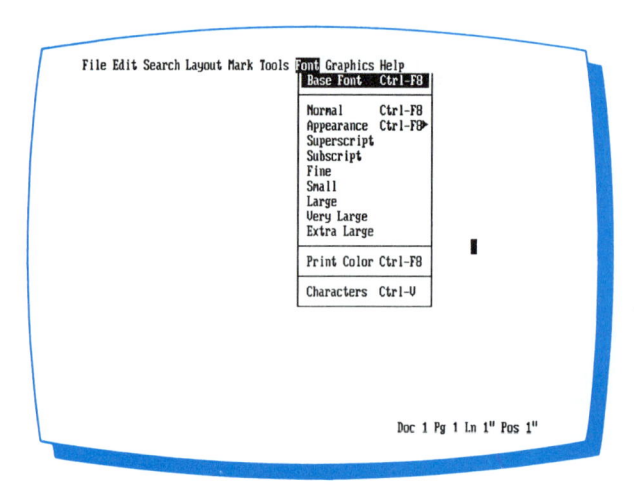

Figure 3-15 Menus
On programs with pull-down menus, when you select a choice from a menu bar at the top of the screen, a list of related commands descends so you can select the one you want.

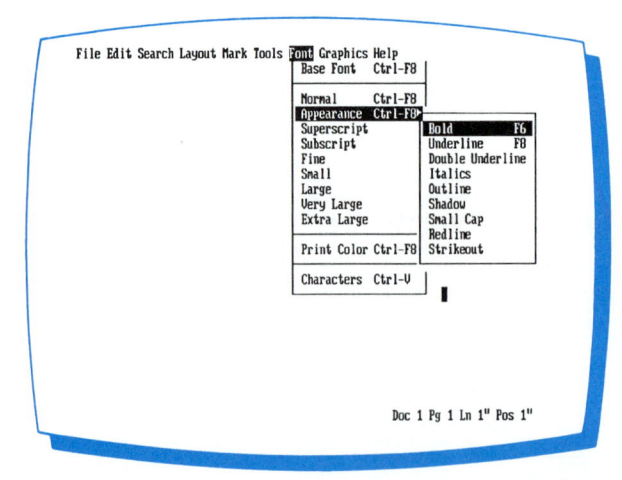

Figure 3-16 Multilevel Menus
Multilevel menus frequently display a submenu when you make a menu choice. For example, WordPerfect's Font menu displays a list of font appearances you can assign.

128   *WORD PROCESSING AND DESKTOP PUBLISHING APPLICATIONS*

Menu tree. An arrangement of menu commands similar to a family tree. Each branch of the menu tree sends you along a particular avenue of operation.

Sticky menu. A menu from which you cannot exit without selecting a quit or exit choice on the menu. Unlike a regular menu, it does not disappear automatically when a command is executed.

Italicize. A character format that emphasizes text by slanting it when printed.

Main menu. The first menu that appears on the screen when you first load some word processing programs. It contains the basic commands that you use to open and print files and perform other procedures.

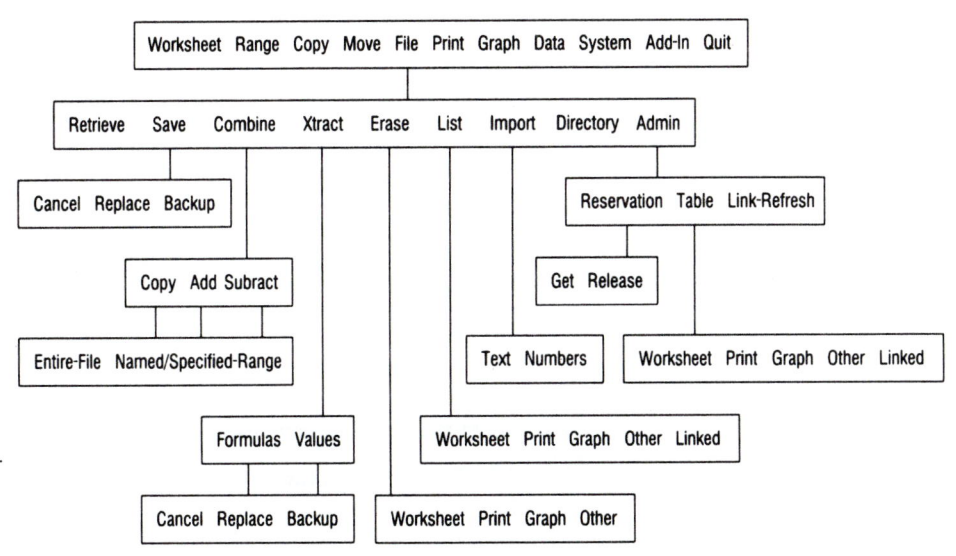

Figure 3-17 Menu Trees
Many menu systems are arranged like a tree. Choosing one command displays another menu.
Courtesy of Lotus Development Corporation

As you make selections from multilevel menus, you are actually working your way through a ***menu tree***, which, like a family tree, is simply an arrangement of menu commands (Figure 3-17). As you work your way through the commands shown on the menu tree, you may find you are on the wrong branch or decide not to continue for some other reason. Usually, **Esc** is designated as the key that cancels a command in progress and returns you to your starting point. Some programs designate **Esc**, or another key, as the key you can use to retrace, a command at a time, your steps to back out of the menu. Sometimes you retrace your steps only part way so that you can continue the command down a different branch of the tree.

Often, the menu disappears when you complete a command, and you are returned to where you were before you began executing the command. In some cases, you must select *Quit* or *Exit* on the menu or press a designated key to remove the menu. These ***sticky menus*** stay on the screen, anticipating you will want to use more than one of the listed choices. For example, you might want to boldface, *italicize*, or underline the same phrase in a document. If the menu were to automatically disappear when you make a selection, you would have to repeat the entire sequence of commands to select again from the same menu. Because the menu remains on the screen, you can make several choices and then remove the menu only when you are finished.

Some programs, when you first load them, display a list of the major program functions. From this ***Main menu*** (Figure 3-18), you initiate most functions, such as opening new files, retrieving existing files, or printing documents. It is also the menu you return to after these functions have been completed.

RESPONDING TO PROMPTS AND DIALOG BOXES

When executing commands, programs often ask you to enter information they need to complete the command, for example, a page number to print, the name of a file to save or retrieve, or a word to be searched for. The text that appears on the screen asking you to supply this information generally appears as either a prompt or a dialog box.

EXECUTING COMMANDS 129

Dialog box. A list of choices or prompts that appears on the screen when you are executing commands.

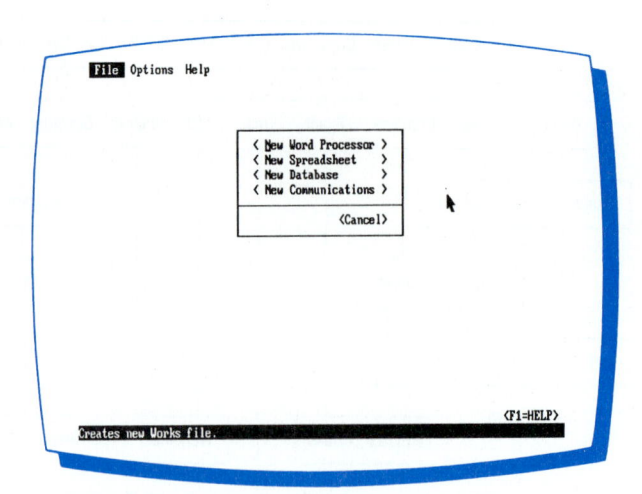

Figure 3-18 A Main Menu
Some programs display a Main menu that lists the program's functions. To select one, you type the number or letter that corresponds to your choice, and then press **Enter,** or click on the choice with a mouse. This illustration shows the Microsoft Works Main menu.

Prompts

Many commands display prompts, lines of text at the top or bottom of the screen that ask you to enter the information the computer needs. You answer prompts in one of three ways.

- You type information from the keyboard, and then press **Enter**. You can type information in lowercase letters, uppercase letters, or both; for example, filename, FILENAME, and FileName are all the same.
- You make a choice from a menu.
- You press **Enter** to accept the default response. Default responses either are entered by the program's designer or are remembered by the program as your previous responses to the same prompts. If the program displays default responses, you can type over them to enter a new response, or you can make another choice from the menu.

Critical commands, such as those that erase a file you are working on or that save files on top of earlier versions, generally prompt you to confirm the command so that you do not inadvertently make a mistake. For example, when saving a file for the second time, many programs display a message telling you the file already exists and asking if you want to cancel the command or replace the file. If you select *Cancel*, you return to where you were before you began the command. If you select *Replace*, the file is saved, and the previous version is erased.

Dialog Boxes

Some programs display ***dialog boxes*** that list command choices much like a form (Figure 3-19). You can enter responses into spaces in the dialog box or make menu choices to indicate, for example, margin widths, page length, or which pages to print. After filling in the form, you press a designated key to continue. The way you move the cursor between the choices on the screen varies. Using a keyboard, the keys most commonly used for this are **Tab** and **Backtab**. When you have made all the necessary changes, you press **Enter** to continue. If using a mouse, you point to a blank and click. You then type the response and press **Enter**, or point to *OK* and click.

130   WORD PROCESSING AND DESKTOP PUBLISHING APPLICATIONS

Mouse. A handheld, movable device that directs a mouse pointer's position on the screen.

Mouse pointer. A highlight on the screen that moves when you move a mouse.

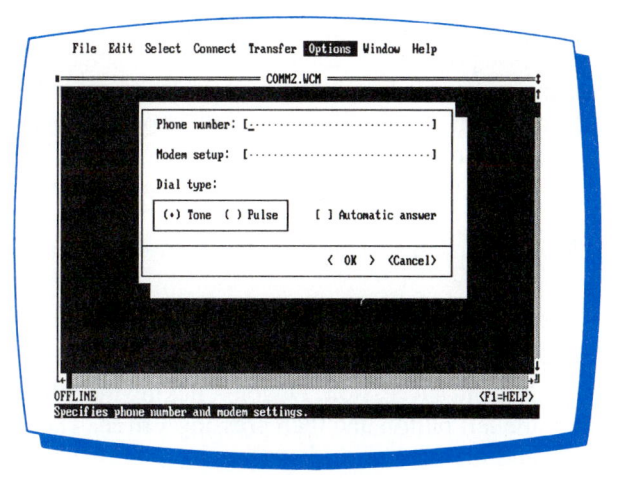

Figure 3-19 Dialog Boxes
Dialog boxes provide spaces that you can enter responses into or lists of choices you can choose from. The Microsoft Works form shown here is used to enter a phone number to call.

USING A MOUSE

An increasingly popular device is the *mouse* (Figure 3-20). As you move the mouse around on a flat, smooth surface, it feeds electrical signals to the computer that move a *mouse pointer* on the screen.

A mouse can be used for several procedures, including the following:

- Selecting commands listed on menus
- Moving the cursor through the document
- Selecting (blocking) text so that it can be copied, moved, deleted, or formatted

When you use a mouse, you roll it across the surface of the desk. This motion tells the mouse which way to move the mouse pointer on the screen. To make the mouse pointer move in a predictable direction, it is important that you hold the mouse so that it is oriented parallel to the middle line of the screen

Figure 3-20 Mouse
A mouse is a device that you move across a smooth surface. As you do so, the mouse pointer moves on the screen so that you can select text or make selections from menus by pressing the buttons on the mouse.
Courtesy of Apple Computer, Inc.

EXECUTING COMMANDS 131

Point. Move the mouse so the mouse pointer points to an item on the screen.

Clicking. Pressing and quickly releasing a mouse's button.

Double-clicking. Quickly clicking and releasing a mouse's button twice in rapid succession.

Drag. Pointing to an object on the screen with the mouse pointer, holding down a button, and then moving the mouse to move the object.

Error message. A message that appears when you make a mistake.

(Figure 3-21). This way, when you move it directly toward and away from you, the mouse pointer moves vertically on the screen. When you move it sideways, the mouse moves horizontally. If you were to hold the mouse at an angle when you moved it in these directions, the mouse pointer would move diagonally on the screen, making it hard to control.

When using a mouse, here are some of the basic terms to remember.

- *Point* means to position the mouse pointer over or on some item on the screen.
- *Clicking* refers to pressing one of the buttons on the mouse.
- *Double-clicking* refers to pressing one of the buttons on the mouse twice in rapid succession. Double-clicking the left button is the same as clicking the left button and then pressing **Enter**. The first click highlights an item, and the second click selects it.
- *Drag* means to hold down one of the mouse buttons while you move the mouse.

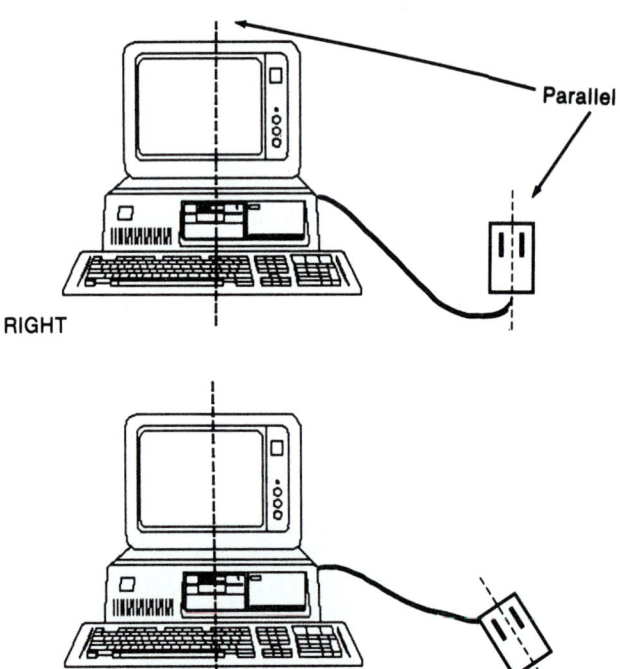

Figure 3-21 Holding and Dragging a Mouse
Hold the mouse parallel to the center line of the screen.

ERROR MESSAGES

If you make any errors when executing commands, the computer often beeps and displays an *error message*. On some programs, you must then press **Esc** or **Enter** before you can enter any further commands or data.

EXERCISE

Exercise 3-4A
PREPARING A QUICK REFERENCE CARD

Refer to a word processing program's user's guide and make a quick reference guide to the commands listed in Table 3-1.

Table 3-1
QUICK REFERENCE CARD

Procedure	Command
Load the program	
Save a file	
Print a file	
Quit the program	

QUESTIONS

1. What is a quick reference card?
2. What are help screens? What does it mean when they are context sensitive?
3. What is a keyboard template?
4. What is a menu?
5. How do you select choices listed on a menu?
6. What is a multilevel menu?
7. What is a sticky menu?
8. What is a Main menu? What are some of the typical commands that would be listed on a Main menu?
9. What are the advantages and disadvantages of commands and menus?
10. What is a prompt? What three ways are there to answer prompts?
11. What is a dialog box?
12. When using a mouse, what does it mean to point? to drag? to double-click?
13. If you make a mistake when using menus or commands, what key is usually assigned to cancel the command?
14. What are error messages?

3-5
ENTERING DOCUMENTS

Scroll. To move text vertically or horizontally on the screen to see different parts of the document.

When you work with a word processing program, you frequently create new documents. However, before you can do so, you must first open a new document file. On most programs, this happens automatically when you load the program. On some programs, you do this by selecting *Create New Document*, or a similar choice, from the Main menu.

If you are already working on a document and want to create a new one, you first save or abandon the current file. This either clears the document screen so that you can enter a new document or returns you to the Main menu so that you can open another new document file.

Once a file is open and the document screen is displayed, entering text with a word processing program is no more difficult than typing it on a typewriter; in many ways, it is easier. With both, you use the keyboard to enter letters, numbers, and symbols.

KEYBOARDING

On a word processing program, the cursor, a bright one-characterwide underline or rectangle, indicates where the next character you type will appear. When you open a new document, the cursor rests in the upper left-hand corner of the screen. As you type characters, they appear where the cursor is, and the cursor moves one space to the right.

As you enter text, the screen gradually fills up. When the last line on the screen is filled, the text begins to *scroll*, or move, up a line at a time so that the line you are entering is always displayed on the screen. To make room for the new text, text at the top of the document scrolls off the top of the screen (Figure 3-22).

Figure 3-22 Scrolling
The document on the screen scrolls when it contains more lines than the screen can display at one time. As you enter new text, the top lines scroll off the top of the screen so that the line you are working on remains displayed.

134 WORD PROCESSING AND DESKTOP PUBLISHING APPLICATIONS

Word wrap. The word processing program's ability to calculate whether the word being entered will fit onto the end of the line. If not, the word is automatically moved to the next line.

Carriage return. A signal sent to the printer telling it to move the print head down one line and back to the left margin. Entered by pressing **Enter** on most programs.

Soft carriage return. A return that the computer automatically enters when it wraps words to the next line as text is entered.

Hard carriage return. A return that you enter at the end of a paragraph by pressing the **Enter** key. You can remove it only by using the program's delete command.

WORD WRAP

When you are typing paragraphs, you do not have to press **Enter** at the end of each line. The program automatically does this for you. Unlike a typewriter, when the end of a line is reached, the word processing program calculates whether the word being entered fits on the line. If it will not fit, the program automatically begins a new line of text by moving the entire word to the next line. Called *word wrap* (Figure 3-23), this function is common to all word processing programs.

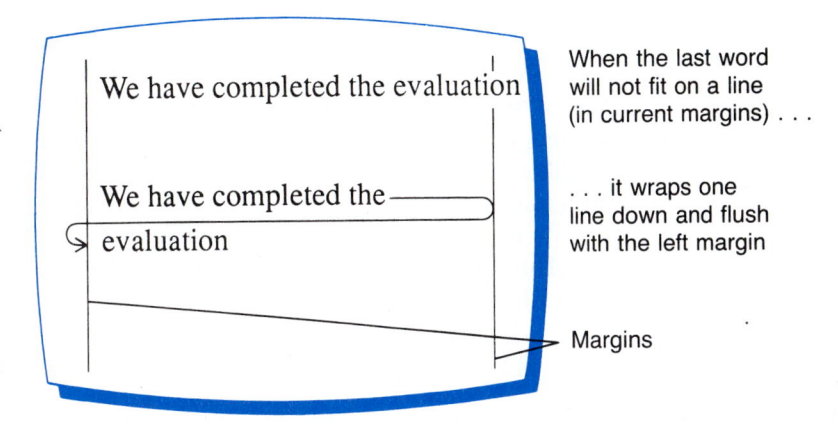

Figure 3-23 Word Wrap
Unlike a typewriter, when you reach the end of a line, the program calculates whether the word you enter fits on the line. If it will not fit, the program moves, or wraps, the entire word to the beginning of the next line.

CARRIAGE RETURNS

Carriage returns are codes in the document that move the cursor and printer down one line and back to the left margin. Word processing programs have two kinds of carriage returns: soft and hard.

Soft Carriage Returns

The computer automatically enters *soft carriage returns* at the end of a line as you enter text whenever it wraps a word to the next line. Soft carriage returns automatically adjust their position if you revise the text so that they no longer fall at the end of a line. For example, when you insert or delete text or when you change the margins, existing soft carriage returns are deleted, and new ones are inserted at the new end of each line.

Hard Carriage Returns

You press **Enter** to enter a *hard carriage return* when you want to end a line before you reach the right margin, for example:

- To enter an inside address, salutations, or headings.
- To insert a blank line, as you do following an inside address, the date, and the closing of a letter. Each time you press **Enter**, you insert another blank line.

Destructive backspace.
The ability of the **Backspace** key to delete a character to its left when pressed.

Tab stop. The stops that provide alignment points across the page so that columns and indents can be created.

▌ To start a new paragraph, you usually press **Enter** twice—once to end the current paragraph and then again to insert a blank line before starting the first line of the next paragraph.

If you then add or delete text, lines that end with hard carriage returns are not automatically adjusted, as are those that end with soft carriage returns.

CORRECTING MISTAKES

There are several ways to correct mistakes, but you usually use the **Backspace** key to do so. If you make any mistakes—and notice them immediately—press **Backspace** to move the cursor to the left and delete the incorrectly typed characters. You can then correctly type the characters. If pressing **Backspace** deletes the character to its left, it is called a *destructive backspace*. But if pressing **Backspace** simply moves the cursor to the left through the text, it is just like the left arrow key. Some programs let you choose how you want the **Backspace** key to work.

You can also move the cursor under or over any character, and then press **Del**. This deletes any character highlighted by the cursor. If you hold the key down, it deletes characters to the right.

TAB STOPS

Tab stops on a word processor are much like those on a typewriter. You can position them at intervals across the width of the screen and beyond. When you press **Tab** in insert mode, the cursor jumps to the next tab stop. When you press **Backtab** (**Shift-Tab**), the cursor moves to the left to the previous tab stop. Programs normally have default tab stops set every five columns or ½ inch. You can change these settings by adding or deleting tab stops. There are two ways to do this.

▌ You can change the tab stops for part or all of an individual document.

▌ You can change the system defaults so that new default tab settings appear when you create a new document.

Text Alignment

Using tab stops to indent or align text is critical. If you indent or align text with the **Spacebar**, your document may print poorly (Figure 3-24). This is because many printers use proportionally spaced type, which means that each character

Figure 3-24 Tabs
When aligning text in columns, you should always use tabs and not spaces.

Item	Number	Price
Disks	200	5.95
Books	100	3.95
Cables	400	9.95

This table prints columns that are out of alignment because they were aligned with spaces rather than tabs.

Item	Number	Price
Disks	200	5.95
Books	100	3.95
Cables	400	9.95

This table prints correctly because tabs were used to align the columns.

Decimal tab. A special tab stop used to enter numbers in columns so that their decimal points are aligned.

occupies a different-width space. For example, the letter "W" takes up more space than the letter "I." Columns that appear aligned on the screen are not aligned on a printout. If you use tab stops to align columns, they print correctly.

Most programs allow you to change tab settings throughout a document by entering a new format line or tab code where you want the settings to change. The new tab stops affect all text that follows until either the end of the document or the next format line or tab code is reached. When you set tab stops, you can set them so that text tabbed to them is left-aligned, centered, or right-aligned (Figure 3-25).

Once you have entered tab stops, you can use them to create tables with aligned columns. You can align text with tab stops as you enter the text or after you have entered it.

- To align text with a tab stop as you enter the text, press **Tab** until the cursor is in the desired tab column, and then type the text. If you type enough text to reach past the right margin, the second and subsequent lines wrap back to and align with the left margin, not with the tab stop.

- To align text with a tab stop after you have entered the text, position the cursor on or under the first character in the text to be aligned. When you then press **Tab**, the cursor and all text to its right moves to the next tab stop. On many programs, you must be in insert mode to do this. If you are in typeover mode, pressing **Tab** may just move the cursor through the text.

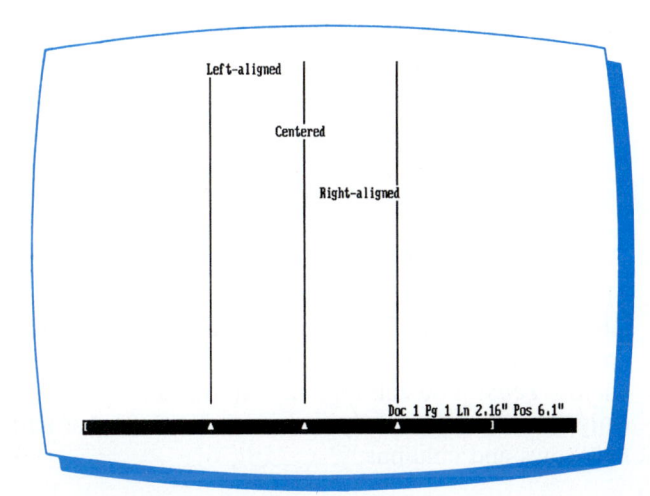

Figure 3-25 Tab Alignment
You can set tab stops so that text tabbed to them is left-aligned, centered, or right-aligned.

Decimal Tabs

Columns of numbers, including those containing decimal points, can be aligned with programs that include a *decimal tab* feature (Figure 3-26). All programs allow you to align decimal points, but some allow you to change the alignment character. This is useful when you want to align dollar signs ($) or when you are writing to a foreign country that uses commas where we use decimal points, and vice versa. (For example, where we write $1,000.50, people in some countries write $1.000,50.)

ENTERING DOCUMENTS **137**

Cells (in tables). The intersections of a table's row and columns into which you type data.

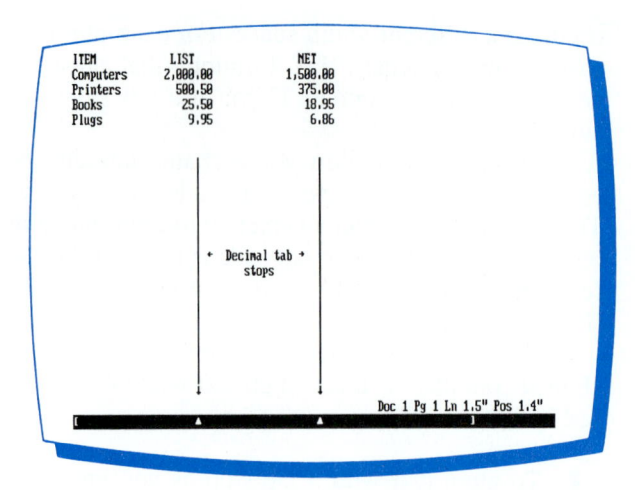

Figure 3-26 Decimal Tabs
Numbers with decimals can be aligned with decimal tab stops so that all the decimals are aligned in the same column.

To align numbers with decimal tabs:

1. Position decimal tab stops in the desired columns.
2. Press **Tab** to move the cursor to the decimal tab position. On many programs, an indicator on the screen shows when the cursor is in a decimal tab column.
3. Enter the part of the number preceding the decimal point. As you do so, the numbers you enter move to the left while the cursor remains in the decimal tab column.
4. Enter a decimal point (using the period key) or other alignment character that you have specified.
5. Type the numbers that follow the decimal point. As you do so, the decimal remains fixed in place, and all numbers are entered to the right of it.

TABLES

The newest programs now contain a table feature that automatically creates tables (Figure 3-27). This procedure automatically adds ruled lines around table entries and you can choose to display or hide these rules. The ruled lines enclose *cells*. You can type data into a cell, and it adjusts its depth automatically. You can also easily make columns wider or narrower, or add and delete new rows and columns.

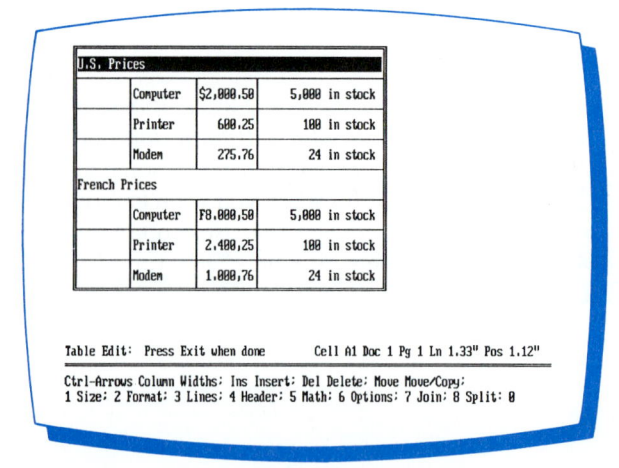

Figure 3-27 Tables
Table features on the latest word processing programs automatically create tables. When you edit a WordPerfect table, the Table Edit menu appears on the screen. You use its commands to modify a table's default settings or insert or delete rows and columns.

138   WORD PROCESSING AND DESKTOP PUBLISHING APPLICATIONS

Hanging indent. A type of indent that places the first line of a paragraph at the left margin, and subsequent lines at a specified tab stop. Also known as reverse indent or outdent.

Enumerations. Indented numbered lists.

Glossary. Those sections of the computer's memory or a file on the disk where you can save sections of text so that it can be quickly inserted over and over again, using only a few keystrokes. Also known as a library or phrase storage area.

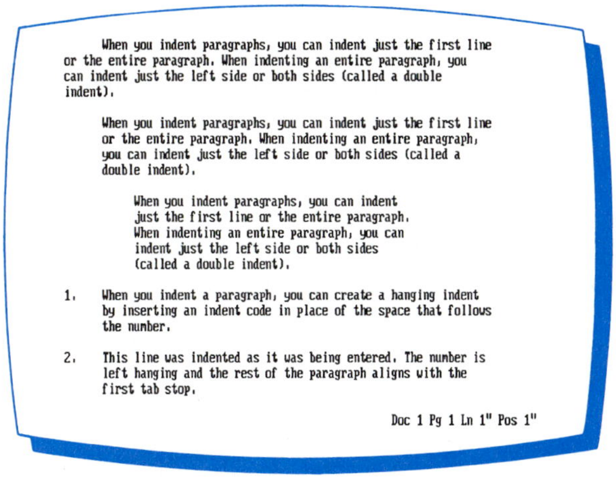

When you indent paragraphs, you can indent just the first line or the entire paragraph. When indenting an entire paragraph, you can indent just the left side or both sides (called a double indent).

When you indent paragraphs, you can indent just the first line or the entire paragraph. When indenting an entire paragraph, you can indent just the left side or both sides (called a double indent).

When you indent paragraphs, you can indent just the first line or the entire paragraph. When indenting an entire paragraph, you can indent just the left side or both sides (called a double indent).

1. When you indent a paragraph, you can create a hanging indent by inserting an indent code in place of the space that follows the number.

2. This line was indented as it was being entered. The number is left hanging and the rest of the paragraph aligns with the first tab stop.

Doc 1 Pg 1 Ln 1" Pos 1"

Figure 3-28 Indents Indents can take several forms. You can indent the first line of a paragraph. You can indent an entire paragraph from the left margin. You can create double indents to indent a paragraph from both the left and right margins. You can create a hanging indent.

INDENTS

You can indent paragraphs in many ways (Figure 3-28). Normally, when you enter text, you execute the Indent command, and it stays in effect until you press **Enter**. At that point, text aligns with the original margins.

One of the major applications of ***hanging indents*** (also called reverse indents or outdents) is for numbered lists, called ***enumerations*** (Figure 3-29). Hanging indents are especially useful when you are preparing numbered outlines or lists. The numbers in the list stand off by themselves, but the text following them is indented and aligned.

On most programs, indents are made to tab stops. To change indents, you may have to change tab stops. On other programs, the amount of the indent is specified independently of the tab stop settings.

GLOSSARIES

Some programs allocate a small portion of the computer's memory so that you can save repeatedly used sections of text, like the date and closing used on letters. To save text in this area of memory, called a ***glossary*** (or a *library* or *phrase storage area*), you highlight it in the document, and then execute the Glossary command. You then assign the entry a name, usually an abbreviation that you can easily remember.

To copy an entry from the glossary into a file, you move the cursor to where you want the text inserted and then execute the Glossary Retrieve or Insert command.

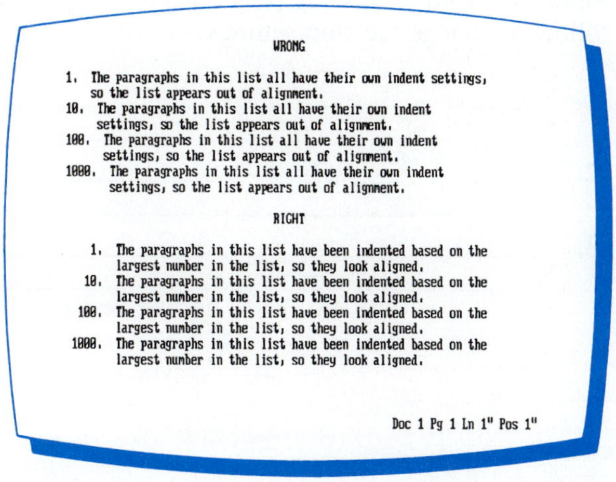

WRONG

1. The paragraphs in this list all have their own indent settings, so the list appears out of alignment.
10. The paragraphs in this list all have their own indent settings, so the list appears out of alignment.
100. The paragraphs in this list all have their own indent settings, so the list appears out of alignment.
1000. The paragraphs in this list all have their own indent settings, so the list appears out of alignment.

RIGHT

1. The paragraphs in this list have been indented based on the largest number in the list, so they look aligned.
10. The paragraphs in this list have been indented based on the largest number in the list, so they look aligned.
100. The paragraphs in this list have been indented based on the largest number in the list, so they look aligned.
1000. The paragraphs in this list have been indented based on the largest number in the list, so they look aligned.

Doc 1 Pg 1 Ln 1" Pos 1"

Figure 3-29 Hanging Indents The largest number determines the amount of the indent for all entries. Set the tab stop so there is room for the largest number followed by a period and one or more spaces. Or, set decimal tab stops to align the periods that follow the numbers.

Glossaries are great time savers. For example, you can enter the phrase *As soon as possible* and attach it to the abbreviation *ASAP*. When you specify that the glossary entry *ASAP* be inserted into the document, the phrase is automatically entered. You can also enter the name and address of someone in the glossary, and then enter it in the document by just specifying his or her last name or initials.

After storing text in the glossary, you can generally save it in a file on the disk. This way you can use the glossary with any document by first loading it back into memory or retrieving it from the disk into the current document when needed. Some programs also let you create different glossaries, each for a special purpose. For example, you could have one glossary for customer inquiry letters and another for contracts.

EXERCISES

Exercise 3-5A
INDENTING TEXT

Refer to a word processing program's user's guide and list the procedures you follow to create a hanging indent.

1. _____
2. _____
3. _____

Exercise 3-5B
SETTING TAB STOPS

Refer to a word processing program's user's guide and list the procedures you follow to change tab stop settings.

1. _____
2. _____
3. _____

QUESTIONS

1. Where does the cursor rest when you load a word processing program or open a new document.
2. When the screen is filled up with text, what happens when you enter another line?
3. Describe word wrap. When does it happen?
4. What are carriage returns? What is the difference between hard and soft carriage returns?
5. What is the most common way to correct mistakes when entering text?
6. When would you use regular tab stops?
7. In what ways can you align text with a tab stop?
8. When would you use decimal tab stops?
9. List and describe three ways to indent text.
10. What is a hanging indent? What is it used for?
11. Describe what a glossary is. Give some examples of when you might use a glossary.

3-6
SAVING AND RETRIEVING FILES

Data file. Any computer file that contains information entered by a user.

When you use an applications program to create a document, spreadsheet model, or database, you store your work on a disk in a *data file* so that you can retrieve it later. Each type of applications program creates its own type of data file. For example, files you create with a word processing program are called document files, those you create with a spreadsheet program are worksheet files, those you create with a database management program are record or database files, and those you create with a graphics program are picture files (Table 3-2).

Table 3-2
APPLICATIONS PROGRAMS AND THEIR FILES

Type of Applications Program	Name of Files
Word processing	Document files
Desktop publishing	Document files
Spreadsheet	Worksheet files
Database management	Database or record files
Graphics	Picture files

SAVING FILES

When you first save a file, you must assign it a filename using the characters and following the rules discussed in Topic 2-4. You should frequently save the file you are working on. If you turn off the computer, experience a power failure, encounter hardware problems, or make a mistake, you may lose files that are in the computer's memory. Your files are not safe from these disasters until you save them onto a disk — a more permanent form of storage. When you save a data file, the program copies it from the computer's memory onto a disk (Figure 3-30). When working on a computer, you should always save your file:

- Before experimenting with unfamiliar commands.
- Before making major revisions.
- Before printing (in case something goes wrong during the process).
- Before quitting the program.

RETRIEVING FILES

After you have created and saved a file on a disk, you can retrieve it later for further work. To retrieve the file, you must

- Insert the disk it was saved on into the disk drive if you are working on a floppy disk system.
- Specify the drive and directory it is stored in if it is not stored on the default drive and directory.

Saving a File

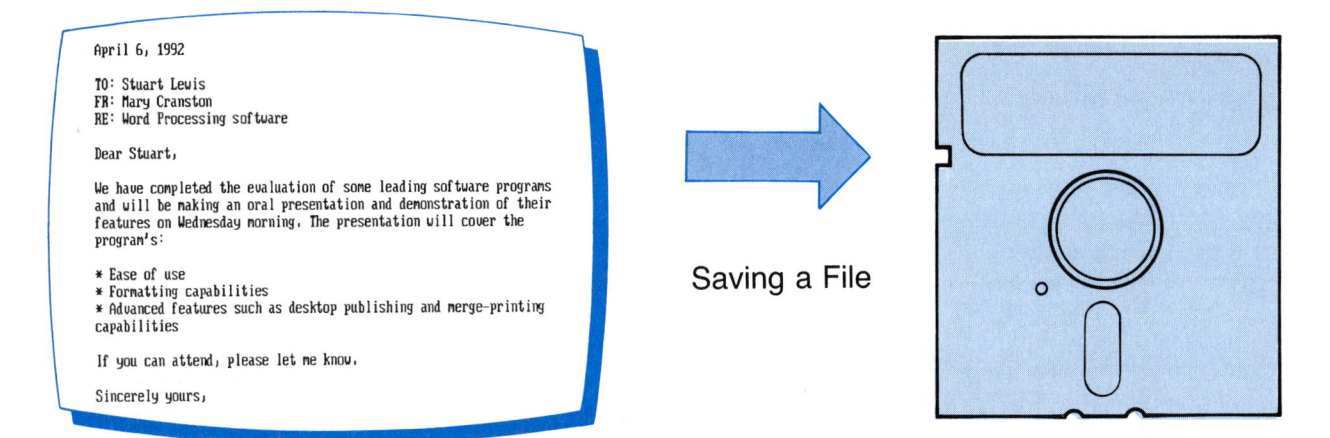

Figure 3-30 Saving a File
When you save a file, the computer copies the version currently on the screen and stored in the computer's memory to a file on the disk. You can retrieve it later by copying it from the disk back into the computer's memory.

When the file is retrieved, the disk drive operates, and the computer copies the file from the disk into the computer's memory and displays it on the screen (Figure 3-31). The copy of the file on the disk remains unchanged until you change the file in memory and then save it back onto the disk, at which time it overwrites the old file.

FILE TYPES

Applications programs are often capable of saving or retrieving files in various formats. With other programs, you have to convert the files if you want to use them with another program.

Retrieving a File

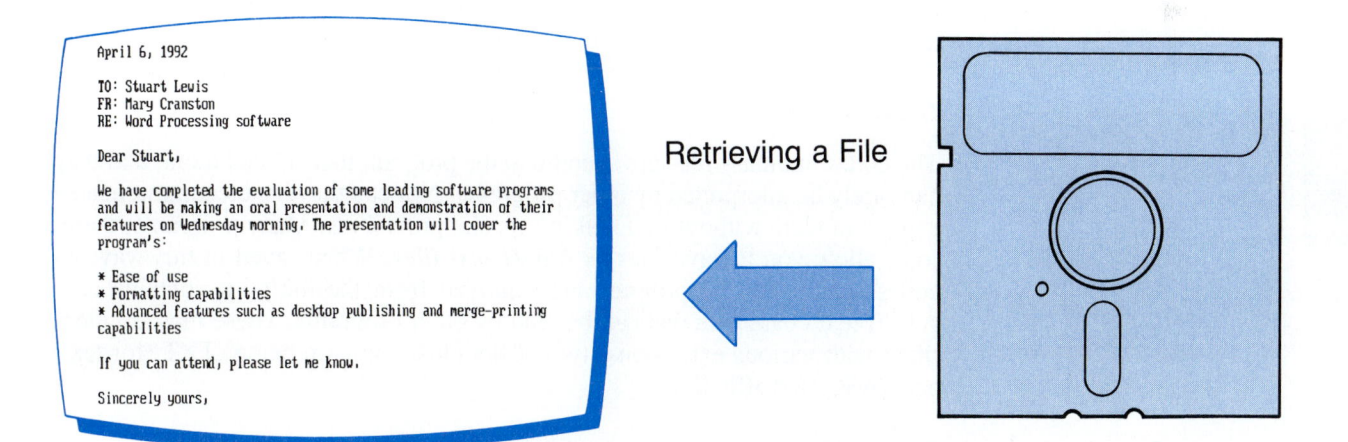

Figure 3-31 Retrieving a File
Retrieving a file from the disk copies it from the disk into the computer's memory. The copy of the file on the disk remains unchanged.

Binary file. A file created with an applications program that contains non-ASCII codes specific to that program.

ASCII text files. Files saved in a format specified by the American Standard Code for Information Interchange. Files saved in this format often can be used by other programs or transmitted by modem because they have a standard format understood by other programs.

Print file. Output that is sent to a file on a disk instead of to a printer. All format commands, like top and bottom margins and headers and footers, are interpreted so that it prints on the disk just as it would on the printer. A print file can then be printed or displayed on the screen directly from DOS.

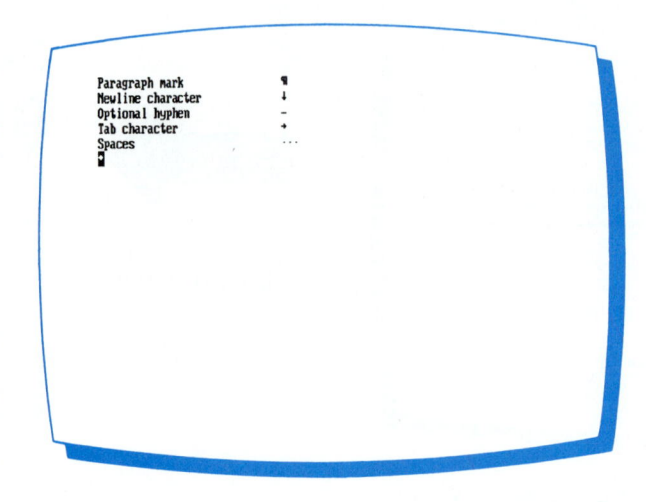

```
Paragraph mark          ¶
Newline character       ↓
Optional hyphen         -
Tab character           →
Spaces                  ...
▯
```

Figure 3-32 Codes in a File
When you change formats in a file, you are actually entering codes that control the printer. On many programs, these codes are hidden from view, but many programs allow you to display them when editing.

Binary Files

Along with ASCII characters such as letters and numbers, most programs use additional bytes that are coded to represent commands (Figure 3-32). These coded characters are used for many formatting commands specific to the program. For example, when you underline words, add page numbers, change margins or line spacing, or add headers and footers, you are actually entering codes into the document. These codes are specific to the program you are using; there is no standard. Thus, these codes cannot be interpreted by other programs. Files containing these codes are called *binary files*. To use binary files with another program, the program-specific codes must be either removed or converted into codes the program will understand. This is generally done by saving them with a command designed for this purpose or by using a separate program to convert them.

Binary files are usually saved with an extension specific to the program you are working on. Some programs automatically add an extension, for example, .DOC (for document) to every file you save. Other programs do not automatically add an extension, but you can add one. Different extensions let you distinguish among files created with different programs.

ASCII Files

The codes in binary files are specific to the program that created them, and they can rarely be interpreted by other programs. Nor can they be telecommunicated using a modem without first making special provisions. Many programs, therefore, allow you to save files as *ASCII text files*. When saved in this way, all codes specific to the program are removed from the file so it contains only ASCII text characters that can be read by other programs. These files are identified with various extensions, two of the most common being .TXT (for text) and .ASC (for ASCII).

Print Files

Print files are like ASCII files, but all format commands you have entered into the file are interpreted. The only difference is that the output is sent to a file on a disk instead of to the printer. For example, headers, footers, page numbers, top and bottom margins, and other formats that would appear on a printout also appear in the print file on the disk. A print file is created just like a printout on the printer. Print files are created so that you can preview the results of format commands before actually printing the file on paper. They can also be printed

ORGANIZING YOUR WORK

The limitations on filenames makes it impossible to identify each document with a fully descriptive name. Most companies and experienced users, therefore, have a rigid system of assigning filenames or numbers to each file. These names or numbers are often entered into a log along with more descriptive information about the files.

If a name is used, it should logically relate to the file's contents. Above all, the system that files are designated by should be consistent and understood by everyone responsible for assigning names or retrieving files.

A typical file-naming system might use the eight filename characters as follows:

- A file number can be assigned. For example, the numbers 00000000 through 99999999 allow 100 million documents to be stored without duplicating a number.
- Abbreviations for the sender and recipient can be used.
- Dates, possibly combined with other information, can be used. For example, a letter by JH completed January 1, 1993, can be coded as JH1193, JH010193, or JH1-1-93.
- Version numbers can be added to filenames. For example, if you revise a file named JOHN1, you can rename it JOHN2 when you save it again.

Besides the filename or file number, a good log will contain some or all of the following information about each file:

- The name of the originator
- The name of the person who did the processing
- The type of file, for example, letter, report, or budget
- A brief description of the file
- The name of the intended recipient
- The name or number of the disk it is stored on
- The retention date, that is, the date on or after which the document can be permanently removed from electronic storage in the absence of other instructions

Other techniques you can use to simplify managing your files include the following:

- The operating system automatically adds the date and time to a file when you save it. These can be seen using the DIR command. These can be used to tell one version of a file from another when they have been saved on different disks using the same filename. Periodically print out directories of the files on your disks.
- Most floppy disks come with a package of labels. Use one of these labels to assign a number and perhaps a descriptive title to each disk, for example, *Disk 1: Letters*; *Disk 2: Spreadsheet Files*; *Disk 3: Reports*.
- If using a hard disk drive, store related files in their own directories.
- Always erase unneeded files from your disks. If you print a file and are certain you will never need it again, delete it immediately. If you leave it, the next time you see the filename, you may not remember if it is important.

Revisable-form text (RFT). A document saved in IBM's Document Content Architecture format so it can be edited or printed on other equipment using a program that utilizes the same format.

directly from the operating system and, in some cases, can be used (as ASCII files can be) by other programs. For example, using print files, you can exchange formatted text between programs. You can create a file using a spreadsheet or graphics program and then print it to the disk. You can then load a word processing program and insert these print files into a document. Print files are usually identified with an extension such as .PRT or .PRN.

Revisable-Form-Text Files

To ease the transfer of files between programs, IBM introduced a set of standards for codes used to format documents. Files coded in this format, called *revisable-form-text (RFT)*, can be retrieved by any other program that also supports the standard. Many programs can now save and retrieve files in this format in addition to their own.

FILE EXCHANGE

What if twenty manufacturers made twenty different kinds of compact disk players and twenty recording companies produced twenty different kinds of compact disks? If you changed players, you might have to buy an entirely new CD disk collection. It is unlikely that the music business would be successful if it operated like this. But as shortsighted as it sounds, this is the way it is in the computer field. Apple computers cannot run IBM PC programs or files. Files created with WordPerfect cannot be edited with WordStar. This incompatibility causes problems for companies that use more than one program. The incompatibility arises from two causes: file storage techniques that limit transfers between computers and file formats that limit transfers between programs.

Exchanging Files Between Computers

The operating system controls the way files are saved on a disk. When you format a disk, you customize it for use with your equipment and operating system. When you then save data onto the disk, the operating system saves it using its own specific storage techniques. If you then take the disk to another computer running a different operating system, you cannot retrieve the files from the disk. For example, a disk used with an Apple Macintosh cannot be read by an IBM PS/2, even though both computers use 3½-inch floppy disks.

To transfer the files, you usually have to send the disk to an outside service that has the hardware and software that can convert the files for you.

When you upgrade from one type of floppy disk to another, the problem is not as serious. For example, millions of users have stored their work on 5¼-inch floppy disks. But many new computers use 3½-inch floppy disks. To use old files on the new machines, users must either add a 5¼-inch floppy disk drive to their new system or have someone who has done so copy their files for them to disks their computer can use.

Exchanging Files Between Programs

As you have seen, the ASCII code stores characters in a computer in a standard way. This standardization lets you exchange files between programs. The problem is that data files you create do not contain only ASCII characters. When you use many formatting commands, for example, those to underline or boldface text, change margins, and enter subscripts or superscripts, the program enters codes that tell the printer what to do. These codes are not standardized. To transfer files to another program, you have two choices: Save the file in a format that can be read by another program, or convert the file into another format using a file conversion program. Many of the latest programs have conversion capabilities built in so files are automatically converted when you retrieve them.

Saving a File in a Format That Can Be Read by Another Program. What if you want to insert a spreadsheet model or database file into a report? Or, what if you want to insert a table in a document into a spreadsheet model or a database file? Do you have to retype everything? The answer is no, if your program allows you to save files in an ASCII text format or other transferable format. When you save a file as an ASCII text file, you remove any special codes so that the file contains only ASCII characters. When you retrieve the file with another program, you have to reformat it.

Converting a File into Another Format. What if you want to transfer a model created on a spreadsheet program to a word processing program or vice versa? Because each program uses its own unique ways to code data, files can't be used directly; they must first be converted using special conversion programs that have been developed. Instead of removing codes, you can use one of these programs to convert the codes entered with one program into those used by another. Some of the latest programs have these conversion programs built in. If you are working on a program like Word for Windows, you can automatically retrieve files in 1-2-3's format without using any special conversion commands. The program does the conversion automatically.

EXERCISES

Exercise 3-6A
SAVING A FILE

Refer to a word processing program's user's guide and list the procedures you follow to save a file.

1. _____
   _____
2. _____
   _____
3. _____
   _____

Exercise 3-6B
RETRIEVING A FILE

Refer to a word processing program's user's guide and list the procedures you follow to retrieve a file.

1. _____
2. _____
3. _____

QUESTIONS

1. What is a data file? List four types of data files.
2. What may happen to a file you are working on if you turn off the computer without first saving the file onto a disk?
3. List four stages at which it is prudent to save your files.
4. Why would you save a file before printing it?
5. What are some of the limitations of filenames?
6. List some things a good log would contain.
7. What is a binary file?
8. What is an ASCII file?
9. What is the difference between files that are stored in ASCII and binary formats?
10. What is a print file? How do print files differ from ASCII files?
11. What prevents you from using the information stored on an IBM disk on an Apple computer?
12. What prevents you from editing a file created on one word processing program with another program?
13. What format do you save files in when you want to exchange them between programs?

3-7
EDITING DOCUMENTS

Block. Any series of adjacent characters, words, sentences, or paragraphs.

After you type a document, you proofread it and then edit or revise it. Editing refers to correcting mistakes and making minor changes. Revising implies more significant changes in organization or approach. To edit or revise a document on the screen, you use the cursor movement keys or commands to move the cursor through the document to delete or insert characters, words, or phrases. You can also select *blocks*, sections of text that you can copy, move, or delete in one step.

MOVING THE CURSOR AND SCROLLING THE SCREEN

Word processing programs provide you with several ways to move the cursor through a document. You can move the cursor a character or line at a time with the directional arrow keys. You can also move the cursor in larger jumps with commands; the longer your document, the more important these commands become. If your computer has **PgUp** and **PgDn** keys, you use them to scroll through the text a screen or a page at a time. Other keys, like **Home** and **End**, move the cursor to the top or bottom of the screen or document or to the beginning or end of a line. Some other commands use **Ctrl**, or another key, as an amplifier. For example, when you press the down arrow key, the cursor usually moves down one line at a time. But when you press the down arrow key while holding down **Ctrl**, the cursor may jump much farther, perhaps to the end of a sentence or paragraph or to the bottom of the screen, depending on the program you are using. When moving the cursor with the designated arrow keys, you will notice that:

- When you move the cursor along a line of text, it moves through the text and does not affect it.
- When you move the cursor past the rightmost character on a line, it usually jumps down to the beginning of the next line.
- When you move the cursor past the leftmost character on a line, it usually jumps up to the end of the line above.
- If the document is longer than the number of lines displayed on the screen, it can be scrolled into view by moving the cursor to the top or bottom of the screen and pressing the up or down arrow keys. Instead of moving off the screen, the cursor stays on the top or bottom line, and the text scrolls into view.
- You cannot move the cursor off the screen, and you usually cannot move it past the last line of text in the document.

You can move the cursor directly to a specific point in a document without having to scroll to it. The way programs do this varies. Some programs let you assign names to lines of text or insert markers that you can instantly move the cursor to. Other programs automatically number every page and line of text so that you can move directly to any page or line you specify.

Some programs and computers are designed so that you can point a mouse. When using a mouse in this way, you see both a cursor and a mouse pointer on the screen. To move the cursor to a new position, you point to that position and click one of the buttons on the mouse. The cursor immediately jumps to the new position. On many programs, you can also scroll the screen by pointing to arrow keys in a scroll bar and clicking on an up or down arrow.

When a document is longer or wider than the screen, you can scroll the screen vertically and horizontally to see it (Figure 3-33).

Figure 3-33 Scrolling the Screen
When a document is wider or longer than the screen, you can scroll it.

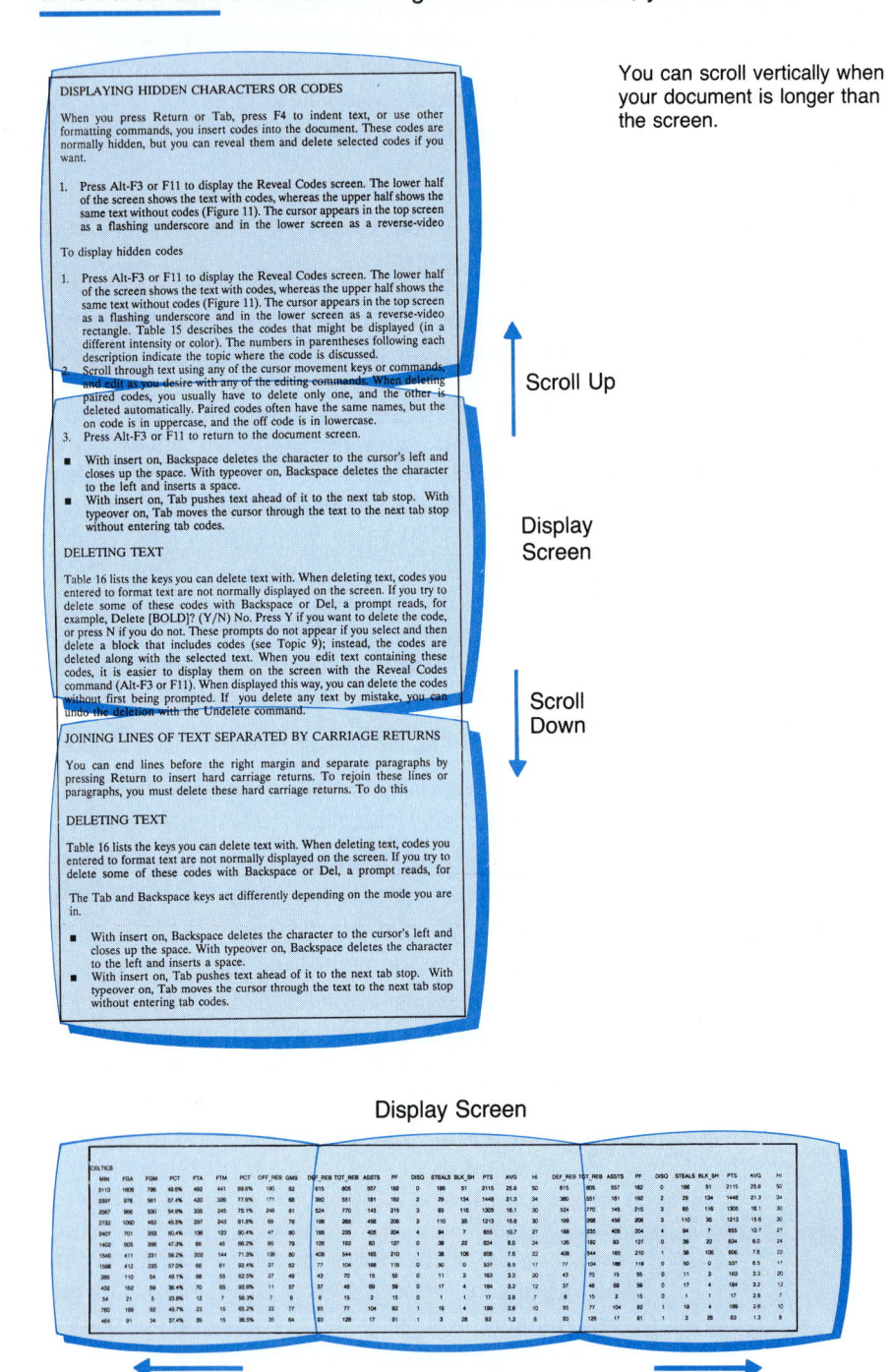

You can scroll vertically when your document is longer than the screen.

You use horizontal scrolling when the document is wider than the screen.

150   WORD PROCESSING AND DESKTOP PUBLISHING APPLICATIONS

Document-oriented program. A word processing program that displays a document as one continuous strip of text.

Page-oriented program. A word processing program that breaks a document into individual pages and does not allow you to see the bottom of one page and the top of the next on the screen at the same time.

Insert mode. A mode where typing new text into existing text causes the existing text to the right of and below it to move aside or down to make room for the new text.

Typeover mode. A mode where data being entered types over and replaces existing text. Also known as replace, strikeover, overtype, or insert-off mode.

Control code. Codes entered into a document to send a command to the printer to control its operation. Typical applications are to change type sizes and character attributes.

■ You use horizontal scrolling when the document is wider than the screen.

■ You use vertical scrolling when the document is longer than the screen. The effects vertical scrolling has depend on whether the program is document oriented or page oriented (some can be both); each reacts differently to vertical scrolling.

- ***Document-oriented programs*** display pages as continuous text; that is, as you type, you can see the bottom of one page and the top of the next at the same time. A line of dashes or other codes indicate where one page will end and the next will begin when you print the document. When working on a document-oriented program, you can move the cursor through the entire document using only the up and down arrow keys.

- ***Page-oriented programs*** treat each page like individual sheets of paper. You cannot see the bottom of one page and the top of the next on the screen at the same time. With the arrow keys, you can scroll through only the displayed page. To scroll through another page, you must execute a command to display the next page or the previous page.

INSERTING OR REPLACING TEXT

To edit text, you move the cursor through the document and delete and insert characters as needed. Most word processing programs allow you to switch between inserting characters and typing over and replacing characters already there.

■ When you enter text in ***insert mode***, any existing text to the right or below moves over and down to make room for the new text. On most programs, you can actually watch text rearrange itself on the screen.

■ When you enter text in ***typeover mode*** (also called *replace*, *overtype*, *strikeover*, or *insert-off*), the new text types over and erases any existing text while text to the right and below does not move. This is useful when entering or editing tables or lists arranged in columns. In typeover mode, you can enter new text without causing characters in columns to the right to shift out of alignment. If you press **Spacebar** in typeover mode, you erase the character highlighted by the cursor.

DISPLAYING HIDDEN CHARACTERS AND CODES

As you create a document, usually just the letters and numbers you type are displayed on the screen. However, you often enter invisible ***control codes*** (also called *printer control* or *format codes*) into the document. On all programs, control codes are entered whenever you press **Enter**, **Tab**, or **Spacebar**. You also enter these codes when you use formatting commands, for example, to center, indent, or underline text. Control codes usually do not appear on the screen and never in the printout. They control how your text is displayed on the screen and printed on a page.

Many programs allow you to display these codes (Figure 3-34), which makes editing much easier. By displaying the codes, you can see where carriage returns and other formatting codes are located, which makes it simple to delete or change them.

EDITING DOCUMENTS

Undo command. A command on some programs that reverses the results of the previous command, in case it was mistakenly entered.

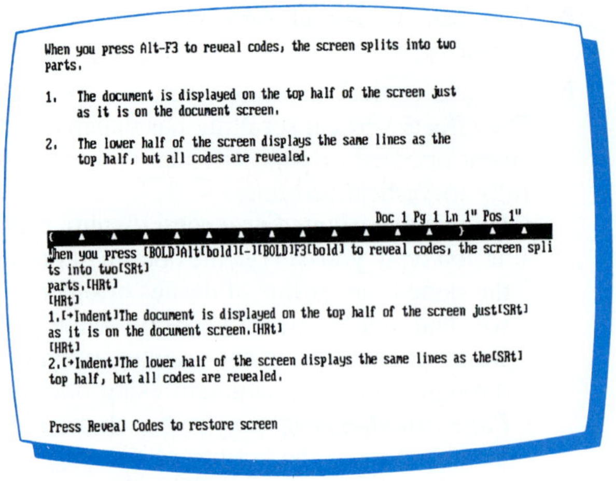

Figure 3-34 Hidden Codes
Displaying hidden codes lets you see the codes that you may want to delete or change. Here, you see some of the hidden codes displayed on WordPerfect. The top half of the screen shows text without codes and the bottom half with them.

DELETING TEXT

As you have seen, you can delete words a character at a time with **Backspace** or **Del**. On most programs, pressing **Backspace** deletes the character to the left of the cursor, whereas pressing **Del** erases the character highlighted by the cursor. If you hold down either key, the computer's autorepeat feature causes it to delete one character after another until you release the key. That is, holding down **Backspace** deletes one character after another to the left of the cursor, and holding down **Del** deletes one character after another to the right of the cursor. When text is deleted, all text to its right and below moves over and up to fill the space vacated.

UNDOING MISTAKES

Deleting text removes it from the screen and the computer's memory. With many programs, this means you lose the text unless you save it before you delete it. Some programs have an ***Undo command*** (also called an *Undelete* command) that stores deletions in a buffer—a small portion of the computer's memory allocated to saving material that you delete. You can recover a deletion if you notice the mistake soon enough.

    Buffers store only the most recent deletions (and sometimes other commands), and they do not permanently store material. Thus, you must undo mistakes immediately. Depending on the amount of material you have deleted and the size of the undo buffer, you may be able to recover only part of the deleted material.

JOINING LINES OF TEXT SEPARATED BY CARRIAGE RETURNS

When editing, you often want to delete blank lines, join two lines, or join paragraphs that were separated by hard carriage returns. Though not necessarily displayed on the screen, hard carriage returns are much like other characters you enter in a document; therefore, you delete them as you would other characters. Some programs let you display hard carriage returns, making it easy for you to find them if you want to delete them.

    To join two lines or two paragraphs (Figure 3-35), move the cursor one space to the right of the punctuation mark at the end of the first line or paragraph. Use your program's delete keys or commands to delete carriage returns until the line or paragraph below jumps up to join the line above. If necessary,

Automatic paragraph reforming. A feature that automatically aligns text with the left and right margins when text is inserted or deleted. Also called line adjust or paragraph aligning.

Repaginate. A command used on a page oriented program when changes are made to a document that affect its length. The command ensures that all text falls on the appropriate page of the printed document.

Figure 3-35 Joining Lines of Text
Joining lines of text is done by deleting the hard carriage returns that keep them separated.

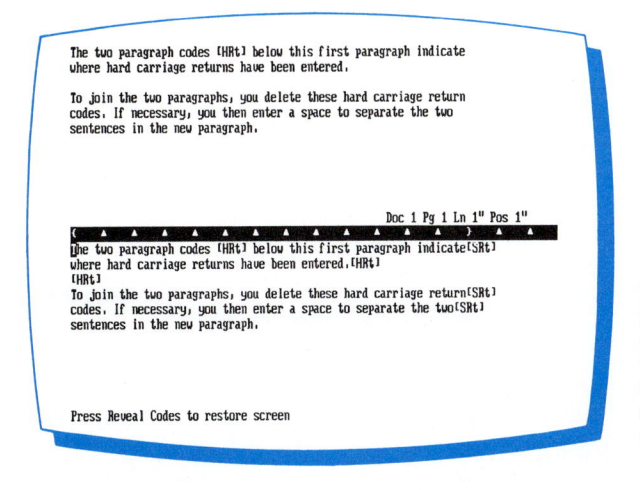

Here, two paragraphs have been separated by two hard carriage returns (indicated by the *[HRt]* codes in the Reveal Codes screen). The *[SRt]* codes are soft carriage return codes.

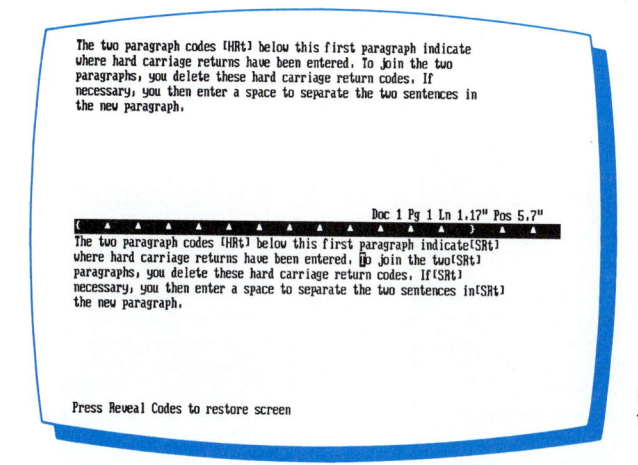

Deleting the *[HRt]* codes joins the two paragraphs.

you then use **Spacebar** to insert spaces between the last word of the first paragraph and the first word of what was the second paragraph.

PARAGRAPH REALIGNING AND REPAGINATION

Paragraph realigning and repagination keep your text adjusted within the page margins as you make changes.

- When you make changes to a paragraph that affect its length or margins, most programs automatically realign it with the margins (Figure 3-36). This is called *automatic paragraph reforming* (also called *line adjust* or *paragraph aligning*).

- If you make any changes that affect a document's length on a page-oriented program, you must *repaginate* your document to display all text on the appropriate pages (Figure 3-37).

EDITING DOCUMENTS 153

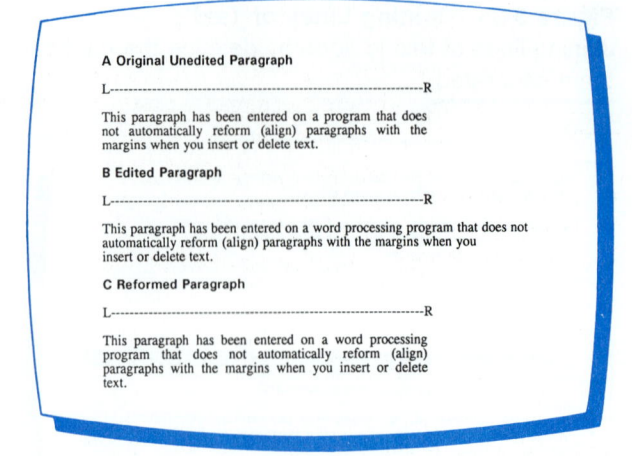

**Figure 3-36
Reforming Paragraphs**
Reforming paragraphs aligns the revised text with the left and right margins. This figure shows the original unedited paragraph, the edited paragraph, and the reformed paragraph.

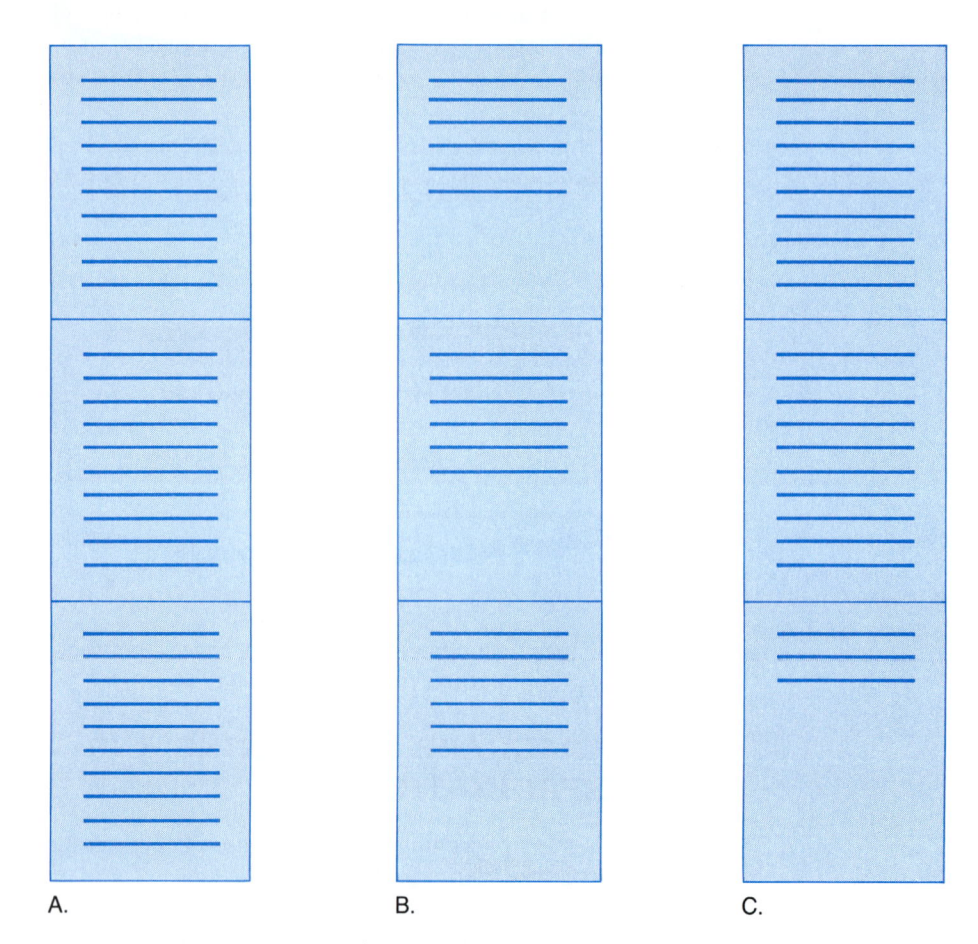

A.   B.   C.

Figure 3-37   Repaginating Documents
Repaging a document is necessary on a page-oriented program when you make changes to a document so that the number of text lines is unchanged. (A) The original document fills all pages equally. (B) The revised document has pages of unequal line length. (C) After repaging the document, the pages are again equally full.

3-7

154   WORD PROCESSING AND DESKTOP PUBLISHING APPLICATIONS

Column mode. A function that allows you to move, copy, delete, or format columns of text rather than lines.

WORKING WITH BLOCKS

If you are revising typewritten copy, at some point, you will likely take a pair of scissors and some glue and reorganize your work by cutting and pasting. With a word processing program, you do this electronically. Blocks of text are the sections you cut from one place in a document and then paste to another place. A block of text can be a character, word, phrase, sentence, paragraph, group of paragraphs, or an entire document.

You can perform several operations on blocks of text, including:

- Copying or moving the block within the document on the screen.
- Copying or moving the block to another file on the disk.
- Deleting the block.
- Formatting the block, for example, boldfacing, italicizing, or underlining it.

When working with blocks of text, you usually copy, move, delete, or format lines of text (Figure 3-38). The block can begin or end anywhere on the lines. Many programs also have predefined blocks that you can select with a single command.

Many word processors also allow you to work with columns of text (Figure 3-39). This feature, called *column mode*, is useful when revising or for-

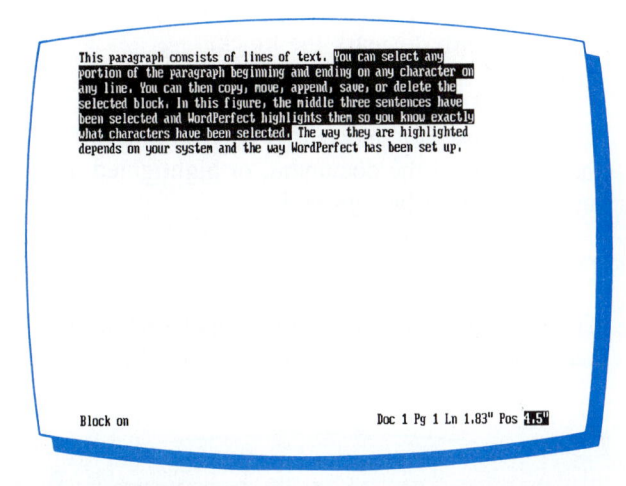

Figure 3-38 Line Block
Line blocks can be characters, words, phrases, sentences, or paragraphs. A block can begin or end anywhere in the document.

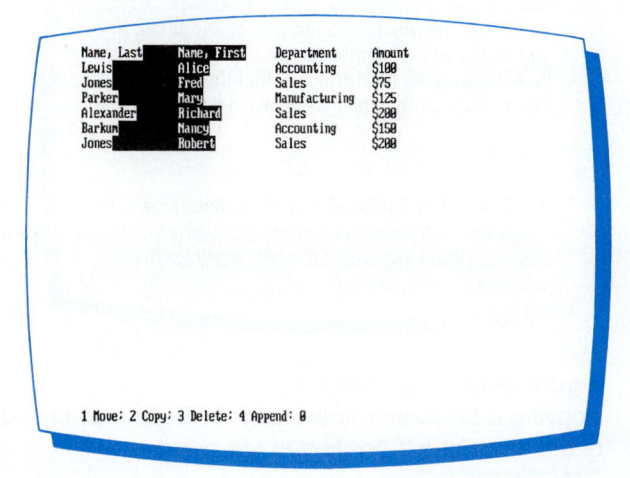

Figure 3-39 Column Block
Using column mode, you can copy, move, delete, or format entire columns in one step. This figure shows the second column highlighted so that one of these operations can be performed on it.

EDITING DOCUMENTS 155

Select. To emphasize text on the screen by displaying it in reverse video (dark characters against a light background) or in a color different from the display's regular color. Also called blocking text.

matting tables or other text aligned in columns. For example, what if you want to reorganize a table by copying, moving, or deleting one of the columns? If the program works only with lines, you must painstakingly copy, move, or delete the entries in the selected column one line at a time. But with column mode, you can select a column and then copy, move, or delete it all at once. Columns are usually defined as text separated by tabs.

Selecting a Block

To *select* a block of text (sometimes called *blocking text*), you indicate the beginning and end of the block. You do this in one of four ways.

- If you are using a mouse, you point to the beginning of the block and hold down one of the mouse's buttons. As you then drag the mouse, you highlight text.
- To select a block with the keyboard keys, you move the cursor to the beginning or end of the block, and then press a function key to enter block mode. You then use the arrow keys to expand the highlight over the text you want included in the block.
- You select specific types of blocks by pressing an amount key that tells the program you want to select the word, sentence, or paragraph the cursor is positioned in.
- You enter control codes at the beginning and end of the block. They are called control codes because you usually hold down **Ctrl** while you type other characters to enter the codes. These codes do not print out; they are used only to mark the block.

A selected block usually appears highlighted so that it stands out from the text you have not selected. It may be in a different color, dimmer or brighter than the rest of the document, or highlighted in reverse video (dark characters against a bright background).

Copying a Block

Copying a block leaves the original block unchanged and duplicates the block in a new position in the document (Figure 3-40). When you copy a selected block

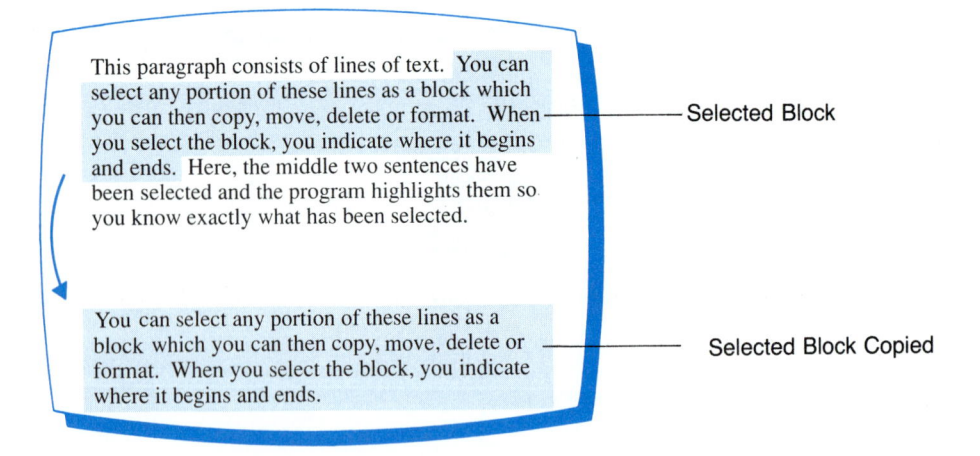

Figure 3-40 Copying a Block
Copying a block leaves the original block unchanged and makes a duplicate of the block at the position of the cursor.

156 WORD PROCESSING AND DESKTOP PUBLISHING APPLICATIONS

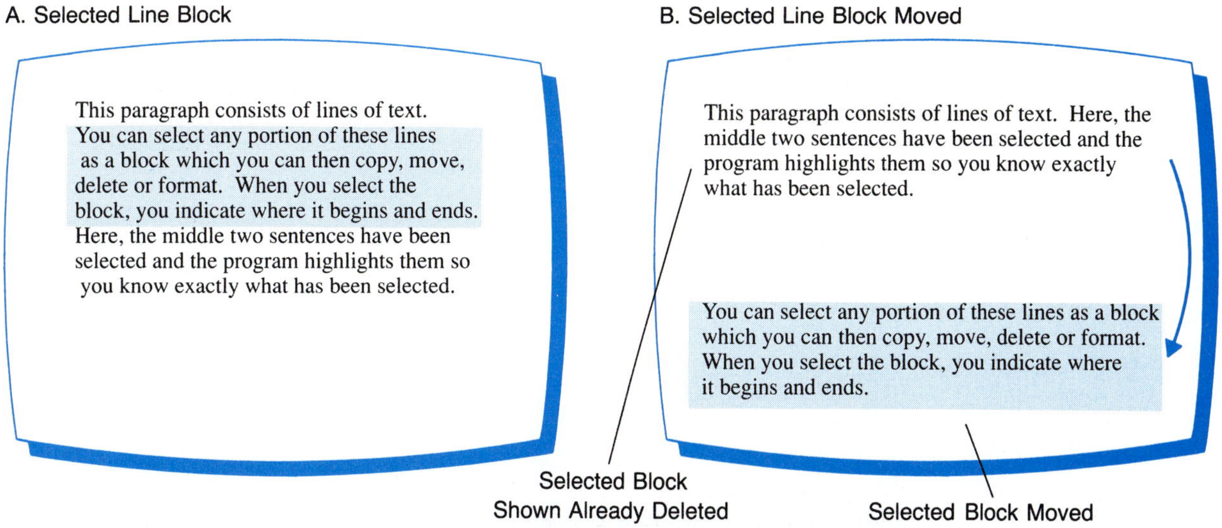

A. Selected Line Block

This paragraph consists of lines of text. You can select any portion of these lines as a block which you can then copy, move, delete or format. When you select the block, you indicate where it begins and ends. Here, the middle two sentences have been selected and the program highlights them so you know exactly what has been selected.

Selected Block Shown Already Deleted

B. Selected Line Block Moved

This paragraph consists of lines of text. Here, the middle two sentences have been selected and the program highlights them so you know exactly what has been selected.

You can select any portion of these lines as a block which you can then copy, move, delete or format. When you select the block, you indicate where it begins and ends.

Selected Block Moved

Figure 3-41 Moving a Block
Moving a block deletes the block from its original position in the document and copies it to the position of the cursor. Text below moves down to make room for it and text closes up to fill the position that it was moved from.

Paste. Moving something that has been copied or cut from a document to another place in the document or to another document.

it is first copied to a buffer (sometimes called a *clipboard*, *scrapbook*, or *scrap*). With the block in the buffer, you move the cursor to where you want to insert the copied text, and then you *paste*, or copy, the block from this buffer. Because the buffer stores only the most recent block, you usually must insert it into the new position before executing any other commands that store text in the buffer. If you copy the block into existing text, the text moves over or down to make room for it. If you copy a column, the columns to the right move over to make room for it.

Moving a Block

Moving a block is just like copying it, but the original block is deleted and the text closes up to fill the space the block was moved from (Figure 3-41).

Deleting a Block

Deleting a block deletes the selected block from the screen and the computer's memory (Figure 3-42). Some programs temporarily store the deleted block in a buffer so that you can undo the deletion if you change your mind. When you execute the Undo command, the deleted block is restored.

Copying a Block to a Disk File

You can copy blocks from the file you are working on to their own files on the disk. Some programs also let you append (copy) them to the end of existing files. You can then retrieve the new or appended file and edit it just like any other document file. Copying blocks is often used to break large documents into smaller, more manageable files.

Formatting Blocks

After selecting a block, you can use any of the program's formatting commands. For example, you can boldface the block or change its margins.

EDITING DOCUMENTS   **157**

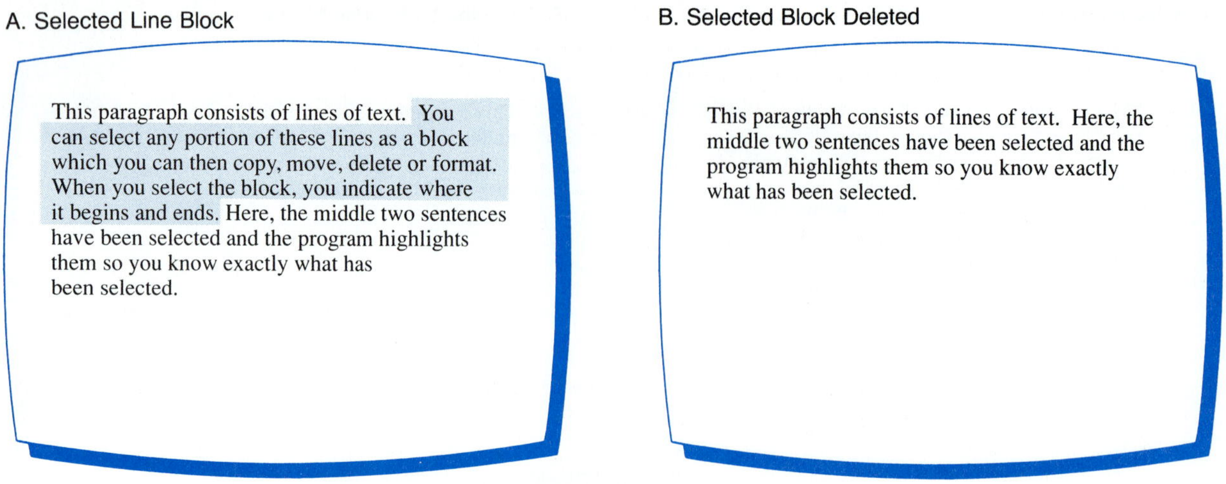

A. Selected Line Block

This paragraph consists of lines of text. You can select any portion of these lines as a block which you can then copy, move, delete or format. When you select the block, you indicate where it begins and ends. Here, the middle two sentences have been selected and the program highlights them so you know exactly what has been selected.

B. Selected Block Deleted

This paragraph consists of lines of text. Here, the middle two sentences have been selected and the program highlights them so you know exactly what has been selected.

Figure 3-42   Deleting a Block
Deleting a block removes it from the document on the screen and the computer's memory. The text below the deleted block moves up to fill the space.

Search.   To look for a string throughout a document or other file.

Replace.   To substitute one string of text for another.

String.   One or more characters (for example, any character, number, word, phrase, sentence, or paragraph) that appear in sequence.

SEARCH AND REPLACE

When you want to find text in a document, you *search* for it. If you want to substitute new text for it, you *replace* it. You can search or replace any *string* of characters. Strings are simply letters, words, numbers, symbols, sentences, codes, spaces, and so on that appear in sequence.

Search

When you use the Search command, you are prompted to enter the string you want to find. If the specified string is found, the program moves the cursor to the beginning or end of the string, or highlights it in some other way. The program may then display a prompt asking if you want to quit the operation or find the next occurrence. Or, the search might end automatically and you then repeat the same command or use another command to continue the search. You might search for strings for several reasons.

- You can use the command to find a section of a document. Just enter a keyword that appears in the section's title or contents, and the Search command finds it.
- You can use the command to check words that you frequently misspell, especially those you misspell in more than one way. For example, using wildcards (see *Wildcards*), you can find all occurrences of the word *similar* even if they have been misspelled as *simalar*, *simeler*, and *similer*.

Replace

When you use the Replace command (sometimes called Search and Replace), you specify the string you want to find and the string you want to replace it with. If the string is found, the action the program takes depends on the options you have selected.

Sometimes, you use the Replace command to replace misspelled words with their correct spelling. But it also has other useful applications, including saving typing time. If a word or phrase appears repeatedly in a document, you can substitute an unusual character (or characters) that are unlikely to appear elsewhere in the document instead of repeatedly entering the word or phrase. Later, you can replace these characters with the actual word or phrase. For example, if you often refer to a book title in a long report, you can enter an abbreviation wherever the title is to appear. Then you can replace the abbreviation with the actual title.

Search and Replace Options

Both Search and Replace are powerful editing tools. Wildcards and other options make them even more so.

Wildcards. When you enter a string to be searched for, you can use wildcards to substitute for any character or characters. The symbols for these wildcards vary from program to program, but the principles are the same.

- The wildcard ? may stand for any character that appears in this position. Searching for *h?t*, would find *hot*, *hat*, *hit*, and so on.
- The wildcard * may stand for any characters in or after this position, for example, *Mac** finds *MacWilliams*, *MacCarney*, *Macintosh*, and so on. And *t*t* finds *tot*, *treat*, and *toast*.

Other Options. When using Search or Replace, you may use several options to control the process. Not every program offers all these options. And programs that do offer them frequently call them other names.

- *Automatic* (also called *Global*) finds all occurrences of a string and automatically replaces them with the new string. You are not prompted to confirm the replacement. Be careful with commands that affect the entire document in this way. Sometimes the command will not differentiate between whole words or parts of words, for example, *row* and *arrow*. This command also ignores context. For example, if the document contains the sentences *He can read very well* and *She read the book just before class*, and you replace *read* with *write*, the second sentence would read *She write the book just before class* and no longer make sense.
- *Manual* (also called *Pause for approval* or *Confirm*) finds the specified string and then pauses. A prompt offers you the choice of replacing the string or leaving it unchanged.
- *Ignore case* finds all occurrences of a string, whether some or all of the characters are uppercase or lowercase. This is useful because words falling at the beginning of a sentence are capitalized, whereas the same word falling elsewhere in a sentence may not be. A few programs ignore the case when searching but replace strings using the same case. That is, if the found string is capitalized, the replacement is capitalized; if the found string is lowercase, the replacement is lowercase.
- *Find whole words only* avoids the problem of replacing parts of words when you intended to replace only whole words. For example, searching and replacing *row* with *column* converts *arrow* into *arcolumn* and *rowboat* into *columnboat*. When you specify this option, you should be aware that searching for a singular will not find plurals or possessives. For example, searching for *desk* will not find *desks*.

EDITING DOCUMENTS 159

Spelling checker. A program containing a dictionary that checks the spelling of any word or words in the document.

Thesaurus. An editing aid that allows you to highlight a word and request that a list of synonyms be displayed.

Document compare feature. A feature that allows you to see the differences between two versions of the same document.

SPELLING CHECKERS

Spelling checkers compare all words in a file against a main dictionary and any supplemental dictionaries that you specify. Any words not found in the dictionaries are either flagged with special characters or highlighted. You can then decide whether to change them, leave them as is, or, in some cases, add them to the dictionary. Good spelling checkers do not simply flag questionable words; they also list spelling suggestions that you can accept or reject.

When a word is flagged because the spelling checker cannot find it in its dictionary, the program offers you options that might include one or more of the following:

- *Replace* replaces the flagged word in the text with one of the words suggested by the program.
- *Skip* or *Ignore* skips the flagged word and continues, leaving the word unchanged. This choice tells the program to assume the word is spelled correctly. On some programs, subsequent occurrences of the word are ignored.
- *Add to dictionary* is selected when the word is spelled correctly and you want to add it to the dictionary. When you add a word to the dictionary, it is usually added to a supplemental dictionary. Most programs let you specify the supplemental dictionary it is to be added to. This way, you can create a series of special-purpose dictionaries. Many users create a supplemental dictionary for names and addresses and another for technical terms used in their fields. At least one program allows you to add a word to a document dictionary. Words added to this dictionary are no longer flagged when you spell check the document again. This dictionary is attached only to the document from which words were added to it.
- *Edit* is used when a word is misspelled so badly that the program cannot suggest alternative spellings.
- *Look up* is used to find specific words, for example, when you are typing and are unsure of a word's spelling. The look-up function allows you to enter the word, and the dictionary suggests possible correct spellings.

Spelling checkers are nice, but you cannot entirely rely on them. They check only for spelling, not usage. For example, spelling checkers would find no problems in the sentence *Eye wood like two except you invitation, butt can not. Unfortunately, their are another things i half too due* or in Hamlet's "*too bee oar knot too bee.*" These may sound funny, but each word is spelled correctly. Because of this limitation, you must proofread documents carefully for content and context.

THESAURUSES

When using a ***thesaurus***, you can highlight a word and request the thesaurus to display a list of synonyms. For example, when the word *wicked* is highlighted, the thesaurus may display the synonyms *sinful*, *erring*, *nefarious*, *wayward*, *dissolute*, *vile*, and *vicious*. You can then select one of the suggested words to replace the word highlighted in the document, look up another word, or quit the thesaurus and return to the document.

DOCUMENT COMPARE

Documents sometimes go through many revisions before the final version is printed and distributed. All changes are not necessarily good ones, but it gets hard to keep track of them from version to version. A ***document compare***

Redlining. A format assigned to text that is inserted into a document so that others can easily see the changes. See also Strikeout.

Strikeout. A format assigned to text in a document that is proposed for deletion. See also Redlining.

feature is therefore useful. This feature compares two versions of a document and highlights the differences between them.

REDLINING AND STRIKEOUT

When a document is written by one person and edited by another, or edited by one person and typed by another, some phrases or paragraphs may have to be flagged for further consideration. Some paragraphs may be proposed for insertion and some for deletion. Some programs allow you to use *redlining* to indicate text proposed for insertion and *strikeout* to indicate text proposed for deletion. Redlining puts markers in the margin on lines that have been redlined or prints a screen over it when you print the document. These highlights indicate that the material is proposed for insertion. Strikeout puts a strikeout character (- or /) through text proposed for deletion.

After final changes are decided on or approved, a special command automatically deletes all text that has been struck out and removes all redlining from text that has been redlined.

EXERCISES

Exercise 3-7A
CURSOR MOVEMENT COMMANDS

Table 3-3 lists some typical cursor movements. List the commands for your program that accomplish each movement.

Table 3-3
CURSOR MOVEMENT COMMANDS

Cursor Movement Commands	Enter Commands for Your Program
To the next character	_____
To the next word	_____
To the next line	_____
To the end of a line	_____
To the beginning of a line	_____
To the end of a sentence	_____
To the beginning of a sentence	_____
To the end of a paragraph	_____
To the beginning of a paragraph	_____
To the end of a document	_____
To the beginning of a document	_____
To the top and bottom of the screen	_____
To a specified line	_____
To a specified page	_____

Exercise 3-7B
DELETE COMMANDS

Table 3-4 lists typical text deletions. List the commands for your program that accomplish each deletion.

Table 3-4
DELETE COMMANDS

Delete Commands	Enter Commands for Your Program
By character	_____
By word	_____
By line	_____
By sentence	_____
By paragraph	_____
To end of line	_____
To beginning of line	_____
To end of sentence	_____
To beginning of sentence	_____
To end of paragraph	_____
To beginning of paragraph	_____
To end of document	_____
To beginning of document	_____

Exercise 3-7C
BLOCK COMMANDS

Many programs have commands that select predefined blocks. Table 3-5 lists typical block selections. List the commands for your program that perform each move.

Table 3-5
BLOCK SELECT COMMANDS

Predefined Blocks	Enter Commands for Your Program
A word	_____
A line	_____
A sentence	_____
A paragraph	_____
To the end of a line	_____
To the beginning of a line	_____
To the end of a sentence	_____

Table 3-5, continued
BLOCK SELECT COMMANDS

Predefined Blocks	Enter Commands for Your Program
To the beginning of a sentence	_____
To the end of a paragraph	_____
To the beginning of a paragraph	_____
To the end of a document	_____
To the beginning of a document	_____

QUESTIONS

1. What is the difference between a document-oriented and a page-oriented program?
2. What is the cursor used for, and how do you move it?
3. What is the basic difference between insert mode and typeover mode? What does to insert text mean? To replace (or type over) text?
4. If you press **Spacebar** to move the cursor, what happens if the program is in insert mode? In typeover mode?
5. What are hidden characters? Why would you want to be able to display them?
6. Describe two keys you can use to delete text. What other procedures can also be used?
7. What is the Undo command? Describe how it works.
8. If two lines or paragraphs were separated by a carriage return, how would you join them?
9. What is paragraph reforming? When is a paragraph reformed?
10. What does repagination mean? When do you repaginate a document?
11. What is a block of text? What kinds of blocks can you work with?
12. What is column mode? When would you use it?
13. What operations can you perform on blocks?
14. How do you select blocks?
15. What is the difference between moving and copying a block of text?
16. What are the advantages of being able to copy or move a block to a file on the disk?
17. What is a string? Give some examples.
18. What is the Search command, and what is it used for?
19. What is the Replace command, and what is it used for?
20. What is a wildcard used for?
21. List and describe four options available when you want to search or replace.
22. What is the purpose of a spelling checker?
23. What is the purpose of a thesaurus?
24. What is the purpose of a style and grammar check?
25. What is a document compare feature, and when would you want to use it?
26. What is redlining? strikeout? How are they related on some programs?

3-8
FORMATTING DOCUMENTS

All applications programs have default settings and provide commands you can use to override them. Figure 3-43 shows some typical word processing default settings. You can use these default settings as is, override them throughout a specific document, or change them for all documents.

A. The top margin is the distance from the top of the page to the first printed line.

B. The bottom margin is the distance from the last printed line to the bottom of the page.

C. Page length is the distance from the top to the bottom of the page.

D. The number of lines of text that can be printed on a page is determined by the size of the type you are using and the spacing between lines.

E. The text is always aligned with the left margin by default. The right margin can be ragged, or justified so that it is evenly aligned.

F. The left margin is the distance in from the left edge of the page that the first character in each line of text prints.

G. The right margin is the distance between the right edge of the page and the last character on a line.

H. The line length is the distance between the left and right margin settings.

I. Page numbers may or may not be printed on each page of a document. If they are printed, the position of the page numbers may vary.

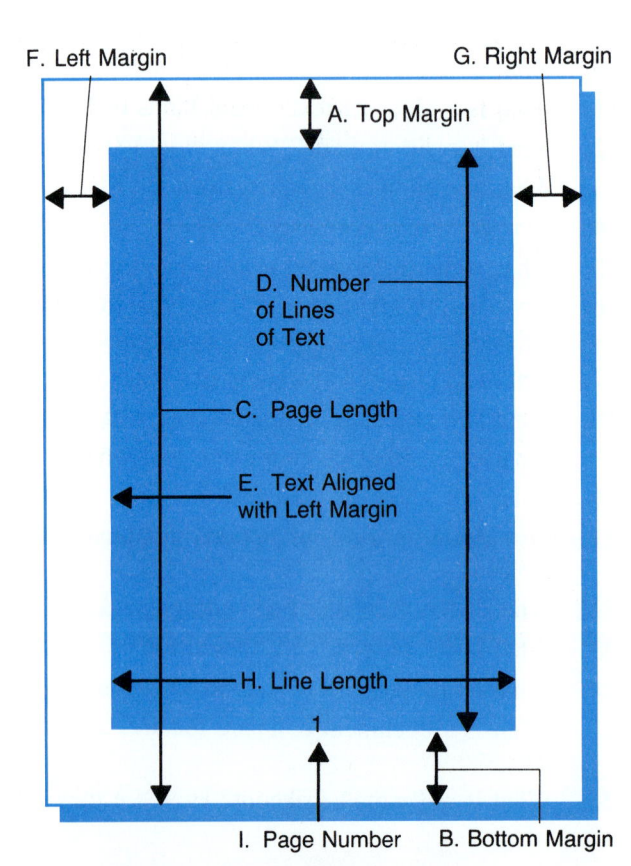

Figure 3-43 Default Document Formats Default settings vary from program to program but include the elements shown in this figure.

164 WORD PROCESSING AND DESKTOP PUBLISHING APPLICATIONS

Open codes. Formatting codes that override default formats from the point at which they are entered to the end of the document or to the next code of the same type.

Format line. The line at the top of (or within) a word processing document that, on some programs, controls the format, for example margins, text alignment, and tab stops. Also known as an embedded ruler line.

Closed codes. Formatting codes that are entered in pairs. The first code begins a format and the second ends it. Also called paired codes.

When you load a word processing program and open a new document, any text you enter is automatically formatted using the default settings. For example, margins may be 1 inch on all sides and text aligned with the left margin and single spaced. If you want different margins or want to center or double space some or all of the text, you must override the default settings at the appropriate place in the document. You can format a document before, while, or after entering it. For example, before entering text, you might change the margins or page length. While entering text, you might boldface and underline keywords and titles. After entering text, you might change the position of page numbers on the page.

You can easily experiment with formats until you find the ones you like. Formatting and text entry are separate operations, so if you want to change margins after you have entered text, you just use the margin commands and all of the text realigns with the new margins. Unlike a typewritten document, you do not have to reenter the text each time you change the format.

Whether or not you see them, many formats are created by entering codes at selected points in the document. For example, common settings, such as hard carriage returns, spaces, tabs, alignment between margins, and emphasized characters, are controlled by codes. When you print the document, these codes arrive at the printer and give it instructions. A code might tell the printer to advance to the top of the next page after printing fifty-four lines, print a page number at the bottom of the page, or indent a paragraph five spaces from the left margin. Usually, these codes are hidden unless you use the program's command that displays them.

There are two types of codes, open and paired. Only one program calls them this (WordPerfect), but the analogy works for all programs.

- ■ *Open codes*, like those used to change tabs or margins, affect all text either from the code to the end of the document or to the next code of the same type (Figure 3-44). Other open codes, like those that indent text, affect all text until the next hard carriage return.

  Some programs group several related open codes together and display them as a ***format line***, sometimes called an embedded ruler line. You can insert these format lines throughout the document wherever you want to change one or more of the settings it controls. Typical format line settings are for left and right margins, tab stops, text alignment, headers and footers, and page numbers.

- ■ *Closed codes* (also called *paired codes*) must be entered in pairs, one code to begin a format and another to end it; for example, one code starts boldfacing, and one code ends it (Figure 3-45).

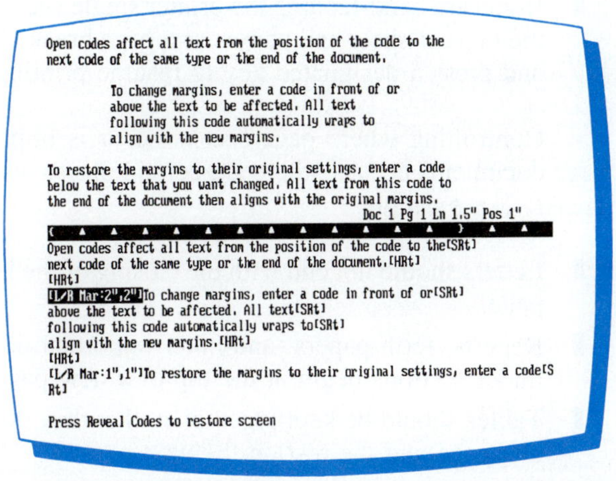

Figure 3-44 Open Codes
Here, an open code has been entered to change the margins after the first paragraph. A second code has then been entered at the beginning of the next paragraph to restore the margins to their original settings.

FORMATTING DOCUMENTS 165

Page break. The point at which one page ends and the printer advances to the top of the next sheet when printing.

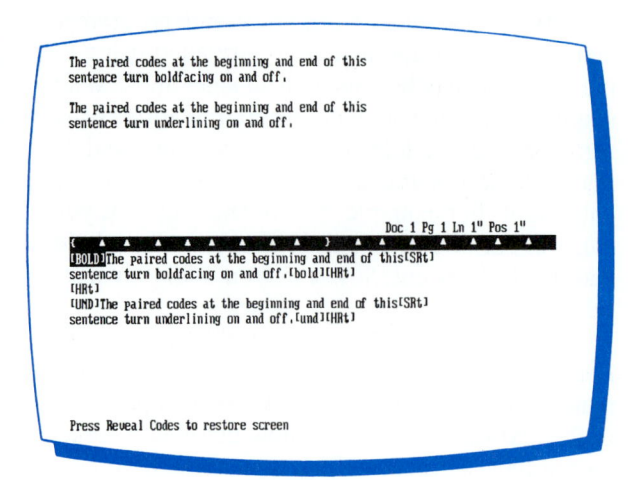

Figure 3-45 Paired Codes
Here, paired codes have been entered to boldface and underline sentences. The first code in the pair turns the format on. The second code in the pair turns the format off.

There are two ways to enter paired codes depending on whether you are formatting new or existing text. To format new text, you enter a beginning code, type text, and then enter an ending code. To format existing text, you select a block of existing text, and then execute the format command that automatically inserts codes at the beginning and end of the selected block.

If you insert text into a document containing paired codes, the position of the cursor determines the format of the text that you insert. If the cursor is between the codes, the text is formatted just like the other text between the code. If the cursor is outside of the codes, the text is not formatted.

PAGE BREAKS

A *page break* is where the printer stops printing lines on the current sheet of paper, advances the paper to the top of the next page, and resumes printing on that page. The way the printer advances to the next page depends on your printer and the kind of paper you are using.

- If you are printing on single sheets of paper on a printer with an automatic sheet feeder, the printer ejects the current sheet, automatically feeds another sheet, and resumes printing.

- If you are printing on continuous form paper, the printer stops printing at a page break, advances the paper to the top of the next page, and then resumes printing.

- If you are hand-feeding the printer single sheets of paper, the printer ejects the current sheet and pauses at a page break. You then insert a new sheet and press a designated key to resume printing.

Controlling where page breaks occur is important when printing multi-page documents because there are certain places where you want to avoid page breaks. For example:

- Letters should not end with the closing of the letter at the top of the second page.

- Reports, term papers, and other important documents should often have major sections begin at the top of a new page.

- Tables should be kept together so that they do not break with one part on one page and the rest on the next page.

Dynamic page display.
A method of displaying on the screen where pages will break when they are printed. To be dynamic, the display must automatically change when adding or deleting text changes the place where pages will break.

Soft page break. A page break that the program inserts automatically when the maximum number of lines on a page is reached. If data are added or deleted so that the number of lines change, a soft page break adjusts automatically.

Hard page break. A page break that you force by entering a command. A hard page break is not moved when you add or delete text above it or repaginate the document. The only way to delete it is with the program's delete command.

Conditional page break. A page format command that moves a specified number of lines to the next page if they all will not fit on the current page when a document is being printed.

Widow. A short line ending a paragraph and appearing by itself at the top of a printed page.

Orphan. The first line of a paragraph that, when printed out, appears as the bottom line of the page.

Page breaks are especially easy to control when your program has a *dynamic page display*, which shows on the screen where page breaks will occur. To control them, word processing programs have three kinds of page breaks: soft, hard, and conditional.

Soft Page Breaks

When you enter or edit a document, most programs automatically insert page breaks and then automatically adjust them when necessary. A few programs do so only when you paginate or repaginate the document. Either way, the inserted page breaks are *soft page breaks*. If you edit the document so that the length of one or more pages changes, the soft page breaks are relocated automatically or when you repaginate the document so each page is full.

Hard Page Breaks

Normally, page breaks occur automatically when a page is full, but you can also force them to fall at selected points in a document. To force a page break, you insert a *hard page break* where you want text to start printing at the top of the next page. To change a hard page break, you must delete the code you entered to create it. If you are using a page-oriented program, repaging the document rearranges soft page breaks, if necessary, but not hard page breaks.

Conditional Page Breaks

Forced page breaks created with hard page break codes give you a lot of control, but they sometimes create problems. For example, if you find a table broken by a page break, you may insert a hard page break just above the table so that it starts printing on a new page. Later, if you add or delete a section of text above the table, it may print on a new page even though there is room for it on the previous page. You can prevent unwanted page breaks like these with a *conditional page break*. This command tells the printer, "If this section fits in the remaining space on this page, print it here; otherwise, advance the paper, and begin printing it at the top of the next page." This command is extremely useful when you want to:

▪ Keep the lines of a table on the same page as the table headings.
▪ Keep an illustration on the same page as its caption.
▪ Keep a heading and at least the first two lines of the following text on the same page.

Widows and Orphans

The first or last line of a paragraph should never be printed by itself at the bottom or top of a page (Figure 3-46). You should always have at least two lines of a paragraph together on a page. If the last line of a paragraph prints by itself at the top of a page, it is a *widow*. If the first line of a paragraph prints by itself at the bottom of page, it is an *orphan*. The same terms are used for lines that print by themselves at the top and bottom of columns when text is printed in two or more columns on a page.

Most programs have a command that prevents widows and orphans from occurring in your printed documents. If the program calculates that only the first line will print at the bottom of the page, it moves the entire paragraph to the next page. If it calculates that only the last line will print at the top of the next page, it moves another line to accompany it. Thus, no three-line paragraphs will be split; the entire paragraph will move to the next page if it will not print on the

A ──▶ and the last line by itself is a widow.

B ──▶ An orphan is the first line of a paragraph that

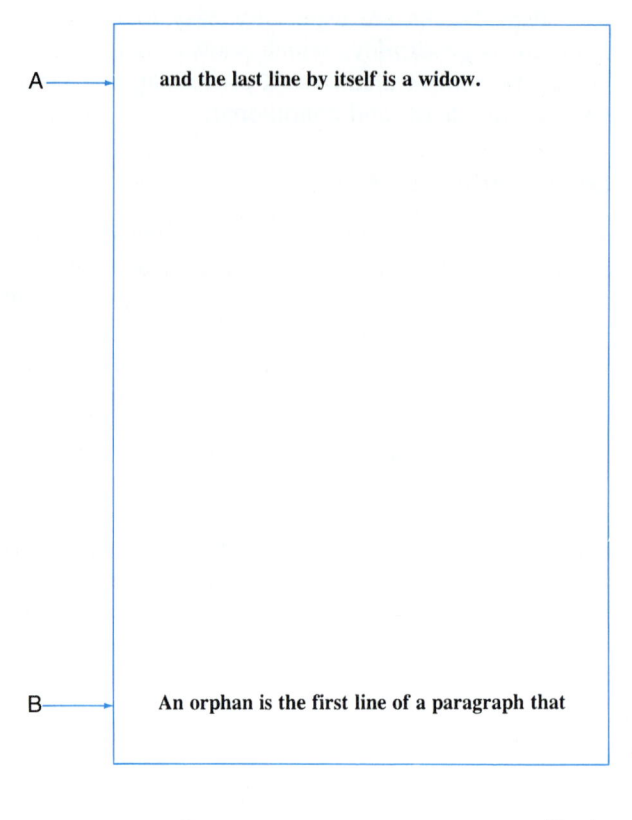

Figure 3-46 Widows and Orphans
Widows and orphans can be prevented. (A) A widow occurs when the last line of a paragraph prints at the top of a new page. (B) An orphan occurs when the first line of a new paragraph prints at the bottom of a page.

current page. On some programs, you can specify the minimum number of lines to appear at the top and bottom of a page.

PAGE NUMBERS

Page numbers can be printed on every page of a multipage document, turned off when printing a single-page letter, or turned off for the first page and on for the second page when printing a two-page letter. This on-off control is sufficient for many documents, but most programs give you much greater control over page numbers. You can control where and how page numbers are printed: centered or aligned with the left or right margin, combined with text, printed on alternate sides of the pages, skipped, started at any desired number, or printed in Arabic or Roman numerals. The way you enter page numbers varies. On some programs, there are special page numbering commands. On others, you enter page number codes in headers and footers.

TEXT ALIGNMENT

Among the most useful features of word processing programs are those you use to align text with the margins. These commands give you a great deal of control over the way your printed document looks. Unlike a typewriter, a word processing program allows you to experiment with alignments without retyping them each time you change them. If you do not like the results you get with one alignment, you can change it without reentering the text. How you align text varies from program to program.

- On some programs, you select the text to be aligned and execute an alignment command.
- On other programs, you enter codes or format lines wherever you want to change the alignment.

168   WORD PROCESSING AND DESKTOP PUBLISHING APPLICATIONS

Flush left. Text aligned with the left margin.

Flush right. Text aligned with the right margin.

Ragged right. Text that has an even left margin and an uneven right margin.

Ragged left. Text that has an even right margin and an uneven left margin.

Justified text. Text that has both right and left margins evenly aligned.

Centered text. Text that is centered midway between the left and right margins or the left and right edges of a spreadsheet cell.

The commands that align text affect entire paragraphs, that is, any section of text that ends with a hard carriage return. To align more than one paragraph, you must either select all the paragraphs and then align them or enter an alignment code above and below the paragraphs to be aligned.

You have four choices when aligning text with the left and right margins (Figure 3-47): You can align it flush with the left margin, flush with the right margin, flush with both margins, or center it between the margins.

- Text is normally aligned with the left margin when you create documents. This text is *flush left*. But there are times when you might want to align it with the right margin, when entering dates and page numbers, for example. This text is *flush right*. If text is aligned with one margin, but the other margin is not, the unaligned margins are **ragged right** or **ragged left**.

- *Justified text* is aligned flush with both the left and right margins. To justify text, the program inserts spaces of varying width between words and letters to expand the lines.

- *Centered text* is normally centered between the left margin and the right margin. But many programs let you change the point that text is centered on. On some, you do this by centering text in a tab stop column. On others, you point to the desired column with the cursor and then execute the centering command. Some programs also have a command that centers text vertically on the page between the top and bottom margins. This command is useful when you are formatting title pages for documents. Generally, the effects of vertical alignment are seen only on the printout of the document; they are not usually displayed on the screen.

A

WordPerfect's default setting is for justified text. Justified text aligns with both the left and right margins. If you turn justification off, text is left-aligned with a ragged right margin. You can also align text with the right margin so that the left margin is ragged, or you can center it between the margins.

B

WordPerfect's default setting is for justified text. Justified text aligns with both the left and right margins. If you turn justification off, text is left-aligned with a ragged right margin. You can also align text with the right margin so that the left margin is ragged, or you can center it between the margins.

C

WordPerfect's default setting is for justified text. Justified text aligns with both the left and right margins. If you turn justification off, text is left-aligned with a ragged right margin. You can also align text with the right margin so that the left margin is ragged, or you can center it between the margins.

D

WordPerfect's default setting is for justified text. Justified text aligns with both the left and right margins. If you turn justification off, text is left-aligned with a ragged right margin. You can also align text with the right margin so that the left margin is ragged, or you can center it between the margins.

Figure 3-47 Aligning Text with the Left and Right Margins
You can (A) full-justify text, or (B) align it left, (C) right, or (D) centered.

Hyphenation zone. The zone on either side of the right margin in which words are hyphenated.

Soft hyphen. A hyphen that appears only in the word (on the printout) if, when a paragraph is reformed before printing, it is required.

HYPHENATION

Programs that automatically reform paragraphs often have a separate Hyphenation command. To hyphenate a document, you move the cursor to the top of the document, and execute the Hyphenation command. The program then scrolls through the text, or you do so manually. When a word falls within the hyphenation zone, the program pauses and suggests where you might place a hyphen. The *hyphenation zone* (Figure 3-48) is a specified number of columns on either side of the right margin setting. If a word begins before or at the left edge of the hyphenation zone and extends past its right edge, you are asked if you want to hyphenate it. You have three options: You can accept the suggestion, use the directional arrow keys to move the cursor to where you want the hyphen, or tell the program not to hyphenate the word.

- If you hyphenate the word, the hyphen is the last character on the line; the rest of the word wraps to the beginning of the next line.
- If you do not hyphenate, the entire word wraps to the next line.

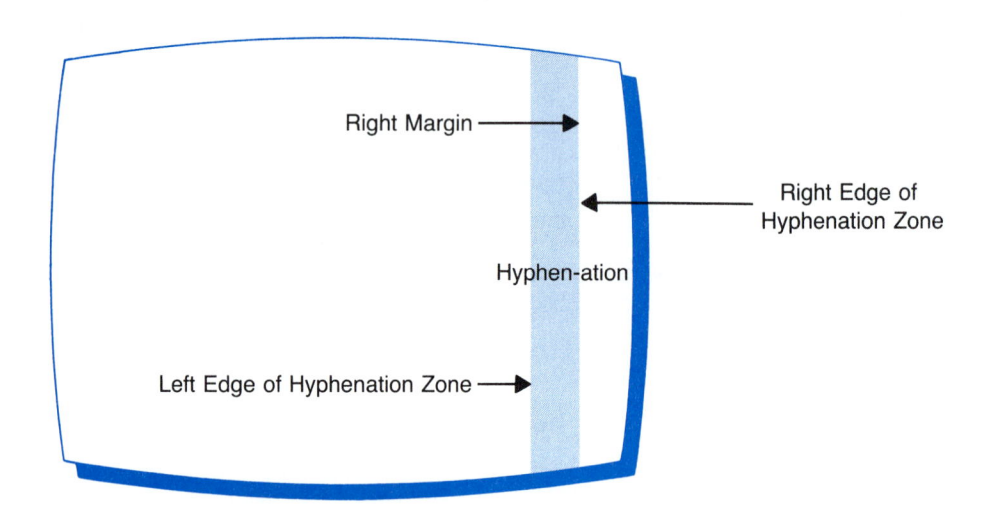

Figure 3-48 Hyphenation Zone
You can revise the hyphenation zone. Here, the left edge of the zone has been set eight columns to the left of the left margin. The right edge of the zone has been set in the same column as the left margin. When a word begins at or before the left edge of the zone and extends past the right edge, you are asked if you want to hyphenate it. The narrower the zone, the more words there are hyphenated.

Bold

Underline

Double Underline

Italic

SMALL CAPS

Figure 3-49 Text Emphasis
Text can be emphasized by changing its style or appearance.

You should always hyphenate just before printing. The slightest change in the wording or punctuation may change the position of words so that hyphenated words no longer fall at the end of lines. Because the hyphens are *soft hyphens*, they do not print out if you revise the text so they no longer fall at the end of the line. To hyphenate the correct words, you have to hyphenate the document again.

TEXT EMPHASIS

Word processing programs offer several formats you can use to emphasize text. For example, you can boldface or underline headings, keywords, disclaimers, and book titles (Figure 3-49). You can use these formats for individual char-

170 WORD PROCESSING AND DESKTOP PUBLISHING APPLICATIONS

- $^1/_2$
- Trademark^{tm}
- Registration^R
- 30^oF
- H_2O
- $1 - ^3/_4 = ^1/_4$

Figure 3-50 Superscripts and Subscripts
Superscripts print above the line, and subscripts below the line. They have several applications. For example, you can use them to create fractions, formulas, trademark symbols, copyright symbols, registration marks, temperature degrees, and footnote symbols.

Boldface. A character enhancement that makes the letter or word appear darker when printed out.

Underline. A format used to emphasize text by printing a line under it. Also called underscoring.

Superscript. A number, word, or phrase positioned above the rest of the line.

Subscript. A number, word, or phrase positioned below the rest of the line.

Gutter margin. A special margin on alternate pages of a document that is to be printed on both sides of the page. The wider gutter margin accommodates a binding.

Margin Release. A command that allows you to enter text to the left of the left margin.

acters, words, lines, paragraphs, or entire documents. You can also combine them; for example, you can both boldface and underline a heading.

- *Boldfaced* text is darker than normal text and can be used to emphasize section and table headings or keywords in a document. Impact printers print boldfaced characters by striking the character two or three times. Laser printers must have access to a separate boldfaced font as they cannot restrike the same characters to create a darker image. Some programs have two boldface commands: One command strikes the character three times for boldface, and another strikes the character twice for doublestrike.

- *Underlining* (also called *underscoring*) can be used to indicate titles of books or articles or to divide sections in financial reports. There are a two basic underscore styles, continuous and noncontinuous, and some programs offer you a choice. Continuous style underscores words and the spaces between the words. Noncontinuous style underscores words but not the spaces between them. Some programs also offer both single and double underline options. These are useful when you are creating financial statements and other documents with subtotals and totals. Although some programs offer these options, they also must be supported by the printer type element or font.

Besides boldfacing, underlining, and striking out characters, some programs offer additional formats. For example, small caps uses all capital letters in different sizes, and shadow print prints each letter with a shadowy effect.

Most word processors allow you to enter **superscripts** above and **subscripts** below the normal line of text. Superscripts and subscripts can be used to print copyright marks, trademark symbols, formulas, and footnote numbers (Figure 3-50).

HORIZONTAL LAYOUT

Margin settings determine where the first and last characters on a line are printed. You can change margins for an entire document or for individual paragraphs (Figure 3-51). The way you specify left and right margins varies.

- On older programs, you set the left and right margins in characters or columns.
- On the latest programs, you set the left and right margins in inches.

Margins set in inches make it much easier to change pitch and fonts and to use proportional spacing because the margins are retained, despite how many characters are printed per inch. The program does all the calculations needed to retain the margins on the printed page.

Gutter Margins

The **gutter margin** command (also called a *binding margin* or *binding width* command) is used when you want to reproduce bound copies of a document that is printed or copied on both sides of the page. This command increases the width of the margin by a specified amount on the side of the pages to be bound or hole punched (Figure 3-52).

Entering Text to the Left of the Left Margin

When you enter text and words wrap, or when you press **Enter**, the cursor always returns to the left margin setting. To enter text to the left of the left margin (Figure 3-53), you use the **Margin Release** command.

FORMATTING DOCUMENTS   **171**

Figure 3-51 Left and Right Margins
You can change margins selectively to improve a document's appearance and impact. For example, this figure shows headings flush with the left margin and text margins changed so that the text stands out from the rest of the document.

VERTICAL LAYOUT

Top and bottom margins determine the space left blank at the top and bottom of a page.

- On most new programs, you set the top and bottom margins and the page length in inches. The program then calculates the space available for text lines.
- On some programs, you set the top and bottom margins in lines, and the number of text lines is set indirectly.

Again, programs that allow you to set top and bottom margins and page lengths in inches make it easier to change type sizes. If you enlarge or reduce the type, the program automatically recalculates how many lines fit on a page.

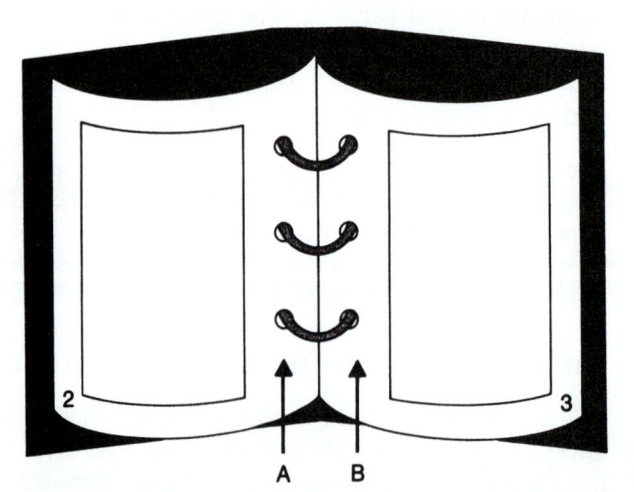

Figure 3-52 Gutter Margin
The Gutter Margin command adds to the width of the margin on the binding side—the right margin on (A) even pages and the left margin on (B) odd pages.

Header. A line or lines of text printed in the top margin of each page of a document. A header may contain the page number, date, time, and so on.

Footer. A line or lines of text printed in the bottom margin of each page of a document. A footer may contain the page number, date, time, and so on.

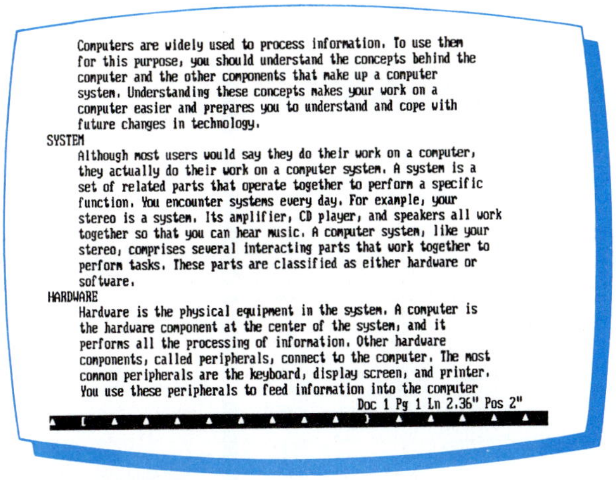
Computers are widely used to process information. To use them for this purpose, you should understand the concepts behind the computer and the other components that make up a computer system. Understanding these concepts makes your work on a computer easier and prepares you to understand and cope with future changes in technology.

SYSTEM

Although most users would say they do their work on a computer, they actually do their work on a computer system. A system is a set of related parts that operate together to perform a specific function. You encounter systems every day. For example, your stereo is a system. Its amplifier, CD player, and speakers all work together so that you can hear music. A computer system, like your stereo, comprises several interacting parts that work together to perform tasks. These parts are classified as either hardware or software.

HARDWARE

Hardware is the physical equipment in the system. A computer is the hardware component at the center of the system, and it performs all the processing of information. Other hardware components, called peripherals, connect to the computer. The most common peripherals are the keyboard, display screen, and printer. You use these peripherals to feed information into the computer

Doc 1 Pg 1 Ln 2.36" Pos 2"

Figure 3-53 Margin Release
You can use the Margin Release command to enter headings or other text in the left margin area. It can also be used for hanging indents, enumerations, and other effects.

Page Length

The page length setting determines where the printer stops printing and advances to the top of the next page. Page length is simply the distance from the top of a sheet of paper to the bottom. When using continuous form paper, envelopes, or labels, you measure the page length from the top of one sheet to the top of the next sheet.

Line Spacing

You can change line spacing for an entire document or for individual paragraphs (Figure 3-54). Some programs display the specified line spacing on the screen; other programs always display single spacing on the screen to make it faster to scroll through the document. When you print the document, the line spacing is whatever you have specified.

Lines per Page

The number of lines printed on a page is based on the length of the paper, the settings for the top and bottom margins, the size of the type used on the page, the line height and line spacing, and the number of lines occupied by headers and footers (Figure 3-55).

HEADERS AND FOOTERS

You can add headers and footers to your document. ***Headers*** are text printed at the top of the page. ***Footers*** are text printed at the bottom of the page. The advantage of using the Header and Footer commands is that you enter the text only once, and it is then printed on any pages you specify. Headers and footers

Line spacing can be changed throughout a document. Here, one paragraph is *single spaced* and another is double spaced.

Line spacing can be changed throughout a document.

Here, one paragraph is single spaced and another is

double spaced.

Figure 3-54 Line Spacing
Line spacing can be changed throughout a document. Here, one paragraph is single spaced and another is double spaced.

Running feet. Footers that print on two or more consecutive pages.

Running heads. Headers that print two or more consecutive pages.

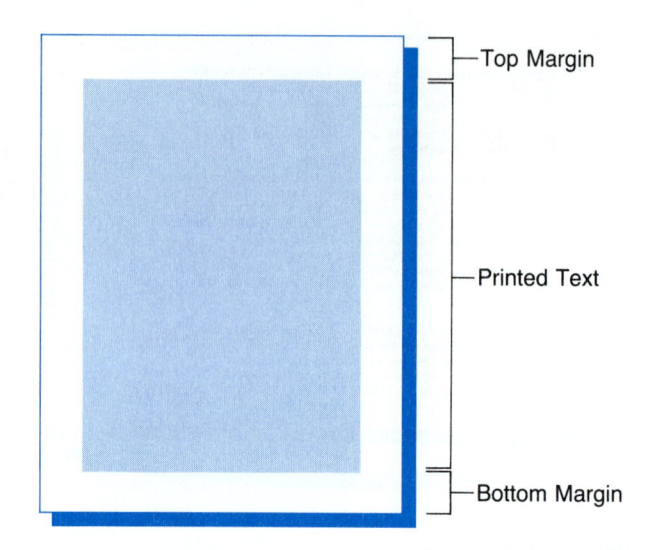

Figure 3-55 Vertical Spacing
Vertical spacing of a document is controlled by the page length, the top and bottom margins, the line spacing, and the size of the type used to print with.

(Figure 3-56) can be printed on a single page or on every page of a document. When printed on more than one page of a document, they are called *running heads* or *running feet*.

When you enter headers and footers, the program normally aligns them flush left on a specific line of the page. However, you can usually align them with the left or right edge of the page or center them between the margins. You can also move them up and down or discontinue them on selected pages.

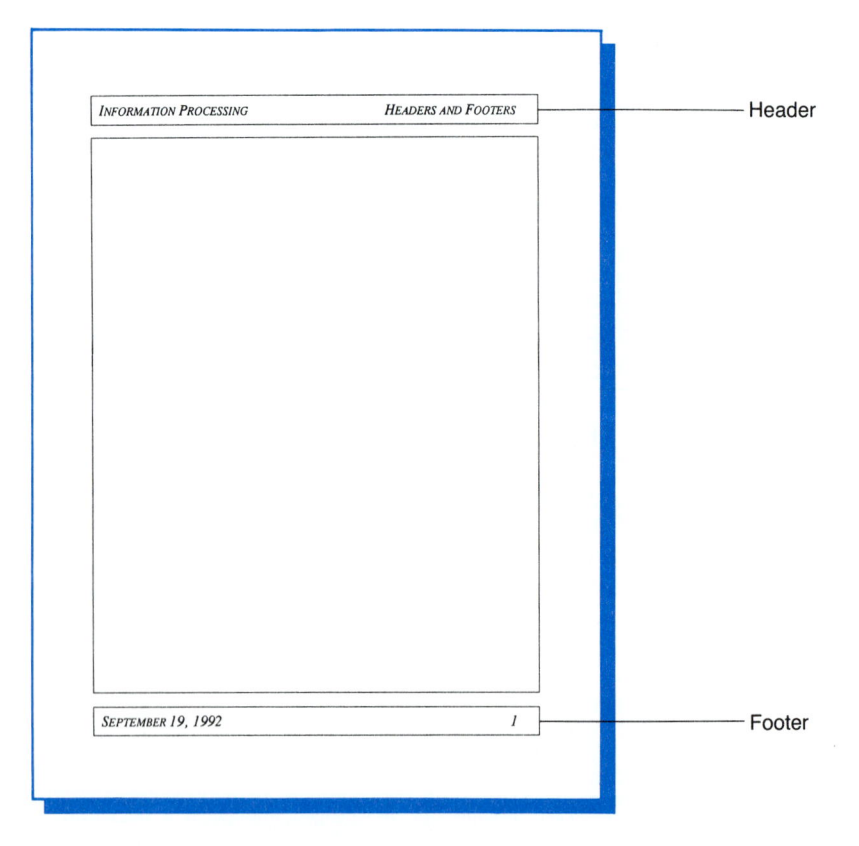

Figure 3-56 Headers and Footers
Headers are lines of text that are printed in the top margin of each page of a document. Footers are the same but are printed in the bottom margin of the page.

174   WORD PROCESSING AND DESKTOP PUBLISHING APPLICATIONS

Footnotes. Numbered notes printed at the bottom of a page that correspond to reference numbers on the same page. See Endnotes.

Endnotes. Numbered notes printed at the end of a document that correspond to reference numbers within the document. See also Footnotes.

Many programs can automatically number, date, and time-stamp pages of a document as it is printed. These features are special forms of headers or footers. Unlike headers and footers that simply repeat text, these features are calculated by the program. You enter special symbols or codes into headers or footers and they calculate and print the current page number or read the current date and time from the computer's clock. The advantage of using the clock is that the dates and times change automatically each time the document is printed; thus, it is easier to keep track of the various versions of the same document.

FOOTNOTES AND ENDNOTES

Footnotes are numbered references printed at the bottom of the page (Figure 3-57). ***Endnotes*** are just like footnotes, but instead of printing at the bottom of the same page that the reference number appears on, they are printed at the end of a section, or at the end of the document. The numbers in the footnotes or endnotes match the numbers in the text that refer to them. For example, immediately following an author's name, you can enter a footnote reference number. When you enter a footnote, a special screen may be displayed where you type it. When you print the document, the codes entered in the document are printed as sequential numbers, and the footnotes they refer to are printed at the bottom of the same page. When you insert new footnotes or delete old ones, all footnote references in the document are automatically renumbered.

FOOTNOTES

In a note system of documentation, the first time you refer to a source in your writing, the note gives complete bibliographic facts as well as the specific place you are referring to or quoting from in that source. Here are first-reference note forms for common sources.

- Book with one author[1]
- Book with two or three authors[2]
- Book with a corporate author[3]
- Work in several volumes or parts[4]
- Works in an anthology or a collection[5]
- Article in a reference work[6]
- Article from a weekly or biweekly magazine or newspaper[7]
- Article from a monthly periodical[8]
- Article from a daily newspaper[9]
- Film[10]
- Interview[11]

After the first note for a source, you should shorten all further references to the source. If you are citing only one work by the author, the author's last name an the page references are enough. If you are citing more than one work by the same author, you must include a shortened form of the title of the particular book-along with the author's last name and the page reference.

- Second Reference to a single work by the same author[12]
- Second reference to more than one work by the same author[13]

---

[1]First Last, Title (City, State; Publisher, copyright date), pages.

[2] Fist Last, First Last, and First Last, Title, (City, state; Publisher, copyright date), pages.

[3]Name of Corporation, Title, (City, state; Publisher, copyright date), pages.

[4] First Last, Title, Volume or Part (City, state; Publisher, copyright date), pages.

[5] First Last, "Title of Article," in Title of Publication, ed. (City, state; Publisher, copyright date), pages.

[6] "Title of section," Title of Book, copyright or edition date.

[7] First Last, "Title of Article," Name of Periodical, date, section, page, column.

[8] First Last, "Title of Article," Name of Periodical, date, section, page, column.

[9] First Last, "Title of Article," Name of Newspaper, date of issue, page.

[10] First Last, dir., Film Title, with Major Actor, Studio, date

[11] Personal interview with Title First Last, date.

[12] Last, page

[13] Last, Title, page

Figure 3-57
Footnotes
Footnotes appear at the bottoms of the same pages as the references to them in the document.

EXERCISE

Exercise 3-8A
FORMATTING DOCUMENTS

Table 3-6 lists typical formatting procedures. List the commands for your program that accomplish each procedure.

Table 3-6
FORMATTING COMMANDS

Procedure	Enter Commands for Your Program
Enter a hard page break	
Add page numbers	
Center text	
Hyphenate a document	
Boldface a word	
Underline a word	
Change line spacing	
Add a header	
Add a footer	
Add a footnote	

QUESTIONS

1. How do you override default formats?
2. What is a page break? Why would you want to control them?
3. What is the difference between a soft and a hard page break?
4. What is a conditional page break command?
5. What are the differences between a hard page break and a conditional page break?
6. What are widows and orphans, and why do you want to prevent their occurring?
7. What are two common ways programs print page numbers?
8. List four ways you can align text, and give some examples of when you might want to use the alignments.
9. Why do you hyphenate a document? When do you do so?
10. What is a hyphenation zone?
11. List two ways to emphasize text.
12. What is the difference between continuous and noncontinuous underlining?
13. Describe superscripts and subscripts, and give examples of when you might want to use them.

14. What two ways are used by programs to set left and right margins?
15. What is a Gutter Margin command, and when would you want to use it?
16. What command do you use to enter text to the left of the left margin?
17. What are headers and footers? Why are they used?
18. What are headers and footers that appear on more than one page called?
19. List and describe some options you have when printing headers and footers.
20. What is the difference between a footnote and an endnote?
21. What happens to a footnote reference number if you insert a new reference number above it?

3-9 MERGE PRINTING

Primary document.
The document used in merge printing that contains the text to appear in all copies and the codes that instruct the program what data to insert during merge printing and where to insert them.

Variables. Personalized data that are inserted into a form letter to customize it.

Secondary document.
A file that stores variables to be merged into a primary file while merge printing to create many customized documents. Secondary files are organized in fields and records.

One advantage of word processing programs is the way they allow you to automate your work. Instead of individually entering and editing tens, hundreds, or thousands of letters, envelopes, mailing labels, forms, or other documents, you can merge print them. Merge printing lets you create one document and then enter personalized data into each copy as it is being printed. This can greatly increase your speed in preparing documents such as form letters for billing or scheduling appointments, which are essentially the same, except for minor changes, from copy to copy.

The first step in merge printing form letters is to create the needed files. When using this feature, you enter the information that is to be printed into every document in the **primary document** (also called the *template*, *shell document*, *main document*, *master document*, or *merge document*). Data to be inserted into this primary document to personalize each copy when it is printed are called *variables* because they vary from letter to letter. You can store these variables in a second file, called a **secondary document** (also called a *data file*, *database*, or *variables file*). When you then **merge print** the primary document, it is printed over and over again, with the variables specific to each copy inserted automatically from the secondary document (Figure 3-58).

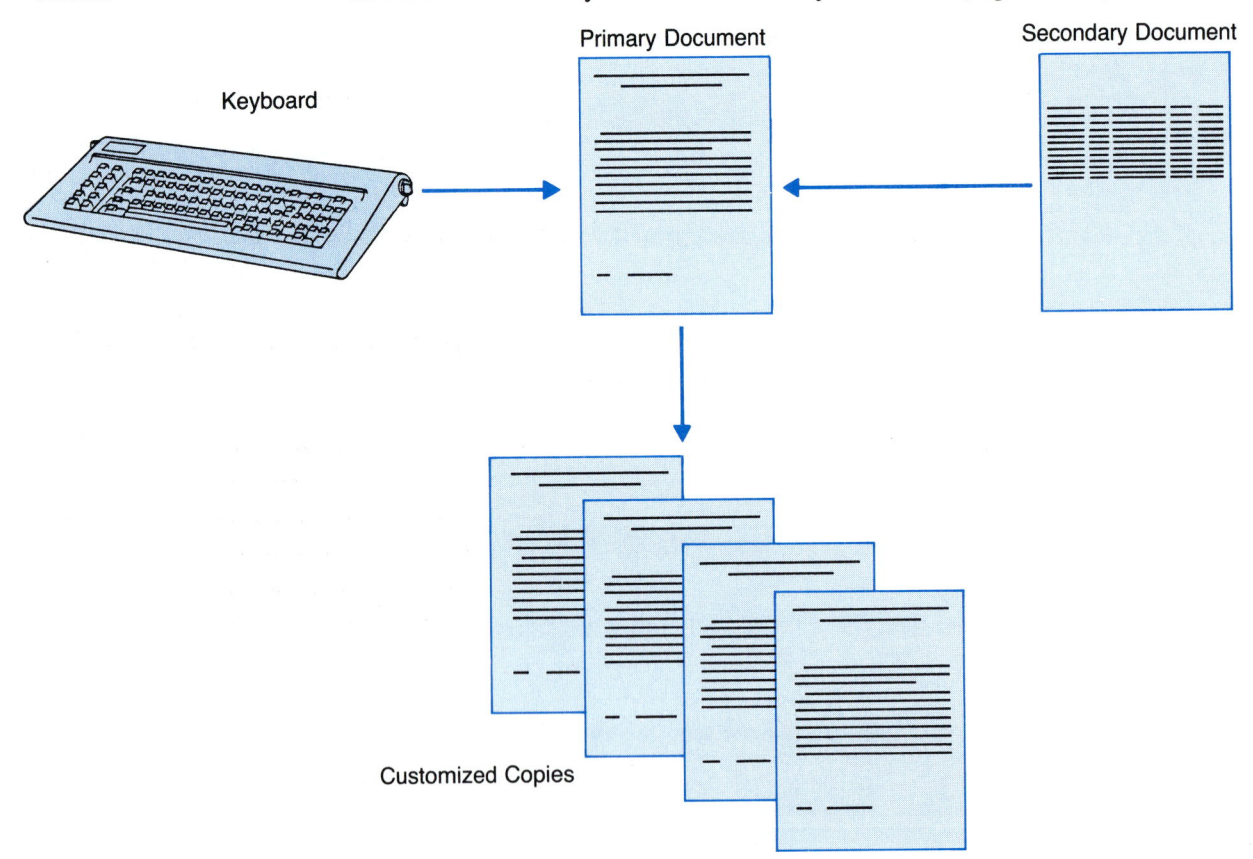

Figure 3-58 Merge Printing
When you merge print a primary document, codes in that file automatically insert data from a data file on the disk or prompt you to insert them from the keyboard. As the data are inserted, multiple customized copies are printed.

Merge printing. Inserting variables into a primary document to produce many customized documents. Variables can be entered from the keyboard or stored in a secondary file from which they are automatically merged into the form document while it is being merge printed.

Merge code. A code inserted into a primary document that specifies what information is to be inserted from the keyboard or from a secondary file. When the primary document is merge printed, the merge code is replaced with data entered manually from the keyboard or automatically from the secondary file.

Field. Any individual item that makes up a record in a record file or database file.

THE PRIMARY DOCUMENT

The program knows where to insert the data because the primary document is coded (Figure 3-59). These *merge codes* refer to information in the secondary document or indicate places where data will be typed in from the keyboard. When the document is merge printed, the codes are replaced with data from the secondary document or with data typed in from the keyboard. For example, one merge code might specify that the person's name is to be inserted from the secondary document, and another code might specify that the person's street address is to be inserted.

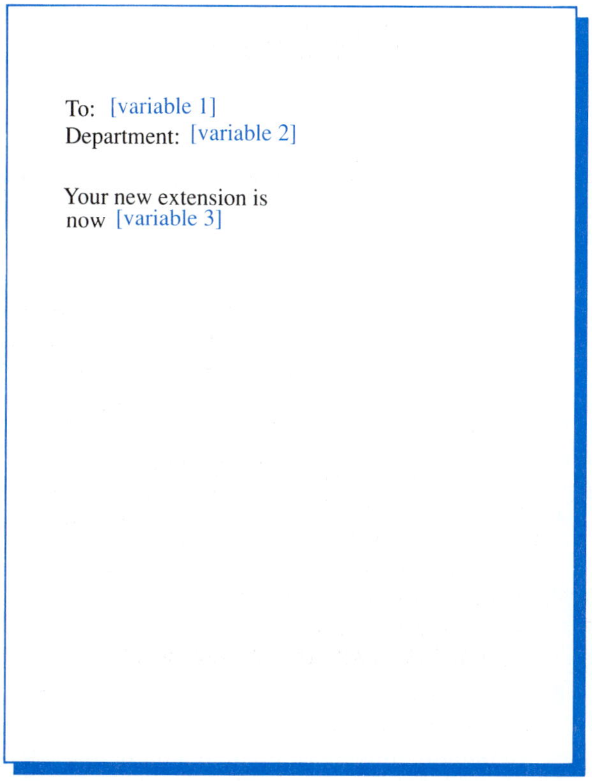

```
To: [variable 1]
Department: [variable 2]

Your new extension is
now [variable 3]
```

Figure 3-59 The Primary Document
The codes in a primary document control the merge-print process. Codes can be entered to tell the program where to insert data automatically from a separate data file or to pause the printer so that data can be entered manually from the keyboard.

THE SECONDARY DOCUMENT

The secondary document (also called a *record file*) stores the variables that you want inserted into each copy of the primary document when you merge print it. The variables are organized in the file into fields and records (Figure 3-60).

Fields

A *field* is a specific piece of information, for example, a person's name. Fields can be names (Smith), numbers (100.10), names and numbers (100 Main Street), or formulas (100*3).

All programs have rules that you must follow when you enter information into the fields in a secondary file. For example,

- If the entry contains commas or colons, you may have to enclose it in double quotation marks. For example, you would enter a name as "Smith, John."

MERGE PRINTING 179

3-9

Record. A group of related fields, such as names and addresses, that make up a database or record file.

Delimiter. A symbol (frequently a comma or colon) that separates two fields in a record file or two cell coordinates in a spreadsheet formula or function.

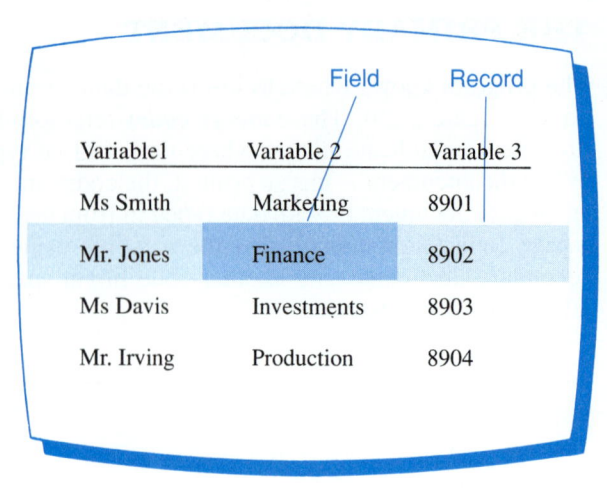

	Field	Record
Variable 1	Variable 2	Variable 3
Ms Smith	Marketing	8901
Mr. Jones	Finance	8902
Ms Davis	Investments	8903
Mr. Irving	Production	8904

Figure 3-60 The Secondary Document Fields and records in a secondary document organize the data in a record file. A field is a specific piece of information, e.g., a name (Mr. Jones), a department (Finance), or a phone extension (8902). A record is a collection of fields that describe a specific item or person, e.g., Mr. Jones, Finance, 8902.

- If the entry contains quotation marks, you might have to enter them in pairs and then enclose the entire entry in another set of quotation marks. For example, "Charles" "Fats" "Waller."
- The entry might have a length limitation.

When you first create a secondary document file, you should plan ahead so that the data are organized in such a way that you can use it effectively.

- If you want to be able to sort a mailing list by ZIP codes, they must be entered in a separate field.
- If you want to use the last name in the salutation, it must be in a separate field. If you have only one field for the entire name, your letter might read "Dear Mr. John Smith" instead of "Dear Mr. Smith."
- The number of lines used in addresses varies. One address might require only three lines, and another might require five. Set up your fields for the maximum number of lines. If a particular address is shorter, you can leave those fields blank.

Records

Related fields are stored together as *records*, for example, a person's name, address, and phone number make up a record. Each record must have the same fields, and data must be entered in the same order into each record. The fields in each record are separated from each other by a *delimiter*, usually a comma or colon or entered into tables.

MERGE PRINTING

When the two documents are completed, you merge print them to print multiple copies of the primary document, each with a different set of variables (Figure 3-61). As the first letter is being printed, the program stops at each code in the primary document, goes to the first record in the secondary document and inserts data from the specified field, and then continues printing. After all the requested fields from the first record have been inserted, the first copy advances from the printer, and the second copy is printed. But this time, the program inserts data from the second record in the secondary document. This continues until all the records in the secondary document have been used.

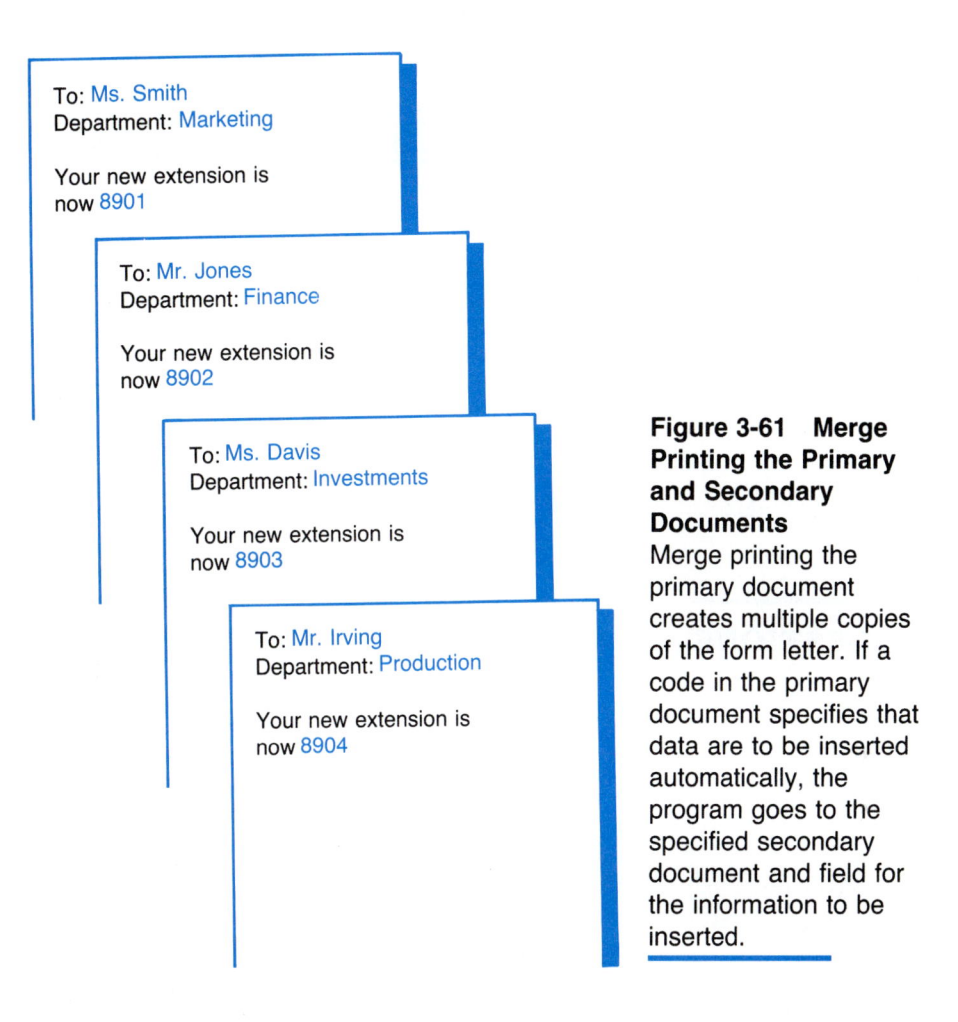

To: Ms. Smith
Department: Marketing

Your new extension is now 8901

To: Mr. Jones
Department: Finance

Your new extension is now 8902

To: Ms. Davis
Department: Investments

Your new extension is now 8903

To: Mr. Irving
Department: Production

Your new extension is now 8904

Figure 3-61 Merge Printing the Primary and Secondary Documents
Merge printing the primary document creates multiple copies of the form letter. If a code in the primary document specifies that data are to be inserted automatically, the program goes to the specified secondary document and field for the information to be inserted.

EXERCISES

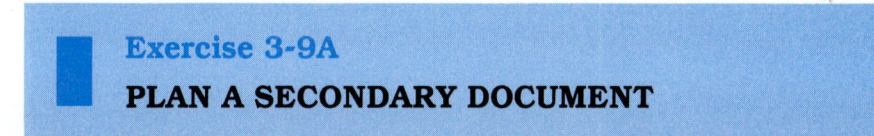

Exercise 3-9A
PLAN A SECONDARY DOCUMENT

You have been assigned the job of merge printing a letter to several important customers. A few of the names on the mailing list are as follows:

Mr. John Lewis, Campbell Corporation, 300 Elm Street, Rochester, NY 10000
Mrs. Shelly Anthony, Fidget, Inc., 100 Main Street, Fresno, CA 10001
Ms. Roberta Cross, President, Computer Corporation, 10010 Oak Road, Bethesda, MD 20000

List and describe the fields you would use to store these names and addresses in a secondary document.

MERGE PRINTING   **181**

Exercise 3-9A
MERGE PRINT A DOCUMENT

Refer to a word processing program's user's guide and list the procedures you follow to merge print a document.

1. _____

2. _____

3. _____

QUESTIONS

1. What are the two files you need for automatic merge printing?
2. Describe a primary document and what its function is.
3. Describe a secondary document and what its function is.
4. Describe fields and records.

3-10 DESKTOP PUBLISHING

In the early days of computers, people who used them for word processing had to use two programs. One program, a text editor, was used to enter and edit text. When the document was completed, a second program, a text formatter, was used to format the document for printing. Today, we find ourselves in a similar position, though at a much higher level. One of the fastest-growing areas within word processing is desktop publishing, which makes it possible to produce documents that look like the documents printed by professional printers. A complete desktop publishing system lets you print text using a variety of fonts (typestyles and typefaces); it also lets you combine line art and photographs on the same page. A complete system lets you print in columns and add special textures, patterns, and lines. Desktop publishing programs that improve the printed quality of documents are being widely used to create forms, newsletters, manuals, charts, brochures, letterheads, logos, catalogs, and reports (Figure 3-62).

Today, word processing and desktop publishing programs overlap more and more. Word processing programs are still better for entering and editing documents, and desktop publishing programs are still better for formatting them. However more and more desktop publishing features are being incorporated into word processing programs. Increasingly, you are able to create, edit, format, and lay out sophisticated documents using only one program.

A complete desktop publishing system includes several components, some of which are also used for other work on the computer. The best systems allow you to preview the results while working on a document, called WYSIWYG (pronounced "whizzy-wig"), or "what you see is what you get." Regardless of the program or system that you use, the features that separate programs with desktop publishing capabilities from those without them include text-handling and graphics-handling features.

Figure 3-62 Desktop Published Documents
Documents created with a desktop publishing program look as if they were professionally prepared and printed.
Courtesy of Aldus Corporation

3-10

Figure 3-63 A Typeball Font
The characters on a typeball are all the same size and all have the same style, so they are a font.
Courtesy of International Business Machines Corporation

Leading. The space between printed lines of text.

Font. A complete set of characters in one type style and type size.

Typeface. A specific type design, for example, Courier or Times Roman.

- You can choose from a wide selection of type fonts.
- You can rotate type to print it in portrait or landscape mode. Some programs allow you to rotate type 360 degrees so that it can be oriented in any direction.
- You can vertically justify text by adding **leading**, that is, space, between lines so that the first and last lines on each page print in the same position even if the number of lines is different.
- You can create multiple columns and justify the text in one or all of them.
- You can print dropout type, white characters against a dark background.
- You can import graphics and print them side by side with text or put them together with text in boxes.
- You can crop, shrink, enlarge, rotate, and move images.
- You can add vertical, horizontal, or diagonal rules of different widths.
- You can use shades of gray to shade boxes or add patterns.

FONTS

One of the hallmarks of professionally prepared documents is the selective use of different styles and sizes of type. This textbook, for example, uses one typestyle and type size for main headings, another for less important headings, another for the text itself, and still another for captions. The visual quality of the final text is much higher than that of the draft it was prepared from.

A *font* is a complete set of the characters you need to print a document in one typestyle and type size. Pick up a typeball from a typewriter, and you are holding a font (Figure 3-63). The importance of fonts has increased as word processing technology has improved and, especially, as printers have become able to print a wide variety of typestyles and type sizes. Fonts are available in many designs or typefaces, each typeface has several typestyles, and each typestyle comes in various sizes (Figure 3-64). Fonts can also have a fixed pitch or be proportionally spaced. Let's look at these characteristics of fonts.

Typefaces

Typeface refers to the type's particular design. Typical typefaces include Elite, Pica, Gothic, Helvetica, Times Roman, and Baskerville.

TYPEFACE	TYPESTYLE	TYPE SIZE
Times Roman Helvetica Courier	Normal **Bold** *Italic*	8 point 10 point 12 point 14 point 18 point

Figure 3-64 Fonts
Fonts come in many typefaces. Each typeface has several variations called typestyles, and each typestyle comes in several sizes.

184   WORD PROCESSING AND DESKTOP PUBLISHING APPLICATIONS

Typestyle. A version of a typeface, for example, bold or italic.

Type size. The size of a printed character, usually specified in points.

Pitch. The number of characters printed per inch. The most frequently used pitches are 10 pitch (pica) and 12 pitch (elite): there are either 10 or 12 characters to the inch.

Points. A unit of measure for type; a point is approximately 1/72 of a inch.

```
This is 10 pitch Courier (Elite).
This is 12 pitch Courier (Pica).
```

Figure 3-65   Pitch
You can change pitch in a document if this command is supported by the printer. For example, you can change from Elite to Pica.

Typestyles

Most typefaces come in several variations called *typestyles*, for example, light, medium, bold, extra bold, italic, expanded, and condensed. These variations are important, especially when you are printing on a laser printer. Because a laser printer cannot backspace over a character to make it darker, it must have access to a normal version of the selected typestyle to print regular text and a bold or italic version to print boldfaced or italicized text. If the printer has access only to Times Roman Normal and Times Roman Bold, you cannot print text in Times Roman Italic.

Type Sizes and Character Spacing

Type size, the size of the printed character, is specified either by pitch or in points.

Pitch. *Pitch* refers to the number of characters printed per inch. If you are typing on a typewriter, you can generally switch from 10 pitch to 12 pitch. This means the typewriter can print either 10 or 12 characters per inch. You can do the same on a word processing program if it has Courier or another fixed pitch typeface (Figure 3-65). Changing the pitch changes letter spacing and affects the number of characters printed per inch and per line.

Points. The size of type is specified in *points*. Each point equals 0.0138 (about 1/72) inch. Because the size of the type determines both its horizontal and vertical size, it determines how many characters can be printed on a line and the number of lines that can be printed on a page (Figure 3-66). On pro-

6 points
8 points
10 points
12 points
14 points
18 points
24 points
30 points
48 points

Figure 3-66   Font Size
Font sizes range from very small to very large.

DESKTOP PUBLISHING   **185**

Fixed pitch allocates the same space to each character whether it is a wide *w* or a narrow *i*.

Proportional spacing allocates more space for wide characters than for narrow ones.

Kerning is a further extension of proportional spacing. It considers the characters a letter is next to. Some characters are printed so that they actually overlap, as an uppercase *T* overlaps an adjacent lowercase *a*.

Figure 3-67   Fixed Pitch and Proportional Spacing
Fonts with fixed pitch differ from those with proportional spacing.

Fixed pitch.   When characters are printed without taking their width into consideration. Each character occupies the same space.

Proportional spacing.   A method of assigning more or less space to characters based on their width. For example, an *m* is given more space than an *i* when it is printed out on a printer.

Kerning.   A way of spacing pairs of printed characters so that they are closer together.

Portrait mode.   Printing a page so that the printed text or image is aligned with the short axis of the paper. See also Landscape mode.

grams where you specify margins in characters and lines, you may have to change the margins when you change the type size. On programs where you specify margins in inches, you do not have to change the margins when you change the type size. The program calculates the number of characters that will fit on a line and the number of lines that fit on a page while retaining the specified margins.

Character Spacing.   Fonts space characters using fixed pitch or proportional spacing (Figure 3-67). ***Fixed pitch*** uses the same space for each letter, whether a wide *w* or a narrow *i*. ***Proportional spacing*** varies the space between the characters, depending on the width of the letter. Proportionally spaced, a *w* is given more space than an *i*. On some programs, you can also kern text. ***Kerning*** controls the spacing between letters to give a very finished appearance to the text.

Portrait and Landscape Modes

Portrait or *landscape* refers to the orientation of the printout on the page (Figure 3-68). ***Portrait mode*** is a normal document; that is, text is printed across the width of the page. ***Landscape mode***, which is useful when you are printing wide tables and illustrations, rotates the image 90 degrees so that it is printed along the length of the page. On some printers, you can switch between modes by changing the orientation of the paper in the printer. On others, landscape mode must be supported by the printer, and all printers do not support this mode because they do not have the necessary landscape fonts.

Changing Fonts

You change fonts for characters, words, or phrases by entering codes into the document. These codes do not appear in your printouts, but they instruct the printer what to do. You enter these codes by typing them or by selecting a font from a menu. When you print the document, the codes tell the printer what font to use. For the printer to change fonts, it must be able to access them. Fully formed character printers can change fonts only if the program allows you to enter ***stop codes***, which instruct the printer to pause so that you can change type elements.

Laser and other dot-matrix printers can change fonts only if the font is available to the printer when needed. Fonts are made available to the printer in four ways: internally, in a cartridge, downloaded into the printer's memory, or scaled to the required size when needed.

- ***Internal fonts*** are stored in the printer's memory and are always available. All the latest dot-matrix printers have a few fonts stored in ROM inside the printer.

- ***Font cartridges*** (Figure 3-69) are cartridges that you plug into the printer. To change a font cartridge, you have to turn off the printer, plug in the new cartridge, and then turn on the printer.

- ***Downloadable fonts*** (also called *soft fonts*) come on disks just like other software. To use them, you download, or transfer, the desired fonts into the printer's memory so that the printer has access to them when it needs them. One technique to increase the available number of fonts is to have the printer load only those fonts needed at the time. When it needs another font, it removes the current font from its memory and downloads another from the disk. Although this slows down the printer, it increases the number of fonts available for a document.

Figure 3-68 Portrait and Landscape Mode
Portrait or landscape refers to the orientation of the printout on the page.

Landscape mode rotates the document 90 degrees so that it is printed along the length of the page.

Portrait mode is like a normal document; that is, text is printed across the width of the page.

Landscape mode. Printing a page so that the printed text or image is aligned with the long axis of the paper. See also Portrait mode.

Stop codes. Codes that tell the printer to pause until a specified key is pressed.

Internal fonts. Fonts that are built into a printer so they are available at all times.

Font cartridge. A cartridge that you plug into a printer that contains fonts.

Downloadable font. A font stored on a disk so that you can transfer it to the printer when needed.

Bit-mapped fonts. Fonts that have a fixed size. See also scalable fonts.

Scalable fonts. Fonts that can be printed in any size within a specified range.

■ Each font can be either a bit-mapped font or a scalable font. *Bit-mapped fonts* are fixed in size. *Scalable fonts* can be set to any size within a specified range. For example, a printer may have a font that can be scaled to any size between 6 points and 99 points. Scalable fonts are ideal because they take up much less space on a hard disk and there are many more available sizes.

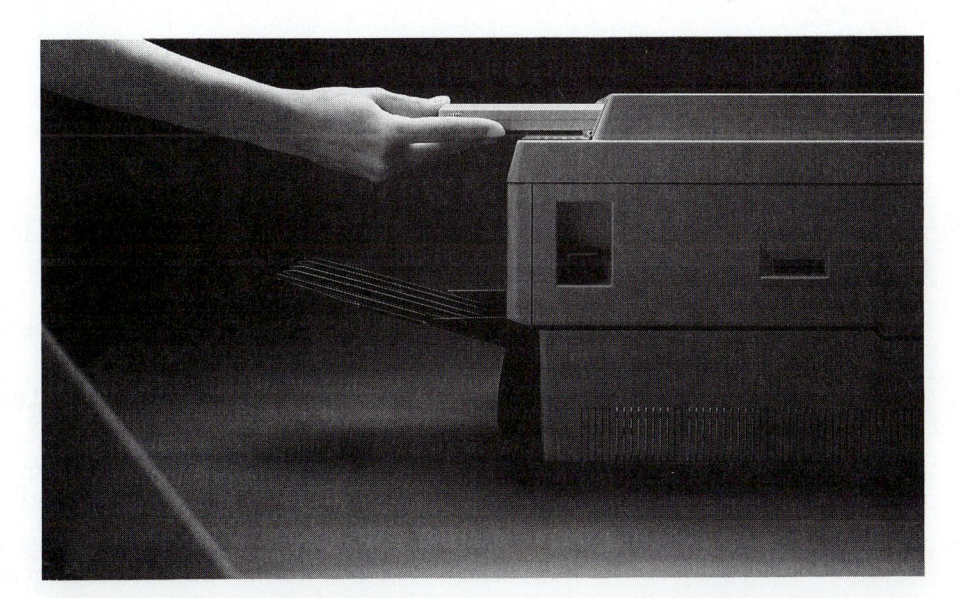

Figure 3-69 Font Cartridges
Font cartridges contain several fonts and are plugged into the printer to make these fonts available when they are specified in a document that you want to print.
Photo courtesy of Hewlett-Packard Company

DESKTOP PUBLISHING   187

GRAPHIC IMAGES

Often, when preparing reports and other kinds of documents, it is necessary to include graphics to illustrate ideas. Traditionally, a page or part of a page in the document was left blank, and the graphic illustration was prepared separately and then inserted or pasted in. Now, it is possible to print graphics right in the document (Figure 3-70). To do so, you must first create the image, and then incorporate it into the document.

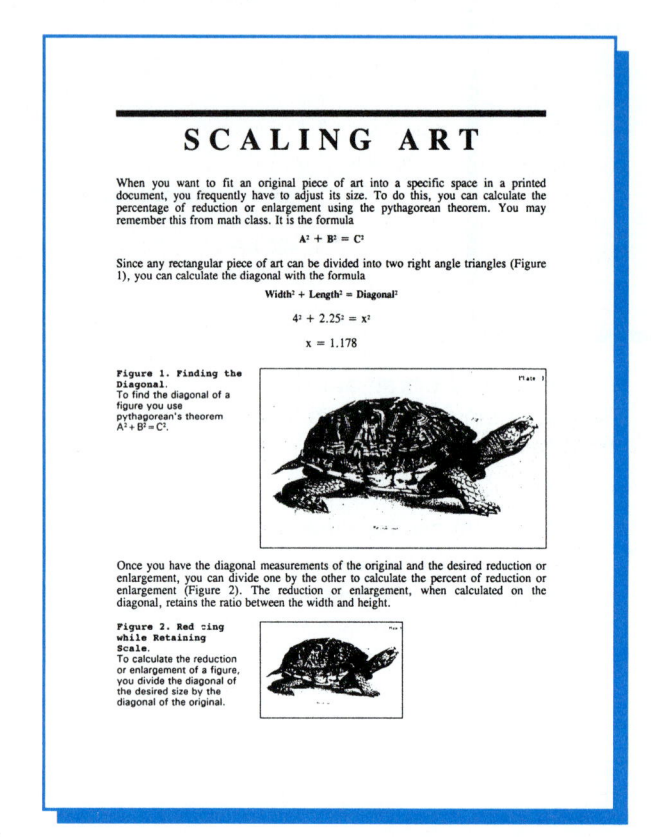

Figure 3-70 Graphics and Text Combined
You can combine graphics with text to illustrate a report or other document.

Creating Graphic Images

There are four ways of obtaining images to be incorporated into a document.

- You can buy ''clip-art'' files on disks that have been specially created for use in desktop publishing.
- You can scan the image into the computer, and then save it in a picture file on the disk.
- You can create the image on the screen with an interactive graphics paint program, and then save it in a picture file on the disk.
- You can use a program that captures any image that can be displayed on the screen. You first load the capture program and then any applications program. You then display on the screen the graphic you want to include in the document. With the graphic on the screen, you press designated keys to save the graphic in a picture file on the disk.

Tagged-Image-File-Format (TIFF). A standard that defines a format in which graphic images are stored on the disk.

Style sheets. Lists of previously defined formats that can be quickly assigned to the parts of a document.

Incorporating Images into Documents

When all the graphics you want to include have been saved in picture files on the disk, you create or retrieve the document file you want to use them in. You insert codes (sometimes called *tags*) into the document that refer to the names of the picture files on the disk that the graphic images are stored in. When the images are the way you want them, you print the document, and the picture files that the codes refer to are merged into the document. If your program has a document preview feature or a WYSIWYG display, you can see the illustrations on the screen, otherwise you just see the codes or outlines.

Graphics Standards

When you create graphic images and then save them, they are saved in a format determined by your hardware and the program. Because there are no established standards for file formats, you can have problems when trying to use an image created on one program with another program. This problem is being addressed in two ways: by the adoption of standards and the development of conversion utilities.

Many programs are now supporting ***Tagged-Image-File-Format*** files (they have the extension .TIF) or PC PaintBrush files (they have the extension .PCX). If files are in one of these formats, most programs will allow you to include them in your documents. Because many programs still have their own unique file formats, conversion programs like Hijack have been introduced to convert one format into another.

STYLE SHEETS

Some programs allow you to define and save the definition of frequently used formats on *style sheets* (Figure 3-71). For example, you can specify that main

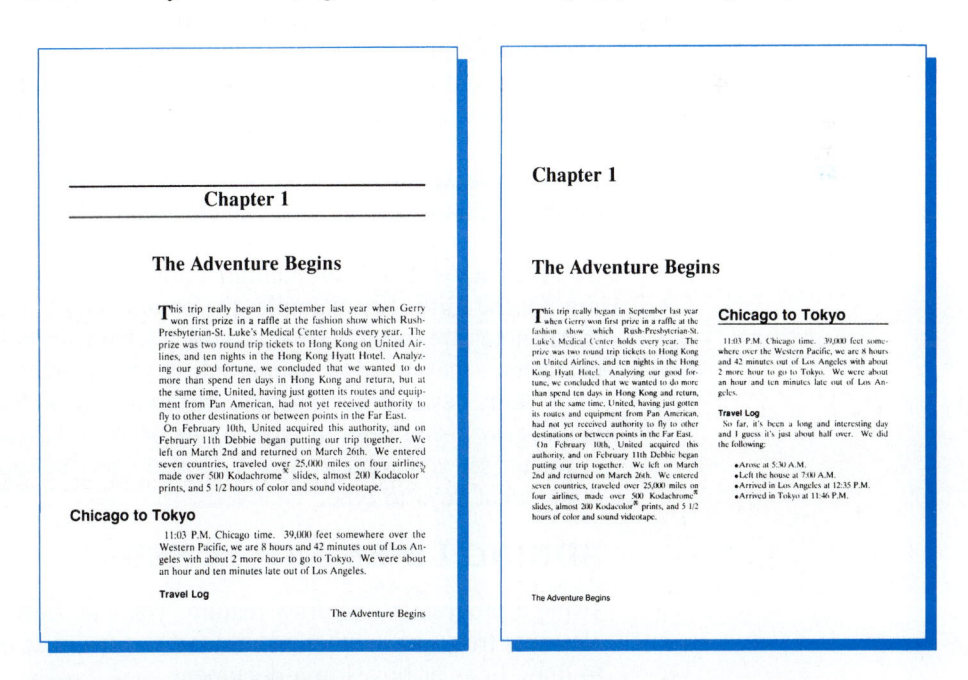

Figure 3-71   Style Sheets
Style sheets are used to define characteristics of typical elements in a document. Each definition is assigned a name. When you format the document, you use these names, not the actual formatting command. If you change the definition, the format of all elements with the same name change.

DESKTOP PUBLISHING   189

headings are to be uppercase and boldfaced, subheadings initial capital only and underlined, and the body of the text printed in 10-point Times Roman type. You specify these definitions on the style sheet.

On most programs, you define the style and add it to a menu that lists all the styles you have defined. When assigning the style to text, you select the style from the menu.

Assume you have formatted a hundred headings and decide that you want to change the format. Without a style sheet, you have to reformat each individually. But with a style sheet, you change only the definition, and all formatted text is automatically changed. For example, you could change the definition of main headings from uppercase and boldfaced to uppercase and underlined, and all main heads are automatically reformatted.

You can also save the style sheet that contains these definitions so that you can use it with any document you create. When you create new documents, you use the existing style sheets to format them for printing, which saves you time and standardizes your formats.

You can create a standard style sheet for each class of documents (memos, letters, reports, and so on) and then use that style sheet each time one of these is created. This ensures that all versions are uniform. You can also create different style sheets for the same class of documents. For example, you can print double-spaced draft copies to make editing easier, and then you can print single-spaced final copies. This lets you print the same document in a variety of formats with little additional effort.

SPECIAL CHARACTERS

Special characters are any characters not on the computer keyboard. These include graphics symbols, Greek letters, foreign currency symbols, foreign language accents, and almost any other character used to communicate information. What if you are preparing a report on international sales and have to express some amounts in pounds sterling? The symbol for this is £, a character not found on many keyboards. Special characters can be created with the printer, composed on the computer, selected from a menu, or entered from the numeric keypad. For example, almost all programs allow you to enter special characters by holding down **Alt** while you type their ASCII decimal codes on the numeric keypad. When you do so, and then release **Alt**, the character is displayed on the screen. You can enter any of the codes shown in Figure 3-72. To find the code, first locate the character you want to enter in that figure, and then read across to the left column numbers for the first two digits and to the top row for the third. For example, the pound symbol is 156, the up arrow is 024, music notes are 013 and 014, and the ½ character is 171. To print these special characters, they must be supported by your printer.

Many newer programs have different sets of characters, many for foreign languages. If you need to type in one of those languages, you can specify the character set you want to use. You also need an appropriate keyboard so you know what keys to type.

ADDING LINES AND BOXES

Using a program's line draw feature, you can draw lines in tables to separate elements from one another and around text to create boxes. There are two ways to draw lines or boxes in a document.

▌ One way is to select the character you want to work with and then use the directional arrow keys to move the cursor around the screen. As you move the cursor, you paint a line with the selected character. There are also commands that let you erase any lines you have mistakenly entered.

	0	1	2	3	4	5	6	7	8	9
00		☺	●	♥	♦	♣	♠	•	◘	○
01	◙	♂	♀	♪	♫	☼	►	◄	↕	‼
02	¶	§	—	‡	↑	↓	→	←	∟	↔
03	▲	▼		!	"	#	$	%	&	'
04	(	)	*	+	,	-	.	/	0	1
05	2	3	4	5	6	7	8	9	:	;
06	<	=	>	?	@	A	B	C	D	E
07	F	G	H	I	J	K	L	M	N	O
08	P	Q	R	S	T	U	V	W	X	Y
09	Z	[	\	]	^	_	`	a	b	c
10	d	e	f	g	h	i	j	k	l	m
11	n	o	p	q	r	s	t	u	v	w
12	x	y	z	{	|	}	~	⌂	Ç	ü
13	é	â	ä	à	å	ç	ê	ë	è	ï
14	î	ì	Ä	Å	É	æ	Æ	ô	ö	ò
15	û	ù	ÿ	Ö	Ü	¢	£	¥	₧	ƒ
16	á	í	ó	ú	ñ	Ñ	ª	º	¿	⌐
17	¬	½	¼	¡	«	»	▒	▓	│	┤
18	╡	╢	╖	╕	╣	║	╗	╝	╜	╛
19	┐	└	┴	┬	├	─	┼	╞	╟	╚
20	╔	╩	╦	╠	═	╬	╧	╨	╤	╥
21	╙	╘	╒	╓	╫	╪	┘	┌	█	▄
22	▌	▐	▀	α	β	Γ	π	Σ	σ	
23	μ	τ	Φ	Θ	Ω	δ	∞	φ	ε	∩
24	≡	±	≥	≤	⌠	⌡	÷	≈	°	•
25	·	√	ⁿ	²	■					

Figure 3-72 The IBM Character Set
This figure illustrates all the characters in the IBM extended character set built into the computer. To determine the decimal code for a special character, first locate the character that you want to enter. Then read across to the left column numbers for the first two digits and up to the top row of numbers for the third digit. For example, the up arrow (↑) is 024, music notes are 013 and 014, and the ½ character is 171.

■ Another way is to select a paragraph, and then use a menu command that places a line on one or more sides or encloses the paragraph in a box. This approach is preferred because the size of the lines or boxes automatically changes if you change margins or add or delete text.

The IBM PC character set has several graphics characters that you can create lines and boxes with. This line-drawing feature can be used to highlight headings, create organization charts (Figure 3-73), and make attractive tables.

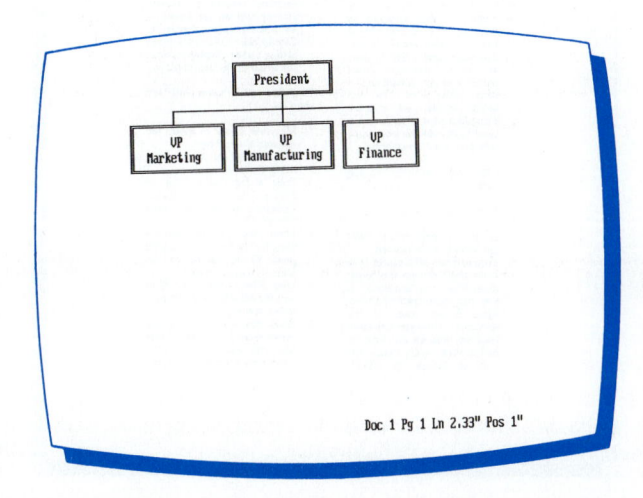

Figure 3-73 Lines and Boxes
Line draw characters can make a document more attractive. For example, you can create illustrations such as organization charts.

DESKTOP PUBLISHING **191**

Newspaper-style columns. Columns of text that flow from the bottom of one column to the top of the next.

Parallel-style columns. Columns arranged side by side.

To print out line drawings, your printer must have a font that contains the line-drawing graphics characters. Because some fonts contain the line draw characters and some do not, you may have to specify a different font to print them if your program allows you to do so.

PRINTING IN COLUMNS

Normally, text is printed in one column on a sheet of paper, but some programs let you specify that it be printed in two or more columns. Some programs display the columns on the screen; others just show the results when you print the document. The two basic types of text columns are newspaper columns and parallel columns.

Newspaper-Style Columns

Newspaper-style columns (Figure 3-74) (also called *snaking columns*) are those you see in newspapers, newsletters, and books. Text flows from column to column. As you enter text, it gradually fills the first column. When that column is full, text flows into the next column. When the last column on the page is full, text starts to fill the first column on the next page. If you add text to or delete text from any of the columns, the remaining text adjusts to keep the columns full.

Parallel-Style Columns

Parallel-style columns (Figure 3-75) (also called *side-by-side columns*) align related text side by side. This style is used when showing the same text in two languages; annotating a script with marginal notes; or creating tables of text for schedules, product descriptions, and the like. Text does not flow from one column to another, as in newspaper columns. You enter and edit text in each column independently.

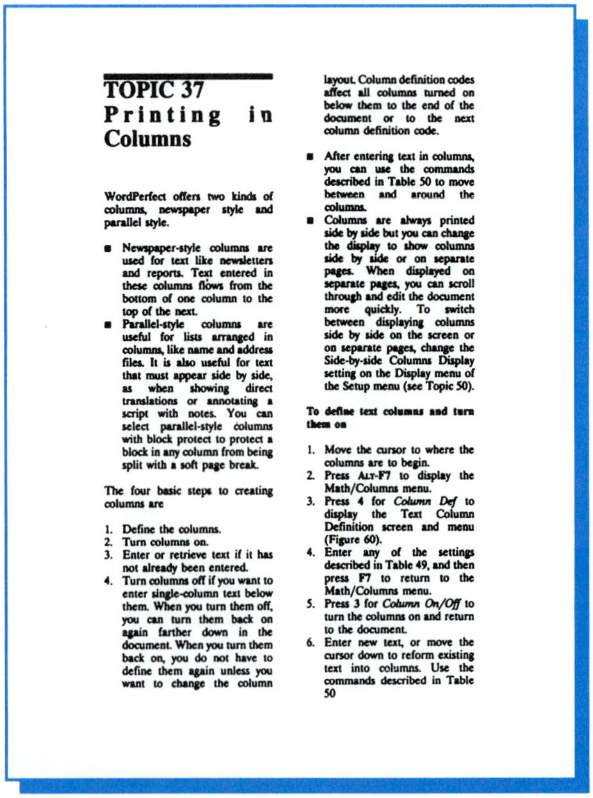

Figure 3-74 Newspaper-Style Columns

Newspaper-style or snaking columns are those you see in newspapers and newsletters. Text flows from the bottom of one column to the top of the next.

192   WORD PROCESSING AND DESKTOP PUBLISHING APPLICATIONS

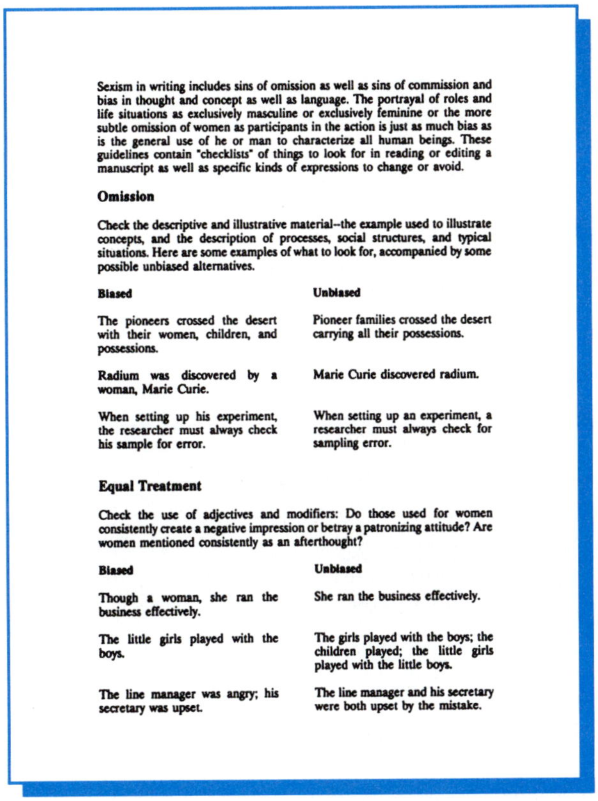
Sexism in writing includes sins of omission as well as sins of commission and bias in thought and concept as well as language. The portrayal of roles and life situations as exclusively masculine or exclusively feminine or the more subtle omission of women as participants in the action is just as much bias as is the general use of he or man to characterize all human beings. These guidelines contain "checklists" of things to look for in reading or editing a manuscript as well as specific kinds of expressions to change or avoid.

Omission

Check the descriptive and illustrative material--the example used to illustrate concepts, and the description of processes, social structures, and typical situations. Here are some examples of what to look for, accompanied by some possible unbiased alternatives.

Biased	**Unbiased**
The pioneers crossed the desert with their women, children, and possessions.	Pioneer families crossed the desert carrying all their possessions.
Radium was discovered by a woman, Marie Curie.	Marie Curie discovered radium.
When setting up his experiment, the researcher must always check his sample for error.	When setting up an experiment, a researcher must always check for sampling error.

Equal Treatment

Check the use of adjectives and modifiers: Do those used for women consistently create a negative impression or betray a patronizing attitude? Are women mentioned consistently as an afterthought?

Biased	**Unbiased**
Though a woman, she ran the business effectively.	She ran the business effectively.
The little girls played with the boys.	The girls played with the boys; the children played; the little girls played with the little boys.
The line manager was angry; his secretary was upset.	The line manager and his secretary were both upset by the mistake.

Figure 3-75 Parallel-Style Columns
Parallel-style columns are those you see in tables or where scripts are annotated. Related text is printed side by side.

AUTOMATICALLY GENERATED LISTS

When working on a long document with many sections, you often need to prepare a table of contents or an index to help readers find the information they need. Both of these lists refer to subjects in the document and provide page numbers for them. Manually preparing these references takes a great deal of time; moreover, if any revisions are made to the document, all page number references might have to be changed. Many programs now allow you to automatically prepare these lists.

In a program that allows you to automatically create indexes and tables of contents, you first enter codes to indicate which items in the text are to be listed. You then generate and print a table of contents (Figure 3-76), an index, or another kind of list, for example, a list of all illustrations or tables in the document. To create automatically generated lists, you normally follow three steps: coding the items to be entered, defining the position of the table and its number of levels, and then generating the table.

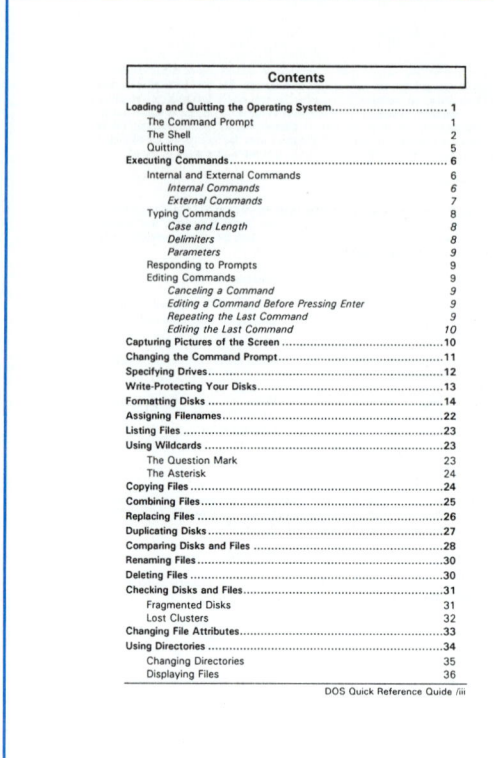

Figure 3-76 Table of Contents
A table of contents can be automatically generated to show not only the headings in the document but also their level and page numbers.

EXERCISE

Exercise 3-10A
DESKTOP PUBLISHING COMMANDS

Table 3-7 lists typical desktop publishing procedures. List the commands for your program that accomplish each procedure.

Table 3-7
DESKTOP PUBLISHING COMMANDS

Procedure	Enter Commands for Your Program
Change fonts	
Add a graphic	
Enter a special character	
Add a box	
Print in columns	
Generate a table of contents	

194 WORD PROCESSING AND DESKTOP PUBLISHING APPLICATIONS

QUESTIONS

1. What is a font? What three terms are used to describe a font?
2. What is pitch? Points?
3. Describe the difference between fixed pitch and proportional spacing. What does the term *kern* mean?
4. List and describe four ways fonts are made available to the printer.
5. List four ways you can get graphic images into the computer so that you can then combine them with a document.
6. Describe how graphic images can be inserted into a document.
7. List some ways a desktop publishing program can manipulate text.
8. List some ways a desktop publishing program can manipulate graphics.
9. What is a style sheet? What is the main advantage of using one?
10. What are the two ways programs let you draw lines and boxes? List as many uses for a program's line draw capability as you can think of.
11. If the line drawings you create do not print out on your printer, what is the reason?
12. How do you enter special characters using their three-digit decimal code?
13. What are two kinds of columns that can be created on some programs? What is the difference between them?
14. What kinds of lists can some programs automatically generate? List three steps you typically follow to automatically generate these lists.

CHAPTER 4

Spreadsheet Applications

OBJECTIVES

After finishing this chapter, you will be able to:

- Describe the terms *spreadsheet*, *model*, and *template*
- List the steps you follow to create and use a typical spreadsheet model
- List and briefly describe some typical spreadsheet programs
- Explain how you move around a spreadsheet and enter labels and numbers
- Describe what ranges are and explain when and how you use them
- Describe how you edit models to change the contents of cells and insert and delete rows and columns
- Describe formulas and explain the principles of entering them
- Describe what built-in functions are and how you use them
- Describe how and why you change column widths and format values
- Explain how you copy and move data on the spreadsheet and describe the differences among relative, absolute, and mixed cell references
- Describe how you create graphs and explain how you select the appropriate graph type for your data
- Describe what macros are and briefly explain how you can create them

What-ifs. The process of changing a value in a spreadsheet to see how the results are affected.

Until recently, accounting, financial analysis, and other mathematical calculations were done by laboriously entering numbers on the pages of an accountant's ruled ledger pad, or spreadsheet. The development of spreadsheet applications programs has taken much of the drudgery out of analysis. It may still take as much time to gather the data needed to analyze a situation, but that is where the similarity between the old and new ways ends. You can quickly create a model of a financial situation on a spreadsheet program by entering labels, numbers, and formulas. Using the program's built-in functions, you can quickly perform complicated calculations such as interest earned and monthly payments on a loan. You can then use the completed model to explore *what-if* questions. If you change any variable—for instance, the price, discount, or sales patterns—the model will recalculate a new result automatically and instantly.

You may think spreadsheets require a strong background in mathematics; after all, they are primarily used to manipulate numbers. Relax—you could not be further from the truth. Spreadsheets use math, but they do the laborious calculations, not you. Spreadsheets allow you to approach problems logically because they make it possible to focus on the problem, not on the calculations. Spreadsheets put tools for analysis and problem solving, once useful only to professionals, within the reach of any interested user.

Any problem that can be quantified can be solved or analyzed with a spreadsheet. In business, spreadsheets analyze the performance of products, salespeople, or dealers. They compare costs, prices, and gross margins of individual products in a product line. They also calculate prices, forecast and make budgets for sales, predict expenses and profits, and make cash-flow projections.

Graphs are powerful analytical tools. They can show trends and relationships between series of numbers that would otherwise be missed. Spreadsheets are an ideal tool to develop the numbers that are then graphed. The combination of spreadsheet and graphics is so powerful that almost all spreadsheet programs come with an integrated graphics capability. This feature makes it so easy to create graphs that they become valuable tools for exploring what-if analyses, not just for presenting the finished results to others.

4-1
SPREADSHEET PROCEDURES — AN OVERVIEW

Spreadsheet. An arrangement of rows and columns that forms cells into which you enter data.

Row. The horizontal line of cells on of a spreadsheet that intersect with a column. Rows are usually numbered down the left side of the screen with row one at the top.

Column. The vertical cells on a spreadsheet (as opposed to the horizontal ones). Usually, columns are labeled with letters across the top of the screen.

Model. A simulation of a real situation. Spreadsheet models are created by entering numbers, labels, and formulas.

Label. An entry in a spreadsheet cell that is meant to be read and not calculated.

Value. A number, formula, or function that is used in calculations.

Template. A model that is designed to be used over and over again. It contains all of the necessary labels and formulas used in a spreadsheet and can be used by anyone who knows how to move the cursor and enter numbers.

One of the primary uses of spreadsheets is to analyze financial or other situations and to explore the effects that any changes may have on these situations. When using a spreadsheet, you should understand three basic terms: spreadsheet, model, and template.

A *spreadsheet* (sometimes called a *worksheet*) is the arrangement of horizontal *rows* and vertical *columns* that appears on the screen when you first load the program.

A *model* is the data you enter into the spreadsheet to solve a problem or perform an analysis. To create a model, you use two basic types of entries: labels and values. **Labels** describe or identify parts of the model. **Values** are the numbers to be analyzed, and the formulas and built-in functions that perform the analysis. You use models to simulate real-world situations. Just as a plastic model of an airplane represents, or simulates, a real plane, a spreadsheet model simulates financial or other situations.

A *template* is a model from which all the numbers have been removed. Because it still retains all the labels, formulas, and functions, you can enter new numbers and the formulas calculate an answer. Mastering a spreadsheet and the business principles needed to analyze a problem takes time. In many firms, people who understand the principles behind an application often collaborate with those who understand a spreadsheet to develop templates of great value to others in the firm. These templates are designed to be used over and over again by anyone who knows how to move the cursor and enter the numbers to be analyzed.

One use of spreadsheet models is to simulate real-world financial situations. Suppose you want to buy a new car and explore how much you can spend while keeping your payments about $170 a month. You probably would not know the actual arithmetic involved, so the first step is to research how monthly payments are calculated. This is the first rule of computer literacy: You cannot use a computer to solve a problem you do not understand. The principles behind the calculations are quite simple. In this example,

- You have between $2,000 and $2,500 for a down payment.
- You know the loan required is the total cost of the car minus the down payment.
- You know the monthly payments are based on the loan amount, interest rate, and term of the loan. These are the numbers you want to explore to see how changes affect the monthly payment. The model you create must have places where you can enter these numbers.
- You have discovered that your spreadsheet program has a built-in function that calculates monthly payments if you tell it what amount, interest rate, and period to use.

This is a typical problem that you can quickly solve on a spreadsheet. Now that you know what you want to do, you create the model.

198   SPREADSHEET APPLICATIONS

Cell. The basic working unit on a spreadsheet. A cell falls at the intersection of a column and a row.

Format. A command you execute to control the way numbers are displayed on the screen. Format also refers to commands used to align labels in their cells.

STEP 1   LOAD THE PROGRAM

The first step in creating a model is to load the program so that the spreadsheet is displayed on the screen (Figure 4-1). If you are planning to save your work, you also insert a formatted data disk into drive B on a floppy disk system or into drive A on a hard disk system.

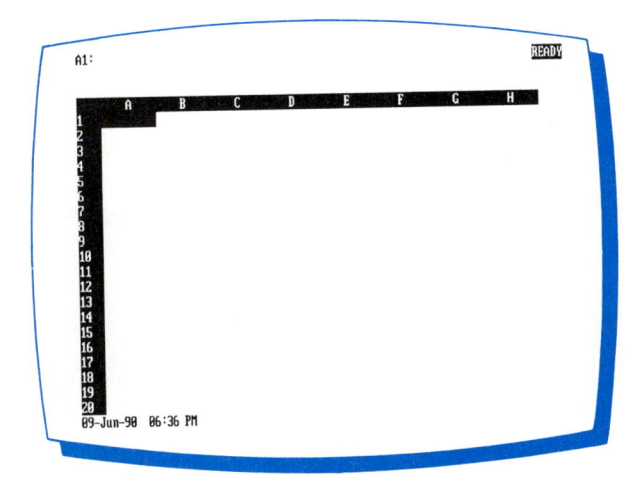

Figure 4-1   The Spreadsheet Screen Display
The spreadsheet on the screen is divided into rows and columns, much like a ledger pad. Each of the rectangles where rows and columns intersect is a *cell*. It is into these cells that you enter labels, numbers, formulas, and functions.

STEP 2   ENTER LABELS

You enter labels into *cells* to identify the contents of rows and columns so that you, and others, can understand the model (Figure 4-2). Labels are simply text characters, much like those you would enter on a word processing program.

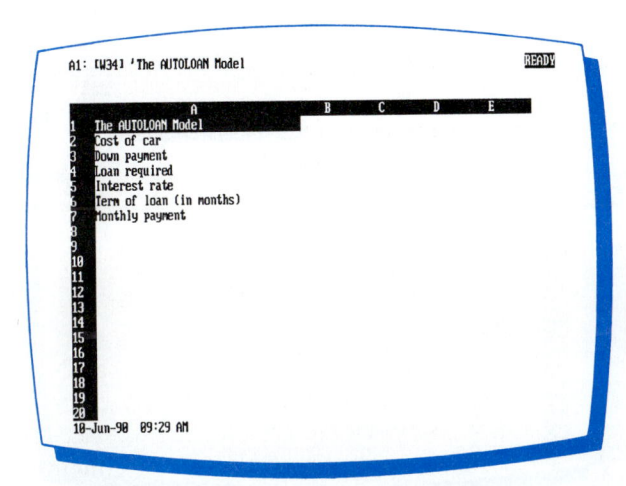

Figure 4-2   Enter Labels
Labels identify the contents of rows (and columns). Here, you enter labels for each row on the auto loan model where you will want to enter numbers, formulas, or functions. To display the labels in their entirety, column A has been widened.

STEP 3   ENTER NUMBERS

You enter numbers to be used in calculations (Figure 4-3). Numbers can be added, subtracted, multiplied, and divided. You can also *format* the numbers (and formulas and functions) so that they are displayed with dollar signs, commas, or percent signs.

SPREADSHEET PROCEDURES—AN OVERVIEW   **199**

4-1

Function. A small program built into a spreadsheet program to make complicated calculations such as interest due, averages, and present value.

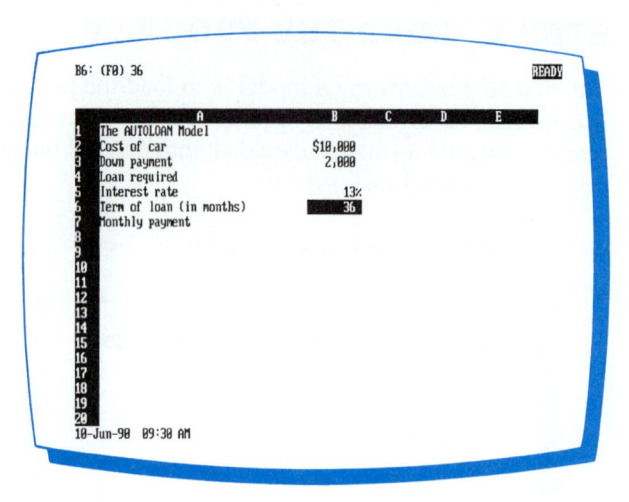

Figure 4-3 Enter Numbers
The numbers entered in the model include the cost of the car ($10,000), the down payment ($2,000), the interest rate (13%), and the term of the loan (36 months).

STEP 4   ENTER FORMULAS

You enter a formula to calculate the amount of the loan required (Figure 4-4). Because you know the cost of the car is $10,000 and your down payment is $2,000, you could subtract the two numbers and enter the result. But if you did this, the loan-required number would not change if you changed either the cost of the car or the down payment. If you enter a formula that refers to the two cells that those numbers are entered in, the loan you require does change if you change the cost of the car or the down payment. The spreadsheet displays the calculated result, not the formula entered into the cell to calculate it. Moreover, the computer remembers the cells you want subtracted, not their values. This way, if you change the values in either of the cells that the formula refers to, the program automatically calculates a new answer.

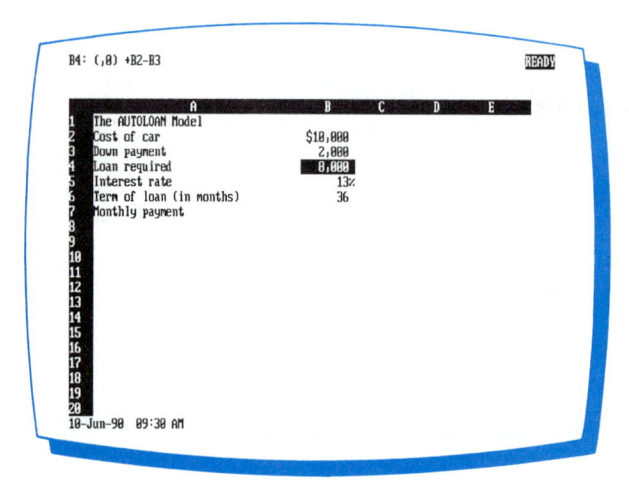

Figure 4-4 Enter Formulas
You enter the formula B2-B3 into cell B4. This formula tells the spreadsheet program to subtract the value in cell B3 from the value in cell B2. The result calculated by the formula is 8,000 (10,000 cost in cell B2 minus the 2,000 down payment in cell B3).

STEP 5   ENTER A FUNCTION

Formulas, like the one that calculates the amount of the loan required, are powerful, but spreadsheets have a special type of formula called a *function* that is even more so. Functions are built into the program and are designed to replace very complicated formulas. In this step, you enter a function that calculates the monthly payment on the loan (Figure 4-5). You'll learn about functions later. For now, all you have to understand is that in English, the function reads "calculate and display the monthly payment based on the amount of the

200   SPREADSHEET APPLICATIONS

loan in cell B4, the annual interest rate in cell B5 (divided by 12 to convert the annual rate into a monthly rate), and the term of the loan in cell B6." The calculated answer is $269.55, way above your goal of $170 a month.

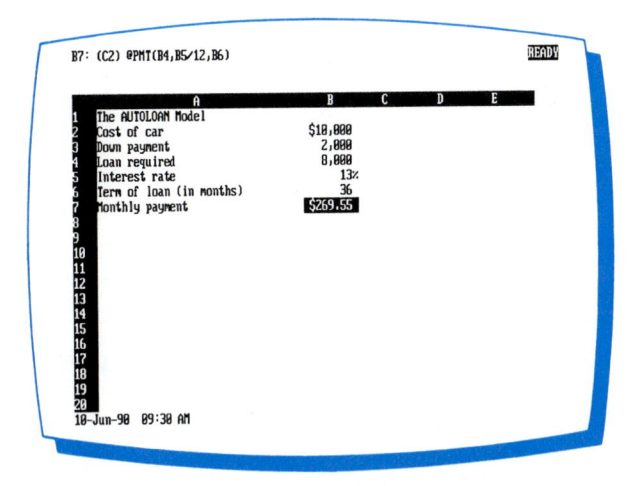

Figure 4-5 Enter Functions
You now enter the program's built-in function that calculates monthly payments into cell B7. The actual function is `@PMT(B4,B5/12,B6)`.

STEP 6 EXPLORE WHAT-IFS

So far, the only exciting things you have seen are that formulas and functions perform calculations. But now we explore the real power of a spreadsheet—its ability to reflect instantly the changes made in variables (called what-ifs or *sensitivity analysis*).

Because the monthly payment based on the original terms is more than you want to pay, let's see if you can achieve your goal of a payment of about $170 a month. You can easily change the terms of the loan or the price of the car until you find monthly payments that are within a few dollars of your goal (Figure 4-6).

- What if you increase the term of the loan from 36 to 48 months?
- What if you increase the down payment from $2,000 to $2,500?
- What if you reduce the cost of the car from $10,000 to $9,000?
- What if you go to a bank that offers a lower interest rate?

Figure 4-6 Explore What-Ifs
Once you have a model completed, you can change any of the variables to find a new result.

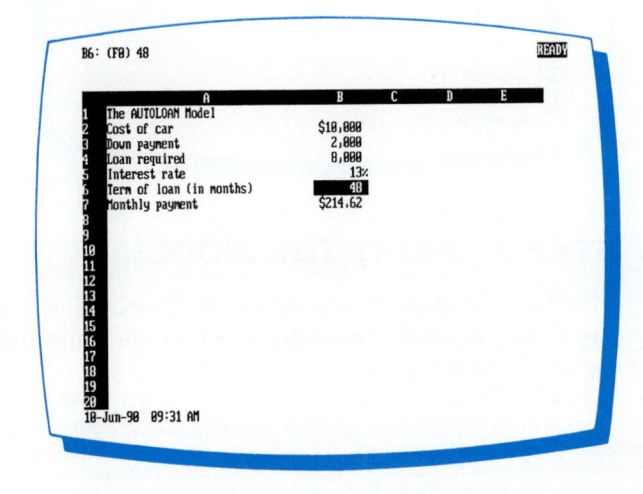

What If You Increase the Term of the Loan? To change the term of the loan, you move the cell pointer to cell B6, type 48 over the current entry, and then press **Enter**. The function in cell B6 calculates and displays the new monthly payment of $214.62.

SPREADSHEET PROCEDURES—AN OVERVIEW   **201**

Figure 4-6, continued

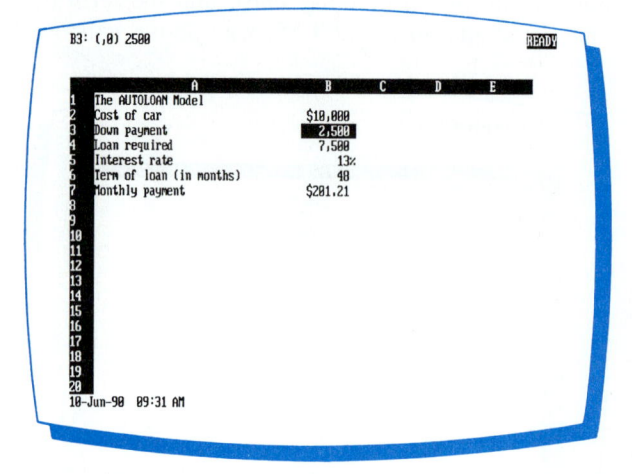

What If You Increase the Down Payment? If you increase the down payment in cell B3 by $500 (from $2,000 to $2,500), the loan required in cell B4 falls from $8,000 to $7,500. The monthly payment in cell B7 decreases to $201.21.

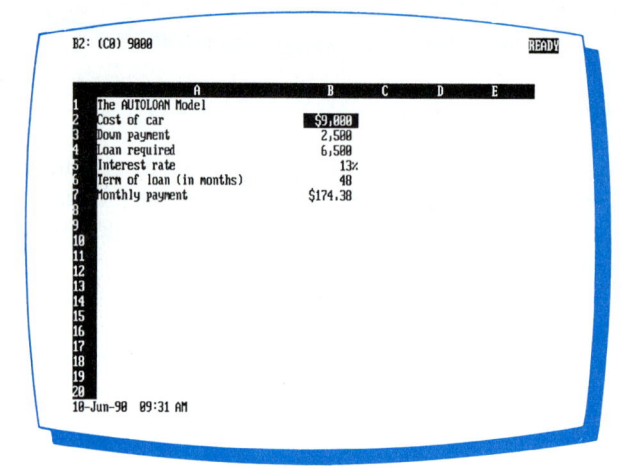

What If You Buy a Less Expensive Car? If you change the cost of the car in cell B2 to $9,000, the loan required in cell B4 falls from $7,500 to $6,500. The monthly payment in cell B7 falls to $174.38.

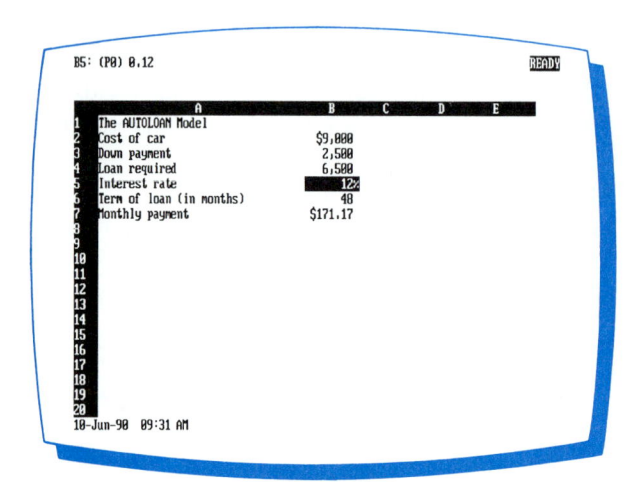

What If You Get a Lower Interest Rate? If you lower the interest rate in cell B5 by 1% (from 13% to 12%), the monthly payment drops to $171.17.

STEP 7   PRINT THE MODEL

If you want to share your results with others, or have a copy for your files, you can make a printout. The spreadsheet's Print command sends data displayed on the screen to the printer.

STEP 8 SAVE THE MODEL

When creating or entering data into models, be sure to save them often—not just when you finish them. Turning off the computer, power failures, hardware problems, or your own mistakes can cause you to lose files that are in the computer's memory. If you erase the numbers (here, the cost of the car, down payment, interest rate, and term of the loan) and then save the model, you convert the model into a template. Anyone can then retrieve the blank template, enter their own data, and analyze their own car purchase plans.

STEP 9 QUIT OR CLEAR THE SCREEN

When you are finished with a model and have saved it, you can work on another model or quit the program.

Clearing the Screen

If you want to stay in the program but begin work on a new model, you clear the old model off the spreadsheet using the program's Clear, Zap, or Erase command. Before you use this command, be sure you have saved the file with the Save command. If you erase data from the spreadsheet without first saving it, the data are lost.

If the model you want to work on has already been created and saved on a disk, you use the program's Retrieve command. On some programs, retrieving a model from the disk automatically clears the old model from the screen and the computer's memory. On other programs, each model is displayed in its own window, so you have to open new windows for each model and then close them when finished.

Quitting the Program

You quit a program when you want to return to the operating system to quit for the day or perhaps to use another program.

When you are finished with a session, you quit the program with the Quit command.

EXERCISE

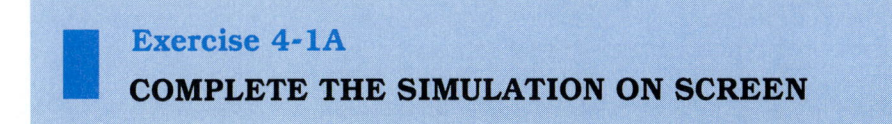

Exercise 4-1A
COMPLETE THE SIMULATION ON SCREEN

The *Information Processing Software Sampler* contains an on-screen simulation of several spreadsheet programs. Run the simulation of Lotus 1-2-3, and then summarize the key features of a spreadsheet program.

QUESTIONS

1. What is the difference between a spreadsheet and a model?
2. What is the difference between a model and a template?
3. What is the purpose of a spreadsheet's functions?
4. What is sensitivity analysis? Give an example.
5. How do you change the data in a cell?
6. What is the model called if you erase all the numbers, leaving just the labels, formulas, and functions?
7. When you retrieve a file on some programs, what happens to the currently displayed model?
8. What is the difference between clearing the screen and quitting the program?

4-2
TYPICAL SPREADSHEET PROGRAMS

Working area. The area of a spreadsheet that contains the cells you enter data into.

Border The letters and numbers that identify columns and rows on a spreadsheet's working area.

Cell address. The cell's coordinates that identify its location on the spreadsheet screen. A cell address is usually given as the column label followed by the row number, e.g. A1, B1.

To use a spreadsheet, you must understand its screen display, how to move the cursor, and how to execute commands.

THE SPREADSHEET SCREEN DISPLAY

When you load a spreadsheet program, the spreadsheet is usually immediately displayed on the screen. Spreadsheet screen displays all have an area, called the *working area* (also called the *worksheet*) where you enter data (Figure 4-7). Data can be lists of names and addresses, inventory items, or models used to explore financial questions. In fact, you can make any of the cell entries described in Table 4-1.

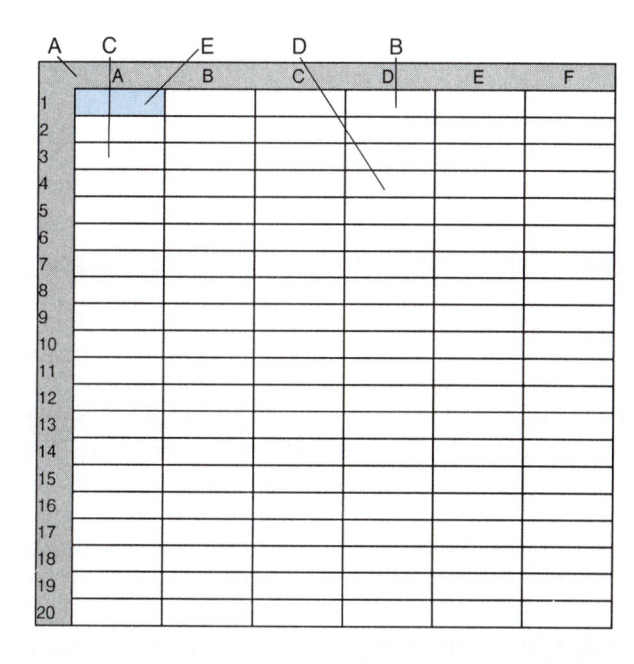

Figure 4-7 The Spreadsheet Working Area
The working area of a spreadsheet contains the following elements:

A. Border
B. Columns
C. Rows
D. Cells
E. Cursor

The working area of a spreadsheet contains the following elements:

A. The *border* contains column letters across the top of the spreadsheet and row numbers down the left side. On some programs, these borders can be turned off so that the column and row labels do not appear on the screen. Borders do not usually appear on printouts, but on some programs you can have them do so.

B. Columns run vertically down a spreadsheet and are labeled consecutively with letters. The first 26 columns are labeled A to Z, the next 26 are labeled AA to AZ, the next 26 are labeled BA to BZ, and so on.

C. Rows run horizontally across a spreadsheet and are labeled consecutively with numbers, starting with row 1 at the top of the spreadsheet.

D. Cells, the basic working units on a spreadsheet, fall at the intersection of each column and row. They are initially empty when the program is loaded and are referred to by their coordinates, or *cell address*. Cell addresses

Active cell. The cell on a spreadsheet in which the cursor is currently positioned.

Boundary. The outer limits of the spreadsheet beyond which you can't move the cursor or enter data.

are indicated by specifying the column letter(s) followed by the row number. For example:
- The cell at the intersection of column B and row 2 is cell B2.
- The cell at the intersection of column A and row 5 is cell A5.
- The cell at the intersection of column D and row 4 is cell D4.

E. The working area contains a bright reverse video highlight, called the cursor, cell pointer, or cell marker. You move this cursor by pressing the cursor movement keys to point to cells when you want to enter, delete, copy, move, or print data. The cell the cursor is positioned in is the *active cell*, or current cell.

Table 4-1
CELL ENTRIES

Entry	Description
Labels	Identify models or individual rows and columns of data
Numbers	Can be used in calculations when referred to by formulas
Formulas and Functions	Can calculate numbers entered into the formula itself or into other cells the formula refers to
Formats	Control the way numbers are displayed on the screen and the way labels are aligned in their cells

GETTING AROUND A SPREADSHEET

The display screen is just a small window on a large spreadsheet (Figure 4-8), but as you will see, you can scroll around the underlying spreadsheet with the cursor movement keys. When you want to enter data into cells or execute other commands, you point to cells. The four directional arrow keys move the cursor a cell at a time and repeat if you hold them down. Other keys, or combinations of keys, move the cursor in larger jumps. The larger your models are, the more important these keys and commands become.

For example, the Goto command moves the cursor quickly to a specific cell. This command displays a prompt that asks you what cell you want to go to. You just type in the cell coordinates, press **Enter**, and the cursor immediately jumps to the specified cell. On many computers, pressing **PgUp** and **PgDn** scrolls you through the spreadsheet a screen page at a time, and pressing **Home** moves the cursor to cell A1 at the upper left-hand corner of the spreadsheet.

Most other commands involve a combination of keys. For example, when using Lotus 1-2-3 on an IBM PC, pressing **Home** moves the cursor to cell A1. But pressing **End** and then **Home** moves the cursor to the lower right-hand corner of the working area of the model. The keys used to make these larger moves depend on the program and computer you are using. Some programs also include a Search command that allows you to move quickly to a specified label, number, or formula.

As you move the cursor down a column or along a row, it eventually runs into one of the edges of the screen display. The next time you press the same key, the cursor stays against the edge of the screen (it cannot be moved off the screen), but the screen display scrolls to reveal the next row or column of the spreadsheet. As it does so, the leftmost column or topmost row scrolls off the other side of the screen. You can see this happen if you watch the row and column labels change as you scroll the screen. If the cursor runs into one of the *boundaries* of the spreadsheet, the computer beeps the next time you press the arrow key that points toward the boundary.

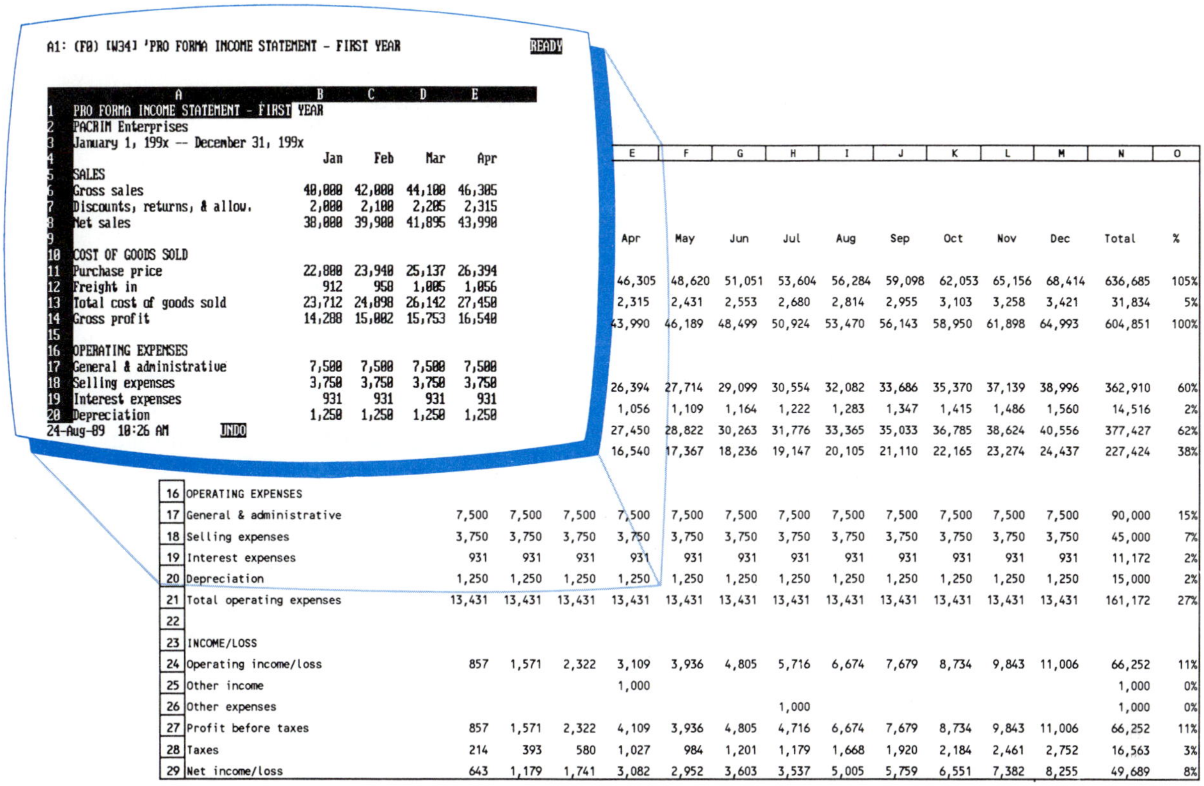

```
A1: (F0) [W34] 'PRO FORMA INCOME STATEMENT - FIRST YEAR                READY

        A                    B       C       D       E
 1  PRO FORMA INCOME STATEMENT - FIRST YEAR
 2  PACRIM Enterprises
 3  January 1, 199x -- December 31, 199x
                            Jan     Feb     Mar     Apr
 4
 5  SALES
 6  Gross sales             40,000  42,000  44,100  46,305
 7  Discounts, returns, & allow.  2,000  2,100  2,205  2,315
 8  Net sales               38,000  39,900  41,895  43,990
 9
10  COST OF GOODS SOLD
11  Purchase price          22,800  23,940  25,137  26,394
12  Freight in                 912     958   1,005   1,056
13  Total cost of goods sold 23,712 24,898  26,142  27,450
14  Gross profit            14,288  15,002  15,753  16,540
15
16  OPERATING EXPENSES
17  General & administrative  7,500   7,500   7,500   7,500
18  Selling expenses          3,750   3,750   3,750   3,750
19  Interest expenses           931     931     931     931
20  Depreciation              1,250   1,250   1,250   1,250
24-Aug-89  10:26 AM     UNDO
```

		E	F	G	H	I	J	K	L	M	N	O
		Apr	May	Jun	Jul	Aug	Sep	Oct	Nov	Dec	Total	%
		46,305	48,620	51,051	53,604	56,284	59,098	62,053	65,156	68,414	636,685	105%
		2,315	2,431	2,553	2,680	2,814	2,955	3,103	3,258	3,421	31,834	5%
		43,990	46,189	48,499	50,924	53,470	56,143	58,950	61,898	64,993	604,851	100%
		26,394	27,714	29,099	30,554	32,082	33,686	35,370	37,139	38,996	362,910	60%
		1,056	1,109	1,164	1,222	1,283	1,347	1,415	1,486	1,560	14,516	2%
		27,450	28,822	30,263	31,776	33,365	35,033	36,785	38,624	40,556	377,427	62%
		16,540	17,367	18,236	19,147	20,105	21,110	22,165	23,274	24,437	227,424	38%
16	OPERATING EXPENSES											
17	General & administrative	7,500	7,500	7,500	7,500	7,500	7,500	7,500	7,500	7,500	90,000	15%
18	Selling expenses	3,750	3,750	3,750	3,750	3,750	3,750	3,750	3,750	3,750	45,000	7%
19	Interest expenses	931	931	931	931	931	931	931	931	931	11,172	2%
20	Depreciation	1,250	1,250	1,250	1,250	1,250	1,250	1,250	1,250	1,250	15,000	2%
21	Total operating expenses	13,431	13,431	13,431	13,431	13,431	13,431	13,431	13,431	13,431	161,172	27%
22												
23	INCOME/LOSS											
24	Operating income/loss	857	1,571	2,322	3,109	3,936	4,805	5,716	6,674	7,679	8,734	9,843	11,006	66,252	11%
25	Other income				1,000						1,000	0%
26	Other expenses					1,000					1,000	0%
27	Profit before taxes	857	1,571	2,322	4,109	3,936	4,805	4,716	6,674	7,679	8,734	9,843	11,006	66,252	11%
28	Taxes	214	393	580	1,027	984	1,201	1,179	1,668	1,920	2,184	2,461	2,752	16,563	3%
29	Net income/loss	643	1,179	1,741	3,082	2,952	3,603	3,537	5,005	5,759	6,551	7,382	8,255	49,689	8%

Figure 4-8 The Screen Is a Window onto the Spreadsheet
The display screen is a window onto a large spreadsheet in the computer's memory.

Macro. A stored sequence of keystrokes that can then be played back by pressing a few keys.

On some programs, you can engage **Scroll Lock** to keep the cursor in the same cell. When you then press the arrow keys, the screen scrolls just as it does when **Scroll Lock** is not engaged, but the cursor does not have to be against the edge of the display to make it do so. When the cursor reaches the edge of the screen, it stays there, and the spreadsheet scrolls under it.

TYPICAL PROGRAMS

There are many spreadsheet programs to choose from. Let's look briefly at the characteristics of a few of the leading spreadsheet programs.

Lotus 1-2-3

Lotus 1-2-3 (Figure 4-9) and similar spreadsheet programs integrate graphics and data management capabilities. These programs also let you write simple programs (called *macros*) that automate many of the commands you use frequently.

Lotus 1-2-3's three-line control panel is located at the top of the screen. The first line indicates the cell in which the cursor is positioned and the cell contents, format, and protection status if any (see the box "Protecting Data" in Topic 4-3). At the far right end of the line is the mode indicator telling you the current state of the program. The second line displays cell data as you enter or edit it. At certain points during command execution, prompts are also displayed on this line.

Menu pointer. A bright highlight moved by the directional arrow keys to point to or highlight a choice on the menu.

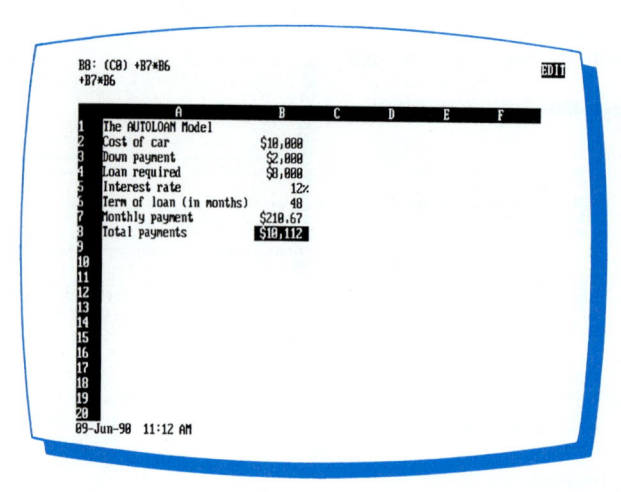

Figure 4-9 Lotus 1-2-3
The 1-2-3 screen display contains a control area at the top of the screen and a working area into which you enter data.

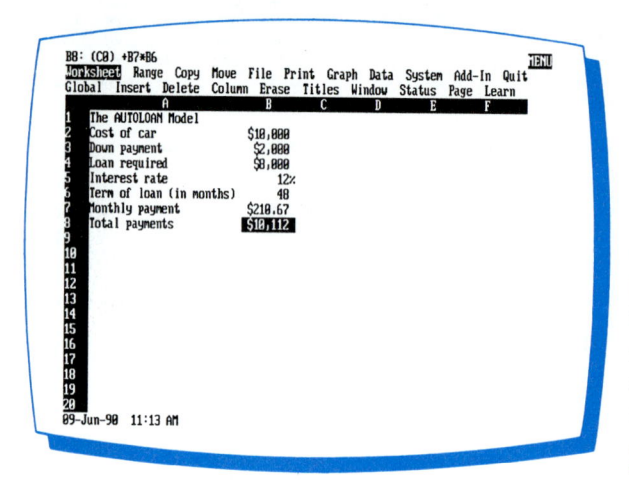

Figure 4-10 1-2-3's Menu
When you press the slash (/) key, a menu is displayed on the second and third lines of the control panel.

When you press the slash key (/) to execute commands, a menu bar appears on the second line of the control panel (Figure 4-10). You can select choices from the menu by using the arrow keys to move a bright highlight, called the *menu pointer*, along the bar, and then press **Enter** to select the highlighted choice. You can also make selections by just typing the first character in the command's name. The third line displays a brief description of highlighted menu selections when the menu is being used to execute commands.

Microsoft Excel

Microsoft Excel was the first modern spreadsheet that achieved widespread use. It has a highly graphic display that operates under the Windows environment (Figure 4-11). It it easy to learn and use because of its pull-down menus. It is very sophisticated and allows you to desktop publish spreadsheet data because what you see on the screen is what you get in a printout. It has built-in graphics that offer a wide choice of graph types and options. Excel also allows you to open multiple windows at the same time so you can compare data or graphs.

Figure 4-11 Microsoft Excel
Microsoft Excel is a state-of-the-art spreadsheet program with built-in desktop publishing features.

Excel features a menu bar at the top of the screen. You use the computer's mouse to point to choices listed on this bar, and then select them by clicking the button on the mouse. A list of related commands then descends, and you select commands from this menu by pointing and clicking.

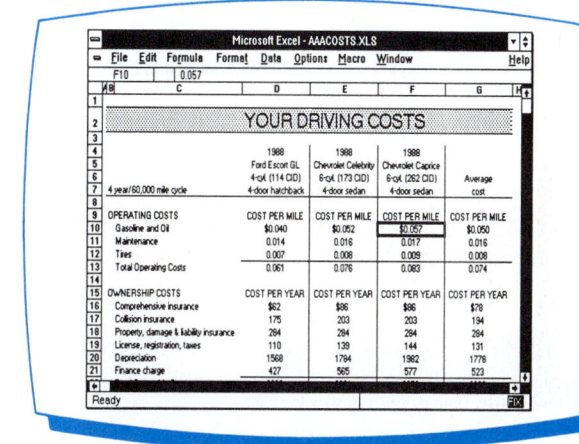

Excel is a graphic program that allows you to desktop publish spreadsheet data; what you see on the screen is what you get in your printouts.

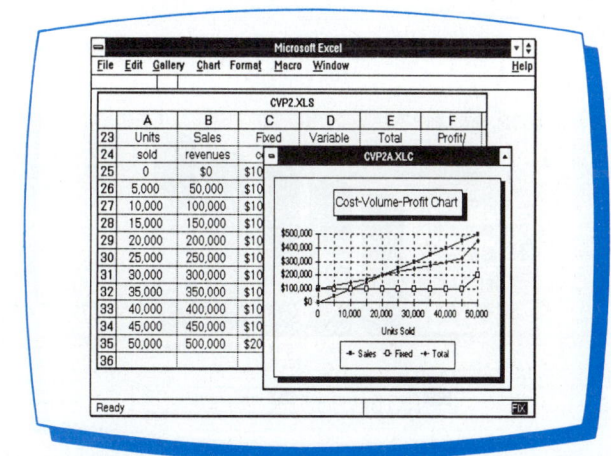

Excel allows you to display several windows on the screen at the same time. Here, a graph is displayed along with the data it represents.

Quattro Pro

Quattro Pro (Figure 4-12) is a full-featured spreadsheet that allows you to operate the program with its own menu commands or with commands identical to those used by Lotus 1-2-3. The input line at the top of the screen displays data

TYPICAL SPREADSHEET PROGRAMS 209

Figure 4-12 Quattro Pro
Quattro Pro is a sophisticated spreadsheet with built in graphics and desktop publishing features.

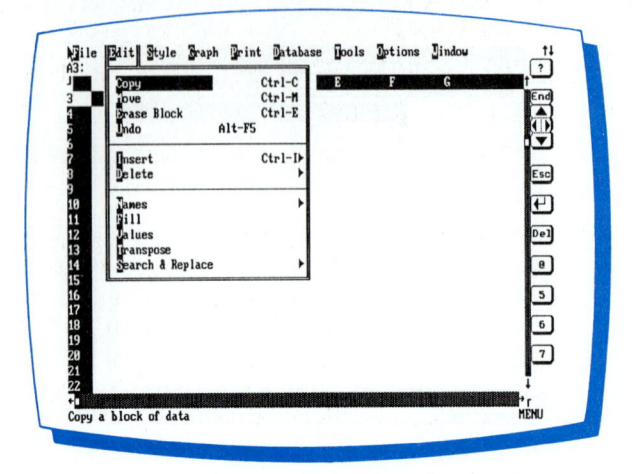

Quattro Pro features a menu bar at the top of the screen and pull-down menus.

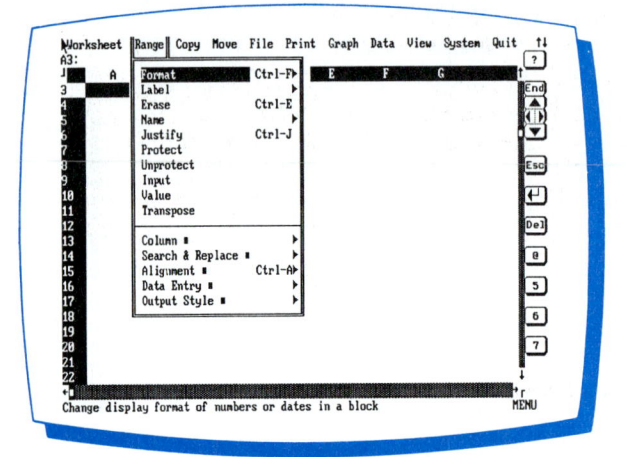

Quattro Pro has a menu system that mimics 1-2-3's. This is very useful for users who are familiar only with 1-2-3 but want to use the program because of its unique advantages. They can do so without learning a new menu structure.

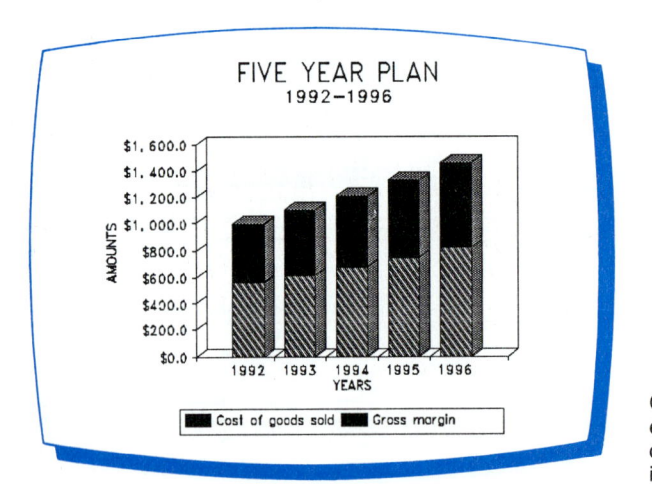

Quattro Pro has an exceptionally fine graphics capability. Here, a bar graph is shown in 3-D.

as you type until you press **Enter** or when you press **Edit (F2)** to return to this line for editing. It also displays a description of the commands that can be selected from the highlighted menu command. The two lines at the bottom of the screen are the descriptor line and the status line. The descriptor line displays

210   SPREADSHEET APPLICATIONS

the contents of the cell containing the cursor. The status line indicates the date and time and the current mode. Quattro also has the ability to display graphs of the data on your worksheet.

Microsoft Works

Besides the standalone programs, spreadsheets are also included in almost all integrated programs, including Microsoft Works (Figure 4-13).

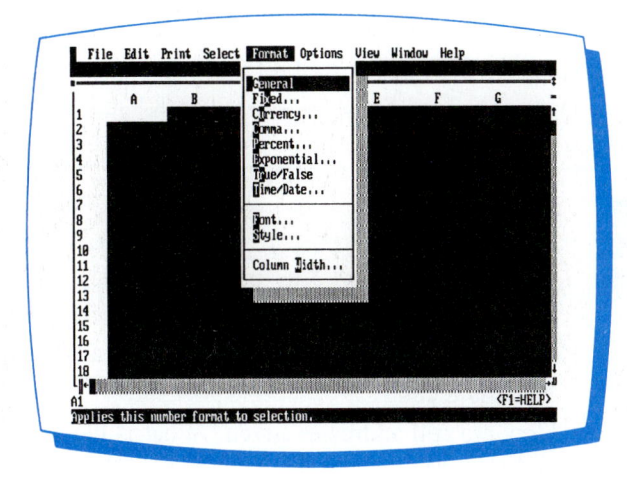

Figure 4-13
Microsoft Works
Microsoft Works is operated by pull-down menus and is much like Excel. It is a powerful, easy-to-use spreadsheet built into an integrated program that also contains graphics, word processing, and telecommunications programs.

EXERCISES

Exercise 4-2A
COMPLETE THE SIMULATION ON SCREEN

The *Information Processing Software Sampler* contains a simulation of several spreadsheet programs. Run the simulations for Lotus 1-2-3, Excel, Quattro Pro, and Microsoft Works. Summarize the key differences among the programs.

Exercise 4-2B
IDENTIFYING CURSOR MOVEMENT KEYS

Refer to a spreadsheet user's guide for instructions on how you move the cursor. Enter the keys you use into Table 4-2.

Table 4-2
CURSOR MOVEMENT KEYS

To Move the Cursor	Enter Commands for Your Program
Right or left one column	_____
Up or down one row	_____
Right one full screen	_____
Left one full screen	_____
Up or down one full screen	_____
To upper left-hand corner (cell A1)	_____
To lower right-hand corner of working area	_____
To a specified cell	_____

4-3 QUESTIONS

1. What is the purpose of the working area?
2. What is a cell?
3. How are cell addresses given? What is the address of a cell in column H and row 30?
4. List and briefly describe the four things that you can enter into a cell.
5. List three typical spreadsheet programs and describe some of their features.
6. Name one integrated program that contains a spreadsheet as one of its components.

4-3
ENTERING LABELS AND NUMBERS

Label prefix. The character you type on a spreadsheet before entering a label that begins with a number, or when you want to align the label in the cell.

You enter data into a spreadsheet by moving the cursor to the cell and then typing in the data. Entries are displayed on the edit line as you type them. When they are displayed on this line, you can press **Backspace** to back over and erase any characters that you have entered incorrectly. You complete the entry by pressing **Enter**, which moves the entry from the edit line to the cell the cursor is positioned in. If the cell already contains an entry, you can replace it by typing a new entry over it and then pressing **Enter**.

Some programs automatically move the cursor to the next cell on the row or column when you press **Enter** to complete an entry. On other programs, you can achieve the same result by pressing one of the cursor movement keys instead of **Enter**; this simultaneously completes the entry and moves the cursor to the next cell in the direction of the arrow key you press. For instance, to enter a number into a cell and automatically move down one row, press the down arrow key (↓) instead of **Enter** after typing the number. When making several entries along a row or down a column, it is faster to enter data this way because you enter the data and automatically move the cursor one cell in the direction of the arrow, saving you a keystroke each time.

When you enter data, many spreadsheet programs distinguish between labels and values (numbers, formulas, and functions) because they use values but not labels in most calculations.

- On 1-2-3, if the first character you type is a letter, the program assumes you are entering a label. If the first character is a number, or one of the characters + − * ($ # @, , it assumes you are entering a value.
- Excel automatically distinguishes between labels and numbers. However, to indicate a formula, you have to press the equal sign (=) as the first character.

ENTERING LABELS

Labels (also called *text*) are any series of characters, including letters, numbers, and symbols. To enter a label, you move the cursor to the cell you want to enter it in, type the label, and then press **Enter**. This is straightforward on most programs, with one exception: labels that begin with numbers or certain other characters used in formulas and functions. For example, on 1-2-3, if the first character you type is a number or a symbol used in formulas, the program assumes you are entering a value. Although this assumption usually saves you time, you sometimes have to override it.

You can override the program's assumptions by typing a designated key or symbol before you type the entry's first character. If you want to enter a label that begins with a number, for example, 100 Elm Street, you first type a *label prefix*, such as an apostrophe ('). This puts the program into label mode. You then enter the label by typing it and pressing **Enter**.

Once a number is entered as a label, it cannot be used in mathematical operations. Be careful when entering text that could also be values. Telephone numbers and ZIP codes, in particular, could cause confusion if entered without a label prefix. For example, if you enter the phone number `554-1212`, the last digits of the number are subtracted from the first digits, and the result, −657, is displayed. No error message results because the program assumes you are entering a formula.

Repeating label. A label that fills the entire width of a cell and that automatically changes width when the column width is changed.

Protect. To prevent the contents of cells from being deleted or changed.

Most programs also have a *repeating label* feature. You can use this to enter lines and borders. For example, on 1-2-3, you press backslash then hyphen (\-) or backslash then equal sign (\=) to fill a cell with a single or double ruled line. The backslash character tells the program to repeat the next character or characters typed so they fill the cell.

ENTERING NUMBERS

You enter numbers just like labels: you move the cursor to the cell where they are to be entered, type them in, and then press **Enter** to enter them in the cell. Numbers must always begin with a character from 0 to 9 or another designated character such as the plus sign (+) or minus sign (-). They cannot contain spaces, letters, or commas (though commas can be added by formatting, as you'll see). You enter percentages as decimals, or sometimes with a percent (%) sign. For example, to enter 10-percent, you type .10 or 10%.

PROTECTING DATA

When you initially create a model, none of the spreadsheet's cells are protected, so that you can enter data into them. If you enter a number or label into a cell containing a formula, the formula is deleted. This can seriously damage a template.

You can *protect* cells so that they cannot be edited, overwritten with new data (by typing, copying, or moving cells into their range), or deleted unless you first remove their protection. If you are planning to use the model as a template, shared by other users, protection is especially important. Others may be less familiar with the model or unfamiliar with the program, thus increasing the likelihood of mistakes.

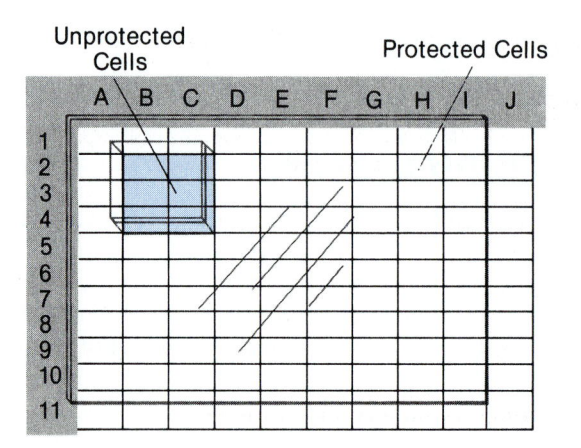

Protecting cells is like placing a protective shield over the model. Many programs display unprotected cells in a different intensity or color so that you can distinguish them from protected cells.

Programs use two different approaches to protect cells.

- Some programs are set up so that all cells are unprotected unless you use a command to protect them.

- Other programs use a two-step process: All cells are protected, but you can turn protection on and off. When protection is off, changes can be made anywhere on the spreadsheet. When protection is on, changes can be made only in cells you have specifically designated as unprotected.

SPREADSHEET APPLICATIONS

EXERCISES

Exercise 4-3A
ENTERING LABELS

Refer to a spreadsheet user's guide for instructions on how to enter labels that begin with numbers. List the procedures here:

1. _____
   _____
2. _____
   _____

Exercise 4-3B
TURNING PROTECTION ON AND OFF

Refer to a spreadsheet user's guide for instructions on how to turn cell protection on and off. List the procedures here:

1. _____
   _____
2. _____
   _____

QUESTIONS

1. How do you enter data into a cell?
2. How does a value differ from text?
3. How do you enter a label that begins with a number?
4. How would you enter the label *123 Spring Street*? the phone number *617-554-1000*?
5. What do numbers begin with?
6. How would you enter the number $6,580.00?
7. Describe two different methods for protecting cells.

4-4 UNDERSTANDING RANGES

Global command. Any command that affects the entire spreadsheet or the entire document.

Global format. A format that affects the entire spreadsheet.

Range command. A command that affects only a selected portion of the spreadsheet. Also called a Local command.

Range. A group of adjacent cells on a spreadsheet program that are selected for an operation.

Many of the commands you use with a spreadsheet affect all cells. These are called global commands. Others affect just single cells or groups of cells. These are called range commands.

GLOBAL COMMANDS

Global commands affect the entire spreadsheet. Some of these commands affect the way information is displayed. For example, there are global commands to set the width of columns, specify how labels are aligned, and control how numbers are displayed. Normally, you specify a global setting based on what works best with most of your data. You then override the global setting, as necessary, wherever you want data to look different from the *global format*.

RANGE COMMANDS

Other commands, called **range commands** (also called *local commands*) affect one or more cells. Understanding ranges is important because you specify them in functions and when formatting, copying, moving, printing, or erasing groups of cells or overriding the global commands in selected cells. When you use range commands, you specify rectangular ranges of cells. A *range* is a group of adjacent cells. Ranges can be as small as a single cell or as large as the entire spreadsheet. The only rule is that the range must be rectangular. There are essentially four rectangular shapes of ranges (Figure 4-14).

- **A.** Individual cells, for example, B2.
- **B.** Rows or parts of rows, for example, D2 to G2.
- **C.** Columns or parts of columns, for example, B5 to B17.
- **D.** Blocks (rectangles) of cells, for example, rows 5 through 17 in columns D through G.

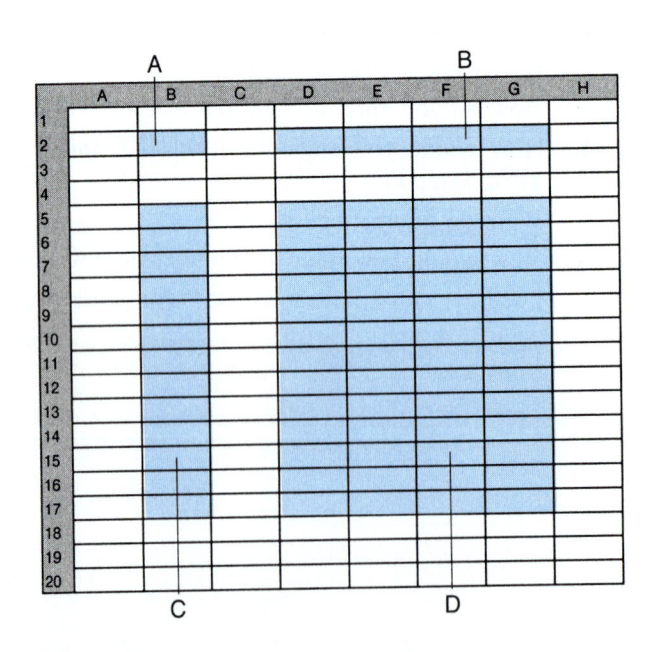

Figure 4-14 Ranges
A range is a group of adjacent cells arranged in a rectangular pattern. Ranges can be as small as a single cell or as large as the entire spreadsheet. The only rule is that the range must be rectangular. There are essentially four shapes of ranges.

216   SPREADSHEET APPLICATIONS

Range name. The name assigned to a range of cells on a spreadsheet.

When you use range commands, you must specify the range of cells to be affected by the command. On some programs, the sequence is:

1. Initiate the command.
2. Specify the range.
3. Complete the command.

On other programs, you complete the same steps but in a different order; for example, the sequence may be:

1. Select (highlight) the range.
2. Execute the command.

You specify or select a range in one of two ways: by typing in the coordinates of the range or by using the cursor or a mouse to point to the cells indicating the range. Figure 4-14 shows the cells that you specify for each type of range in a second color.

- To select a range by typing, you type two cell addresses that define the range, the upper left-hand and lower right-hand cells in the range. When more than one cell is in the range, you type two cell addresses separated by a delimiter, usually a period or colon. On Lotus 1-2-3, you type `A1.C3` to indicate the cells falling in the columns between A and C and the rows 1 and 3. On Excel, you type `A1:C3` to indicate the same range.
- To select a range by using the cursor, you press the arrow keys to point to the upper left-hand and lower right-hand corners of the range. On Lotus 1-2-3, you move the cursor to one of the corners of the range (when the prompt tells you to select the range), and then press the period (.) to anchor that corner of the range. You then use the cursor movement keys to highlight the desired range. On Excel, to select a range by pointing, you use the mouse to point to one corner, hold down one of the buttons, and then drag the highlight over the range.

NAMING RANGES

Some programs allow you to assign names to ranges of cells. Programs that let you name ranges have menu commands that you use to name or remove names from cells. *Range names* are useful because you can refer to the range name and not have to remember or point to its cell coordinates over and over again. Range names are very useful when you are:

- Entering formulas. For example, you can enter a formula such as SALES-COSTS if you have assigned those names to ranges of cells.
- Formatting cells. For example, you can specify a currency format for the range of cells named SALES.
- Printing a selected part of the model. For example, you can tell the program to print the range named Summary.
- Copying or moving cells. For example, you can tell the program to copy the range named 1989 to column F.
- Answering the prompt to the Goto command. For example, when prompted to enter the cell to go to, you can type SALES, and the cursor jumps to the upper left-hand corner of the range with that name.

EXERCISE

Exercise 4-4A
SPECIFYING RANGES

Refer to a spreadsheet user's guide for instructions on how to specify ranges when erasing cells. List the procedures here:

1. _____

2. _____

3. _____

QUESTIONS

1. What is the difference between a global format and a range or local format?
2. What is a range? Describe some typical shapes of ranges.
3. Describe two ways you can specify ranges.
4. What is a delimiter? When is it used? What characters are usually used for delimiters?
5. What are range names? When might you use them?

4-5 EDITING MODELS

If you want to improve or expand a model, you can edit or erase the contents of cells or insert or delete rows and columns.

EDITING CELL CONTENTS

The procedure you use to edit the contents of a cell depends on whether you notice the mistake while entering it or after having entered it.

Editing Data That Are Being Entered

If you notice a mistake while entering data, you generally have four choices.

- You can press **Backspace** to delete one or more characters to the left of the edit cursor. The key repeats if you hold it down so that you can delete characters one after another until you release the key.
- You can press **Esc** to abandon the entry and then correctly reenter it.
- You can press **Enter** and then correctly reenter the entry.
- You can press the **Edit** key to display the entry on the edit line, correct the entry, and then press **Enter**.

Editing Data That Have Been Entered

After you have pressed **Enter** to enter data into a cell, the entry must be returned to the edit line before you can edit it. You first move the cursor to the cell you want to edit, and then you press a designated key. For example, on Lotus 1-2-3 and Excel, you press **Edit** (**F2**). This displays the cell's contents on the second line of the control panel, along with a one-characterwide edit cursor. You can then freely move the edit cursor through the data and insert or delete characters as needed, much as when you are working on a word processing program.

Newer spreadsheet programs also have Search and Search and Replace commands that operate just like those on word processing programs. Using these commands, you can search or replace text, formulas, or functions.

Erasing Cell Contents

Most programs have a command you use to erase the contents of one or more cells. This command does not delete the cells themselves, just their contents. To erase the contents of cells, you first select the cells to be erased, and then you execute the Erase command (sometimes called the Blank or Clear command) or specify a range of cells when prompted to do so. For example, on Lotus 1-2-3, you press **/RE** (for *Range, Erase*), and a prompt asks you to specify the range to be erased. When you do so, and then press **Enter**, the contents of the cells in the range are erased. The Erase command on some programs erases only the labels, numbers, or formulas, not the formats assigned to the cells. On other programs, you can specify what you want erased from the cell. A few programs also let you specify that only numbers be deleted, leaving formulas and labels. This command automatically creates a template that can be used with other data.

INSERTING AND DELETING ROWS AND COLUMNS

One of the advantages of working with spreadsheet models is being able to revise and improve them as you gain more experience with the program and more understanding of an analysis. Most programs insert or delete an entire row or column. Others allow you to insert or delete partial rows or columns.

Inserting Rows and Columns

Often, you may find it necessary to insert rows or columns into the middle of an existing model. You can easily do this, and all formulas below the inserted rows, or to the right of the inserted columns, automatically adjust so that they continue to refer to the correct cells. When inserting rows and columns, keep the following points in mind:

- Rows are usually inserted above the cursor, and columns are inserted to the left of the cursor.
- On programs that insert an entire row or column, the cursor can be in any cell in the row or column you are inserting into. On programs that insert partial rows or columns, you must highlight all the columns you want to insert a row into or all the rows you want to insert a column into.
- If rows or columns are inserted within a print range or a range referred to by a formula, the range expands to include the new rows or columns. If rows or columns are inserted on the edge of the range, they are not included.

Deleting Rows and Columns

Deleting rows or columns has almost the same effect as inserting them. The spreadsheet closes up, and all formulas automatically adjust to refer to the correct cells. However, if you delete any cells that formulas that are not deleted refer to, those formulas will display some form of error message. These messages tell you that the cells they refer to have been deleted. It is therefore wise to save a model before making deletions. After making deletions, be sure to recalculate the spreadsheet to see if any error messages appear in the cells. If you have any doubts, save the model under a new filename so that you do not store it on top of, and erase, the original.

You may also want to convert formulas that refer to parts of the model to be deleted into their currently displayed values before deleting the cells they refer to. Most programs have a special command that converts formulas into their calculated values in situations like this. For example, on Lotus 1-2-3, you can convert formulas into their calculated values so that they do not change during later recalculations if the cells they refer to are changed or deleted. To do this, move the cursor to the cell containing the formula, press the **Edit** (**F2**) key to move the formula to the edit line, and then press the **Calc** (**F9**) key. To enter the calculated value into the cell, press **Enter**.

When deleting rows and columns, keep the following points in mind:

- If you do not delete the upper left-hand or lower right-hand corner of a range, the range contracts or expands to accommodate the change. If these corners are deleted, the range is no longer defined, and formulas referring to it display error messages.
- Rows and columns cannot be deleted when cells in the range are protected.

EXERCISES

Exercise 4-5A
EDITING CELL CONTENTS

Refer to a spreadsheet user's guide for instructions on how to edit the contents of a cell. List the procedures here:

1. _____
2. _____
3. _____

Exercise 4-5B
INSERTING A COLUMN

Refer to a spreadsheet user's guide for instructions on how to insert a column. List the procedures here:

1. _____
2. _____
3. _____

QUESTIONS

1. Explain four ways of editing data while they are being entered.
2. How do you edit data that have been entered?
3. What command do you use to delete the contents of a range of cells?
4. How do you insert blank rows into a spreadsheet model?
5. What happens when you delete cells that existing formulas refer to?

4-6 FORMULAS

Formula. A group of symbols (in a spreadsheet program) that expresses a calculation. Formulas can contain constants (4*3) or can refer to variables entered in other cells (4*A1). Operators, such as +, −, *, and /, in the formula indicate the arithmetic calculations to be performed.

Operator. A symbol used in a formula that tells the spreadsheet program what calculation to perform. The + operator, for example, tells the program to perform addition.

You can enter *formulas* in spreadsheet cells that either calculate numbers directly or refer to cells elsewhere on the spreadsheet into which you enter numbers or other formulas. When entering formulas, you must understand a few principles, namely, how operators and the order of operations work and the difference between constants and variables. Once you understand these principles, you can enter formulas by typing them in or by pointing.

OPERATORS—THE BASIC BUILDING BLOCKS

When you enter formulas, certain keys (and the symbols they generate on the screen) tell the program what calculations to perform. These symbols, or *operators*, are used in conjunction with numbers or cell references to create formulas. Table 4-3 lists typical spreadsheet operators, and Table 4-4 shows how you can use these operators to create formulas.

Table 4-3
SPREADSHEET OPERATORS

Operator	Use
+	Performs addition
−	Performs negation and subtraction
*	Performs multiplication
/	Performs division
^	Specifies an exponent

Table 4-4
SPREADSHEET FORMULAS

Formula	Displayed Result
10+10	20
10*4	40
30−5	25
200/5	40
A1+A2	The value in cell A1 plus the value in cell A2
A1*A2	The value in cell A1 multiplied by the value in cell A2
A1−A2	The value in cell A1 minus the value in cell A2
A1/A2	The value in cell A1 divided by the value in cell A2
−10+A1	-10 plus the value entered in cell A1
2*A1	2 multiplied by the value entered in cell A1
4−A1	4 minus the value entered in cell A1
200/A1	200 divided by the value entered in cell A1
10^2	100; that is, 10 raised to the 2nd power
10^A1	10 raised to the power entered in cell A1

Order of operations.
The sequence in which a formula is calculated. Every program has a specific sequence to follow.

Precedence. The priority assigned to operators that determines the sequence in which they are calculated when a formula contains more than one.

THE ORDER OF OPERATIONS

When you enter formulas that contain more than one operator, another concept, the *order of operations*, becomes important. Every program has a specific order that operators are calculated in.

- Some programs automatically calculate operations from left to right in the order they appear in the formula unless you use parentheses, in which case the numbers in parentheses are calculated first.

- Most programs follow algebra's rules of order of procedure. Operators are assigned a *precedence*, or priority: those with a higher precedence are performed before those with a lower precedence. For example, multiplication and division have equal precedence but a higher precedence than addition and subtraction, which also have equal precedence. Operators with the same level of precedence are calculated from left to right.

Suppose you want to add the numbers 1 and ½. To do this, you can enter the formula `1+1/2`. The formula contains two operators, one to add (+) and one to divide (/).

1. If calculations are performed from left to right, the answer is 1. First addition is performed, so 1+1=2; then division is performed, so 2/2=1.

2. If algebra's rules of precedence are followed, the answer is 1.5. First division is performed, so 1/2=0.5; then addition, which has a lower precedence, is performed, so 1+0.5=1.5.

You can enter formulas so that operations occur in the desired sequence, but it is usually easier to use parentheses because they control the order of operations regardless of the rules followed by the program. For example, entering the formula as `1+(1/2)` calculates the correct answer because the operations within the parentheses are always performed first. If parentheses are nested for example, `1+(1/(1/2))` the operations are performed from the innermost parentheses outward; in this formula, the answer would be 3.

Figure 4-15 shows how the order of operations works when controlled and uncontrolled by parentheses. The three formulas are all attempts to calculate the net price based on the list price of $10 and the discount of 20%. The formula requires two operators: multiplication and subtraction. Because multiplication will occur before subtraction if parentheses are not used, the way the formula is entered in important. As shown here, the same cell references and operators can be used in three different combinations, and only one of them will calculate the correct result.

	A	B	
1	List price	$10.00	
2	Discount	20%	
3	Net price #1	$8.00	← (1-B2)*B1
4	Net price #2	($1.00)	← 1-B2*B1
5	Net price #3	$9.80	← +B1*1-B2

Figure 4-15 Order of Operations
The formula in cell B3 subtracts the discount in cell B2 (20%) from 1 (100%) and multiplies the result (80%) by the list price ($10.00) in cell B1. Only the calculated result for Net Price #1, $8.00, is correct.

FORMULAS **223**

Constants. Numbers that are contained (embedded) in formulas, instead of being entered in cells to which formulas refer.

Variable. Any data entered into a model's cell, to which formulas in other cells refer. It's called a variable because it can easily be changed (varied) during a sensitivity analysis.

CONSTANTS AND VARIABLES

When you enter formulas, they can contain both constants and variables (Figure 4-16).

- *Constants* are numbers you do not expect to change. For example, the formula `5*10` contains only numbers; there are no references to other cells. Numbers contained in formulas are called constants because you can change them only with some difficulty, by reentering or editing the formula, for example, by changing it to `6*10`.

- *Variables* are numbers you do expect to change. For example, the formula `6*A1` contains a constant and a cell reference. The number in the cell referred to by the formula can be easily changed and is thus a variable. Numbers like this are called variables because you expect to change them to see what effect different numbers have on the outcome.

When creating a model, you first decide what variables you want to explore, and then structure your models accordingly. Formulas can be all constants. But these formulas do not take advantage of a spreadsheet's unique ability to explore what-ifs. To change a formula entered in this way, you must edit or reenter it. You build more powerful models by entering formulas that refer to other cells. This way, you can change the values in the cells the formula refers to, and it calculates them just as if they were part of the formula. For example, formulas can be part constant and part variable, or they can be all variables. You should consider almost every number a variable for three reasons.

	A	B
1	Net price	$8.00

← (1-0.2)*10

Formulas with all constants are like those you enter on a calculator. To enter a formula that contains only constants, you might type **(1-.2)*10** into cell B2. The formula calculates and displays the number *$8.00*. Because the numbers are part of the formula, you cannot change the discount or price to calculate a new result.

	A	B
1	List price	$10.00
2	Discount	20%
3	Net price	$8.00

← (1-B2)*B1

To enter a formula that contains constants and variables, you might enter **$10.00** into cell B1 and **20%** into cell B2. You then enter the formula **(1-B2)*B1** into cell B3. The formula subtracts the percentage in cell B2 from 100% and multiplies the result by the price in cell B1. The numbers in cells B1 and B2 are now variables. You can change them to explore what-ifs.

	A	B
1	List price	$10.00
2	Discount(%)	20%
3	Discount ($)	$2.00
4	Net price	$8.00

← +B2*B1
← +B1-B3

To enter a formula that contains only variables, first calculate the discount in dollars in cell B3 with the formula **+B2*B1**. You then enter the formula **+B1-B3** into cell B4. Both formulas contain only variables.

**Figure 4-16
Constants and Variables**
Formulas can contain all constants, part constants and part variables, or all variables.

224 SPREADSHEET APPLICATIONS

Cursor pointing. Using the cursor to point to cells to be included in a formula.

- Embedding a number in a formula is making an assumption either that it should not or cannot be changed or that it is unimportant to the outcome of the analysis. When exploring the model, you may find it is very sensitive to changes in that number—a phenomenon you would never discover if the number were embedded in a formula.
- The next time you use the model, you may forget there is an embedded number and not take it into consideration.
- Printouts of models generally print out only the displayed values, not the formulas behind them. Anyone else trying to follow your analysis might get lost if too many numbers are embedded in formulas rather than displayed on the printout.

WAYS TO ENTER FORMULAS

There are two ways to enter formulas: by typing them in or, if they refer to other cells, by pointing with the cursor to the cells referred to.

Typing in Formulas

You can type in a formula that refers to another cell, for example, `A1*A2`. But this formula begins with a letter, so if you type that letter first, many programs assume you are entering a label. To enter formulas that begin with letters on these programs, you must first type the plus sign (`+`) to enter the formula as `+A1*A2`. On Excel, you have to type an equal sign to begin any formula. For example, you would type `=.1*10` to find 10% of 10.

Pointing to Cells

You can use *cursor pointing* to point to cells referred to in the formula. Pointing is especially useful when working on larger spreadsheets where the cells you want to refer to are not displayed on the screen. Experienced users almost always build formulas by pointing because it is faster, more accurate, and easier than typing. Figure 4-17 shows how cursor pointing is used with Lotus 1-2-3 to enter a formula.

Figure 4-17 Using Cursor Pointing to Enter Formulas
The numbers 3 and 4 have been entered into cells A1 and A2. Here's what happens when you use pointing to enter a formula into cell A3 that adds the value in cell A2 to the value in cell A1.

A3:
+

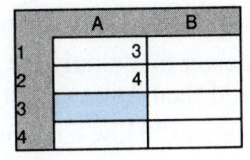

1. Move the cell pointer to cell A3, and then press + (the plus sign) to begin the formula.
   - The first line of the control panel indicates the cell pointer's position.
   - The formula on the second line of the control panel reads +.

A1: 3
+A1

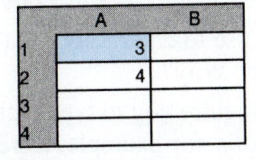

2. Press ↑ twice to move the cell pointer to A1.
   - The first line of the control panel indicates the cell pointer's position and the contents of the cell.
   - The formula on the second line of the control panel reads +*A1*.

Figure 4-17, continued

A3:
+A1+

	A	B
1	3	
2	4	
3		
4		

3. Press + (the plus sign).
   - The first line of the control panel indicates the cell pointer's position and the contents of the cell.
   - The formula on the second line of the control panel now reads +A1+.

A2: 4
+A1+A2

	A	B
1	3	
2	4	
3		
4		

4. Press ↑ to point to cell A2, the cell you want to add to A1.
   - The first line of the control panel indicates the cell pointer's position and the contents of the cell.
   - The formula on the second line of the control panel now reads +A1+A2.

A3: +A1+A2

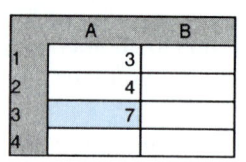

	A	B
1	3	
2	4	
3	7	
4		

5. Press **Enter** to complete the entry.
   - The formula appears on the first line of the control panel.
   - The formula leaves the second line of the control panel.
   - The formula is entered into cell A3 and displays the result 7.

EXERCISE

4-6

Exercise 4-6A
POINTING TO ENTER FORMULAS

Refer to a spreadsheet user's guide for instructions on how to enter a formula by pointing with the cursor. List the procedures here:

1. _____
2. _____
3. _____

QUESTIONS

4-7

1. What are operators? List and describe the functions of four of them.
2. What formula would you enter to multiply the values in cells A1 and C3? to divide A1 by C3? to add them? to subtract A1 from C3?
3. What is the order of operations? How can you change the order?
4. What is the difference between a constant and a variable?
5. What is a constant? When would you use one?
6. What is a variable? When would you use one?
7. What two ways can you use to enter a formula? Which approach do most experienced users prefer? Why?
8. Why do most programs require you to type a plus sign before entering the first character in a formula, for example, +B2−B3?

4-7
FUNCTIONS

Syntax. The rules that must be followed when entering a function or query.

Function name. The name assigned to a function that must always precede it.

Argument. Part of the syntax of a spreadsheet function. Arguments can be values, cell references, ranges, other functions or other cells.

All spreadsheet programs contain built-in functions designed to perform commonly used calculations. Many of the calculations they can perform are quite complicated, so functions simplify model building by simplifying the formula you must enter. Functions have a structure, or *syntax*, that you must follow.

- A *function name* must begin every function. The name is usually the full name or a contraction of the full name. On some programs, the @ must precede the function's name. For example, a function that sums the values in a series of cells might be called @SUM or SUM, and a function that averages the numbers in a series of cells might be named @AVG or AVG.
- *Arguments* must follow the name and be enclosed in parentheses. Arguments can be numbers, cell references, ranges, formulas, or other functions. If the function contains more than one argument, each part is separated from the other by commas or semicolons.

For example, to calculate monthly payments on a loan in 1-2-3, the function syntax is `@PMT(`*Principal, Interest, Period*`)`. The prefix is @PMT (for **P**ay-**M**en**T**). The arguments are *Principal*, *Interest*, and *Period* and are separated by commas and enclosed in parentheses. If you substitute numbers in the function, for example, the function `@PMT(10000,.14,48)` calculates and displays monthly payments of $1,402.60.

Instead of entering the values into a function, you can enter them into other cells, and then enter references to those cells into the function (Figure 4-18). The values in these cells are calculated just as if they were a part of the function. Entering the values into their own cells makes them into variables that you can easily change to explore what-ifs. Functions can also be used in combinations (Figure 4-19).

The number and types of functions vary from program to program, as do the exact name of the function and the way its arguments are structured. Functions can usually be grouped into categories such as financial, statistical, mathematical, and date and time. Here we describe and illustrate some of the functions available on most programs.

	A	B
1	Principal	$10,000
2	Interest	14%
3	Periods	48
4	Payment	$273.26
5		
6		

← @PMT(B1,B2/12,B3)

Figure 4-18 Functions That Refer to Other Cells
The function in cell B4 includes references to cells B1, B2, and B3. The references are separated by commas and arranged in the same order as if the values themselves had been entered into the function. The function calculates the same result as if the values had been in the function, but now you can easily change any of the three variables, and the function calculates a new result.

	A	B
1	Principal	$10,000
2	Interest	14%
3	Periods	48
4	Payment	$273.26
5	Payment (rounded)	$273.00	← @ROUND(@PMT(B1,B2/12,B3),0)
6		

Figure 4-19   Functions in Combinations
This figure shows the same function entered in Figure 4-18 nested in another function that rounds the result of the first function's calculation to zero decimal places. The function reads "Round the value of the function @PMT(B1,B2/12,B3) to zero decimal places." The original function calculates the value $273.26, but the new one rounds it to $273.00.

FINANCIAL FUNCTIONS

Financial functions are used to make calculations related to money (Figure 4-20). For example, you can calculate the future or present value of money, or calculate monthly payments due on a bank loan. For example,

- **Present Value** (@PV) calculates the present value of a series of payments (called an ordinary annuity). Arguments are the payments, interest rate, and period.
- **Payments** (@PMT) calculates the monthly payments needed to amortize a loan. Arguments are the principal, interest rate, and period.

	A	B
1	Financial Functions	
2		
3	Present value	
4	Payments	$1,000
5	Interest	12%
6	Term	12
7	Present value	6,194.37	← @PV(B4,B5,B6)
8		
9	Payments	
10	Principal	$50,000
11	Interest	12%
12	Term	360
13	Payments	514.31	← @PMT(B10,B11,B12)

Figure 4-20   Typical Financial Functions
This figure shows how functions can calculate present values and payments.

STATISTICAL FUNCTIONS

Statistical functions are used to make calculations about groups of numbers (Figure 4-21). For example, you can calculate averages, or determine the number of values, or lowest and highest values in a list.

- **Count** (@COUNT) calculates the number of nonblank cells in a range of values.
- **Maximum** (@MAX) calculates the largest value in a range of values.
- **Minimum** (@MIN) calculates the smallest value in a range of values.
- **Average** (@AVG) calculates the average value of a list of values.

Serial numbers. The numbers calculated by a date or time function.

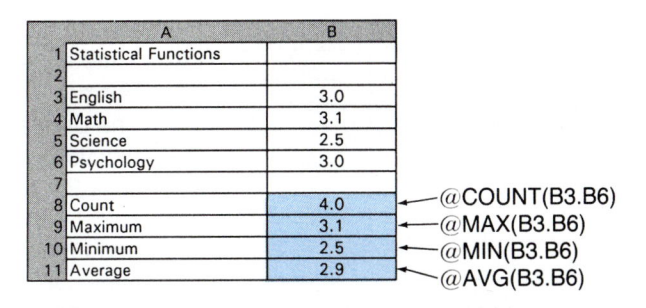

	A	B
1	Statistical Functions	
2		
3	English	3.0
4	Math	3.1
5	Science	2.5
6	Psychology	3.0
7		
8	Count	4.0 ← @COUNT(B3.B6)
9	Maximum	3.1 ← @MAX(B3.B6)
10	Minimum	2.5 ← @MIN(B3.B6)
11	Average	2.9 ← @AVG(B3.B6)

Figure 4-21 Typical Statistical Functions
This figure shows how functions can calculate counts, maximums, minimums, and averages.

NUMERIC AND MATHEMATICAL FUNCTIONS

Numeric and mathematical functions are used to make arithmetic and trigonometric calculations (Figure 4-22). For example, you can calculate totals, square roots, sines, cosines, and round off numbers.

- **Sum** (@SUM) calculates the total sum of a range of values. For example, @SUM(A1.A5) adds the values in cells A1 through A5.
- **Round** (@ROUND) rounds a number to a specified number of decimal places. The arguments are a number with at least one decimal place and the number of decimal positions you want to round it to.
- **Square root** (@SQRT) calculates the square root of a number.
- **Sine** (@SIN) calculates the sine of a radian angle.

	A	B
1	Mathematical Functions	
2		
3	Sums	
4	1989	$125,000
5	1990	273,453
6	1991	323,467
7	Sum	$721,920 ← @SUM(B4.B6)
8		
9	Number	1.10
10	Round	1.00 ← @ROUND(B9)
11	Square root	1.04881 ← @SORT(B9)
12	Sine	0.89121 ← @SIN(B9)

Figure 4-22 Typical Mathematical Functions
This figure shows how functions can calculate sums, round numbers off, and calculate square roots and sines.

DATE AND TIME FUNCTIONS

Date and time functions display dates and times as *serial numbers*. The serial number can be formatted so that the date and time are displayed in a variety of other formats. Figure 4-23 shows the results of formatting dates calculated with date functions.

The number of date and time functions available varies from program to program, as does their syntax. For Lotus 1-2-3, two of the most frequently used date functions are @NOW and @DATE.

Figure 4-23 Date and Time Functions and Formats
The date and time functions entered into cells B1 and B9 calculate the serial date and time numbers shown in cells B2 and B10. The cells below each serial number show how the available formats affect the number's display.

	A	B
1	Date Function	@DATE(92,1,11)
2	Serial number	33614
3	DD-MMM-YY	11-Jan-92
4	DD-MMM	11-Jan
5	MMM-YY	Jan-92
6	Long Intn'l	01/11/92
7	Short Intn'l	01/11
8		
9	Time Function	@TIME(12,1,45)
10	Serial number	0.501215278
11	HH:MM:SS AM/PM	12:01:45 PM
12	HH:MM AM/PM	12:01 PM
13	Long Intn'l	12:01:45
14	Short Intn'l	12:01

- **@NOW** calculates the current date or time if it was entered into the computer system's clock when starting up.
- **@DATE** calculates the serial number for the specified date. For example, `@DATE(92,1,30)` calculates the serial number 33663 on 1-2-3 — the number of days since December 31, 1899.
- **@TIME** calculates the serial number for the specified time. For example, `@TIME(23,59,59)` calculates the serial number .9999, or 11:59.59 P.M.

The serial numbers can also be added and subtracted, for example, to find the number of days between two dates or the numbers of hours, minutes, and seconds between two times (Figure 4-24). The serial numbers are usually calculated by counting from a date at the turn of the century. (For example, Lotus 1-2-3 counts from December 31, 1899, Excel from January 1, 1900, and SuperCalc from March 1, 1900.)

	A	B	
1		Unformatted	
2	Date of birth	25598	← @DATE(70,1,30)
3	Current date	32949.82539	← @NOW
4	Number of days	7351.825394	← +B3-B2
5	Number of years	20.14198738	← +B4/365

You enter the function @**DATE(70,1,30)** into cell B2 and the function @**NOW** into cell B3. The formula **+B3−B2** in cell B4 calculates the number of days between the two dates—in effect, how many days you have lived. The formula **+B4/365** in cell B5 calculates the number of years you have lived.

	A	B	
1		Formatted	
2	Date of birth	30-Jan-70	← @DATE(70,1,30)
3	Current date	17-Mar-90	← @NOW
4	Number of days	7351.825394	← +B3-B2
5	Number of years	20.14198738	← +B4/365

Here, the model has been formatted to make it possible to read the dates.

Figure 4-24 Date Arithmetic
What if you were born on January 30, 1970, and wanted to find out how many days you have lived as of today? You enter these two dates, and then subtract the earlier from the later to calculate the number of days.

EXERCISE

Exercise 4-7A
FUNCTIONS THAT SUM AND AVERAGE

Refer to a spreadsheet user's guide for instructions on how to enter functions that calculate sums and averages. List the procedures here:

Sum _____

Average_____

QUESTIONS

1. What are functions? What are they used for?
2. How would you enter a function to round the value 1.11234? to round the value in cell B4?
3. What will the function SUM(B4.B6) do? What is the term SUM called? What is the reference B4.B6 called (other than a range)?
4. What arguments are needed to calculate the monthly payments needed to amortize a loan?
5. What is a date function?
6. What does @NOW calculate on 1-2-3?
7. What are two 1-2-3 date and time functions? When would you use them?
8. Describe the model you would build to calculate the number of days you have been at college so far.

4-8
CHANGING A MODEL'S APPEARANCE

When you want your models, whether on the screen or in printouts, to be attractive and easy to read, you use formats to align text and format numbers. When you do this, you can use global or range format commands.

- A global format affects all cells on the spreadsheet. Generally, you select a global format based on the format that will be used most often in a model and then override it in selected cells to display them as desired.
- To override the global format in selected cells, you use range formats.

Range formats have priority over global formats. For example, if you use a range command to format a group of cells and then change the global format, the format of the cells you formatted with the range command does not change. To make the cells in the range respond again to global commands, you must first reset them to the global format using a command designed for this.

COLUMN WIDTHS

You can change the width of individual columns or of all columns on the spreadsheet, and you can change them before or after you enter data into them. If you use a global command, it changes the width of all columns except those previously changed with a range command.

The width of a column, as measured in characters, determines how many characters can be displayed in cells falling in the column. When you first load a spreadsheet, all columns are usually nine characters wide. You can change the width of any or all columns to between one and the maximum width specified by your program.

Narrow columns let you see more on the screen and squeeze more into a printout. Some programs even let you set columns widths to 0 so that their contents are hidden on the screen and don't appear in printouts. Because column width is always set for an entire column — it cannot be wider or narrower at the top than at the bottom — a column must be set to the width required by the longest entry in the column.

FORMATTING TEXT

You can align text (and, on some programs, numbers) in cells. They can be aligned with the right or left edge of the cell or centered in the cell. On some programs, you can change the font used for text so that it prints in a different typestyle, in boldfaced or italic type, underlined, or in color.

FORMATTING VALUES

Spreadsheet programs provide several formats you can use when formatting values on your spreadsheet. When formatting numbers, you can often specify the number of decimal places to be displayed. Formatting numbers does not affect the way they are used in formulas. Numbers are always accurately calculated up to the number of decimal places offered by the program, usually fifteen or so. For example, you can format the number `1000.1425` so that it is displayed as *$1,000, $1,000.14, 1000.142,* and so on, but it is always calculated by any formulas that refer to it as 1000.1425. Figure 4-25 illustrates some typical formats.

	A	B	C	D
1	Global format	1.5		
2				
3	Decimal places	None	One	Two
4	Fixed	2	1.5	1.50
5	Scientific	2E+00	1.5E+00	1.50E+00
6	Currency	$2	$1.5	$1.50
7	, (comma)	2	1.5	1.50
8	General	1.5	1.5	1.5
9	+/-	+	+	+
10	Percent	150%	150.0%	150.00%
11	Text	+$B$1	+$B$1	+$B$1

Figure 4-25 Value Formats
This figure shows some typical formats and how they are displayed when the number of decimal places is changed. The number 1.5 is entered in each cell.

EXERCISES

Exercise 4-8A
CHANGING COLUMN WIDTHS

Refer to a spreadsheet user's guide for instructions on how to change the width of a column. List the procedures here:

1. _____
2. _____
3. _____

Exercise 4-8B
FORMATTING NUMBERS

Refer to a spreadsheet user's guide for instructions on how to format numbers. List the procedures here:

1. _____
2. _____
3. _____

QUESTIONS

1. If you format cells with a range command and then change the global format, what happens to the cells formatted with the range command?
2. Why would you want to change the width of a column?
3. List and briefly describe five formats you can use for values.

CHANGING A MODEL'S APPEARANCE

4-9 COPYING AND MOVING DATA

Copying. Making a duplicate copy.

Moving. Copying data to a new location and then deleting them in the original location.

Source range. The cells containing data that are to be copied or moved to another range. See Target range.

Target range. The cells specified as the new location for the contents of cells in the source range when they are moved or copied. Also called the destination range.

You can copy or move the contents of cells to other locations on a spreadsheet. *Copying* lets you save time by entering a formula once and then copying it as needed. *Moving* lets you reorganize models as you create or revise them. These are two of the most powerful spreadsheet features.

COPYING DATA

Copying allows you to enter formulas once and then copy them where needed, greatly speeding up the process of model building. For example, you can create a monthly budget by entering the necessary formulas into the first monthly column and then copying them to the other monthly columns.

When you copy a range of cells, a duplicate set of the range's contents and formats is copied from the original cells, called the ***source range***, to a new location, called the ***target range*** (also called the *destination range*). The data in the cells in the source range are left unchanged (Figure 4-26). If any cells in the target range contain data, they are overwritten by the copied data.

When you copy ranges, you must specify cell addresses that define the source and target ranges (Figure 4-27). When you copy the contents of cells to which formulas in other cells refer, those formulas continue to refer to the original cells, not to the copies.

MOVING DATA

When you move a range of cells, a duplicate of the cell's contents and formats is moved to the target range, and then the contents of the cells in the source range are automatically deleted (Figure 4-28). If the cells in the target range contain

Figure 4-26 Copying a Range
When you copy a range of cells, a duplicate set of the range's contents and formats is copied from the source range to the target or destination range. Data in the cells in the source range are left unchanged.

**Figure 4-27
Specifying Ranges
When Copying**
The cells you specify as the source and target ranges are shown in a second color. Some combinations of source and target ranges are not possible, for example, copying a column to a cell. These impossible combinations are indicated by being overprinted in color on the figure. (Some programs have a Transpose command that allows you to copy data from columns to rows and vice versa.)

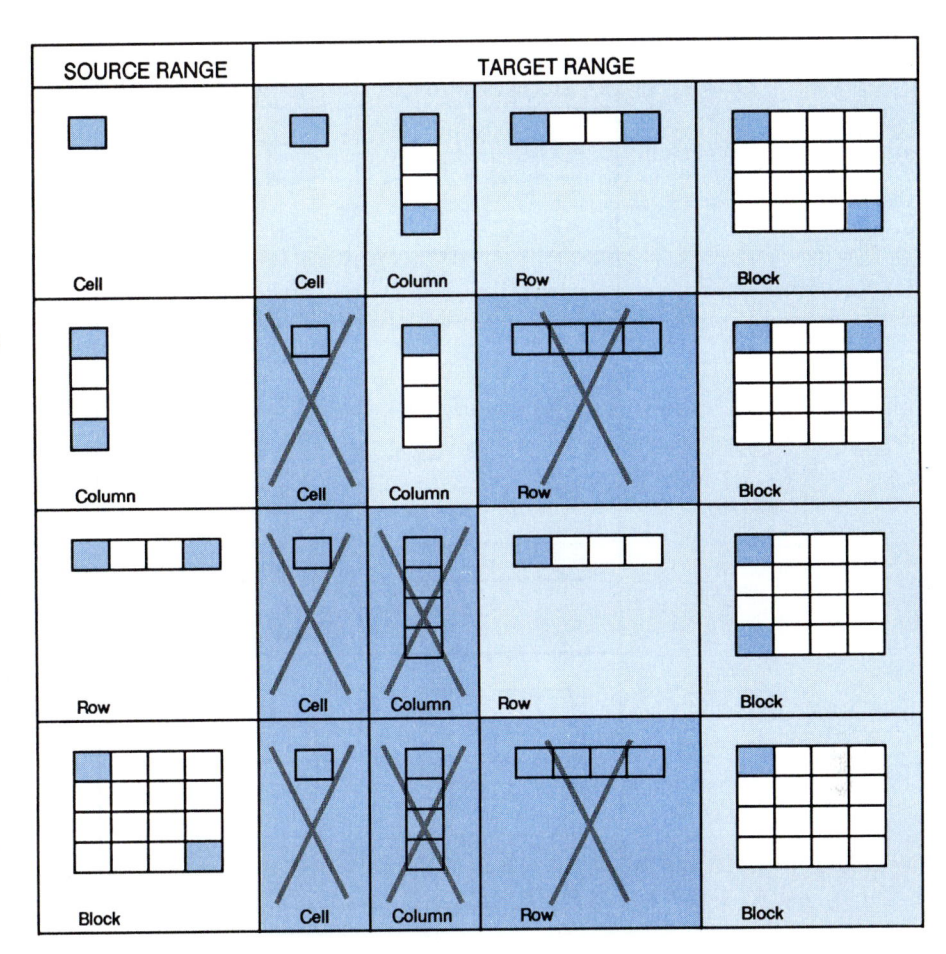

Figure 4-28 Moving a Range
When you move a range of cells, a duplicate of the cell's contents and formats is moved to the target range, and then the contents of the cells in the source range are automatically deleted.

COPYING AND MOVING DATA   **235**

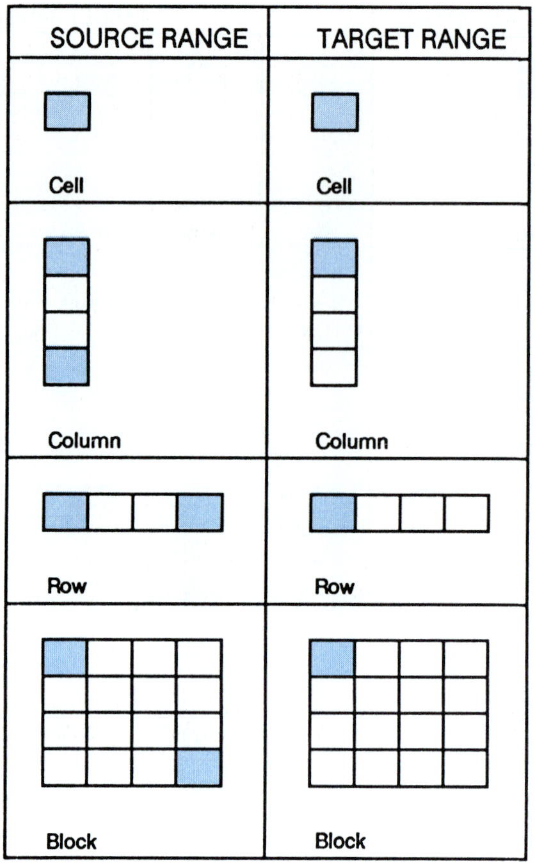

**Figure 4-29
Specifying Ranges When Moving**
When you specify ranges to move, you specify the upper-leftmost and lower-rightmost cells in the source range and the upper-leftmost cell in the target range.

any data, they are overwritten by the data that are moved in. If any formulas refer to cells in the target range, they display error messages.

When you move the contents of cells, you must specify cells that define the source and target ranges. The cells you specify vary depending on the shape of the range (Figure 4-29).

- If you are moving a single cell, the source range is the address of that cell, and the target range is the address of the cell you move it to.
- If you are moving a column, you specify the top and bottom cells in the source range and only the top cell in the target range.
- If you are moving a row, you specify the first and last cells in the source range and only the first cell in the target range.
- If you are moving a block, you specify the upper left-hand and lower right-hand cells in the source range and only the upper left-hand cell in the target range.

RELATIVE AND ABSOLUTE CELL REFERENCES

If you typed in every formula and function that you needed, you would not have to be concerned about relative and absolute cell references. But they become very important when you enter a formula in one cell and then copy it to others to save time.

Relative References

When you create formulas, they often refer to other cells on the spreadsheet. The program does not "remember" the actual cell coordinates (for example,

Relative reference. A spreadsheet formula reference to another cell that refers to its position relative to the cell containing the formula, for example, two rows up and one column over. When the formula is copied it will refer to a cell in the same relative position to the cell to which it is copied. See also Absolute reference.

Absolute reference. A reference in a formula to a row or column that remains unchanged when copied to other cells. Absolute reference is frequently specified with dollar signs ($), for example $A$1. See also Relative reference.

A1); instead, it remembers the position relative to the cell the formula is entered in, for example, one column to the left and two rows up. When you copy the formula to another cell, it refers not to the original cell but to whatever cell is one column to the left and two rows up from the cell you copied it to (Figure 4-30). This automatic adjustment occurs because the reference to the cell is a *relative reference*; that is, the position of the cell referred to is relative to the position of the formula. The program's default setting is relative references; all formulas you enter have relative references unless you specify otherwise.

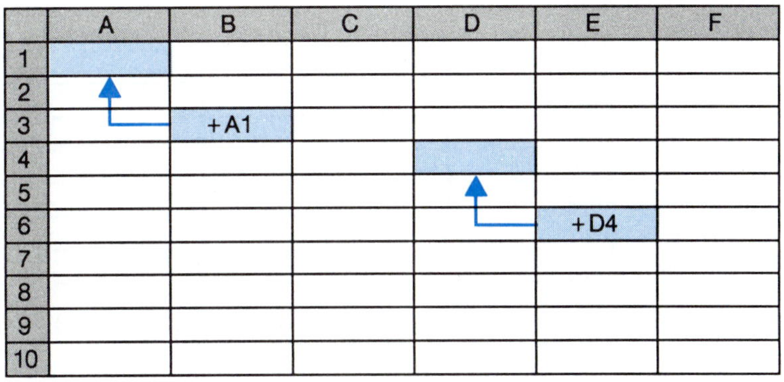

Figure 4-30 Copying Relative References
When you enter the cell reference +A1 into cell B3, any value or label in cell A1 is carried to cell B3. But when you copy the formula to cell E6, it no longer refers to cell A1 but to cell D4 because the formula always refers to the cell one column to the left and two rows up.

Absolute References

You do not always have to keep references to cells relative. You can also make them *absolute references* so that a formula refers to the same cell wherever it is copied on the spreadsheet (Figure 4-31). On many programs you specify an absolute reference by preceding it with a dollar sign. For example, $A$1 means that both the column and row references are absolute.

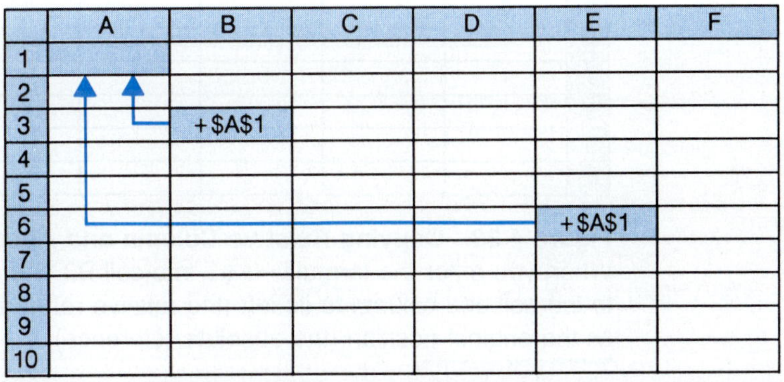

Figure 4-31 Copying Absolute References
When you enter the formula +$A$1 into cell B3 (the dollar signs indicate both the row and column references are absolute), it has the same result as entering +A1, but it behaves differently when you copy it. It no longer remembers the cell it refers to relative to its position. It remembers the absolute position, in this case, cell A1. When you copy it to another cell, say, cell E6, it still refers to cell A1.

4-9

Mixed reference. A cell reference in a spreadsheet that is part relative and part absolute.

Mixed References

You can also use *mixed references*, which keep the reference to the row or column relative while making the other reference absolute (Figures 4-32 and 4-33).

	A	B	C	D	E	F
1						
2						
3		+A$1				
4						
5						
6					+D$1	
7						
8						
9						
10						

Figure 4-32 Copying Absolute Column and Relative Row References
You enter the formula `+$A1` (the column reference is absolute, but the row is relative) into cell B3. When you copy the cell reference to cell E6, part of it changes, and part of it does not.

- The column reference, which was made absolute by adding a dollar sign in front of it, does not change when copied. It always refers to column A.

- The row reference, the part of the formula that is relative, does change. It always refers to a cell two rows up, just as it did in the original position.

	A	B	C	D	E	F
1						
2						
3		+$A1				
4						
5						
6					+$A4	
7						
8						
9						
10						

Figure 4-33 Copying Relative Column and Absolute Row References
When you enter the formula `+A$1` into cell B3 and copy it to cell E6, it refers to the cell one column to its left (the relative reference) and on the same row as the original position (the absolute reference).

Specifying References

The way you specify that a cell reference is absolute varies from program to program. On most programs, you specify absolute references by adding dollar signs ($) in front of the column or row references.

Many programs also assign a function key the task of cycling through four possible combinations of cell references so that when you are using cursor pointing to build a formula, you can point to a cell and press the key to select the type of reference you want. When you are pointing to a cell in point mode, the cell reference you are pointing to changes its reference each time you press the specified key. As you cycle through the reference types, the cell reference on the edit line changes. Table 4-5 describes the sequence of available choices.

Table 4-5
ABSOLUTE AND RELATIVE CELL REFERENCES

Cell Reference	Column	Row
A1	Relative	Relative
$A1	Absolute	Relative
A$1	Relative	Absolute
$A$1	Absolute	Absolute

EXERCISES

Exercise 4-9A
COPYING DATA

Refer to a spreadsheet user's guide for instructions on how to copy data from one cell to another. List the procedures here:

1. _____
2. _____
3. _____

Exercise 4-9B
MOVING DATA

Refer to a spreadsheet user's guide for instructions on how to move data from one cell to another. List the procedures here:

1. _____
2. _____
3. _____

QUESTIONS

1. What is the difference between copying and moving a range?
2. When copying or moving cells, how to you specify the range to be moved?
3. If you copy or move data into a range that already contains data, what happens to the old data?
4. What is the difference between a relative and an absolute cell reference?
5. What are mixed references?
6. How do you specify absolute references on most programs?
7. What key do you use on most programs to cycle through the four possible combinations of cell references?
8. If you enter the formula B3 into cell D4 and then copy it to cell G6, what cell will it refer to in its new position?
9. If you enter the formula $B$3 (the $ indicates an absolute reference) into cell D4 and then copy it to cell G6, what cell will it refer to in its new position?
10. If you enter the formula $B3 (the $ indicates an absolute reference) into cell D4 and then copy it to cell G6, what cell will it refer to in its new position?
11. If you enter the formula B$3 into cell D4 and then copy it to cell G6, what cell will it refer to in its new position?

4-10
BUSINESS GRAPHICS

Graph. A visual representation of verbal or numeric information. There are various types of graphs including line graphs, bar graphs, stacked-bar graphs, and pie charts.

Data range. A range of cells containing values to be graphed.

Using the graphics capabilities built into almost all spreadsheets, you can create *graphs* to analyze financial and statistical data. For example, you can use graphs to find trends and relationships between sets of numbers such as sales, expenses, and profits over a period. Once graphs are created;

- You can print out the final results for distribution to others. Many word processing programs now read graphs created on programs such as 1-2-3 so you can incorporate them into your documents.
- You can store a series of graphic images so that you can display them one after another on your computer's screen (or project them onto a larger screen) to support an audiovisual presentation.
- You can transfer the graphs to a program that enhances them, for example, to add text, select from a variety of typefaces, add boxes around them, and add shades or colors.
- You can use a slide program designed to polish and present them in sequence.

Graphs are important tools in business because managers and analysts often need to find or illustrate patterns in sets of numbers. Many people who do not like interpreting tables of numbers find that business graphs can provide the same information more quickly and efficiently.

For instance, if your profits increased from $5,000 to $25,000, this would seem to be a successful trend. But if sales increased from $25,000 to $500,000 over the same period, the growth in profits wouldn't seem nearly as impressive. Obviously, a single set of numbers by themselves tells only part of the story; their relationship to other sets of numbers tells another. How then can numbers be easily related and compared? One way is to present the numbers as graphs that pictorially represent the relationship. When you create graphs, the trend in profits looks great until you plot them to show their relationship to sales (Figure 4-34).

CREATING GRAPHS

There is usually one requirement when creating a graph. You must specify a range of cells, called the ***data range***, that contains the data (called a *data set*) to be graphed (Figure 4-35). When specifying data ranges to be graphed, keep the following points in mind:

- The graph plots whatever values are in the cells in the data range. If you change the values in the range, the graph changes.
- To compare data, you can graph more than one data range on the same graph. The only exception is pie charts, where you plot only one data range.
- The data can be in rows or columns.
- The ranges should all have the same number of cells. For example, if you graph six cells of sales data to compare it with expenses, you must graph six cells of expense data.

Figure 4-34 Trend in Profits
Graphs can reveal relationships between sets of numbers.

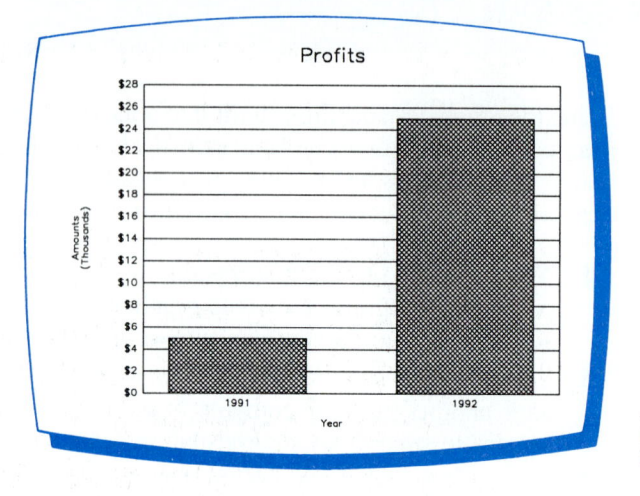

Just the company's profits have been plotted. The increase looks dramatic.

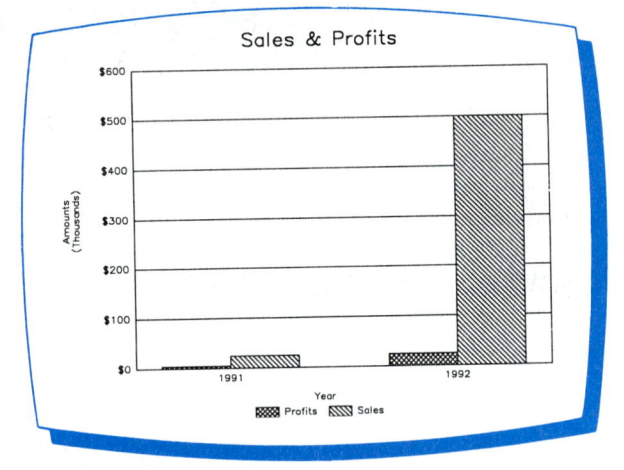

The profits have been plotted against sales. Now it becomes obvious that there is a problem. The company's growth in profits is lagging behind its growth in sales.

	A	B	C	D	E	F
1	Part 1. Variables					
2	Initial sales	1,000				
3	Sales growth rate	10%				
4	Cost of goods sold	56%				
5						
6	Part 2. Model					
7	Year	1992	1993	1994	1995	1996
8	Sales	1,000	1,100	1,210	1,331	1,464
9	Cost of goods sold	560	616	678	745	820
10	Gross margin	440	484	532	586	644

Row 7 ← X-axis range
Row 8 ← First data range
Row 10 ← Second data range

Figure 4-35 Graph Data Ranges
Graph data ranges are cells in a column or row. Each range must include the same number of cells.

Graph Options

When you want to add various refinements to your graph, most programs provide many options (Figure 4-36):

242 SPREADSHEET APPLICATIONS

Discrete data. Data that consist of values measured at a series of selected points. The data between these selected points is meaningless. See Continuous data.

Time-series graphs. Graphs that show how something changes its quantity over a period of time.

Continuous data. The data that are sampled and measured to determine a trend. The values between the measured data points can be estimated. See also Discrete data.

A. *Titles* can be added to the graph and to the X and Y axes. (The X axis is the horizontal axis and the Y axis is the vertical axis.)
B. *Scale formats* change the way numbers are displayed on the X and Y axes.
C. *Legends* identify data ranges.
D. *Grid lines* can be added horizontally or vertically to the graph.
E. *Data labels* can be added to identify or annotate data points.

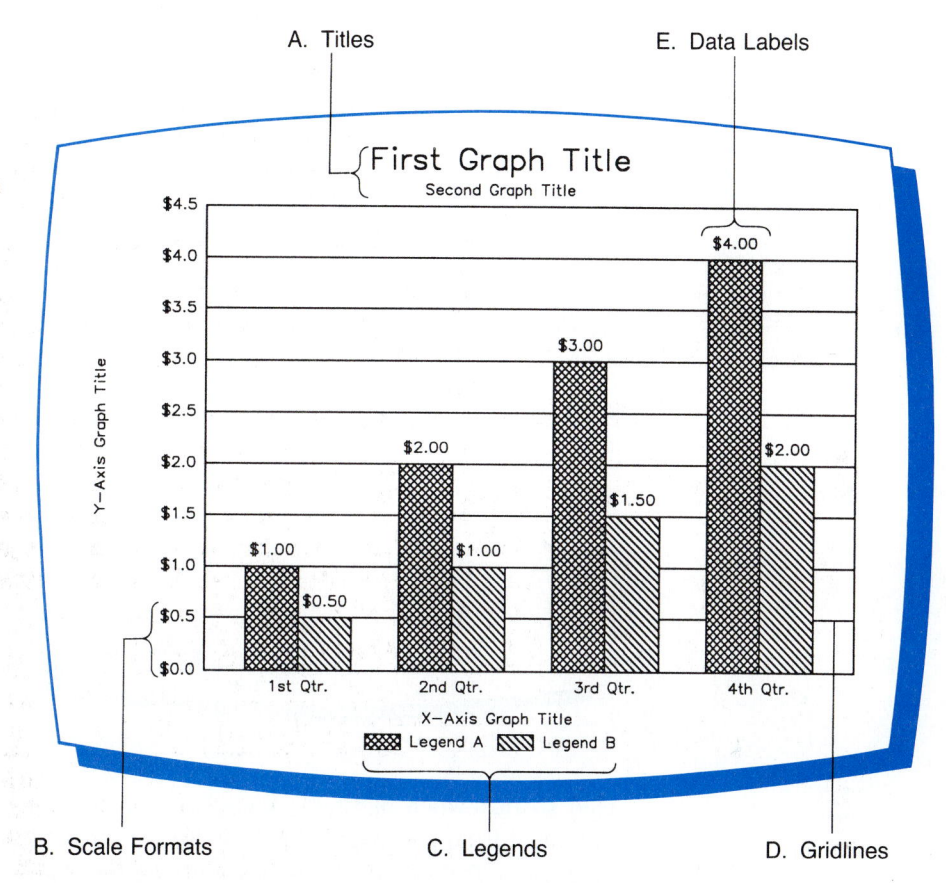

Figure 4-36 The Graph
You can use graph options to improve the look of your graphs and increase their readability for others.

TYPES OF BUSINESS GRAPHS

When creating a graph, you select the type of graph that best illustrates the data. You can instantly change the type of graph without reentering the data. You can experiment with several graph types to find the one that best illustrates the data. When creating graphs, you are usually graphing discrete or continuous data.

Discrete data consist of values measured at a series of selected points. When plotted on a graph, the space between the data points are meaningless. Graphs of this kind are frequently called *time-series graphs* and are used in business to plot sales, profits, inventory, and other important financial values (Figure 4-37).

Continuous data occur when measurements have been sampled to determine a trend. Although each data point is a discrete value, the points are sam-

BUSINESS GRAPHICS 243

Interpolation. Calculating a data point based on the data points on either side.

Figure 4-37 Discrete Data
In this example, sales can be plotted for a seven year period. If you pick a point on the X (horizontal) axis that falls between periods and read up to the line connecting data points and then across to the Y axis, you will not locate the results at that point in time.

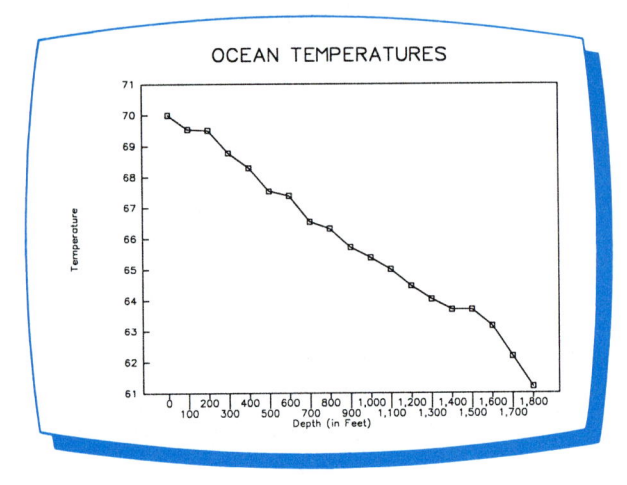

Figure 4-38 Continuous Data
In this example, water temperatures can be estimated for any depth by reading up from the X axis, which shows depth, and across to the Y axis, which shows temperature.

pled so that when plotted, values between the measured data points can be estimated from the graph (Figure 4-38). In this graph, for example, an oceanographer can measure the temperature of the water at various depths in the ocean. If samples are measured at increments of 100 feet from the surface down to 1,800 feet, a graph can be plotted using the available data points. This estimation of values falling between data points that were actually measured and plotted is called *interpolation*. When graphing continuous data, a general rule is that the more data points you have measured and plotted, the more accurate the graph is.

Spreadsheet programs offer a variety of graph types that you can use to plot your data. Figure 4-39 illustrates the basic types found on all programs.

Figure 4-39 Graph Types
Spreadsheet programs allow you to plot your data as line graphs, bar graphs, stacked-bar graphs, or pie charts.

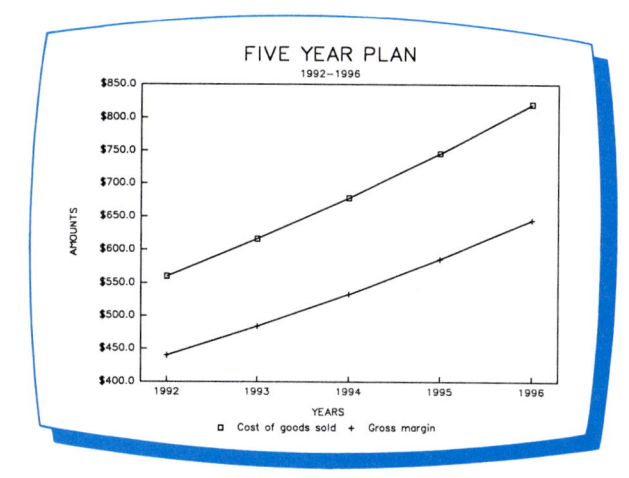

Line Graph. A line graph plots a series of values, against the X axis (the horizontal axis) and can be used to plot discrete and continuous data. The X axis contains a series of descriptive labels with no numeric value.

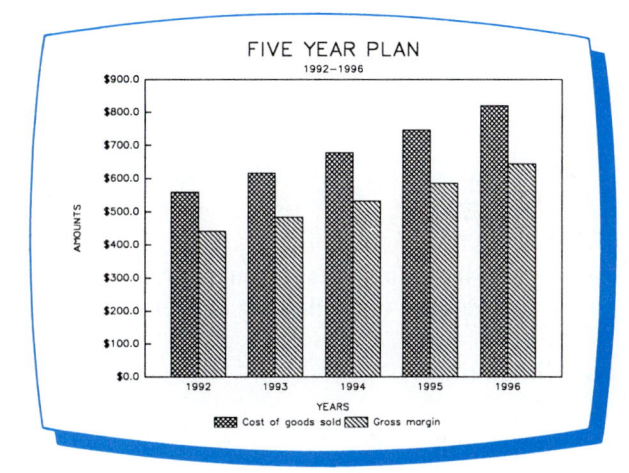

Bar Graph. Bar graphs are like a series of snapshots taken at intervals. All bars on a bar graph start at the zero line. Positive values are indicated by bars that extend up from this base line; negative values, by bars that extend down. Bar graphs are particularly appropriate for discrete data, for example, if you want to graph a comparison of sales by product.

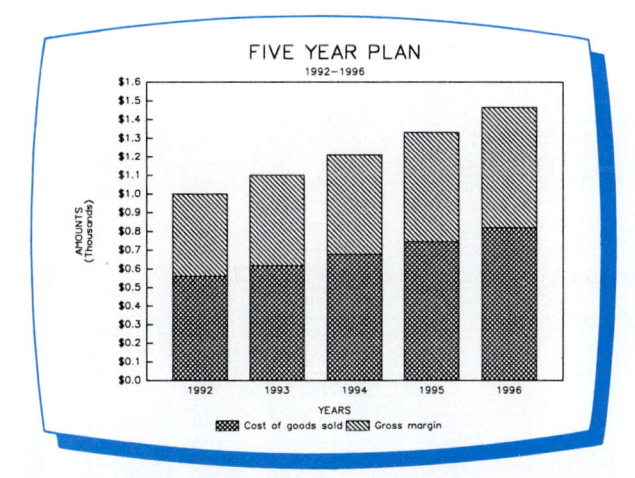

Stacked-Bar Graph. Stacked-bar graphs are similar to bar graphs, but instead of the bars being arranged side by side, they are stacked on top of each other. A stacked-bar graph can show several sets of data at the same time.

BUSINESS GRAPHICS   245

Figure 4-39, continued

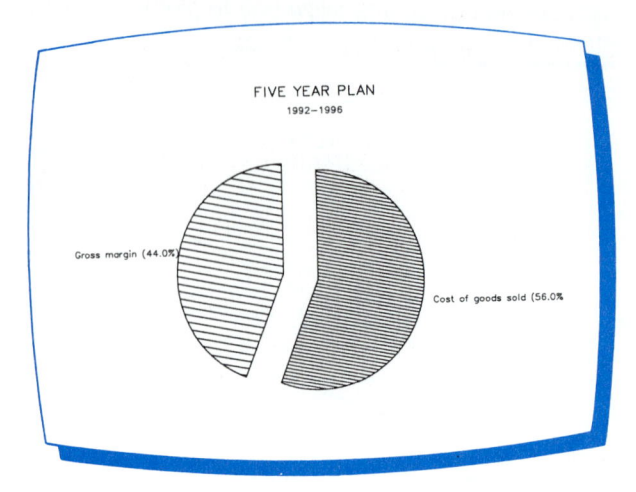

Pie Chart. A pie chart is like a single bar on a stacked-bar graph; it can show only one set of data at a time. Pie charts are generally used to illustrate relationships such as sales of various products in a product line. The pie represents the "whole" or 100 percent, and the slices represent parts of the whole. The relative sizes of the parts are indicated by the size of the pie slices.

4-10

EXERCISES

Exercise 4-10A
IDENTIFYING GRAPH OPTIONS

Figure 4-40 shows a typical business graph. Label parts of the graph with the letters that identify the following elements:

A. Graph title
B. X axis
C. X-axis title
D. Y axis
E. Y-axis title
F. Data ranges
G. Legends
H. Grid lines

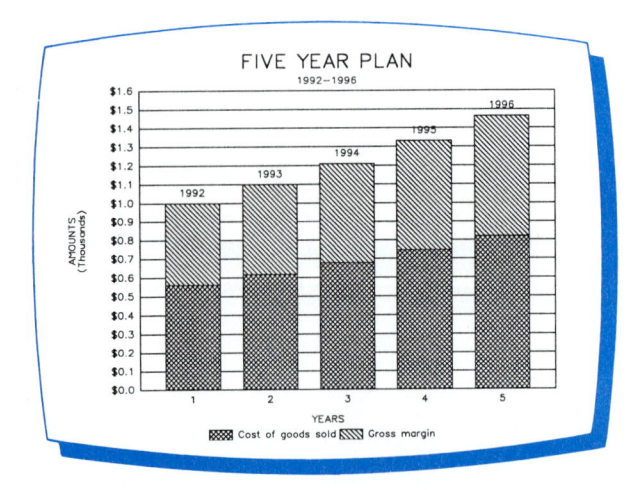

Figure 4-40 A Typical Business Graph

246   SPREADSHEET APPLICATIONS

> **Exercise 4-10B**
> **SELECTING GRAPH TYPES**

Using Figure 4-39 as a guide, identify the type of graph you would use to plot the data in the table below. If you could use more than one type, list all those that you might try.

MATCHING DATA WITH THEIR GRAPH TYPES

Type	Graph
Profits and sales	_____
Breakdown of sales by division	_____
Increase in sales over five years	_____
Measurements in a scientific experiment	_____
Daily temperatures	_____

QUESTIONS

1. What is the main advantage of creating graphs with a spreadsheet?
2. List and briefly describe three options you can use to improve the appearance of your graphs.
3. How does discrete data differ from continuous data? What types of graphs or charts would you use for each?
4. What is interpolation?
5. List four basic graph types, and discuss briefly what each type is used for.
6. If you were going to plot monthly sales and expenses for a twelve-month period, which type of graph(s) would best represent this data?

4-11
AUTOMATING WITH MACROS

Record mode. The mode used to record keystrokes so you can play them back. Used to automate procedures when working with applications programs.

Macro language. Key words and other elements that allow you to create macros.

Keyword. A word in a macro language that represents one of the keys on the keyboard.

Macros are simply a way to store keystrokes so that they can be played back later. They can save you from having to rekey repetitive data or commands. It is like making a piano into a player piano; the only difference is that the computer's keys do not move up and down—it is all done electronically. Macros are created in two ways: by recording them or by using a macro language.

RECORDING MACROS

Recording macros is usually a two-step process.

1. Record keystrokes. You execute a command to begin recording keystrokes. On some programs, this is called *record mode* (also called *learn mode*). You then enter the data or commands you want to use again. The keystrokes are automatically recorded as you run through the sequence of commands or characters you want to record.

2. Attach the keystrokes to a key. After the keystrokes are recorded, you are prompted to select a key they will be attached to. You then turn off the record mode.

Whenever you want to play back the recorded keystrokes, you hold down one of the special keys on the keyboard (usually **Alt**), and then press the key you attached the macro to. The entire sequence of keystrokes will be automatically replayed.

MACRO LANGUAGES

On some programs, you can also enter macros by typing them in, assigning names to them, and then executing them. When entering them like this, you are actually using a *macro language*. You then enter the keystrokes needed as a label and name the label. The language contains *keywords* used to indicate keys on the keyboard (see Table 4-6). Until you have all commands memorized, the best way to create a macro is to enter the entire command keystroke by keystroke, noting on a sheet of paper the keys you press.

Table 4-6
1-2-3'S MACRO KEYWORDS

Macro	Keyword Equivalent	Macro	Keyword Equivalent
Function Keys		*Other Keys*	
Edit (F2)	{edit}	←	{left}
Name (F3)	{name}	→	{right}
Abs (F4)	{abs}	↑	{up}
Goto (F5)	{goto}	↓	{down}
Window (F6)	{window}	Home	{home}
Query (F7)	{query}	End	{end}
Table (F8)	{table}	Backspace	{bs}
Calc (F9)	{calc}	Del	{del}
Graph (F10)	{graph}	Esc	{esc}
		Enter	~ (the tilde)

User-defined menus.
Menus created by users of applications programs rather than by the program's authors.

Let's look at an example. To print a worksheet using 1-2-3, you must press the slash key (/), and then select *Print, Printer, Align, Go, Page,* and *Quit*. But you can create a macro so that this same series of commands is executed when you hold down **Alt** and press the letter **P** (or any other key you assign the series of keystrokes to). This macro would be written as `{HOME}/ppagpq`.

- `{HOME}`, enclosed in braces, tells the program to move the cursor to cell A1.
- The slash (/) calls up the Main menu.
- The sequence of letters (`ppagpq`) is the same sequence you would type to print the model from the keyboard.

After entering the macro, you assign it a name; in this example, you name it so that it is executed when you hold down **Alt** and press **P**.

Macros can be made to pause during execution and accept operator input. For example, on Lotus 1-2-3, you use the `{?}~` command to pause the macro for operator input. The macro continues only after you press **Enter**.

USER-DEFINED MENUS

Programs that provide you with a macro language also allow you to create your own menus. These *user-defined menus* (Figure 4-41) can be displayed and executed just like the menus built into the spreadsheet program. They are useful additions for models used over and over again or by many people. For example, you can create a menu that lists commands to print the model, display graphs, or even display areas of the spreadsheet where you have entered text describing the model.

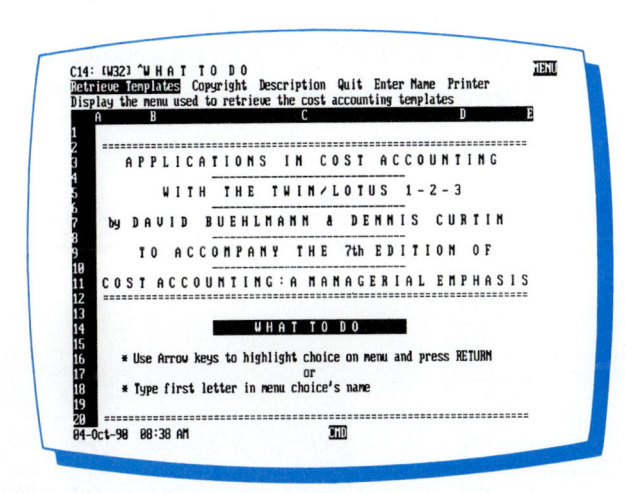

Figure 4-41
User-Defined Menus
User-defined menus can be displayed and executed just like the menus built into the spreadsheet program.

AUTOMATING WITH MACROS

EXERCISE

Exercise 4-11A
CREATING A GRAPH

Refer to a spreadsheet user's guide for instructions on how to create a graph. List the procedures here:

1. _____
2. _____
3. _____
4. _____

QUESTIONS

1. What are two ways you can create macros?
2. Describe the purpose of keyboard macros.
3. List the steps you would follow to record a macro.
4. How do you play back a recorded macro?
5. When you use a macro language to write a macro, what are the special terms called that you enter to indicate what keys should be executed?
6. What is the macro command for pressing **Enter**?
7. Why might you want to create a user-defined menu?

CHAPTER 5

Database Management Applications

OBJECTIVES

After finishing this chapter, you will be able to:

- List the steps you follow to create and use a typical database
- List and briefly describe some typical database programs
- Describe how you create a database by defining its fields
- Describe how you enter and update records
- Describe how you can display one or more records using a query language
- Describe how you sort and index database files and explain the differences between these two approaches
- Explain the parts of a typical report and list the steps you follow to print a report
- Explain how new database files can be created from old ones

5-1

Sort. To arrange a file into a desired order using keys. For example, a mailing list can be sorted by descending numeric order by ZIP codes, or in ascending alphabetic order by last name.

The concept behind database management programs is simple. They allow you to store information in your computer, retrieve it when you need it, and update it when necessary. You can store large amounts of information such as mailing lists, inventory records, or billing and collection information in database files. You can then manipulate the information in these files with the database management program. For example, you can:

- Add new information.
- Find specific information.
- Update information that has changed.
- *Sort* the information into a specified order.
- Delete information that is no longer needed.
- Print out reports containing all or some of the information contained in the file(s).
- Create new files that contain information from two other files or part of the information in one file.

Because of the power and flexibility of database management programs, the applications are almost endless.

- You can maintain mailing lists for sales and marketing purposes. The data can be used to automatically print letters, envelopes, and mailing labels. You can also ask the program questions such as, ''What phone numbers are listed for SMITH?'' or ''What phone numbers are listed in area code 617?''
- You can manage inventory by recording products or supplies moving into and out of a business. The program can give you answers to questions such as, ''How many parts are left in inventory?'' or ''How many were shipped this month?''
- You can manage assets such as stock portfolios so that you always know what stocks you have and what their value is. You can ask the program questions such as, ''What IBM stocks do I have?'' ''What stocks have increased in value since I bought them?'' or ''What stocks have I sold this year?''
- You can store and retrieve illustrations such as photographs or line drawings. The illustrations are first scanned into the computer and then labeled or described with text. You locate a specific illustration by searching for one or more words used in its label or description.

5-1

DATABASE MANAGEMENT PROCEDURES — AN OVERVIEW

Database. Information stored in one or more files and organized into fields and records.

Database management program. A program that organizes, manipulates, and retrieves information from one or more database files. Also called record or file management programs.

The management of databases is one of the most important applications of microcomputers. A *database* is simply one or more interrelated files that contains an organized body of information. To create, maintain, and use a database, you use a *database management program*. (When reading about databases, you will often find the terms spelled as database or data base. There is no difference between the two terms; the spelling hasn't been standardized.)

Before discussing database management in detail, we look briefly at the procedures you would follow to create and use a database file that contains names and addresses. We discuss all the procedures introduced here in greater detail in the following sections, but this overview should give you a feel for how these programs work and how you can use them.

STEP 1   PLANNING THE DATABASE

You want to keep track of names and addresses, so you must first plan exactly what information is to be included in the database. This planning is important because the way the information is broken down determines how you can access it later. You begin by listing the information you want to store.

- Name and ID number
- Street
- City
- State and ZIP code
- Phone number

After thinking about the information, you realize you may want to sort it later by last name, ZIP code, or area code. To do so, you need to break down the list still further so each of these items is a separate listing.

- ID number
- Last name
- First name
- Street
- City
- State
- ZIP code
- Area code
- Phone number

STEP 2   DEFINING THE DATABASE

Once you have a list of the information that you want to store, you create a database file to store it in. This information is not stored randomly in a file; it must be stored in a highly organized way so that the program can find it later. The way data are organized in a database is really quite simple. They are always organized into fields and records (Figure 5-1).

5-1

ID	LASTNAME	FIRST	STREET	CITY	ST	ZIP	AREA	PHONE
101	June	Gary	100 Elm Street	New Haven	CT	10000	203	555-1000
102	Benjamin	Nancy	25 Oak Street	Cambridge	MA	20000	617	555-1212
103	Kendall	Liz	26 Rosewood	Chicago	IL	20000	312	555-1200
104	Hogan	Dennis	40 Main Street	Edgewater	NJ	30000	201	555-1003
105	Lyons	Susan	168 Bridge Road	Beverly	MA	20000	617	555-1004
106	Baxter	Michelle	110 Millbrook	Austin	TX	50000	512	555-1009
107	Sobel	Carol	45 Porter Ave.	Fairlawn	NJ	30000	201	555-1005
108	Surridge	Nancy	10 Preston Lane	Oakland	CA	40000	415	555-1007
109	Fiske	Robert	1500 Storybrook	Boston	MA	02198	617	555-1008
110	Werthman	Ted	25 Stuart Road	Miami	FL	60000	305	555-1010

Figure 5-1 Fields and Records
Databases are organized into (A) fields, each of which has (B) a name and (C) records.

- A record is a description of a person, thing, or activity. In this example, a record is the complete name, address, and phone number for a person.
- A field is one part of the description stored in the record. In our file, the fields are those you broke down in Step 1.

When you first create a database file, you have to tell the program what fields you plan on storing so that it can allocate room for them. This step is called defining the database. When you define a database, you describe each field by specifying its name, length, and the type of data to be stored, for example, text, dates, or numbers that can be calculated. You enter these descriptions using the program's create database or define database screen (Figure 5-2).

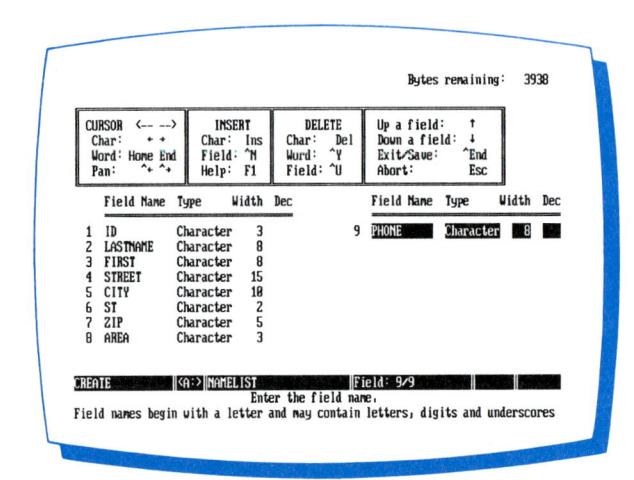

Figure 5-2 Defining a Database
When you execute the dBASE command that creates a new database file, the screen where you define fields is displayed. You move the cursor from field to field, and enter each field's name, type, and width. If the field is numeric, you can also specify the number of decimal places.

STEP 3 ENTERING DATA

Once you have defined the database file, you can enter data for each person. Many programs display forms on the screen that display the field names you assigned. To enter data, you move the cursor from field name to field name and type in the data. The data you enter into the form are automatically entered into the database (Figure 5-3).

254   DATABASE MANAGEMENT APPLICATIONS

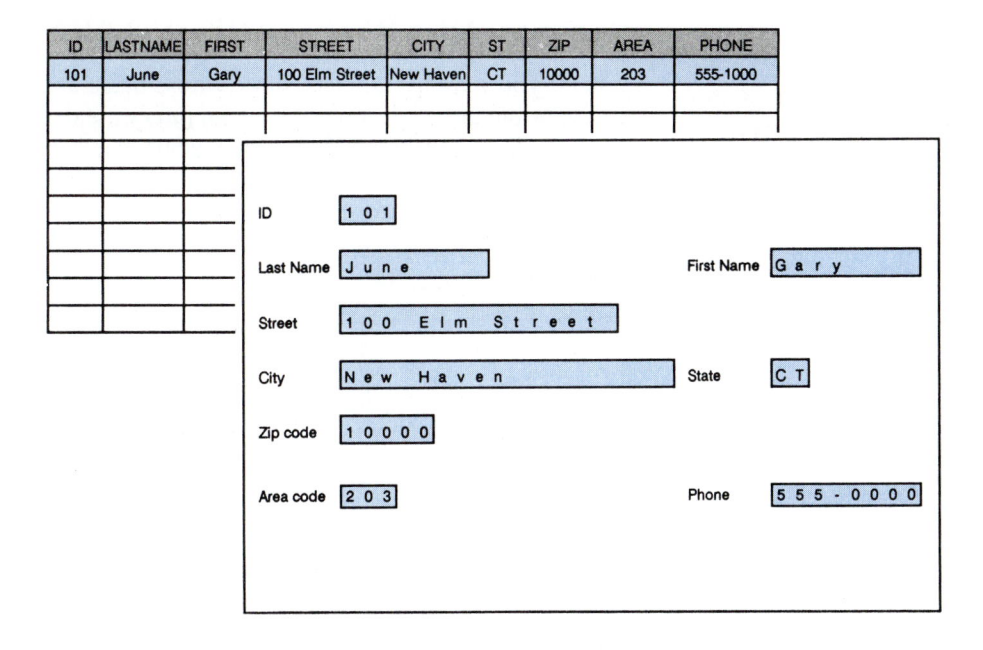

Figure 5-3 Entering Data
As you enter data, the information is stored in a table in memory and on the disk. Each fill-in blank is a field, and all the fields make up a record.

STEP 4   UPDATING THE DATABASE

Whenever people described in your database move or change their names, their records must be updated to reflect the changes. To make these changes, commands are used to locate the records, and the new data are entered in place of the old (Figure 5-4).

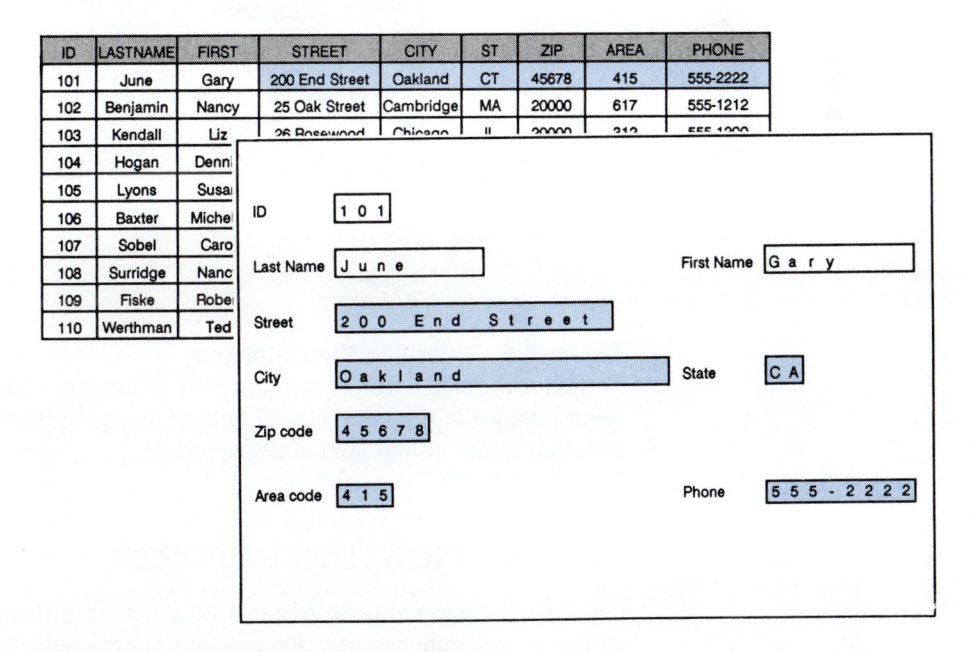

Figure 5-4 Updating the Database
To change data in a database, you display the record you want to change, and enter the new data into the appropriate fields. The data in the database are then changed.

DATABASE MANAGEMENT PROCEDURES—AN OVERVIEW   255

5-1

Query. A question posed to a database.

Report. A printed document containing the contents of a record file or database. The report can include all of the data or just the data in selected fields and selected records.

STEP 5   QUERYING THE DATABASE

What if you want to call Gary June, whose name and address have been entered into your database? To do so, you can *query* the database for all records where the last name is June. When you execute the command, the record for any person whose last name is June is displayed on the screen. If there is more than one June, the first record for that name is displayed, and then you can scroll though all other records that have June in them until you find the correct record (Figure 5-5).

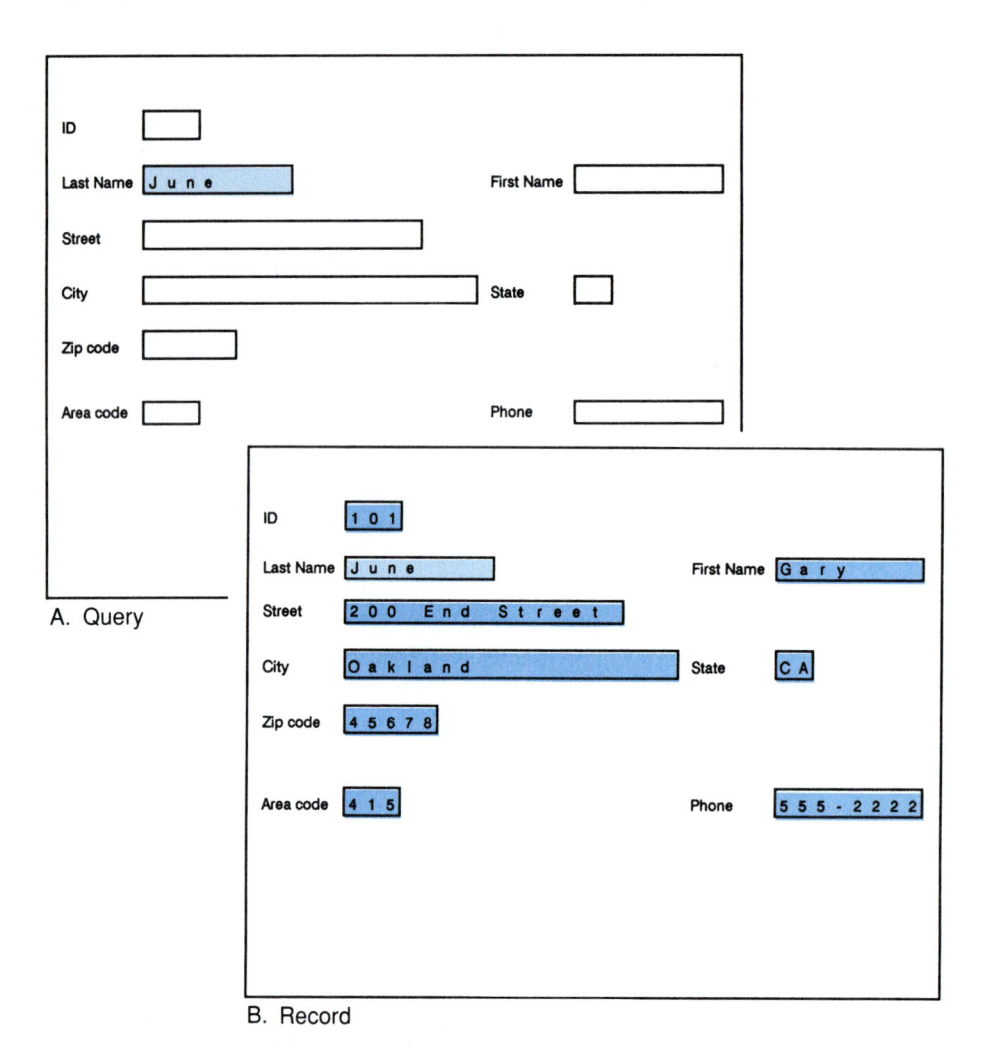

A. Query

B. Record

Figure 5-5   Querying the Database
To find a specific record, you query the database. Here the name June has been entered in the LASTNAME field of the query screen (A), and the record with that name in that field is displayed (B).

STEP 6   PRINTING REPORTS

One of the most valuable features of a database management program is its ability to generate reports. *Reports* are simply selected parts of the database displayed on the screen or printed out in a specified way. For example, using our database, you can print mailing labels that include complete addresses (Figure 5-6) or a report that lists just names, phone numbers, and amounts due (Figure 5-7).

Gary June
100 Elm Street
New Haven, CT. 10000

Nancy Benjamin
25 Oak Street
Cambridge, MA. 20000

Liz Kendall
26 Rosewood
Chicago, IL. 20000

Dennis Hogan
40 Main Street
Edgewater, N.J. 3000

Susan Lyons
168 Bridge Road
Beverly, MA. 20000

Michelle Baxter
110 Millbrook
Austin, TX. 50000

Figure 5-6 Printing Reports — Mailing Labels
The same database can also be used to print simpler reports, such as mailing labels.

```
Page No.    1
11/03/89
                    AMOUNTS DUE

First       Last        Area    Phone           Amount
Name        Name        Code    Number          Due

** Amounts due from state: CA
James       Poe         415     555-1007         10.00
** Subtotal **
                                                 10.00

** Amounts due from state: CT
Tina        Culman      203     555-1000         10.00
** Subtotal **
                                                 10.00

** Amounts due from state: FL
Jose        Alverez     305     555-1010         61.00
** Subtotal **
                                                 61.00

** Amounts due from state: IL
Liz         Kendall     312     555-1200         35.00
John        Davis       312     555-1020         75.00
** Subtotal **
                                                110.00

** Amounts due from state: MA
Nancy       Benjamin    617     555-1212         15.00
Daphne      Swabey      617     555-1004         30.00
Robert      Fiske       617     555-1008         18.00
** Subtotal **
                                                 63.00

** Amounts due from state: NJ
Dennis      Hogan       201     555-1003         25.00
Carol       Sobel       201     555-1005         50.00
** Subtotal **
                                                 75.00

** Amounts due from state: TX
Lars        Porsena     512     555-1009         43.00
** Subtotal **
                                                 43.00
*** Total ***
                                                372.00
```

Figure 5-7 Printing Reports — Amounts Due
Reports can be comprehensive, even calculating totals and subtotals.

EXERCISE

Exercise 5-1A
COMPLETE THE SIMULATION ON SCREEN

The *Information Processing Software Sampler* contains an on-screen simulation of several database programs. Run the simulation of dBASE III Plus, and then summarize the key features of a database program.

QUESTIONS

1. What is a field? A record? Give examples of each.
2. What is the first step in creating a new database file? the second? What do you do in each step?
3. What appears on the screen when you enter data into the database?
4. What is it called when you change information in the database?
5. What is it called when you look for data in the database?
6. What is a printout of information in the database called?

5-2

TYPICAL RECORD AND DATABASE MANAGEMENT PROGRAMS

Record management programs. A program that manages information like a database management program but that isn't as powerful.

The term *database* describes the files containing data. Frequently, the term *database program* is used to describe all programs used to manage those files. Actually, these programs fall into one of two main categories: record management or database management programs.

RECORD MANAGEMENT PROGRAMS

Record management programs (sometimes called *file management* or *flat file* database programs), including those integrated into many word processing and spreadsheet programs, store, maintain, and use data stored in single files (Figure 5-8). If you use a record management program to store data on various aspects of a business, you must store the data for different applications in separate files. If you want to make changes, you must make them in each file when information is duplicated. Let's say you have one file for names, addresses, and phone numbers and another file for payroll information. If a person's name occurs in both files, the name must be separately entered into each file. If the name must be changed or deleted later, it must be separately changed in or deleted from each file.

RECORD MANAGEMENT PROGRAM

FLIGHT	TO	FROM	DEPART	ARRIVE
AA100	Boston	Los Angele	10:00	14:00
AA200	Boston	Chicago	11:00	15:00
AA300	Boston	NY	12:00	16:00
UA100	Los Angele	Chicago	13:00	17:00
UA200	Chicago	NY	14:00	18:00
UA300	Atlanta	NY	15:00	19:00
PANAM1	NY	London	16:00	20:00
PANAM2	NY	Paris	17:00	21:00
PANAM3	NY	Toronto	18:00	22:00

Figure 5-8 Record Management Programs Record management programs can address only one file at a time. To manage information in another file, you must clear the first file from memory and retrieve the new one.

DATABASE MANAGEMENT PROGRAMS

As the amount of information being processed increases, the record management method of using separate files to store information becomes cumbersome because information must be extensively duplicated. An employee's name might appear in several different files, for example, payroll, vacation, and expense accounts. There are disadvantages to this duplication.

Relational database. A database where data are organized into tables.

- It increases the risk of errors in the information. Because a person's name would have to be entered more than once, any changes in status would have to be made in different files, perhaps by different people. Over time, the data's accuracy deteriorates. For example, changes might be made in some files and not in others, or some data might be entered correctly into one file and incorrectly into another.
- It increases the amount of data entry because some information must be entered more than once.
- It requires more storage space, which causes problems when the database is large.

The concept of a database, introduced in the early 1970s, eliminates these problems. In a database, the data are stored so that there is no duplication of data. For example, a person's name can appear in the database only once, so a change must be made only once. Database management programs (also called *data base management systems*, or *DBMS*) are used to manage these databases. They can do everything a record management program can do and much more. The main difference is that a database management program can use interrelated data stored in one or more files (Figure 5-9), thus eliminating the duplication of data and the need to enter updates more than once into different files. Database management programs, therefore, have a major advantage over record management programs as many applications they are used for require more than one file. For example, the accounting process requires separate files for the general ledger, accounts receivable, and accounts payable.

There are many ways to organize the data in a database, but most programs organize them as a *relational database*. A relational database organizes its data into tables that contain rows and columns much like a spreadsheet (Figure 5-10).

A. The columns are fields, and the labels at the top of each field are the field names. Each column on the table has a fixed length.

B. There is one or more rows of data, and each row is a record.

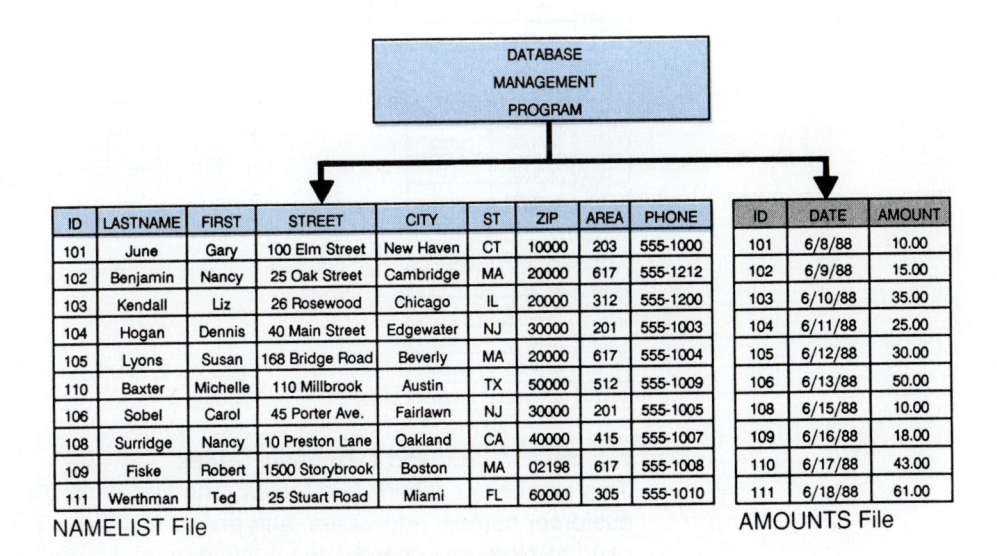

DATABASE MANAGEMENT PROGRAM

NAMELIST File

ID	LASTNAME	FIRST	STREET	CITY	ST	ZIP	AREA	PHONE
101	June	Gary	100 Elm Street	New Haven	CT	10000	203	555-1000
102	Benjamin	Nancy	25 Oak Street	Cambridge	MA	20000	617	555-1212
103	Kendall	Liz	26 Rosewood	Chicago	IL	20000	312	555-1200
104	Hogan	Dennis	40 Main Street	Edgewater	NJ	30000	201	555-1003
105	Lyons	Susan	168 Bridge Road	Beverly	MA	20000	617	555-1004
110	Baxter	Michelle	110 Millbrook	Austin	TX	50000	512	555-1009
106	Sobel	Carol	45 Porter Ave.	Fairlawn	NJ	30000	201	555-1005
108	Surridge	Nancy	10 Preston Lane	Oakland	CA	40000	415	555-1007
109	Fiske	Robert	1500 Storybrook	Boston	MA	02198	617	555-1008
111	Werthman	Ted	25 Stuart Road	Miami	FL	60000	305	555-1010

AMOUNTS File

ID	DATE	AMOUNT
101	6/8/88	10.00
102	6/9/88	15.00
103	6/10/88	35.00
104	6/11/88	25.00
105	6/12/88	30.00
106	6/13/88	50.00
108	6/15/88	10.00
109	6/16/88	18.00
110	6/17/88	43.00
111	6/18/88	61.00

Figure 5-9 Database Management Programs
Database management programs can manage the data in more than one file.

5-2

ID	LASTNAME	FIRST	STREET	CITY	ST	ZIP	AREA	PHONE
101	June	Gary	100 Elm Street	New Haven	CT	10000	203	555-1000
102	Benjamin	Nancy	25 Oak Street	Cambridge	MA	20000	617	555-1212
103	Kendall	Liz	26 Rosewood	Chicago	IL	20000	312	555-1200
104	Hogan	Dennis	40 Main Street	Edgewater	NJ	30000	201	555-1003
105	Lyons	Susan	168 Bridge Road	Beverly	MA	20000	617	555-1004
106	Baxter	Michelle	110 Millbrook	Austin	TX	50000	512	555-1009
107	Sobel	Carol	45 Porter Ave.	Fairlawn	NJ	30000	201	555-1005
108	Surridge	Nancy	10 Preston Lane	Oakland	CA	40000	415	555-1007
109	Fiske	Robert	1500 Storybrook	Boston	MA	02198	617	555-1008
110	Werthman	Ted	25 Stuart Road	Miami	FL	60000	305	555-1010

Figure 5-10 Relational Database
A relational database table contains rows and columns much like a spreadsheet.

Because a database can contain more than one table, the tables can be linked to one another, as Figure 5-11 shows. As you'll see later, you manipulate the data in these tables to enter, update, and find information stored in the database. You can also combine two or more files into a new file.

Record or database management programs are available in several versions, including:

- Standalone programs, such as dBASE or Paradox, that are designed to be used independently.

ID	LASTNAME	FIRST	STREET	CITY	ST	ZIP	AREA	PHONE
101	June	Gary	100 Elm Street	New Haven	CT	10000	203	555-1000
102	Benjamin	Nancy	25 Oak Street	Cambridge	MA	20000	617	555-1212
103	Kendall	Liz	26 Rosewood	Chicago	IL	20000	312	555-1200
104	Hogan	Dennis	40 Main Street	Edgewater	NJ	30000	201	555-1003
105	Lyons	Susan	168 Bridge Road	Beverly	MA	20000	617	555-1004
106	Baxter	Michelle	110 Millbrook	Austin	TX	50000	512	555-1009
107	Sobel	Carol	45 Porter Ave.	Fairlawn	NJ	30000	201	555-1005
108	Surridge	Nancy	10 Preston Lane	Oakland	CA	40000	415	555-1007
109	Fiske	Robert	1500 Storybrook	Boston	MA	02198	617	555-1008
110	Werthman	Ted	25 Stuart Road	Miami	FL	60000	305	555-1010

A.

ID	DATE	AMOUNT
101	6/8/88	10.00
102	6/9/88	15.00
103	6/10/88	35.00
104	6/11/88	25.00
105	6/12/88	30.00
106	6/13/88	50.00
107	6/15/88	10.00
108	6/16/88	18.00
109	6/17/88	43.00
110	6/18/88	61.00

B.

Figure 5-11 Linked Database Tables
This database contains two tables. The first table (A) is used to store customer names, addresses, and phone numbers. The second table (B) is used to store any charges the customers make and the date they made them. When more than one table is used, they are linked using a common field that contains unique data, in this case, the customer's ID number.

- Applications programs, such as word processors and spreadsheets, that frequently have record management capabilities built in.
- Integrated programs that almost always have a record management program as one of their components.

Here, we look at some examples of each of these types of programs. One, dBASE, is a true relational database management system, so it can work with more than one file. All the others are record management programs that can work with only one file at a time.

dBASE

dBASE is a standalone relational database program and, for years, has had the largest share of the market. It was originally published as dBASE II and has been revised several times. Each version has improved on previous ones by making the program easier to use. On dBASE II, only a dot appeared on the screen, and all commands had to be typed. Later versions are much simpler because they include easy-to-use pull-down menus (Figure 5-12).

A. A menu bar at the top of the screen contains a series of menus that can be pulled down.

B. The status bar displays the command in progress, the current default drive, the name of the current file, and the number of records. It also indicates if **Caps Lock** and **Num Lock** are engaged or not.

C. The navigation line, just below the status bar, displays messages listing the keys and commands you can use.

D. The message line, the bottom line on the screen, displays messages when the program wants you to enter information. When the menu bar is displayed, this line briefly describes the highlighted menu choice.

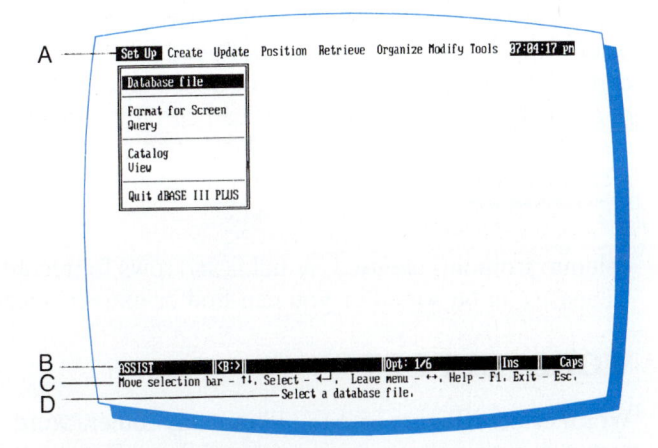

Figure 5-12 dBASE III Plus
The dBASE screen display has the elements shown here.

SPREADSHEETS

Many spreadsheets, such as Excel and Lotus 1-2-3, contain limited record management capabilities. A database is created right on the spreadsheet (Figure 5-13). A row is used for headings (field names) indicating the contents of each

	A	B	C	D	E
1	STATE	POP1080	POP1086	PCIO1079	PCIO1085
2	WYOMING	469,557	507,000	7,927	9,782
3	ALASKA	401,851	534,000	10,193	13,650
4	VERMONT	511,456	541,000	6,177	9,619
5	DISTRICT OF COLUMBIA	638,432	626,100	8,959	13,530
6	DELAWARE	594,338	633,000	7,449	11,375
7	NORTH DAKOTA	652,717	680,000	6,417	9,635
8	SOUTH DAKOTA	690,768	707,000	5,696	8,553
9	MONTANA	786,690	819,000	6,589	8,781
10	NEVADA	800,508	964,000	8,453	11,200
11	RHODE ISLAND	947,154	975,000	6,897	10,892
12	IDAHO	944,127	1,003,000	6,248	8,567
13	NEW HAMPSHIRE	920,610	1,027,000	6,966	11,659
14	HAWAII	964,691	1,062,000	7,740	11,003
15	MAINE	1,125,043	1,174,000	5,766	9,042
16	NEW MEXICO	1,303,303	1,479,000	6,120	8,814
17	NEBRASKA	1,569,825	1,598,000	6,934	10,546
18	UTAH	1,461,037	1,665,000	6,305	8,535
19	WEST VIRGINIA	1,950,183	1,919,000	6,142	8,141
20	ARKANSAS	2,286,358	2,372,000	5,613	8,389
21	KANSAS	2,364,236	2,461,000	7,349	10,684
22	MISSISSIPPI	2,520,770	2,625,000	5,182	7,483

Row 1 — Field name. Row 5 — Record. Column C — Field.

Figure 5-13 Spreadsheets
On this spreadsheet, records are entered on rows and fields are entered into columns. The column headings are used for the field names. At any time you can sort the data into ascending or descending order based on the contents of any column. For example, you can sort it into alphabetical order by last names or by city. You can also quickly find a specific record or extract records in whole or in part from the database.

column. Columns are used for fields and rows for records. Data entered into the database can be sorted or you can find or extract selected records.

WORDPERFECT

WordPerfect (Figure 5-14), like many other word processing programs, includes a record management capability. This built-in database is used to maintain lists of names and addresses and other information to be inserted into primary documents during merge printing.

MICROSOFT WORKS

Microsoft Works is an integrated program that includes spreadsheet, word processing, record management, and telecommunications functions. When you select the database function from the Main menu, you can create forms on the screen that you then use to enter data into the database (Figure 5-15).

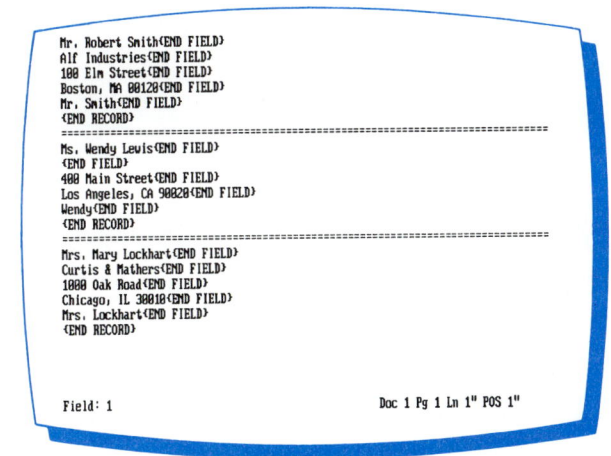

**Figure 5-14
WordPerfect**
WordPerfect database files use special characters to end fields and records. The {END FIELD} codes indicate the end of fields, and the {END RECORD} codes indicate the end of records.

**Figure 5-15
Microsoft Works**
When you display the database function on Microsoft Works, a blank screen appears. You then enter field names to lay out an on-screen form. When completed, you use the form to enter data into the database file.

EXERCISE

Exercise 5-2A
COMPLETE THE SIMULATION ON SCREEN

The *Information Processing Software Sampler* contains a simulation of several database programs. Run the simulations for dBASE III Plus, Lotus 1-2-3, WordPerfect, and Microsoft Works and summarize how the programs differ.

QUESTIONS

1. What is a database?
2. What is the difference between a record management program and a database management program?
3. What are two or three disadvantages of duplicating information when using a record management program?
4. Name one program that is a relational database program.
5. When database capabilities are built into applications programs, are they usually relational database programs?

5-3 DEFINING A DATABASE FILE

5-3

The first step in using a database management program is to define the database file you want to store data in. To define a database, you must know how the program stores the data that you plan on entering. Moreover, because databases are hard to revise after you have entered data into them, you should know how to carefully plan a database before you actually define it.

THE ORGANIZATION OF A DATABASE

When you enter information with a database management program, it is stored in a file. The information you enter must be organized so that the program can easily manipulate it. To understand how a program manages information, you must first understand the five levels of organization used to store and manipulate data (Figure 5-16).

1. When you enter information into a computer, you type it in from the keyboard. The first level of organization is, therefore, the alphanumeric characters you type, for example, numbers and letters.
2. You use one or more characters to enter fields. A field is a piece of the information about a person or item. For example, fields can be used to store a person's name, an address, a phone number, or a price. Fields can be numbers (101), names (June), names and numbers (100 Elm Street), or formulas (100*3).
3. Related fields are stored together as records. A record is like an index card: it contains all the information about a product, person, or other item.

1.

ID	LASTNAME	FIRST	STREET	CITY	ST	ZIP	AREA	PHONE
1								

2.

ID	LASTNAME	FIRST	STREET	CITY	ST	ZIP	AREA	PHONE
101								

3.

ID	LASTNAME	FIRST	STREET	CITY	ST	ZIP	AREA	PHONE
101	June	Gary	100 Elm Street	New Haven	CT	10000	203	555-1000

4.

ID	LASTNAME	FIRST	STREET	CITY	ST	ZIP	AREA	PHONE
101	June	Gary	100 Elm Street	New Haven	CT	10000	203	555-1000
102	Benjamin	Nancy	25 Oak Street	Cambridge	MA	20000	617	555-1212

5.

ID	LASTNAME	FIRST	STREET	CITY	ST	ZIP	AREA	PHONE
101	June	Gary	100 Elm Street	New Haven	CT	10000	203	555-1000
102	Benjamin	Nancy	25 Oak Street	Cambridge	MA	20000	617	555-1212

ID	DATE	AMOUNT
101	6/8/88	10.00
102	6/9/88	15.00

Figure 5-16 Levels of Data Organization in a Database
When you create a database, you enter characters, fields, records, files, and related files.

Key field. The field in a database that contains key attributes.

For example, it might contain a person's ID, last name, first name, street, city, state, ZIP code, area code, and phone number.

4. Related records are stored together as files, for example, a list of customers.

5. Related files are stored together as a database. The database contains interrelated files that can be combined or from which information can be drawn.

PLANNING YOUR DATABASE FILES

When you first create a database, you must tell the program what information you are going to keep. This is not as straightforward as you might think. When asked what information they need, many managers will say "Everything." But it is usually impossible to include everything because of the limited availability of the information, the cost of collecting the information if it is available, and the cost of recording and holding the information if it can be collected. Therefore, when deciding what information to keep, you should spend some time thinking about what type of questions you wish to ask and have answered by the data. This, in turn, will tell you what data you need to keep.

As you compile a list of the data you want to store, you can sketch it out, specifying what you want to store about each item or person. You then assign field names and specify the type and length of the data to be entered into each field. When planning a database, you must also consider the limitations of the program you are using. Programs differ in the types of fields they provide, the number of fields allowed per record, the length of fields, and the length of records.

In some cases, you might divide certain basic information into more than one field so that you can manipulate it more easily. The fields you use to sort the file and find specific records are called *key fields*. For example, if you used only one field for both the persons' first and last names, and then entered names like John Smith, Betty Lewis, and Roger Wentworth, your file would be limited. You could not sort names based on the persons' last names. To sort the persons' names, you set up two fields, one for the first name and one for the last name. The same is true of addresses. For example, if you do not enter ZIP codes into a separate field, you will not be able to sort the records by ZIP codes.

Designing a relational database requires very careful planning because more than one file can be involved. Not only does each file need to be well planned, but the relationships between files must also be carefully thought through. Figure 5-17 shows the plan for a database that contains two files, one to manage a list of customer names and addresses and the other to manage charges that they make and the dates they were made.

DEFINING A DATABASE FILE

When you define a database file, a definition screen appears on the screen. You enter the definition of each field into the form. For example, you specify field names, field types, field lengths, and validity checks.

Field Names

When naming fields, you always use unique field names. The same field name cannot be used more than once in the same file. Typical field names might be LASTNAME, FIRST, STREET, CITY, STATE, ZIP, AREA, and PHONE. Besides being unique, field names must follow other rules required by the program. For example, most programs will not allow spaces in field names.

FILE: NAMELIST

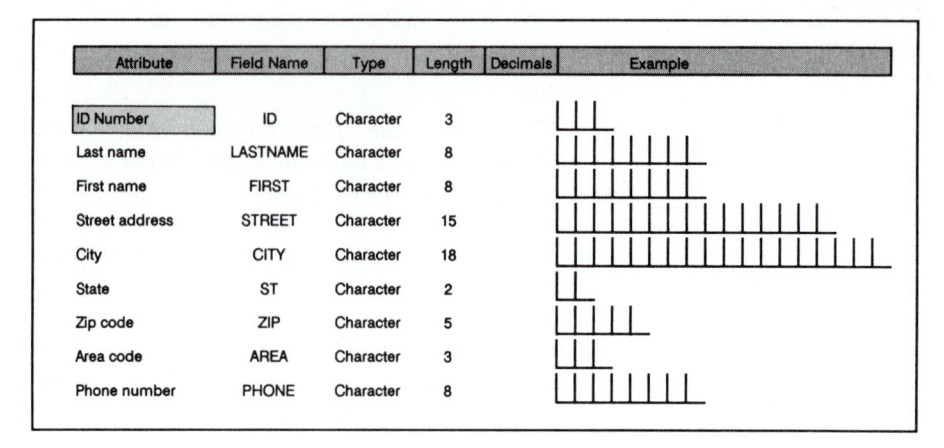

Attribute	Field Name	Type	Length	Decimals	Example
ID Number	ID	Character	3		
Last name	LASTNAME	Character	8		
First name	FIRST	Character	8		
Street address	STREET	Character	15		
City	CITY	Character	18		
State	ST	Character	2		
Zip code	ZIP	Character	5		
Area code	AREA	Character	3		
Phone number	PHONE	Character	8		

FILE: AMOUNTS

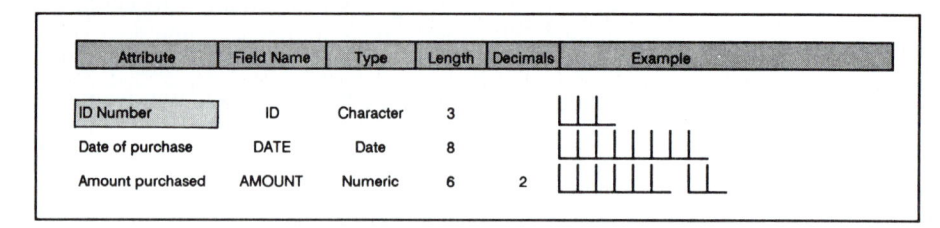

Attribute	Field Name	Type	Length	Decimals	Example
ID Number	ID	Character	3		
Date of purchase	DATE	Date	8		
Amount purchased	AMOUNT	Numeric	6	2	

Figure 5-17 Planning a Database
When planning a database, you list the fields you want to include for each item or person. You then plan the name of each field, its type, and its length.

Field Types

Your decision about what fields to set up will be influenced by the field types provided by your program. All programs let you store characters and numbers, but some also let you store dates, times, or comments. Some even let you create fields that calculate an answer based on the entries in other fields. Typical fields types include the following:

- **Character fields** (also called text fields) store all characters you can enter from the keyboard, including letters, numbers, symbols, and spaces. When numbers are entered into these fields, for example, ZIP codes, they are treated as text and cannot be used in calculations.

- **Numeric fields** store values, including numbers, signs, and decimals. There are two kinds of numeric fields, integers (numbers without decimal places) and decimals. Numbers entered into these fields can be used in calculations.

- **Calculating fields** make calculations based on numbers in other fields. For example, if you are tracking a student's progress through college, you would want to store all of his or her courses and corresponding grades. Because many student activities depend on grade point averages, one field can be designated to automatically calculate these for each course or each semester.

- **Logical fields** (sometimes called Boolean fields) are used to enter only true or false notations. For example, on dBASE, you enter true as T, t, Y, or y and false as F, f, N, or n.

266 DATABASE MANAGEMENT APPLICATIONS

Validity check. A method of checking database input data for accuracy. For example, you might specify that text of only a certain length can be entered in a field. Also called editing checks.

- **Date fields** store dates, which you can display in several formats. When dates are entered into these fields, they can be used in calculations. Dates can be added and subtracted, or numbers can be added to or subtracted from them. This allows you to get answers to questions such as, "What is the average number of days between orders?"
- **Time fields** operate just like date fields but are used to enter hours and minutes instead of days.
- **Memo fields** (also called *comment fields*) are used to enter descriptive text, much as you would enter notes to yourself into a notebook. Though all other fields are used for specific information, these fields are for general information. For example, you can enter a note that a price or address is expected to change and the date this is expected to happen. To preserve memory, a memo field often has a variable field length. As you enter text, the size of the field and the amount of memory or data storage space used increases automatically.

Field Lengths

When planning the file, you need to decide how many characters long each field has to be. Deciding field lengths ought not to be taken lightly. If you make the field too short, you will lose information. For instance, if you allowed only seven characters for the name, you could enter the name Smith but not the name Hamilton. But if you make the field too long, you waste memory and space on the disk used to store the file, limiting the number of fields in the record or the number of records in the file. Therefore, you need to balance the amount of information held with the space required to hold that information.

The length of the field specifies the number of characters allowed. If the field is numeric, you must specify the total number of digits in the number and the number of decimal places. The program needs to know this so that it can store the values entered into these fields in a way that you can use them in calculations. When designating the length of numeric fields, include room for a minus sign, the total number of characters, and a decimal point. For example, if you specify the field is five characters long with two digits to the right of the decimal point, you can enter values from −9.99 to 99.99. You cannot enter numbers lower than −9.99 (for example, −10.00) and greater than 99.99 (for example, 100.00) because they contain six characters.

Validity Checks

Validity checks (also called *editing checks*) are provided by some programs to help prevent you from making mistakes when you enter data. For example, you can specify that only text of a certain length or numbers entered in a specific way can be entered into a given field. Specifying the largest value that can be entered into a payroll field will prevent your writing a paycheck for $3000.50 when it was meant to be $300.50. If you enter data that violate the rules you specify, they will not be accepted, and the computer will beep, or a prompt will appear telling you to reenter the data.

EXERCISES

5-3

Exercise 5-3A
PLANNING A DATABASE FOR NAMES AND ADDRESSES

Sketch out a database file you would use to maintain a file containing your friends' names, addresses, and telephone numbers. Assume you want to be able to sort the file by last name and ZIP code.

Exercise 5-3B
PLANNING A DATABASE FOR RECORDS OR CDs

Plan a database that you would use to catalog all of your record albums or compact discs. List the field names you would use, and indicate their type and length. What do you think would be the best field to use as the key field so that you could always find a specific song?

5-4

QUESTIONS

1. List the five levels of data in a database.
2. Why would you not be able to sort names based on last names if you entered both first and last names into one field?
3. What is a key field? Why is it important?
4. Briefly describe each of the following types of fields:
   Character
   Numeric
   Logical
   Date
   Memo
5. What length would you specify for a field into which the largest number you were going to enter was 100.00? 10.00? 1000.00?
6. Why not specify the maximum length available for each field so that you do not have to plan field lengths so carefully?
7. What is the purpose of validity or editing checks?

5-4
ENTERING AND UPDATING RECORDS

Once you have defined a database file, you can enter data into it. You can enter records in any order you want. There is no need to worry about the order, because you can sort the file into any desired order at any time. The number of records you can enter is determined by the size of each record and the program's limitations. Generally, programs that create disk-based data files can store more records because the number is limited only by the available disk space. Programs that create memory-based data files are limited by the amount of memory in your computer.

When you enter or update data, you can display them in one of two ways: as a list or as a form.

The list view of a database displays as many records and fields as will fit on the screen (Figure 5-18). To enter or edit records, you move the cursor through the fields, and type data in. If the database is wider or longer than the screen, you can scroll through it both horizontally and vertically.

The form view (Figure 5-19) displays only a single record but you can use it to scroll through the database record by record. Its advantage is twofold. You can see more fields on the screen, and descriptive text can be added to the form to describe the types of data that should be entered. To fill out or edit the form, you move the cursor to the data entry spaces (fields) following the descriptive text. The length of the data entry space usually indicates the field length so you can tell when you are running out of space to enter data. When finished, you press a specified key to display another blank form so that you can enter the next record.

STATE	AREANAME	POP1080	POP1086	PCIO1079	PCIO1085	POP12086	PCI11085
56	WYOMING	469,557	507,000	7,927	9,782	8	23.4
02	ALASKA	401,851	534,000	10,193	13,650	32.9	33.9
50	VERMONT	511,456	541,000	6,177	9,619	5.8	55.7
11	DISTRICT OF COLUMBIA	638,432	626,100	8,959	13,530	-1.9	51
10	DELAWARE	594,338	633,000	7,449	11,375	6.5	52.7
38	NORTH DAKOTA	652,717	680,000	6,417	9,635	4.2	50.1
46	SOUTH DAKOTA	690,768	707,000	5,696	8,553	2.3	50.2
30	MONTANA	786,690	819,000	6,589	8,781	4.1	33.3
32	NEVADA	800,508	964,000	8,453	11,200	20.4	32.5
44	RHODE ISLAND	947,154	975,000	6,897	10,892	2.9	57.9
16	IDAHO	944,127	1,003,000	6,248	8,567	6.2	37.1
33	NEW HAMPSHIRE	920,610	1,027,000	6,966	11,659	11.6	67.4
15	HAWAII	964,691	1,062,000	7,740	11,003	10.1	42.2
23	MAINE	1,125,043	1,174,000	5,766	9,042	4.4	56.8
35	NEW MEXICO	1,303,303	1,479,000	6,120	8,814	13.5	44
31	NEBRASKA	1,569,825	1,598,000	6,934	10,546	1.8	52.1
49	UTAH	1,461,037	1,665,000	6,305	8,535	14	35.4
54	WEST VIRGINIA	1,950,183	1,919,000	6,142	8,141	-1.6	32.5
05	ARKANSAS	2,286,358	2,372,000	5,613	8,389	3.7	49.5
20	KANSAS	2,364,236	2,461,000	7,349	10,684	4.1	45.4
28	MISSISSIPPI	2,520,770	2,625,000	5,182	7,483	4.1	44.4

Figure 5-18   The List View
The list view of a database displays a large number of records.

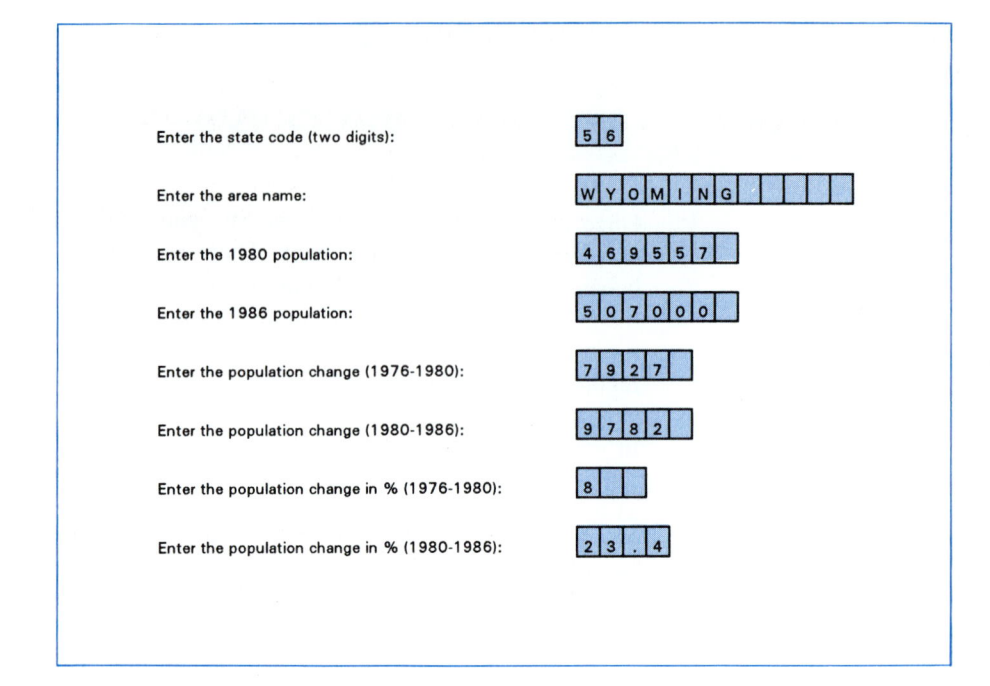

Figure 5-19   The Form View
The form view allows you to enter or edit information by filling out a form on the computer screen.

When creating an on-screen form, be sure to consider its design. It should provide for the most efficient movement of the cursor from one field to the next during the entry of information. For example, if you are transferring data from customer purchase orders into a file, your on-screen form should parallel the structure of the purchase order forms as closely as possible.

The form used for entering data is not always the best form for other purposes. For example, an accountant might want to view the information differently from the person who enters order information. Thus, some programs allow you to create more than one form, or view, for each record file. These forms can make the record files easier to use by excluding unneeded information from the screen. They can also prevent information from appearing in certain forms so that unauthorized users cannot see certain data. Other forms can be designated as "read only" so that users can view but cannot enter or change data.

UPDATING RECORDS

Besides death and taxes there is at least one other certainty in life. The sooner you collect all the information you need, the sooner it will be outdated and require modifications to make it up to date. With card files, this is quite straightforward. All you have to do is to read through a card file until you find the card that is in error, and then replace it with a corrected card. Though straightforward, finding the card is not necessarily fast. Think of the problem of updating a card file with 500 cards in it, even if they are in alphabetical order. To update the file, you would have to sort through all 500 cards each time you wanted to find the one to update. A database management program lets you update your records much more easily. You can just edit the information in fields, or add or delete complete records.

Adding Records

When you want to add new records to a file, you display a blank record on the screen and then type in a new record, just as you entered the initial records into the file. Unlike a card index file, where you would want to insert the card in the proper order, the database management program will generally add it to the end of the file (Figure 5-20) or insert it into a space where you have previously deleted a record. New records can be added one after another without worrying about the order they are added in or where they are inserted into the file. After they have been entered, they can easily be sorted into any desired order.

Inserting Records

Some programs let you insert a record into a file at a specific point. First you display the record that you want the new record to be inserted below, and then you use the program's Insert command to enter the new record. Inserting records takes more time than adding them to the file because the program must make room for them between already existing files (Figure 5-21). It is like trying to squeeze one more person into a crowded elevator—the new file has to elbow its way in. To make room for the new record, the file must be resorted by the program, and this takes time.

Rec #	ID	LASTNAME	FIRST	STREET	CITY	ST	ZIP	AREA	PHONE	
1	101	June	Gary	100 Elm Street	New Haven	CT	10000	203	555-1000	
2	102	Benjamin	Nancy	25 Oak Street	Cambridge	MA	20000	617	555-1212	
3	103	Kendall	Liz	26 Rosewood	Chicago	IL	20000	312	555-1200	
4	104	Hogan	Dennis	40 Main Street	Edgewater	NJ	30000	201	555-1003	
5	105	Lyons	Susan	168 Bridge Road	Beverly	MA	20000	617	555-1004	
6	106	Baxter	Michelle	110 Millbrook	Austin	TX	50000	512	555-1009	
7	107	Sobel	Carol	45 Porter Ave.	Fairlawn	NJ	30000	201	555-1005	
8	108	Surridge	Nancy	10 Preston Lane	Oakland	CA	40000	415	555-1007	
9	109	Fiske	Robert	1500 Storybrook	Boston	MA	02198	617	555-1008	
10	110	Werthman	Ted	25 Stuart Road	Miami	FL	60000	305	555-1010	
11	111	Edwards	Jim	50 Locust St	Teaneck	NJ	30000	201	555-1111	← Added Record

Figure 5-20 Adding Records
When you add records, they are added at the end of the file.

Rec #	ID	LASTNAME	FIRST	STREET	CITY	ST	ZIP	AREA	PHONE	
1	101	June	Gary	100 Elm Street	New Haven	CT	10000	203	555-1000	
2	102	Benjamin	Nancy	25 Oak Street	Cambridge	MA	20000	617	555-1212	
3	103	Kendall	Liz	26 Rosewood	Chicago	IL	20000	312	555-1200	
4	104	Hogan	Dennis	40 Main Street	Edgewater	NJ	30000	201	555-1003	
5	105	Lyons	Susan	168 Bridge Road	Beverly	MA	20000	617	555-1004	
6	106	Baxter	Michelle	110 Millbrook	Austin	TX	50000	512	555-1009	
7	111	Edwards	Jim	50 Locust St	Teaneck	NJ	30000	201	555-1111	← Inserted Record
8	107	Sobel	Carol	45 Porter Ave.	Fairlawn	NJ	30000	201	555-1005	
9	108	Surridge	Nancy	10 Preston Lane	Oakland	CA	40000	415	555-1007	
10	109	Fiske	Robert	1500 Storybrook	Boston	MA	02198	617	555-1008	
11	110	Werthman	Ted	25 Stuart Road	Miami	FL	60000	305	555-1010	

Figure 5-21 Inserting Records
When you insert records, they are entered into the specified position in the file, and all the following records are renumbered.

ENTERING AND UPDATING RECORDS

Flagged record. A database record that has been marked for deletion but not yet actually deleted.

Packing. An operation that permanently removes deleted records from a database file.

Updating Records

It is often necessary to update records in a database file, for example, when customers change addresses. To do this, you first use the command to find the specific record to be updated and display it on the screen. You then revise the contents of the appropriate fields. You can also use a command that updates all the records in a file. For example, you can add a number to all the numbers in a numeric field or change all the dates in a date field. When combined with query commands that establish criteria, this command can update groups of records that match the specified criteria.

Deleting Records

If a customer no longer buys from the company, a product is no longer manufactured, or an item is no longer in inventory, its record in a database file is no longer needed. These unwanted records should be deleted from the file. To do this, you first display the record and then execute the Delete command. Some programs do not immediately delete records from the disk when you specify that they be deleted. The deleted record is just marked with an electronic flag. These *flagged records* are ignored when other file operations are used, and they can often be recovered if needed. They can be permanently removed by an operation called *packing*.

5-4 EXERCISE

Exercise 5-4A
ADDING RECORDS

Refer to a database user's guide for instructions on how to add a new record to your database. List the procedures here:

1. _____
2. _____
3. _____
4. _____

5-5 QUESTIONS

1. In what order do you enter records?
2. What is the difference between a list view and a form view?
3. What is an on-screen form? Why do some programs offer more than one type?
4. When you add new records to a file, where are they stored in the file?
5. What is the difference between inserting a record and adding one?
6. Why does inserting a record take longer than adding one to the end of the file?
7. When you delete a record, what does the program do before permanently deleting the record? How do you permanently delete them?

5-5 DISPLAYING RECORDS

Query language. A language used to specify which records and which fields are displayed or printed.

Query by example. A form displayed on the screen so that you can enter queries to a database by filling out the appropriate spaces.

Criteria. The conditions that you want met when the computer performs a specific task.

Once data have been entered into a database file, you generally work with specific records. For example, you may want to look up the phone number of Gary June, change the address of someone who has moved, or delete a record for someone who has been dropped from your customer list. To do this, you use commands that display only a selected record on the screen, or you use designated keys to scroll through groups of records contained in the file, much as you would flip through the cards in an index card file. If the file has just been created, the records will appear in the order they were entered in. If the file has been sorted, the records will appear in the order they were sorted into.

QUERY LANGUAGES

Scrolling through a file to look at records one after another in the order they are stored or sorted can take a long time if the file has many records. What if a customer calls about his or her account and wants to know what date a purchase was made? Using the customer ID number and the amount of the purchase, you can immediately locate the date of the purchase by asking the program to display any charges to the customer's account for the specified amount. Questions like this, when addressed to a database, are called queries. You can use queries to display, update, delete, and insert records into a database file.

The way you pose queries varies from program to program, but there are essentially two ways to do so, with a query language or a query-by-example form.

Query languages are special languages you use to ask questions and execute commands. Query languages can be simple or complex. On powerful database management programs, they are similar to programming languages. For example, they can contain functions that calculate sums; count records; or indicate maximum, minimum, and average values in an entire file. They can also contain arithmetical operators such as +, -, *, or / and relational and logical operators (see below).

Writing queries is difficult and requires an understanding of the program's query language. Many of the newer programs have adopted an approach that simplifies working with the database. This approach, called *query by example* (*QBE*), uses a fill-in form that lists all the fields in the file. Using this form, you pose queries. For example, if you enter Gary in the first name field, all records with that name in that field will be displayed.

USING CRITERIA TO DISPLAY RECORDS

When using queries, you often specify *criteria* that narrow your search. Only those records that match the criteria are then displayed. Criteria specify a field to look in and a value to look for. The value can be a text string or a number. Ideally, the field you use to search the file contains unique values. Unique values, such as a driver's license number, an employee number, or a social security number, are unlikely to be duplicated in more than one record. In some cases, you may have trouble identifying a field where all the data would be unique. For example, if your file contains names, addresses, and phone numbers, the only unique field is likely to be the phone number. If that is what you are looking for, it is unlikely you would want to look it up in the phone book and then search the file for the number that you now already know. In these

Relational operator. Operators that indicate relationships such as equal to, greater than, or less than.

situations, you have to be creative when first designing the database. For example, if you store first names in one field and last names in another, you can search the file using both of these fields as keys or search fields. This way, the program will find a specific record where the first name is Dennis and the last name is Hogan.

After specifying the fields to be searched and the criteria to be used, the program searches the specified field in all the records in the file. If it finds a match, it displays the entire record on the screen. If more than one record meets the criteria, you execute the program's command that displays the next record.

In addition to displaying selected records, you can display selected fields from those records. For example, if your database has names, addresses, and phone numbers, and you are interested only in the last name and phone number, you can display just fields that contain those elements.

Relational Operators

When searching numeric, date, or time fields, you can use the *relational operators* less than, greater than, equal to, and not equal to. For example, when searching for text strings, you can look for records that meet equal or nonequal criteria. In a search using an equal criteria, the search will look for all records that match the criteria you specify. For example, you can ask the program to find a record with June in the field named LASTNAME. Any record with June in this field will be displayed. In a search using an unequal criteria, all records but the one you specify will be displayed. For example, you can ask the program to find all records that do not have June in the LASTNAME field. Table 5-1 describes relational operators you can use to specify criteria.

Table 5-1
RELATIONAL OPERATORS

Operator	Description
>	Finds all records greater than the criteria you specify. For example, `AMOUNT>10.00` finds all records where the AMOUNT is more than 10.00; `DATE>1/10/92` finds all records where the DATE is later than January 10, 1992; and `NAME>"June"` displays all records alphabetically after June.
<	Finds all records less than the criteria you specify. For example, `AMOUNT<10.00` finds all records where the AMOUNT is less than 10.00; `DATE<1/10/92` finds all records where the DATE is earlier than January 10, 1992; and `NAME<"June"` displays all records alphabetically before June.
=	Finds all records equal to the criteria you specify. For example, `LASTNAME="June"` finds all records with June in the field named LASTNAME; `AMOUNT=10.00` finds all records where the AMOUNT is 10.00; and `DATE=1/10/92` finds all records where the DATE is January 10, 1992.
>=	Finds all records greater than or equal to the criteria you specify. For example, `LASTNAME>="June"` finds all records with June or any name alphabetically later in the field named LASTNAME; `AMOUNT>=10.00` finds all records where the AMOUNT is 10.00 or more; and `DATE>=1/10/92` finds all records where the DATE is January 10, 1992, or later.

Logical operator. An operator that joins two statements so they must both be true (AND), or one must be true (OR), or they must both be false (NOT).

Compound statements. Two or more statements connected by AND or OR logical operators.

Table 5-1, continued

Operator	Description
<=	Finds all records less than or equal to the criteria you specify. For example, `LASTNAME<="June"` finds all records with June or any name alphabetically earlier in the field named LASTNAME; `AMOUNT<=10.00` finds all records where the AMOUNT is 10.00 or less; and `DATE<=1/10/92` finds all records where the DATE is January 10, 1992, or earlier.
<>	Finds all records not equal to the criteria you specify. For example, `LASTNAME<>"June"` finds all records except those with June in the LASTNAME field, and `DATE<>1/10/92` finds all records not dated January 10, 1992.

Logical Operators

Sometimes, you want to find a record or a group of records that meet more than one criterion. To do so, you construct a search condition that contains several criteria using the *logical operators* AND, OR, and NOT.

To understand logical operators, you should understand a little about logic. For example, you can combine the two statements "This is Chapter 5" and "The topic is logic" using an AND or OR logical operator. These statements connected with logical operators are called *compound statements* and their truthfulness can be determined with a truth table. For example, if the compound statement is "This is Chapter 5 AND The topic is logic," its truth table would be like the one in Table 5-2. For this compound statement to be true, both statements within it must be true.

Table 5-2
TRUTH TABLE FOR AN AND STATEMENT

Chapter 5	Topic Logic	Chapter 5 AND Topic Logic
T	T	T
T	F	F
F	T	F
F	F	F

If the compound statement is "This is Chapter 5 OR The topic is logic," its truth table would be like the one shown in Table 5-3. For this compound statement to be true, either statement within it must be true.

Table 5-3
TRUTH TABLE FOR AN OR STATEMENT

Chapter 5	Topic Logic	Chapter 5 OR Topic Logic
T	T	T
T	F	T
F	T	T
F	F	F

One way to look at logical operators is the way an engineer would when designing an electrical circuit, such as those used in your computer system (Figure 5-22). In this scenario, the designer is using switches to control the flow of current from left to right in the circuit. For current to flow through the network, the appropriate switches must be closed.

Figure 5-22 Electrical Circuits and Logical Operators
Electrical circuits that contain switches are a graphic way to illustrate logical operators.

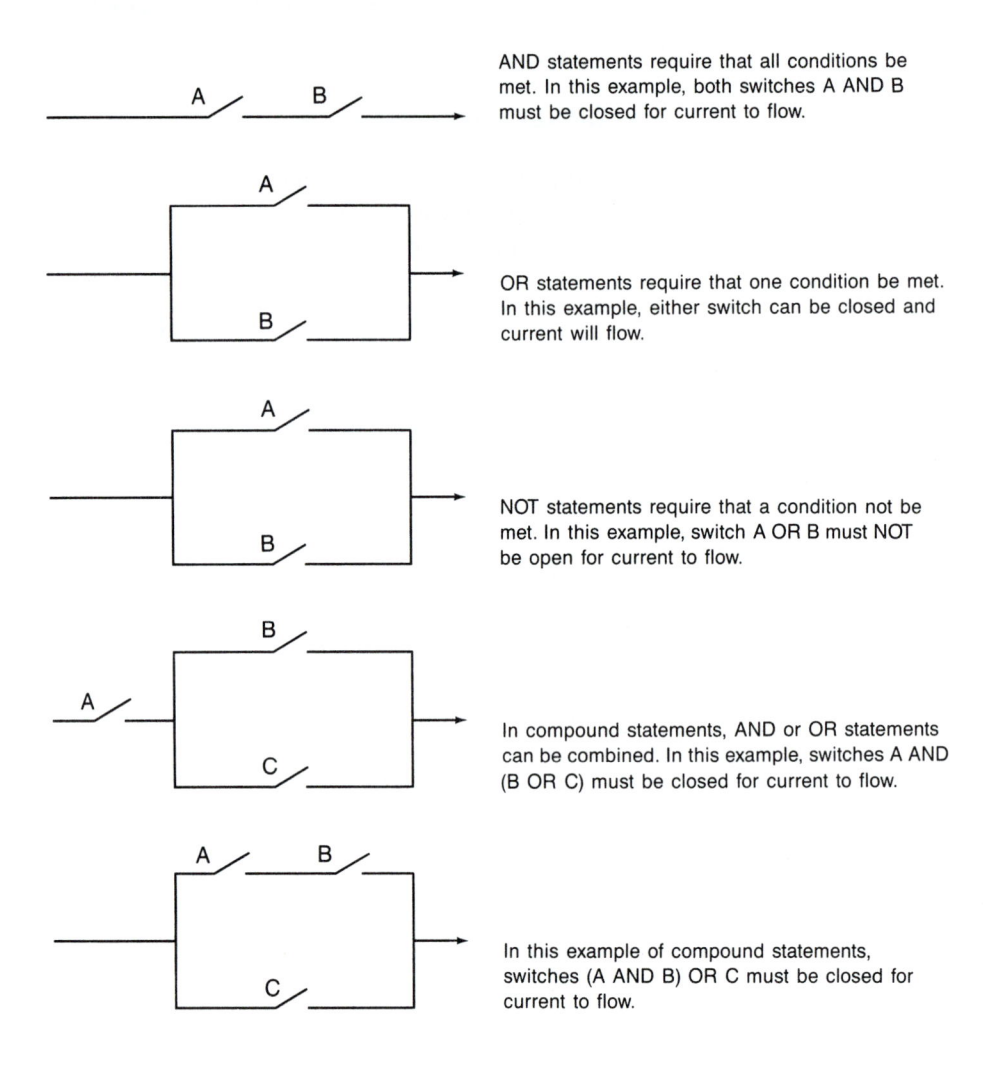

AND statements require that all conditions be met. In this example, both switches A AND B must be closed for current to flow.

OR statements require that one condition be met. In this example, either switch can be closed and current will flow.

NOT statements require that a condition not be met. In this example, switch A OR B must NOT be open for current to flow.

In compound statements, AND or OR statements can be combined. In this example, switches A AND (B OR C) must be closed for current to flow.

In this example of compound statements, switches (A AND B) OR C must be closed for current to flow.

5-5

276 DATABASE MANAGEMENT APPLICATIONS

EXERCISE

Exercise 5-5A
QUERYING A DATABASE

Assume you have a database file with the following fields:

Last_name:
First_name:
Company:
Phone:
Last_contact:
Last_sale:
Items_purchased:

How would you set up search criteria to find all customers named Jones? to find all customers to whom you made a last sale after January 1, 1992? to find all customers named Jones who bought a book?

QUESTIONS

1. Why might you want to display specific records?
2. What is a query language?
3. How do you enter a query by example?
4. What are criteria? What do they do?
5. What are relational operators? List and describe some.
6. What are logical operators? List and describe some.
7. What are compound statements?

5-6
SORTING AND INDEXING RECORDS

Ascending order. A method of sorting documents and files beginning with A (or 0) up through Z (or 10).

Descending order. A method of sorting documents and files beginning with Z (or 10) up through A (or 0).

Primary key. The field by which a file is sorted first.

One of the major advantages of a database management program is that you can enter data in any order, and then rearrange it later. The two most important ways to rearrange files are by sorting and indexing.

SORTING FILES

Sorting a file rearranges the records into a specified order. Because the file is actually rearranged on the disk, sorting a large file can take a great deal of time. To sort a file, you specify what field is to be reordered and in what order its data are to be sorted. For example, you can sort the file so that the names are arranged alphabetically, or you can sort it so that a given set of numbers is arranged in *ascending* or *descending order*. When the file is sorted based on a specific field, all the records are copied to a new file, where they are rearranged in the specified order. When you specify the field to be used, you are designating it as the key. You can often specify more than one key — one primary key and one or more secondary keys.

Primary Keys

The *primary key* is the field that is sorted first. If you are sorting a list of names in the original file, the primary key will sort it so that all the names are in ascending alphabetical order (Figure 5-23). Ideally, a primary key contains unique information, for example, a driver's license number, an employee number, or a social security number.

#	LASTNAME	FIRSTNAME
1	Smith	Vance
2	Jones	Marie
3	Lewis	John
4	Jones	Stuart
5	Curtin	Dennis
6	Smith	Adam
7	Stanford	David
8	Smith	Robert
9	Benjamin	Nancy
10	Swabey	Daphne
11	Vogel	Terry
12	Smith	Frank
13	Jones	Lewis

A. Original Order

#	LASTNAME	FIRSTNAME
9	Benjamin	Nancy
5	Curtin	Dennis
2	Jones	Marie
4	Jones	Stuart
13	Jones	Lewis
3	Lewis	John
1	Smith	Vance
6	Smith	Adam
8	Smith	Robert
12	Smith	Frank
7	Stanford	David
10	Swabey	Daphne
11	Vogel	Terry

B. Primary Key Is LASTNAME

Figure 5-23 Sorting a File on a Primary Key
When you sort a file, you specify a primary key that is to be used as the basis of the sort. Here, the original file (A) shows the order in which the file was originally arranged. After sorting using the LASTNAME field as the primary key, the file is sorted in ascending order by last name. But note how the primary key did not perform a complete sort. The files are not organized correctly by first name. For example, Jones, Stuart is listed before Jones, Lewis.

278   DATABASE MANAGEMENT APPLICATIONS

Secondary key. A key that breaks ties when a file is sorted by the primary key.

Secondary Keys

Sometimes, a unique field does not exist or serve your purpose, for example, when you sort a file by last names and more than one record contains the same last name. In these cases, a *secondary key*, such as the first name, must be used to break ties in the file after it has been sorted by the primary key (Figure 5-24).

Sort Orders

When you sort a file, you can specify that it be sorted into ascending or descending order. Figure 5-25 shows a file sorted by number.

#	LASTNAME	FIRSTNAME
1	Smith	Vance
2	Jones	Marie
3	Lewis	John
4	Jones	Stuart
5	Curtin	Dennis
6	Smith	Adam
7	Stanford	David
8	Smith	Robert
9	Benjamin	Nancy
10	Swabey	Daphne
11	Vogel	Terry
12	Smith	Frank
13	Jones	Lewis

A. Original Order

#	LASTNAME	FIRSTNAME
9	Benjamin	Nancy
5	Curtin	Dennis
2	Jones	Marie
4	Jones	Stuart
13	Jones	Lewis
3	Lewis	John
1	Smith	Vance
6	Smith	Adam
8	Smith	Robert
12	Smith	Frank
7	Stanford	David
10	Swabey	Daphne
11	Vogel	Terry

B. Primary Key Is LASTNAME

#	LASTNAME	FIRSTNAME
9	Benjamin	Nancy
5	Curtin	Dennis
13	Jones	Lewis
2	Jones	Marie
4	Jones	Stuart
3	Lewis	John
6	Smith	Adam
12	Smith	Frank
8	Smith	Robert
1	Smith	Vance
7	Stanford	David
10	Swabey	Daphne
11	Vogel	Terry

C. Primary Key Is LASTNAME and Secondary Key Is FIRSTNAME

Figure 5-24 Sorting a File on a Secondary Key
By specifying the same primary key, and then specifying that the FIRSTNAME field be used as a secondary key, the file is correctly sorted.

#	LASTNAME	FIRSTNAME
1	Smith	Vance
2	Jones	Marie
3	Lewis	John
4	Jones	Stuart
5	Curtin	Dennis
6	Smith	Adam
7	Stanford	David
8	Smith	Robert
9	Benjamin	Nancy
10	Swabey	Daphne
11	Vogel	Terry
12	Smith	Frank
13	Jones	Lewis

A. Ascending Order

#	LASTNAME	FIRSTNAME
13	Jones	Lewis
12	Smith	Frank
11	Vogel	Terry
10	Swabey	Daphne
9	Benjamin	Nancy
8	Smith	Robert
7	Stanford	David
6	Smith	Adam
5	Curtin	Dennis
4	Jones	Stuart
3	Lewis	John
2	Jones	Marie
1	Smith	Vance

B. Descending Order

Figure 5-25 Sort Orders
Here is the same file sorted by number into (A) ascending and (B) descending orders. Notice how the name fields are rearranged so that they stay on the same line as the number they are associated with.

SORTING AND INDEXING RECORDS **279**

Sequential file. A file that is accessed in a linear fashion so that to get to a record, you have to go through all of the records that precede it.

dBASE	Excel
(space)	0
!	1
"	2
#	3
$	4
%	5
&	6
'	7
(	8
)	9
*	(space)
+	!
,	"
-	#
.	$
/	%
0	&
1	'
2	(
3	)
4	*
5	+
6	,

dBASE	Excel
7	-
8	.
9	/
:	:
;	;
<	<
=	=
>	>
?	?
@	@
A	A a
Z	B b
[	Z z
\	[
]	\
^	]
_	^
`	_
a	`
z	{
{		
		}
}	~
>	

Figure 5-26 Sort Sequence
The sequence into which characters are sorted is based on the procedures used by the program. Excel assigns a lower place in the sequence to numbers than dBASE does. dBASE sequences the uppercase letters A through Z above the lowercase letters a through z. Excel sequences them as A a, B b, C c, and so on.

When you sort numbers, this is straightforward. If you sort the numbers 0 to 9 in ascending order, they are arranged from 0 to 9; in descending order, they are arranged from 9 to 0. But the way letters and other symbols are arranged can vary depending on the procedure used by the program. Figure 5-26 lists the order into which characters are sorted by dBASE and Excel.

INDEXING FILES

Sorting is not always the best way to arrange a list. For example, it can take a long time to sort an entire file if the list is long. Also, a file can be sorted in only one order at a time. For example, a name and address file used for mailings might be sorted by last name to produce a reference list. It would then be sorted by ZIP code for printing mailing labels because the post office gives reduced rates for mailings that are presorted. To maintain lists like these in more than one order, you would need separate files, each sorted differently.

To overcome these problems, many database management programs have an index capability. To understand the difference between sorting and indexing, let's look at how a database management program finds a specific record without, and then with, an index.

Sequential Files

Records are physically stored in a file on the disk much like pages are organized in a book. When you search a *sequential file* for a specific record, the program begins at the beginning of the file and reads each record until it finds the one you want. If you create a file with many records, the data cannot all fit in the computer's memory at the same time. Much of them will be stored on one or more disks and read into memory as needed. When the program tries to find a file sequentially, it begins to read these records into memory in batches, looking for the record it wants. If it does not find the record, it replaces the first batch of records in memory with others from the disk and continues to look. Retrieving data from disks is slow compared to the speed of processing the records once they are in memory. It can take a long time just to find a specific record. If the program is also sorting the file into a specific order, it can go on for hours rearranging the records a few at a time.

Indexed file. A file that is sorted quickly by means of an index rather than sorting the files physically on the disk.

Direct access. The computer's ability to locate specific data in a file directly, without having to search though all of the data in the file.

Suppose your file has 10,000 records in it, and you want to find a specific record. Sequentially finding this record would be time consuming, especially if it were near the end of the file. On average, the program would have to read half the file, 5,000 records, before it found the record you wanted. Sequential file scans are fine if you always need to look at or process all the records in a file. But if you want to find only specific records, this method may be unsatisfactory.

Indexed Files

Indexed files were developed to overcome the problems of using sequential files. The idea behind an indexed file is similar to that of an index at the back of a book. The index lets you look up a term and go directly to where it is discussed. This is called ***direct access***. Then you can sequentially search from there to find the exact place on the page.

As you enter records into a file, the program sequentially numbers them. These numbers represent the order in which they are physically stored in the file. This order is usually the one that the records were entered in unless the entire file has been sorted.

To index a file, you select the field you want it indexed by and the program creates a shorter companion file for the index. The index contains only the record numbers assigned by the program and the contents of the field that the file has been indexed on (Figure 5-27). The index is sorted into ascending or descending order.

When you use an index to find a particular record, the program first reads the index file and scans the records there. Because the index is generally much smaller than the file, this can be done quickly. When it finds a record that matches the search criteria you entered, it looks for its record number, and goes directly to where that record is stored on the disk. The computer then starts reading data records from that point until it finds the record it is looking for.

Indexes allow you to keep a file in order by several primary keys without having to physically resort it each time or maintain duplicate files. For example, the original file can have two indexes, one sorting it by department and another by phone number (Figure 5-28). You can also index a file on more than one field. This is similar to sorting a file using a primary and secondary key. The index can be compiled by concatenating two or more fields, for example, to index a file by both first and last names (Figure 5-29).

Record #	ID	LASTNAME	FIRST	STREET	CITY	ST	ZIP	AREA	PHONE
1	101	June	Gary	100 Elm Street	New Haven	CT	10000	203	555-1000
2	102	Benjamin	Nancy	25 Oak Street	Cambridge	MA	20000	617	555-1212
3	103	Kendall	Liz	26 Rosewood	Chicago	IL	20000	312	555-1200
4	104	Hogan	Dennis	40 Main Street	Edgewater	NJ	30000	201	555-1003
5	105	Lyons	Susan	168 Bridge Road	Beverly	MA	20000	617	555-1004
6	106	Baxter	Michelle	110 Millbrook	Austin	TX	50000	512	555-1009
7	107	Sobel	Carol	45 Porter Ave.	Fairlawn	NJ	30000	201	555-1005
8	108	Surridge	Nancy	10 Preston Lane	Oakland	CA	40000	415	555-1007
9	109	Fiske	Robert	1500 Storybrook	Boston	MA	02198	617	555-1008
10	110	Werthman	Ted	25 Stuart Road	Miami	FL	60000	305	555-1010

A. Database File

Record #	LASTNAME
6	Baxter
2	Benjamin
9	Fiske
4	Hogan
1	June
3	Kendall
5	Lyons
7	Sobel
8	Surridge
10	Werthman

B. Indexed on LASTNAME

Figure 5-27 An Indexed File
Here, a database file (A) has been indexed by LASTNAME (B). The file remains in its original order, but the index is arranged alphabetically by last name. When searching for a record, the program searches the index file and then uses the record number it finds there to find the matching record in the database.

Figure 5-28 A File with Multiple Indexes
You can create indexes for more than one field so that you can quickly access records using either field as the basis for a query. Here the database file (A) has been indexed on both the LASTNAME (B) and ST (C) fields.

Figure 5-29 A File Indexed on More Than One Field
You can index a file on more than one field name so that you can access records in an order similar to that provided by a sort on a primary and secondary field. Here the database file (A) has been indexed on both the LASTNAME and FIRST fields (B). Notice how the index concatenated the two fields into one.

Once you have created an index, some programs automatically maintain it. If you add, insert, or delete records in the file, these programs automatically update the index. Some programs also allow you to index large indexes so that they can be scanned faster. This breaks a search into two steps. The program uses the first index to find a record in the second index and, from there, finds its location in the file.

Indexes do have drawbacks. Because they are automatically updated, making a small change in a field takes longer than it would without the index. You can have more than one index for each file, so changes can take a long time. And indexes are like any other file; they take up disk storage space.

5-6

282 DATABASE MANAGEMENT APPLICATIONS

EXERCISE

Exercise 5-6A
SORTING A DATABASE

Refer to a database user's guide for instructions on how to sort a database. List the procedures here:

1. _____
2. _____
3. _____
4. _____

QUESTIONS

1. Why might you want to sort a file?
2. Explain the purpose of a key field.
3. What is the purpose of a primary key? a secondary key?
4. Into what orders can you sort a file?
5. What is the difference between sorting and indexing a file?
6. What are two major advantages of using indexes? What is the primary disadvantage?
7. What is the difference between sequential and direct access?

5-7
PRINTING REPORTS

Most businesspeople do not actually use the database file itself. Generally, they use reports created from part of the information stored in the file. The file might contain information about all aspects of the business. Reports are then designed to organize specific information needed by different people, such as the sales manager, the president, or the finance department. Each report provides only the information needed by those it is printed for. Reports are not always complicated. For example, checks prepared on computers are reports. Many reports appear in tabular form, with information arranged in rows and columns. The typical tabular report contains the information shown in Figure 5-30.

A. A heading that identifies the report
B. A heading for each column
C. The columns that contain data from selected fields
D. Totals and subtotals (for groups of records), which can be printed by entering "report breaks" to indicate what records are to be included

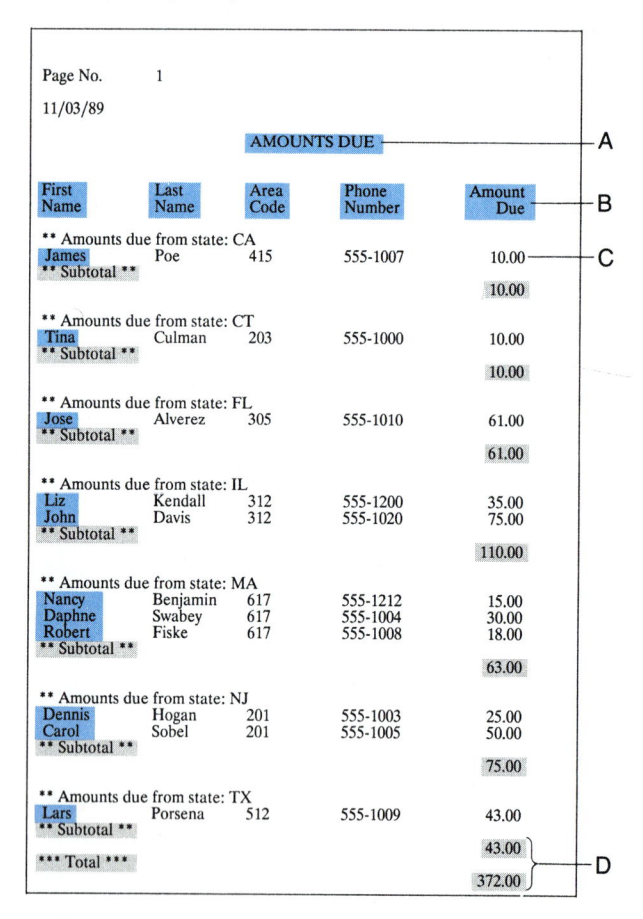

```
Page No.      1
11/03/89
                              AMOUNTS DUE                           ── A

First         Last      Area        Phone           Amount
Name          Name      Code        Number          Due             ── B

** Amounts due from state: CA
James         Poe       415         555-1007        10.00           ── C
** Subtotal **
                                                    10.00

** Amounts due from state: CT
Tina          Culman    203         555-1000        10.00
** Subtotal **
                                                    10.00

** Amounts due from state: FL
Jose          Alverez   305         555-1010        61.00
** Subtotal **
                                                    61.00

** Amounts due from state: IL
Liz           Kendall   312         555-1200        35.00
John          Davis     312         555-1020        75.00
** Subtotal **
                                                   110.00

** Amounts due from state: MA
Nancy         Benjamin  617         555-1212        15.00
Daphne        Swabey    617         555-1004        30.00
Robert        Fiske     617         555-1008        18.00
** Subtotal **
                                                    63.00

** Amounts due from state: NJ
Dennis        Hogan     201         555-1003        25.00
Carol         Sobel     201         555-1005        50.00
** Subtotal **
                                                    75.00

** Amounts due from state: TX
Lars          Porsena   512         555-1009        43.00
** Subtotal **
                                                    43.00        ┐
*** Total ***                                                    ├─ D
                                                   372.00        ┘
```

Figure 5-30
Typical Report
The typical report contains a heading for the report, a heading for each column, columns of data, and subtotals and totals.

Report format. The design specifications for a printed database report.

You can create reports in five basic steps and then print them.

1. Decide what fields are to be included in the report. A report does not have to print out all the data contained in a database file. Selected fields can be printed so that you can tailor the report for specific uses. For example, you might have a file that contains names, addresses, and phone numbers but you would not print the phone numbers when printing addresses on forms.

2. Lay out the order of the fields to be printed. Reports are arranged in rows and columns much like a table. But you can specify the order the columns are arranged in. Some programs allow you to design an on-screen form that shows exactly what the report will look like when printed. This lets you design a report that can fill in preprinted forms such as purchase orders, invoices, or paychecks.

3. Sort or index the file so that it will print data in a desired order.

4. Specify the criteria, if any. This allows you to print selected records and selected fields from those records.

5. Specify if there are to be totals or subtotals calculated for numeric fields. To do this, you specify the field that will be totaled. This field is not the field that contains the numbers to be totaled but any field that contains duplicate data. For example, in the report shown in Figure 5-30, the file contains a field named ST (for state) and a field named AMOUNT. To prepare a report that subtotaled amounts by state, it would be sorted or indexed by state, and then the ST field would be specified as the criterion for subtotals to generate the report shown. Some programs let you create subtotals at various levels.

Because it takes time to lay out a report, most programs let you save the *report formats* you create so that they can be used again. You assign each format a name, and then save it onto the disk so that it can be retrieved.

EXERCISE

Exercise 5-7A
PRINTING A REPORT

Refer to a database user's guide for instructions on how to print a report. List the procedures here:

1. _____
2. _____
3. _____
4. _____

QUESTIONS

1. What is a report? How does it compare to a database file?
2. What information does a typical report contain?
3. What are the five basic steps to create reports?
4. Assume you had a database file with two fields: a field named ITEMS that contained the ID numbers of items purchased, and a field named AMOUNT that contained the price of each. What field would you specify that subtotals be grouped on if you wanted a report listing sales by item?

5-8 MAKING NEW DATABASES FROM EXISTING FILES

Join. A database procedure that combines two existing databases into one new one.

Link. Querying two or more database files at the same time.

Because data in a relational database are stored independently from how they are viewed, you can change your view of the data at any time. This is done by creating new tables from existing tables in different combinations. The result of combining tables is always another table. In many ways, this is much like a cut-and-paste operation where rows or columns are cut from different tables and combined into a new table.

If you have two files with a common field, you can *join* or *link* them into a third table (Figure 5-31). These commands construct a new table by combining fields in one table with fields in another table, provided both tables have the same value in a specified common field. All records that fail to have the same value in the common field are deleted from the new table. When linked in memory, you can query both files at the same time. You can also save the joined file onto the disk if you want to reuse it again. If you do save the joined file on the disk, you assign it a new name and the original files from which it was created remain unchanged.

In addition to joining or linking files you can also save selected records or fields in an existing database to their own file on the disk. This creates a smaller database that is faster to query and use.

ID	LASTNAME	FIRST	STREET	CITY	ST	ZIP	AREA	PHONE
101	June	Gary	100 Elm Street	New Haven	CT	10000	203	555-1000
102	Benjamin	Nancy	25 Oak Street	Cambridge	MA	20000	617	555-1212
103	Kendall	Liz	26 Rosewood	Chicago	IL	20000	312	555-1200
104	Hogan	Dennis	40 Main Street	Edgewater	NJ	30000	201	555-1003
105	Lyons	Susan	168 Bridge Road	Beverly	MA	20000	617	555-1004
106	Sobel	Carol	45 Porter Ave.	Fairlawn	NJ	30000	201	555-1005
107	Surridge	Nancy	10 Preston Lane	Oakland	CA	40000	415	555-1007
108	Fiske	Robert	1500 Storybrook	Boston	MA	02198	617	555-1008
109	Baxter	Michelle	110 Millbrook	Austin	TX	50000	512	555-1009
110	Werthman	Ted	25 Stuart Road	Miami	FL	60000	305	555-1010

A. NAMELIST Database File

ID	DATE	AMOUNT
101	6/8/89	10.00
102	6/9/89	15.00
103	6/10/89	35.00
104	6/11/89	25.00
105	6/12/89	30.00
106	6/13/89	50.00
107	6/15/89	10.00
108	6/16/89	18.00
109	6/17/89	43.00
110	6/18/89	61.00
101	6/18/89	30.00
101	6/19/89	45.00

B. AMOUNTS Database File

ID	LASTNAME	FIRST	STREET	CITY	ST	ZIP	AREA	PHONE	DATE	AMOUNT
101	June	Gary	100 Elm Street	New Haven	CT	10000	203	555-1000	6/8/89	10.00
101	June	Gary	100 Elm Street	New Haven	CT	10000	203	555-1000	6/18/89	30.00
101	June	Gary	100 Elm Street	New Haven	CT	10000	203	555-1000	6/19/89	45.00
102	Benjamin	Nancy	25 Oak Street	Cambridge	MA	20000	617	555-1212	6/9/89	15.00
103	Kendall	Liz	26 Rosewood	Chicago	IL	20000	312	555-1200	6/10/89	35.00
104	Hogan	Dennis	40 Main Street	Edgewater	NJ	30000	201	555-1003	6/11/89	25.00
105	Lyons	Susan	168 Bridge Road	Beverly	MA	20000	617	555-1004	6/12/89	30.00
106	Sobel	Carol	45 Porter Ave.	Fairlawn	NJ	30000	201	555-1005	6/13/89	50.00
107	Surridge	Nancy	10 Preston Lane	Oakland	CA	40000	415	555-1007	6/15/89	10.00
108	Fiske	Robert	1500 Storybrook	Boston	MA	02198	617	555-1008	6/16/89	18.00
109	Baxter	Michelle	110 Millbrook	Austin	TX	50000	512	555-1009	6/17/89	43.00
110	Werthman	Ted	25 Stuart Road	Miami	FL	60000	305	555-1010	6/18/89	61.00

C. Tables Joined on ID to Create New File

Figure 5-31
Joining Tables
Here, the (A) NAMELIST and (B) AMOUNTS files contain a common ID field that can be used to join them into (C) a new table. All records that fail to have the same value in the common field are deleted from the new table.

EXERCISE

Exercise 5-8A
CREATING A NEW DATABASE

Refer to a database user's guide for instructions on how to create a new database containing only selected records from an existing one. List the procedures here:

1. _____
2. _____
3. _____
4. _____

QUESTIONS

1. Explain what joining two files does and why you would want to do it.
2. When joining two existing tables, what conditions must be met?

CHAPTER
6

Communications Applications

OBJECTIVES

After finishing this chapter, you will be able to:

- Describe why computers and peripherals are connected together into local area networks so they can communicate with each other
- Describe how computers can be connected together over long distances into wide area networks using telephone lines
- Describe the kinds of equipment you need to communicate between computers
- List and briefly describe some typical communications programs
- List and describe the communications settings you use to connect computers together
- Explain how you can transfer files between computers and describe the types of files you can send and receive
- Describe other ways to communicate with computers, including facsimile and voice mail

6-1

Computers are useful by themselves, but their power increases when they are connected to other computers so that users can communicate with each other. There are two ways to connect computers. One way is for computers located on the same campus or in the same building to be wired together into a local area network. The other way is for computers anywhere in the world to be connected into wide area networks using the regular telephone lines. Depending on how the computers are connected, the resource available to you can increase significantly. For example, you can:

- Exchange electronic mail with other users.
- Transfer programs or data files from another computer onto one of your own disks so that you can run those programs or access those data files on your computer.
- Call up commercial databases or information services such as Compu-Serve, Prodigy, and other, more specialized service, such as Dow-Jones News Retrieval.
- Hold conferences with one or more other users.

6-1 LOCAL AREA NETWORKS

There is a saying that "the whole is greater than the sum of its parts." This is certainly true of microcomputers. Individually, they are useful, but when linked into a local area network, they become even more so. Local area networks can connect computers within a single building or in several nearby buildings. For example, many colleges have connected the computers in their offices, classrooms, labs, and dorms into local area networks. It is estimated that almost six million computers are already connected into local area networks, and that number is growing.

CENTRALIZED INFORMATION PROCESSING

Computers have been used in businesses since the early 1950s. These first mainframe computers were large, expensive, and complicated. As a result, separate facilities were set aside, and a professional staff was hired to program and operate them (Figure 6-1). These facilities and this staff are called the data processing (DP), management information systems (MIS), or information systems (IS) department—referred to hereafter as the DP department. These departments manage and operate the firm's centralized computer facilities and in many cases its microcomputers.

In the 1960s, smaller, less expensive minicomputers were developed. These smaller computers allow information processing to be done at the department level. In both cases, the systems are centralized and users work at dumb terminals. These terminals lack the ability to process data on their own. They have only a screen and a keyboard. To work, a dumb terminal must be con-

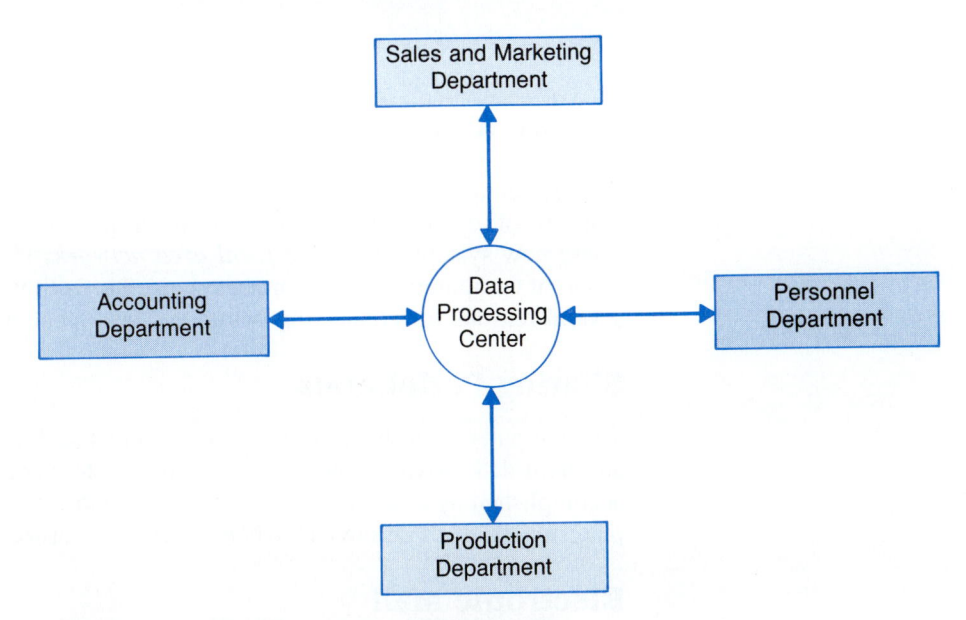

Figure 6-1 Data Processing Departments
Data processing departments are operated by a specialized staff. These service departments perform data processing for other departments throughout the firm.

6-1

Standalone microcomputer. A computer system that is not connected to other computers.

Local area network (LAN). A method of connecting computers and peripherals, in a relatively small area, so that they can communicate with one another and exchange data.

Electronic mail (E-mail). Mail sent directly from one computer to another using a network or a modem connected to the telephone line.

nected to a mainframe or minicomputer that can process data for it. The terminal is used only to send information to the computer and receive information from it.

DECENTRALIZED INFORMATION PROCESSING

With the development of low-cost microcomputers, information processing became more decentralized. *Standalone microcomputers*, which were not tied into a larger system, began to appear throughout the corporation. Each standalone microcomputer is a complete system that includes a computer, keyboard, display screen, and printer (Figure 6-2). A standalone system like this is used by a single person or shared by several people who use it at different times. Although the standalone units are not operated by a specialized staff, they may be supervised by a manager from the company's DP department. This manager approves the purchase of hardware and software and provides training and support to the users.

Figure 6-2 Standalone Workstations
A standalone workstation has everything an operator needs to do word and information processing. The workstation is not connected to other computers.
Courtesy of IBM Corporation

LOCAL AREA NETWORKS

With recent advances in technology it has become possible to combine the best features of centralized and decentralized information processing systems. These new systems are called *local area networks* (*LAN*), which is simply a group of computers that are connected together with wires or cables. There are several reasons for connecting computers into local area networks.

Sharing Peripherals

The computers can share expensive peripherals such as plotters, laser printers, and hard disk drives. Where there are only a few computers this can also be accomplished by mechanical or electronic switches that connect a specific computer to one of these devices when a switch is turned (Figure 6-3).

Electronic Mail

The computers can communicate with each other, and users can exchange messages and electronic mail. *Electronic mail* (also called *E-mail*) allows users to send messages to other users on the network. These messages can be composed using the E-mail program, or on any word processing program. The message

292   COMMUNICATIONS APPLICATIONS

Broadcast. To transmit copies of your document to several recipients at the same time via electronic mail service.

Store and forward. The ability to store a message until the addressee reads it.

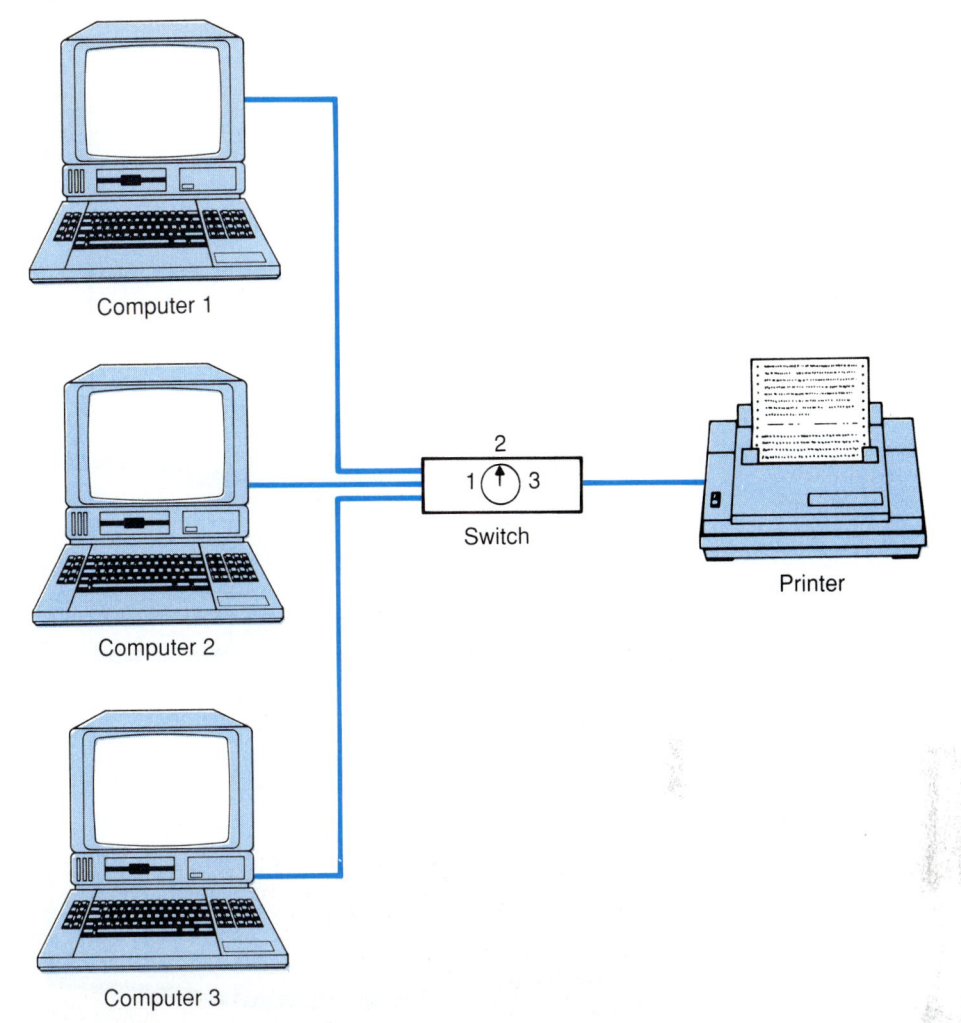

Figure 6-3 Switches
Switches that connect computers to devices such as printers and modems are like a simple network. Mechanical switches require you to turn a selector knob and can print the output from only one computer at a time. Electronic switches automatically route print jobs from any of the connected computers.

---

can then be sent to one user or *broadcast* to many users. To simplify the process, many programs include address books that contain other users' IDs so you can point to the user's address rather than type it in. Also, users can be grouped together so messages can be broadcast over and over to the same groups with a single address.

When a message is sent, many E-mail programs let you include attachments with your message. These items can be grouped together in an electronic "envelope" and can be all of the same type or mixed media, for example, letters, graphics, or spreadsheet files created on other programs.

E-mail programs (Figure 6-4 and 6-5) are usually memory resident so you can press some specified keys (called hot keys) to pop up the E-mail menu in the middle of an application. You can then send or receive mail and return to what you were doing. If a message arrives when you are working on a word processor, spreadsheet, or other program, a beep or message on the screen indicates its arrival.

When you send a message, it is stored on the file server until the addressee reads it. This process is called *store and forward* because the message is stored

LOCAL AREA NETWORKS 293

6-1

Encrypt. To code data in such a way that an unauthorized user cannot see or use it.

Message Handling Service (MHS). A standard agreed to by many manufacturers so that the exchange of messages between networks is possible.

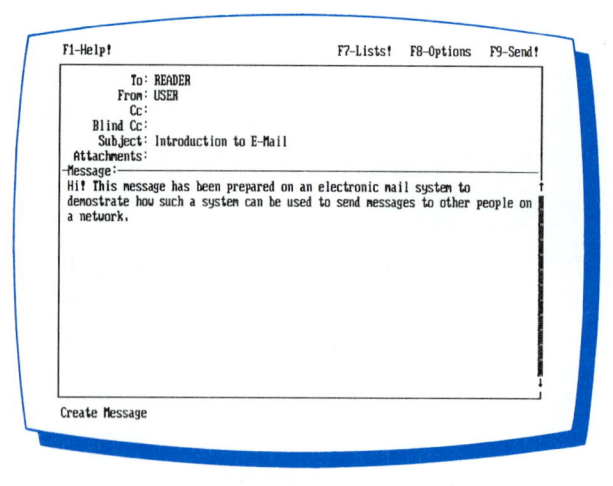

Figure 6-4 E-mail Message
Here a message has been prepared on the Da Vinci eMAIL Electronic Mail program.

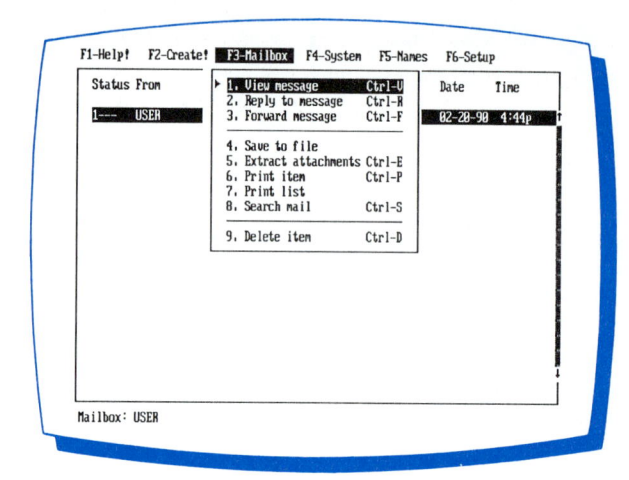

Figure 6-5 E-mail Commands
Here, a pull-down menu lists Da Vinci's electronic mail commands.

until the addressee signs on to the network or accesses the electronic mail service. On good programs, the messages are *encrypted* as soon as they are sent so that if data are accessed by an unauthorized user, they appear unintelligible on the screen.

Once a message has been read, it can be printed, replied to, saved, archived, or deleted. If you save messages, you can then use special search commands to locate specific messages by looking for keywords, names, or message dates.

Electronic mail on a network can be sent to other networks, or accessed by modems, if the network has an electronic mail gateway to those services. This way you can send a message around the world by addressing it to a service such as MCI. To make this exchange of messages between networks possible, a standard called *Message Handling Service* (*MHS*) is being used by many electronic mail program developers. This standard was developed by Novell and Action Technology to simplify the exchange of messages.

Sharing Files and Programs

Applications programs used on a network work best when they are designed to be "network aware." For example, many operations must be regulated because two or more users may want to work on the same file at the same time. For example, suppose only one unit of a particular inventory item is in stock, and two order-entry people try to accept an order for it at the same time. If this is not

294   COMMUNICATIONS APPLICATIONS

File locking. Preventing two users from accessing and changing the same file at the same time.

Authorized user. Any person authorized to work with a computer, program, or file. Authorization is usually granted by the MIS department or a network or department manager.

Read-only access. A file that can be displayed but not changed or deleted.

Log on. To connect up with a network or a service with which the computer telecommunicates.

Network manager. The person assigned the responsibility of resolving any problems with a network or the people who use it.

controlled by the program, one of these updates will be lost and one customer will be left with an unfilled order. To prevent this from happening, *file locking* (also called *record locking*) is used. When the first user selects a file or record for updating, the system locks that file or record to prevent access by other users until it is released, in its updated form, by the first user. When the file is locked, other *authorized users* can view it (called *read-only access*) but not modify it.

USERS AND ADMINISTRATORS

When a computer is connected to a network, users have access to programs and files based on rights granted by the network administrator.

Users

To use a network, users first *log on* with an ID and a password. The ID is assigned by the network administrator. The password is selected by the user and can (and should) be changed by them at any time to improve security. Because network software can be customized, what users see when they log on depends on the system's design. Usually, a menu appears to load applications programs and execute operating system commands such as those used to copy files or format data disks.

Administrators

Systems organized into a network are usually supervised by a *network manager*. This person can be a member of either the department the network is located in or the DP department. The network manager is responsible for the efficient management of the network and sets up procedures for the users. He or she adds and removes users and assigns passwords and levels of access. Passwords can be used to provide different types of access. One user, for example, may be authorized access to correspondence files but denied access to financial analysis files. Some users can be given just read-only access, whereas others can be allowed to enter and update the files. This prevents unauthorized users from altering files. The network administrator is also responsible for troubleshooting problems should they arise and assisting both new and experienced users with problems.

No security system is perfect; when data are extremely sensitive, an *audit trail* is essential. An audit trail is a record of who accessed the network and what files they altered. A typical entry on the audit trail may include:

- The operation that was performed
- The computer it was done from
- The identification of the user who performed it
- The date and time it was done
- The database, table, record, and field that were affected
- The original entry of the changed fields
- The new entry of the changed fields

Although most networks are quite secure, you should always assume that what you send can be seen by others. Even if the network administrator cannot see the contents of messages, others on the network may try to gain access. With enough time, computational resources, and experience, they may be able to.

6-1

SNEAKER NET

Networks are often either too expensive or too complicated for some users to take advantage of. These people sometimes refer to their "network" as Sneaker Net or Walk Net. On these networks, the computers are not connected by wires but by users who walk from one workstation to another to deliver a file on a disk or a printout. Not only are these networks less expensive and less complicated, but the users get some exercise.

6-2

EXERCISE

Exercise 6-1A
COMPLETE THE SIMULATION ON SCREEN

The *Information Processing Software Sampler* contains an on-screen simulation of several communications programs. Run the simulation of the Da Vinci eMAIL program, and then summarize the key features of an electronic mail program.

QUESTIONS

1. What is the difference between centralized information processing and decentralized information processing?
2. What does the acronym LAN stand for?
3. What are the advantages of having computers and other hardware connected to a network?
4. What is the difference between a dumb terminal and a computer that is connected to a network?
5. Describe two reasons why networks are used to connect computers.
6. Give three things an audit trail entry might include.

6-2
WIDE AREA NETWORKS

Public Switched Telephone Network (PSTN). The telephone network that you use when you make a phone call.

Wide area network. Computers equipped with modems and connected together by telephone lines.

Host computer. The controlling computer that one or more other computers are connected to.

Answer mode. A setting on modems and/or communications programs that tells the computer to answer the phone when it rings.

Auto-answer. A modem or communications program setting that tells the modem to answer the phone automatically when it rings.

Null-modem cable. A cable used to directly connect the serial ports on two computers so they can exchange data.

Many users call computers that are not connected into a network. To do so, they dial up these computers using their modems, which are connected to the telephone lines. These telephone lines are also referred to as the *Public Switched Telephone Network* (*PSTN*) or *wide area network*. Using this network, you can call another computer, called a *host computer*. The host computer can be a mainframe computer, a minicomputer, or a microcomputer. The thousands of computers that you can call fall into four classes.

- Information services, such as CompuServe, offer a variety of databases and other services. You must subscribe to the service and are then billed for the time you are connected to the service.

- Electronic mail services, such as MCI Mail, are available for sending messages and mail. Your message is stored by the computer and then forwarded to the person it is addressed to when he or she logs on to the service.

- Bulletin boards are set up by individuals or groups. You can call them without charge.

- Private wide area networks are set up by corporations or others, and are open only to members of the company or affiliated institutions. For example, Internet (also called ARPANET) connects 936 networks, 175,000 computers, and 35 countries. It is used by people in government, business, and academia.

CALLING OTHER COMPUTERS

You can call any other computer that is also equipped with a modem. To do so, the computer you are calling must be on, running a communications software program, and set to *answer mode*. You can also use your computer to answer incoming calls. This is handy if, for instance, you want to set up your own bulletin board so your branch office can send in reports electronically.

To use your computer to answer and record incoming calls, you need an *auto-answer* modem, which answers the phone when a call comes in. Some communications programs let you protect your system from unwanted callers by assigning passwords. Callers are prompted to enter the password and are usually given three tries to get it right. If they enter the correct password, communications continue. If not, the modem disconnects and hangs up the phone.

HARD-WIRED COMPUTERS

You can wire two computers together so that they act just like a wide area network. This is useful when you want to exchange files between two computers that are not part of a network and are located close to each other. To do this, you use a special cable called a *null-modem cable* to connect the two computers. This cable is just like the one you use to connect a standalone modem to your computer, but two wires have been reversed. When calling a computer connected in this way, you follow all the same procedures you use to call one over the phone lines, but you don't enter a phone number. The other computer answers automatically when you select it for a call.

Teleconference. Exchanging messages with other computer users over the phone lines.

CALLING INFORMATION SERVICES

There are many commercial information services that you can subscribe to. You can use these services to locate important information, or to exchange electronic mail with other subscribers. You can also *teleconference* by leaving messages to be read later, or if two users call at the same time, they can type messages back and forth.

Prodigy

The Prodigy service was introduced by IBM and Sears to provide low-cost information services to home users. Access to the service is based on a relatively low monthly charge, the trade-off being that you are continually confronted with advertisements when using the service. Despite this minor drawback, it does provide useful services such as stock market quotations and news service stories at a very low cost.

CompuServe

CompuServe was established in 1979 and has since become the largest information service in the world that is accessible by any computer user. Some of the services it offers are:

- News bulletins from AP and the *Washington Post*
- Weather reports for any area of the country
- Sports scores
- An electronic encyclopedia
- Electronic mail
- Home shopping and banking
- Discussion forums on various topics
- Computer games
- Home management programs (for example, Balancing Your Checkbook)
- Travel reservations
- Business news
- Stock quotations
- Standard & Poor's analysis
- Brokerage service
- Electronic conferencing
- A business reference library
- Personal finance programs (for example, Calculating Your Next Raise)
- Forums for personal computer users
- Services for professionals in aviation, law, medicine, engineering, and so on

CALLING ELECTRONIC MAIL SERVICES

We've seen how electronic mail is useful for local area networks. Wide area networks also distribute E-mail. E-mail services are provided by both commercial and private networks. MCI is typical of the commercial electronic mail services available to microcomputer users. MCI offers various ways for you to send mail.

Bulletin board system (BBS). A computer you can call (usually for free) to send and read messages. Also called public access message system.

System operator (SYSOP). The person who manages and operates a bulletin board.

Chat mode. A mode that allows people to type messages back and forth when they are connected to a bulletin board or information service.

- An Instant Letter is used to send a letter to another subscriber. It is immediately available for retrieval by the person it is addressed to.
- An MCI Letter is sent to the computer just like an Instant Letter, but MCI transmits it to the MCI postal center closest to the person it is addressed to, prints it, and then gives it to the U.S. Postal Service for delivery.
- Overnight Letters and Four-Hour letters are similar but are delivered by courier.

MCI Mail also lets you use your computer as a telex station to connect with more than one million other telex users around the world. Moreover, MCI lets you broadcast your mail to a mailing list that you store on the service. When you send the message to the service, it routes it to everyone on the specified list. Several private E-mail services also exist for special uses.

- Bitnet connects many colleges and universities.
- Arpanet connects government researchers in colleges and industry.
- BIX connects serious computer users.

CALLING BULLETIN BOARDS

Bulletin board systems (*BBS*) (also called *public access message systems*) are set up by firms or individuals. For example, Figure 6-6 shows the main menus of the bulletin board service operated by Public Brand Software. Many of these bulletin boards are run by an intriguing assortment of individuals whose interests include exchanging computer know-how, arranging dating services, exchanging gossip, and sharing programs and games that you can transfer to your own disk. Many bulletin boards also have a public message base where you, or any other caller, can write anything your heart desires (unless you break the law) and which any other caller can read. Many also provide electronic mail services that allow you to assign a password to a message so that it can be read only by the person it is addressed to. These messages can also be read by the *system operator* (*SYSOP*), the person who runs the system. This person can see everything on the bulletin board. Most systems also have a *chat mode* (also called CB mode) so that you can exchange messages in real time with the SYSOP or with other users if the bulletin board accepts calls on more than one line.

Locating the first bulletin board to call is the hardest part. You can often get numbers from magazines, users' groups, and friends. Because most bulletin boards list other bulletin boards, you will soon be aware of hundreds. If you call

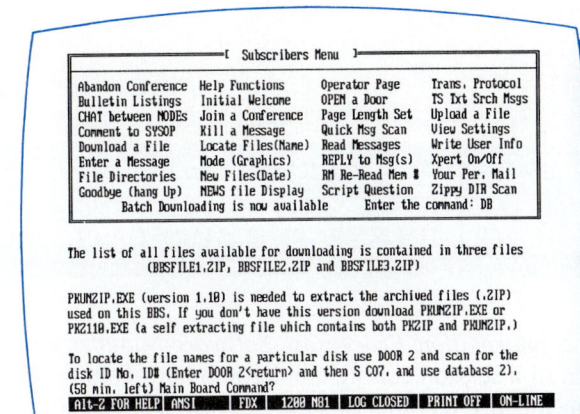

FIGURE 6-6 The Public Brand Software Opening Menu Public Brand Software distributes low-cost software by catalog or through a subscription to their bulletin board. The service is also used to exchange messages between members. This figure shows the main menu that appears when you log on to the service.

WIDE AREA NETWORKS 299

Packet-switching networks. Networks that send data from more than one user at the same time.

Access points. The local phone number that you dial to connect your computer into a network. Also called nodes or ports.

one, though, do not be surprised to find that the number is no longer in service. Because most of these boards are operated by individuals, they open as people become interested and close when they lose interest or run out of money to support the cost of maintaining the system. Many software companies also run bulletin boards. Users can call in to get the latest information from the company, exchange ideas with other users, and download programs.

PACKET-SWITCHING NETWORKS

When you call an outside service such as CompuServe, you can call one of its local access points. These calls are frequently local, and not long-distance calls. If there is not one of those in your area, you still do not have to pay a long-distance rate if you use a service such as TeleNet or Tymnet. These services, called *packet-switching networks*, are designed to connect computers around the country. They have *access points* (also called *nodes* or *ports*) in hundreds of cities throughout the world. For example, Tymnet has more than 10,000 access points in 500 cities and 67 countries. To use the service, you dial the phone number of the local access point using a local telephone number. If your town does not have one, you may have to place a long-distance call to the nearest town that does. When you connect with the network, you indicate the service you are calling. The network then takes your local call and sends it to that service. These services work only if the computer you are calling is also on the system.

Packet-switching networks are generally cheaper than placing a long-distance call directly to the computer over any available phone line. When you are connected to a phone line, you use only a small part of its capacity, and much of the time you are connected, no data are being sent or received. Packet-switching networks package your data along with those of other users. By time-sharing the lines, more data can be sent, and the lines are used more efficiently, which lowers the cost for all users. Moreover, the networks charge you based on the amount of data you transmit rather than the time you are connected.

Because packet-switching networks generally connect fixed points at the host end, packet-switching companies have introduced a type of service that lets you connect with any phone number in a given area. These services, such as TeleNet's PC Pursuit and Tymnet's Outdial, allow you to dial a local number to access the network. You then dial the area code you want to call, and you are connected to a modem at that end from which you can dial any number in the remote city. These systems are widely used to connect with out-of-town BBSs that are not fixed nodes on the network.

EXERCISE

Exercise 6-2A
COMPLETE THE SIMULATION ON SCREEN

The *Information Processing Software Sampler* contains an on-screen simulation of a session calling a bulletin board. Run the simulation and then summarize the key features of such a session.

QUESTIONS

1. When using a wide area network, what is the computer that you call, called? What mode must it be set to?
2. What is a null-modem cable used for?
3. What is E-mail?
4. What is a bulletin board? What is chat mode?
5. What is the advantage of using a packet-switching network? How does it work?

6-3
TELECOMMUNICATIONS EQUIPMENT

Modem. A device that converts signals from digital to analog and back again so computers can exchange data over telephone lines.

Telecommunication. A method of communicating between computers using telephone lines and a modem.

To telecommunicate with another computer, you need a modem and a communications program. A modem lets your computer transmit information over a cable or telephone line. You will need a serial port, which is frequently built into the computer, and a cable to connect it to the modem. You will also need a wire to connect the modem to the phone line.

MODEMS

A *modem* is a communications device that links computers connected by telephone lines. With modems, you can send data from your computer to another similarly equipped computer located anywhere you can reach by phone (Figure 6-7). This is called *telecommunications*.

The reason you need a modem to telecommunicate is simple: The computer generates digital signals, but telephone lines are designed to carry analog signals. When you transmit a message, the modem at the sending end converts the computer's digital signals into analog signals (modulation) so that they can be transmitted effectively over telephone lines. The modem at the receiving end then converts the analog signals back into digital signals (demodulation) so that they can be used by the computer. The name *modem* derives from *mo*dulate-*dem*odulate.

All electronic data are transmitted as electrical voltages that periodically change in form. A receiver then interprets, or decodes, these changing voltages to reconstruct the original message.

Microcomputer — Modem — Phone Line — Modem —

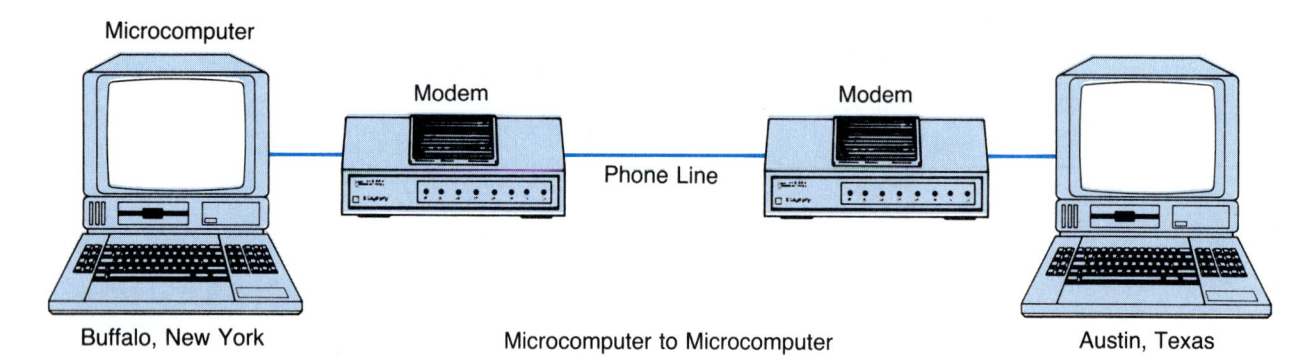

Buffalo, New York   Microcomputer to Microcomputer   Austin, Texas

Figure 6-7 Modems
Modems must be used at both ends of the telephone circuit. The sender can then transmit data over the telephone lines to the modem at the other end. The receiving modem can be connected either to another computer or to a printer.

TYPES OF MODEMS

The type of modem determines how it is connected to the computer and phone lines.

Acoustic coupler modem. An inexpensive modem that has two rubber cups into which you press a telephone handset to make a connection between the computer and the telephone line.

Direct-connect modem. A modem that connects to the computer with a wire or cable. See also Acoustic coupler modem.

Integrated Services Digital Network (ISDN). The digital telephone network being installed worldwide to replace the existing analog network. This network enables the transmission of voice, data, and video without modulation.

Acoustic Coupler Modems

An *acoustic coupler modem* (Figure 6-8) is a low-speed modem that has a rubber cradle into which you place the telephone's handset. A speaker in the sending end of the modem "talks" into the microphone in the telephone's mouthpiece. These signals are then transmitted over the telephone lines. A microphone in the receiving end of the modem "listens" at the telephone's earpiece for data received from the remote computer. The data are then passed on to the computer.

Though generally inexpensive, acoustic couplers have several drawbacks. They often require you to manually dial the number you want to call. And when you connect with another computer, you must flip a switch to go from voice to data transmission. These modems have fairly high error rates because the modem picks up any background noise in the room, and this can garble the data transmission. Moreover, a telephone always feeds some of the transmitted signal back into the earpiece so that you can hear what you are saying. This telephone feedback confuses acoustic coupler modems. The transmit volume has to be set very low so that the modem does not interpret this feedback as a signal.

The one big advantage of acoustic coupler modems is that they can be used from any phone. For example, they are essential on portable or laptop computers when you want to use them to make calls from hotel rooms or public telephones that are not otherwise equipped for modems. This is because most of these phones do not allow you to plug the modem directly into the phone line.

Figure 6-8 Acoustic Coupler Modems
Acoustic coupler modems have cups into which you press the telephone's handset.
Courtesy of Radio Shack, a division of Tandy Corporation

Direct-Connect Modems

A *direct-connect modem* (Figure 6-9) is connected to the computer and phone lines with cables so that no background noise can interfere with the data. Because there is less noise, data can be transmitted faster than with acoustic couplers. There are two types of direct-connect modems: a modem on a board

INTEGRATED SERVICES DIGITAL NETWORK

The *Integrated Services Digital Network* (*ISDN*) is the latest development in telephone communications. This proposed network will gradually replace the traditional telephone wires that you use whenever you make a phone call. The ISDN international standards allow users to simultaneously send voice, data, and video over local, national, and international telephone networks. Because this network is digital, and not analog like the current system, modems are not required. Data can be sent directly from the computer at up to 64 kilobits per second, which is much faster than today's modems can send data.

**Figure 6-9
Direct-Connect Modems**
Direct-connect modems plug directly into the phone line so you do not need a phone to use them. One type plugs into an expansion slot in the computer. This standalone modem connects to the computer's serial port.
Courtesy of U.S. Robotics

6-3

that plugs into an expansion slot in the computer, and a standalone modem that connects to the computer's serial port with a cable. Both types are then connected to the telephone's wall jack with a standard phone cable.

One type of direct-connect modem is built into the computer just like any other component. These modems cannot be removed from the computer.

6-4

EXERCISE

Exercise 6-3A
READ A REVIEW

Locate a review or an advertisement in a computer magazine that discusses a modem. List the features that are described.

QUESTIONS

1. What equipment do you need to telecommunicate?
2. What function does the modem serve?
3. List two types of modems, and describe the differences between them.
4. What is the difference between analog and digital signals?
5. What is a carrier wave? What is it used for?
6. What is ISDN?

6-4
COMMUNICATIONS PROGRAMS

Hayes compatible. Modems that use the same set of instructions developed for Hayes modems.

Dialing directory. A list of phone numbers and communications settings stored in a communications program.

Auto-redial. A modem or communications program setting that has the modem redial phone numbers when busy signals are encountered.

Script languages. A programming language built into communications programs so users can automate procedures.

When you use a modem to call other computers, you use a communications program. Here we introduce you to some popular communications programs and the principles behind them.

INTRODUCTION TO COMMUNICATIONS PROGRAMS

When you use a communications program with a modem, most of the process is automated for you.

Command Sets

Most modems use commands that are based on those developed by Hayes, a major manufacturer of modems. Modems that use this command set are called *Hayes compatible*. Typical Hayes commands include the prefix AT (for Attention) followed by special characters that stand for commands. For example, because phones are either tone or pulse, ATDT (Attention, Dial, Tone) tells the modem to dial a number using tone mode. ATDP (Attention, Dial, Pulse) tells the computer to dial the number using pulse mode. ATH (Attention, Hangup) tells the computer to break the connection and hang up the phone.

Dialing Directories

If you often call the same computers, you can enter their names and addresses into the program's *dialing directory*, along with other information such as the communication parameters that the system uses. When you want to call the computer, you retrieve the dialing directory file and select the number to be called. The number is then dialed automatically using the communications parameters you specified in the file.

Auto Redial

Many programs have an *auto-redial* feature. If you get a busy signal on the first try, you can use this to automatically redial the number at specified periods until a connection is made. When the computer is reached, the computer beeps to signal you that a connection has been made. Some programs allow you to specify a list of numbers to be dialed in sequence. If the first number is busy, the program automatically dials the second. This process is repeated until a connection is made with one of the numbers.

Script Languages

Most communications programs have *script languages* that allow you to automate many operations. Script languages are similar to macros in word processing and spreadsheet programs. You can either write a small program or record your keystrokes for playback later. One of the most common uses for these script languages is to automate dial-up and log-on sequences when calling information utilities. If you enter and save these sequences, you can automatically dial and be logged on to the system when you call it. To protect yourself, you should not include your password in these saved sequences if others have access to your program disk. Programs that allow you to write scripts are more

COMMUNICATIONS PROGRAMS 305

powerful. For example, you can write a script that dials a number at a specified time, logs on, checks for mail, downloads it to your computer, and then logs off. Because the entire process is automated, and can be done when phone charges are lowest, this automation can save you a good deal of money.

TYPICAL COMMUNICATIONS PROGRAMS

Many communications programs are available. Here is a brief description of some of the most widely used.

PROCOMM PLUS

PROCOMM PLUS is a powerful, full-featured, communications program (Figure 6-10). It includes a dialing directory, several error-correcting file transfer protocols, and a script language you can use to automate the program. It has built-in context-sensitive help screens that guide you through its operation.

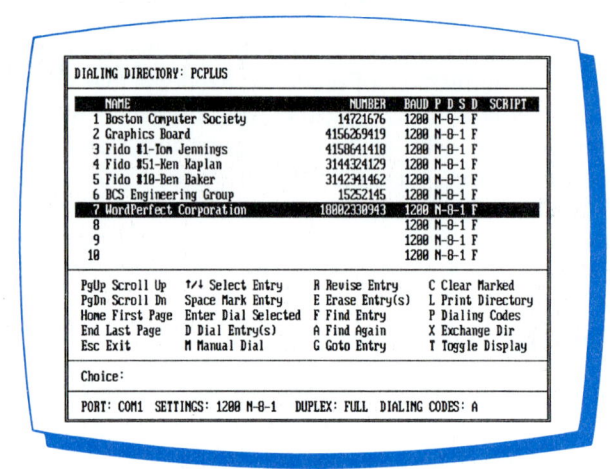

Figure 6-10 PROCOMM PLUS PROCOMM PLUS is a very powerful shareware communications program that includes a dialing directory and script language that you can use to automate your telecommunications procedures.

Crosstalk

Crosstalk is another popular communications program. When loaded, it displays a status screen listing the name and communications settings for a computer you want to call (Figure 6-11). You can create files for each service you call and store them in their own files. When you want to make a call, you load the file you created for that service, type **DIAL**, and then press **Enter** to make the call. The latest version is menu operated, but you can also still use the same commands introduced in earlier versions.

Microsoft Works

Microsoft Works, an integrated program, includes telecommunications as one of its features (Figure 6-12). It allows you to store dialing information in files that you then retrieve when you want to call another computer. It is operated with pull-down menus that list all the program's commands.

Navigation Programs

Services such as CompuServe can be both difficult and time consuming for beginners to get around in. To make this service easier and cheaper to use, navigation programs have been developed. Two of the most popular are TAPCIS (Figure 6-13) and the CompuServe Information Manager (Figure 6-14).

Figure 6-11 Crosstalk
Crosstalk for Windows is easy to operate because of its pull-down menus.

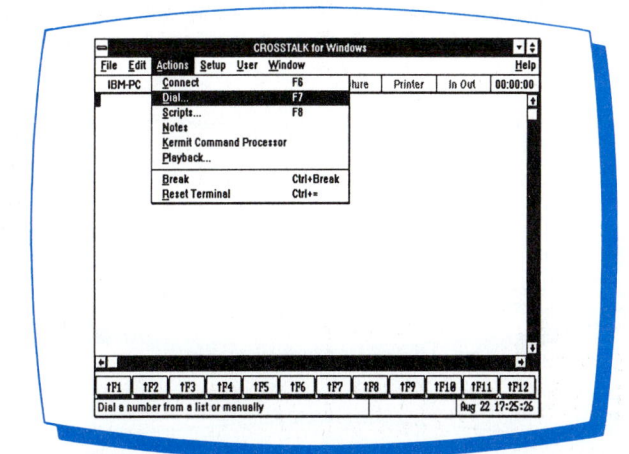

When you pull down the Actions menu, the Dial command is displayed.

When you select Dial, a window opens listing all of the other computers that you can call.

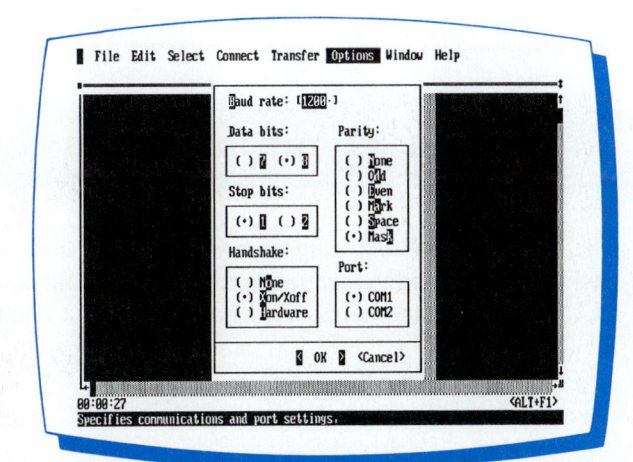

**Figure 6-12
Microsoft Works**
Microsoft Works includes a menu-driven telecommunications program.

COMMUNICATIONS PROGRAMS   307

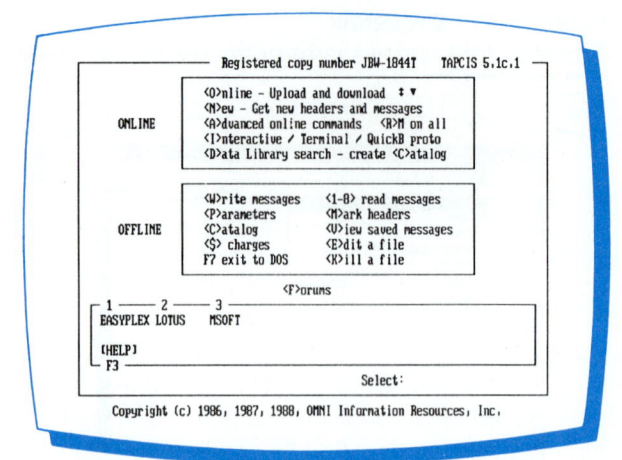

Figure 6-13 TAPCIS TAPCIS will automatically dial CompuServe, upload and download mail and files, and then sign off. This automation greatly reduces the cost of accessing the service.

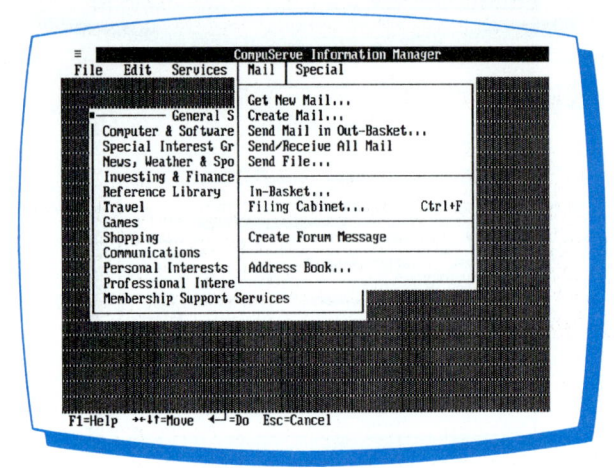

Figure 6-14 CompuServe Information Manager CompuServe Information Manager allows you to navigate the service using pull-down menus.

6-4
6-5

EXERCISE

Exercise 6-4A
COMPLETE THE SIMULATION ON SCREEN

The *Information Processing Software Sampler* contains an on-screen simulation of several communications programs. Run the simulation of PROCOMM PLUS and then summarize the key features of a communications program.

QUESTIONS

1. What is the purpose of a communications program?
2. What is a command set? What does Hayes compatible mean?
3. What is the purpose of a dialing directory? an auto-redial feature?
4. What is a script language used for?
5. List three typical communications programs.
6. What do navigation programs do?

308   COMMUNICATIONS APPLICATIONS

6-5
TRANSFERRING FILES

Upload. To send a file to a mainframe or other microcomputer.

Download. To transfer a file from one computer to another.

Text capture. Storing in a disk file the text that appears on your screen when telecommunicating with other computers.

When sending files to another computer, you can type them from the keyboard, and when receiving them, you can view them on the screen. But these methods are not always suitable. For example, you may want to send a message after you have carefully written and revised it. You might also want to transmit or receive more complicated documents such as programs or spreadsheet files. To do this, you can create and edit the files on regular applications programs and then transmit them to the other computer. When you send or transmit a file to another computer, it is called *uploading*. When you receive a file from another computer, is called *downloading*.

Before uploading or downloading files, you have to understand the two kinds of files you can send or receive: text and binary.

ASCII FILES

As you saw in section 3-6 in Chapter 3, text files are files that have been saved in an ASCII format. Many applications programs have a command that saves files in this format. The command generally includes the expression *Text file* or *ASCII file*. You can also create these files using an applications program's command to print to the disk.

BINARY FILES

Binary files require a more sophisticated transmission procedure because, unlike text files, a single missing or incorrect bit can make them unusable. To transmit or receive these files, you must use 8 data bits with no parity and the XMODEM error checking protocol.

Binary files include two basic types of files.

- Executable program files, which can usually be identified by their .EXE or .COM extensions
- Encoded (formatted) files, like those produced on WordPerfect, dBASE, Lotus 1-2-3, and other applications programs

DISPLAYING ASCII FILES ON THE SCREEN

When your computer is connected to another computer, you can scroll through messages or download ASCII text files so that they are displayed on your screen. You can also route copies of these files either to your printer or to a file on a disk. This is called *text capture*, and no error checking is done by the program.

Most programs provide two ways to send the data to the printer. You can send just what is currently on the screen, or you can send anything that appears on the screen during a session. To do either, you press specified keys on the keyboard or make menu selections. You use the same keys or menu choices to turn the printing off. Continuously sending data to the printer slows you down because the printer prints more slowly than you can receive.

Because large files take a long time to read on the screen or print out, it is usually faster to store them in a file on the disk so that you can read them or print them out later. To do so, you execute the program's Save command and specify

Compress. A procedure that removes unnecessary bytes from a file so it takes up less room on a disk or can be transmitted more quickly.

Uncompress. Expanding a file that has been compressed so that it can be read by the program for which it was designed.

Communications protocol. The method used to ensure that the messages and files exchanged between computers are accurately received.

a filename. Anything that appears on your screen, whether originating from your keyboard or the remote computer, will be stored in the specified file. The data received from the other computer will also be displayed on your screen unless you are using a communications protocol that displays messages that tell you which block is being received and verifies its receipt.

UPLOADING AND DOWNLOADING ASCII AND BINARY FILES

One way to communicate with another computer is to send and receive program and data files that are stored on a disk. For example, a software company can send you an update to their program, or a sales manager can send a sales report to the home office. To send or receive files, you must use the communication program's command to upload or download a file, and then specify both the name of the file to be uploaded or downloaded and the communications protocol to be used in the file transfer.

Many files that are exchanged over the phone lines are *compressed* by the sender so that they can be transmitted more quickly. The recipient then uses a program to *uncompress* the files once they are received. Depending on the type of files being sent, compression can save a great deal of time and dramatically lower phone costs. For example, a graphics file that might normally take 20 minutes to transmit can be transmitted in 5 minutes if it is first compressed. Programs that compress and uncompress files are found on many bulletin boards. The most popular program of this kind is called ARC. You can try this program for free, then, if you like it, you send the developers a fee to continue using it.

There is a cliché that if anything can go wrong, it will. This certainly applies to the high-speed transmission of digital data over telephone lines that are designed to carry voice communications. If even 1 bit of data is received incorrectly, all the following data may be garbled. It's like a high-speed train hitting a bump in the track and derailing. Until phone circuits are improved for digital data, *communications protocols* (also called *link protocols*) are used to check for errors and correct them during transmission. There are a large number of error checking schemes in use, including ones with names such as Kermit, YMODEM, and CompuServe B. To see how these work in principle, let's look at XMODEM, written by Ward Christianson of Chicago. This is a public-domain program, essentially a gift to the computing community. This program uses a simple technique. To use XMODEM, communications parameters must be set to no parity and 8 data bits.

1. It sends data in blocks of 128 bytes. The data are not displayed on the screen as they are being sent or received.

2. Each of the bytes contains an ASCII character, which is identified by its ASCII number. For example, the letter *A* is ASCII 01000001, *B* is 01000010, and so on.

3. The program adds the values of all the ASCII characters in the block and sends the ASCII character for that value last. This value is called the checksum character.

4. The receiving end adds the values of all ASCII characters in the block it receives and checks it against the checksum character to see if they match.

5. If they match, the receiving computer sends an acknowledgment back to the transmitting computer, which then sends the next block. If it detects an error, the receiving computer requests that the block be retransmitted.

QUESTIONS

1. What do downloading and uploading refer to?
2. What two types of files can you transfer between computers?
3. When text is displayed on your screen, what is it called when you save it in a disk file?
4. Why are files compressed before they are transferred?
5. What are communications protocols, and what role do they play in telecommunications? Name two.

6-6
OTHER CONNECTIONS

Facsimile. A device that can send a copy of a printed document to another facsimile machine or microcomputer over the telephone lines. Also called FAX.

In addition to networks and modems, there are other ways to communicate between computers or between computers and people or other devices. The two most popular are facsimile and voice mail.

FACSIMILE MACHINES

Until recently, you could distribute the documents that you created on your computer in only two ways, either as electronic digital signals or as printed copy. Today, you can distribute them electronically over a network, or you can use a modem to connect to a remote computer. And you can distribute printed copy through the mail, or you can use a *facsimile* (*fax*) machine (Table 6-1).

Table 6-1
METHODS OF DOCUMENT DISTRIBUTION

Sender	Recipient	Method of Distribution
Printout	Printout	Facsimile to facsimile
Digital	Digital	Computer to computer
Digital	Printout	Computer to facsimile
Printout	Digital	Facsimile to computer

A facsimile machine (Figure 6-15) is like a copy machine where you insert the

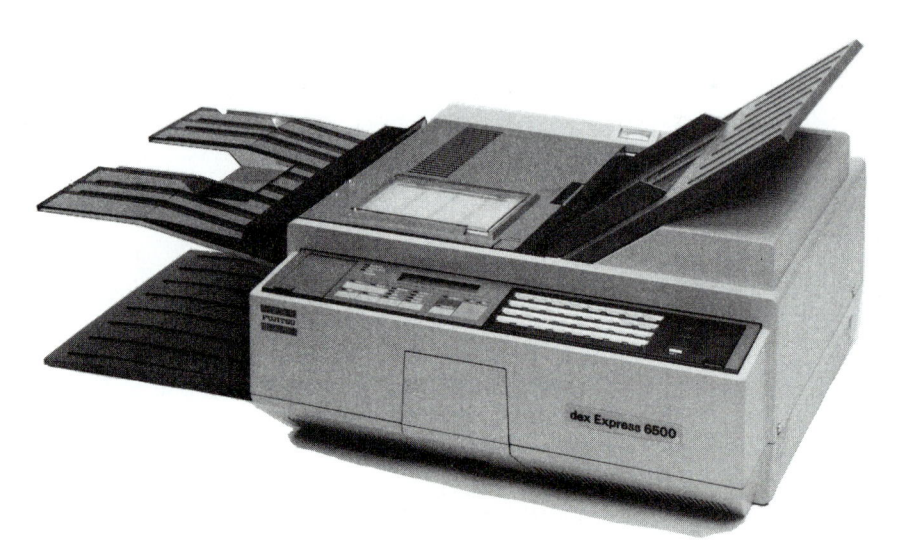

Figure 6-15 Facsimile Machines
Facsimile machines have a document tray into which you place the document you want to send. You dial the number of another fax, and the document is drawn through the scanner and converted into digital signals. These signals are sent over the telephone lines, and the receiving fax reverses the process and converts the signals back into a printed image. *Courtesy of Fujitsu Imaging Systems of America, Inc.*

COMMUNICATIONS APPLICATIONS

Voice mail. The digital storage and routing of phone messages.

Automated attendant. The part of a voice mail system that directs you to the person you are trying to reach.

original document into your machine, and a copy comes out on another facsimile machine anywhere else in the world.

Because the cost of fax machines has dropped, they have become widespread. To send a document on a fax machine, you insert the document into the fax's document tray, and then dial the phone number of another fax machine. When the other fax answers the call, your fax automatically feeds the document through its scanner. This scanner converts the document into digital signals. These signals are sent over the phone line to the recipient's fax machine, which reverses the process. It converts the digital signals back into an image, which it prints out. When the transmission is completed, both machines hang up.

With an add-on board, it is even possible for you to send a document to someone's fax machine directly from your computer, or for someone with a fax machine to send a document directly to your computer. This speeds up the process as you don't have to first make a printout and then walk to a fax machine. These add-on boards are installed into one of the expansion slots in your computer and then connected to the telephone jack on the wall with a cable.

VOICE MAIL

One of the big problems in business is "phone-tag." This is where you call someone, discover he or she isn't there, and then leave a message for the person to return your call. When the person does call back, you aren't there, so he or she leaves a message for you. A microcomputer-based solution to this problem has been introduced. Called *voice mail*, it automates phone answering and messaging. To use these systems, you insert an add-on board and run the voice mail software. When someone calls your phone, the computer answers, and a digitized voice tells the caller to leave a message. When the caller does so, it is digitized and stored on your disk. You can then play back recorded messages by pressing a few keys on the computer's keyboard or by dialing your phone from a touch-tone phone. Sophisticated systems also have an *automated attendant* that routes callers to the right person when they press the keys of a touch-tone phone. For example, the attendant answers the phone and tells the caller to press 1 to reach marketing, 2 to reach service, or 3 to place an order. The voice mail system then routes the call to the appropriate department. If no one answers, a digitized voice asks the caller to leave a message.

EXERCISE

Exercise 6-6A
READ A REVIEW

Locate a review or an advertisement of a computer-based facsimile add-on board in a computer magazine. List the features that are mentioned in the ad or review.

QUESTIONS

1. What is the purpose of a facsimile machine?
2. What is voice mail, and, briefly, how does it work?
3. Give an example of how an automated attendant works.

CHAPTER 7

Computers and Careers

OBJECTIVES

- Describe the causes of health problems that might arise when working on a computer, and explain how to avoid them
- Describe some security issues that arise when computers are used
- List and describe ways to protect and secure your data
- Describe some of the positions for which computer-trained people qualify and how they may get training

Once you have gained computer experience, there is still more to learn. First of all, there are the health problems that arise, many of which can be prevented by knowing what causes them. Then, you usually use computers in a relatively public setting, and others may have access to your work. You have to know how to protect sensitive information. But foremost is the need to find ways to put your knowledge to work in a business environment, after locating the position that most closely matches your interests.

7-1 ERGONOMICS AND HEALTH

Ergonomics. The study of the interaction of people and machines so the machine is designed to accommodate the needs of the user.

The medical and physical effects of working long hours on a computer are not fully known. It is suspected that some problems can result. Complaints generally concern vision and muscle strain. But you can avoid most, if not all, of these problems.

Your eyes were made to see most efficiently at a far distance. Working on a computer calls for intense concentration on a task close at hand, usually no more than a couple of feet away. When your eyes change focus from far, their natural state, to near, several different muscles are called into action. A muscle inside the eye changes the shape of the eye's lens to focus sharply and clearly on the display screen. Other muscles turn both eyes inward, pointing them together at the same character on the screen, and still other muscles move the eyes quickly from one character or word to another. Users complain most often of headaches, blurred vision at both near and far viewing distances, itching and burning eyes, eye fatigue, flickering sensations, and double vision.

Researchers in *ergonomics*, the study of the interaction of people and machines, have developed several suggestions that users should follow to reduce or eliminate any potential problems.

- Use an adjustable chair, which allows you to sit at a proper angle to the display screen (Figure 7-1). Generally, the top of the display screen should be 10 degrees above, and the center of the screen 20 degrees below, your straight-ahead seeing position. The distance from your eyes to the screen should be 14 to 20 inches.

- Place your reference material as close as possible to the display screen to avoid frequent or large eye and head movements. A copy stand is very useful for this.

- Place your reference material the same distance from your eyes as the display screen is to avoid having to change focus when you look from one to the other. Every time your eyes change focus, it requires muscles to work inside the eye. Frequent changes may cause you to feel tired.

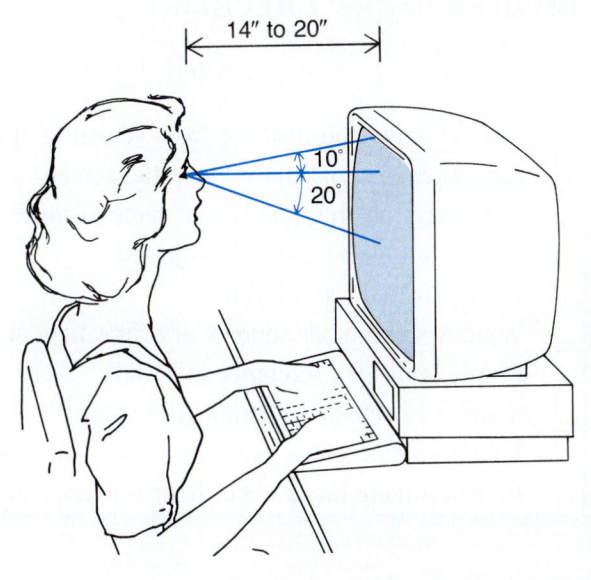

**Figure 7-1
Positioning Your Materials**
Positioning your display screen correctly can reduce the strain of working at a computer and make your work healthier and more enjoyable.

ERGONOMICS AND HEALTH   315

7-1

Lighting and glare control can also make a difference. The following recommendations are designed to maximize comfort, accuracy, and productivity and to minimize eye fatigue and other complaints:

- Although lighting needs vary from person to person, check that overall illumination for video display equipment is between 30 and 50 foot-candles, which is less than the customary office lighting level. Display screen brightness should be three or four times greater than room light. A lower level of room lighting can be achieved by using fewer bulbs or fluorescent lights and by replacing cool white fluorescent tubes with cool white deluxe tubes that provide less light but a more comfortable and pleasing atmosphere.
- Adjust the characters on the display screen to contrast well with the screen background.
- Minimize reflected glare on display screens by placing the screens so that windows and other sources of light are behind you. Do not sit facing an unshaded window or other bright light source. Make use of drapes and shades to reduce glare. Small hoods can be attached to extend above the display screen to shield it from overhead light if necessary. You can also use nonreflective surfaces or buy antiglare filters that fit over the screen.
- Use localized lighting such as flexible lamps for other desk work as required. They are shielded and must be placed to avoid glare on the work surface of the display screen.
- Avoid white or light-colored clothing if it causes a reflection on the screen.

Taking rest breaks can often solve many problems. Because information processing generally requires intense concentration on the document and screen, rest is important. The National Institute of Occupational Safety and Health (NIOSH) recommends a fifteen-minute break after two hours of continuous work for users having moderate visual demands or moderate workload (less than 60 percent of your time looking at the screen) and a fifteen-minute break every hour for users having high visual demands, high workloads, or repetitive work tasks.

COMPUTER USERS' CHECKLIST

Your workspace and vision care habits: Do they measure up?

- [ ] Correct angle and distance from screen to eyes (see Figure 7-1)
- [ ] Reference material placed near the screen
- [ ] Reference material and screen same distance from eyes
- [ ] Screen brightness properly adjusted
- [ ] Proper overall room lighting
- [ ] Windows and other sources of bright light shielded
- [ ] Proper lamps for reference material
- [ ] Sources of screen reflection eliminated
- [ ] Fifteen-minute break every two hours for moderate users
- [ ] Fifteen-minute break every hour for frequent users

EXERCISES

Exercise 7-1A
COMPLETING AN ERGONOMICS CHECKLIST

Sit at one of the computers in the lab, and compare the Computer Users' Checklist with the computer's setup. How could the setup be improved if you had to work there for many hours at a stretch?

Exercise 7-1B
ORGANIZING A WORK AREA

Using a ruler and Figure 7-1 as a guide, organize a work area in the lab so that you are properly positioned in relation to the equipment.

QUESTIONS

1. What is ergonomics? Why is it important?
2. List three things you can do to avoid vision and muscle strain problems when working at a computer.

7-2 ETHICS AND MORALITY

Centralized. Any process or organization that is grouped together into a single unit.

Password. A form of protection that allows access only to users who know the assigned password.

In the early days of computing, the computer and its information were tightly controlled. Only a professional staff was allowed access. With computers now located everywhere and accessible to everyone, security and other issues have become very important.

SECURITY

When computer power is *centralized*, security can be ensured. Only people authorized to have access to information are allowed to see it. Security is important for everyone, not just management. For example, no one should be able to see your salary or medical records stored on the computer unless there is a genuine need to and management authorizes it. When computers are sitting on desks throughout the firm, security becomes a serious problem. The DP department can use access codes to prevent unauthorized people from seeing information in the main computer, but these can be lost or stolen. Moreover, people often use their microcomputers for sensitive work, and most microcomputers have very poor security devices, if any at all. However, there are ways to protect your work.

Occasionally, you work at display terminals that people can see as they walk by, or you make printouts that are to be widely circulated, or you share your printouts with other users. What if sensitive data are on the screen, perhaps a list of salaries? You can hide this data from other users by hiding the windows the data are displayed in if your program allows you to do so.

Hiding information on the screen does not protect the files themselves. Some programs provide a higher level of security by letting you assign *passwords*. Without the password, the files cannot be retrieved. If you assign a password and then forget it, you cannot retrieve the files, so be sure to use passwords that you will remember.

If you work on a computer with floppy disk drives, you can secure your work by removing the floppy disks and taking them with you. On a hard disk system, this is not possible. Protecting sensitive data on hard disks from other

---

PASSWORDS

- Don't share your password—with anyone.
- Choose a password that is hard to guess. Mix letters with numbers, or select a famous saying and choose every fourth letter.
- Don't use a password that is your address, pet's name, nickname, spouse's name, telephone number, or one that is obvious—such as sequential numbers or letters.
- Use longer passwords because they are more secure; six to eight characters are realistic.
- Be sure that your password is not visible on the computer screen when you enter it.
- Be sure that your password does not appear on printouts.
- Don't tape passwords to desks, walls, or terminals. Commit yours to memory.

Encryption program. A program that encrypts data.

License. What you actually buy when you purchase a computer program. You do not own the program, you just purchase the license to use it.

Copy protection. A technique that prevents users from making copies of disks.

Piracy. The act of copying a copyrighted program for sale or use by others without the permission of the copyright holder.

Site license. A license from a publisher that allows you to make copies of their program for use at a specific site, or to run their program on a network used by more than one user.

Virus. A program designed to reproduce itself onto other magnetic media with the goal of destroying a user's data.

Trojan horse. A program in which someone has planted a virus in the hopes that when you run the program, the virus will damage your data or cause you other problems.

users who have access to the computer is difficult. One way to provide security is to encrypt (or code) files using an *encryption program*. Then, only users who know an assigned password can gain access to the files.

THEFT OF SOFTWARE

When you walk into a computer store and pay $100 or more for a program, you may think you have bought the program, but usually you would be wrong. You have actually bought the *license*, or right, to use the program and its documentation. The physical materials still belong to the publisher. Read these licenses carefully; they spell out your rights in detail. Most specify that you can use the program only on one computer and cannot make copies for distribution to others. You can however, make copies for your own use, because you should never run the program from the original disk.

To discourage the illegal copying of programs, some software publishers *copy protect* their program disks so that users cannot copy them. Several firms have produced special programs designed to copy disks that have been copy protected. The rationale for these programs is that users need backup copies in case something goes wrong with the primary disk. But some users, and almost all software companies, feel a different rationale predominates — that these programs are used to copy programs so that they can be distributed to others. Called *piracy*, this practice costs software companies lost revenues, and they are increasingly taking legal action to prevent the distribution, sale, and use of these disks, especially in large corporations. Corporations are even being held accountable for the actions of employees who use these programs to copy disks.

A *site license* allows a company or school either to run programs on networks without having a copy for each computer or to make a limited number of copies for use within a single department or location. Site licenses reduce the company's total software costs, lessen the likelihood of violating the publisher's legal rights, and make it easier on all network users because they do not need individual copies of the program.

VIRUSES

One of the fastest growing problems in the microcomputer field is the introduction of *viruses* by antisocial users. A virus is a small program, either stored on a disk by itself or appended to an existing file called a *Trojan horse*. When the file is loaded or the Trojan horse program is run, the virus loads itself into the computer's memory. Once there, it can secretly attach itself to other files or programs or store itself on any other disks run on the computer, including the hard disk. What happens next depends on the intent of the vandal who created the virus.

- The virus may cause problems immediately.
- It may count specific occurrences, for example, how many times it is copied, and then cause damage.
- It may look at the computer's clock and cause damage on a specific date.
- It may reproduce itself and then cause damage. Like a biological virus, a computer virus can infect other files and then spread from them (Figure 7-2).

ETHICS AND MORALITY

7-2

1. A programmer creates a program that can secretly bind to another program or a computer operating system and copy itself.

2. The program is placed on a floppy diskette or hidden in a program sent to an electronic information service, or electronic bulletin board, where information is exchanged by computer over telephone lines.

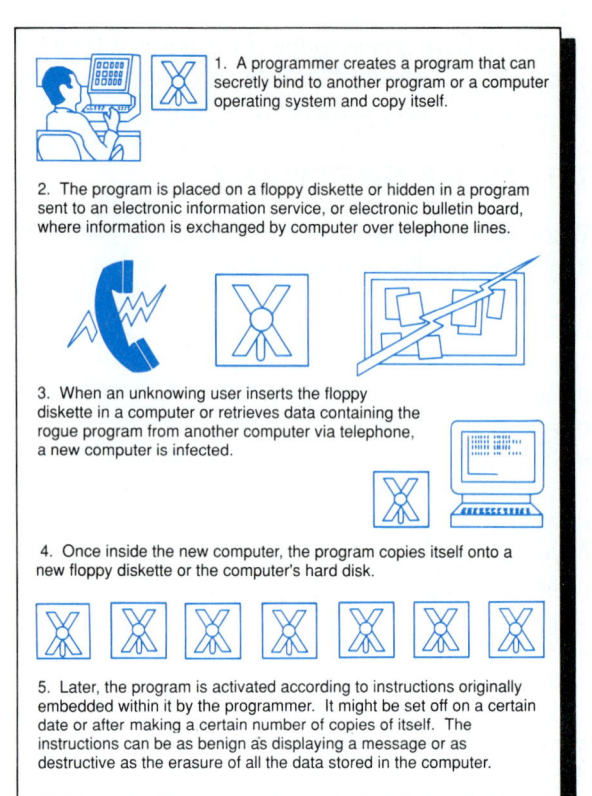

3. When an unknowing user inserts the floppy diskette in a computer or retrieves data containing the rogue program from another computer via telephone, a new computer is infected.

4. Once inside the new computer, the program copies itself onto a new floppy diskette or the computer's hard disk.

5. Later, the program is activated according to instructions originally embedded within it by the programmer. It might be set off on a certain date or after making a certain number of copies of itself. The instructions can be as benign as displaying a message or as destructive as the erasure of all the data stored in the computer.

Figure 7-2 How a Virus Program Spreads.
Reprinted by permission of The New York Times

THE ELECTRONIC SUPERVISOR

Computer technology makes possible the continuous collection and analysis of management information about work performance and equipment use. This information can be useful to managers in managing resources, planning workloads, and reducing costs. It can be advantageous to employees as well, by providing timely feedback on performance and an objective basis for evaluation. Despite these possible advantages, however, there is controversy about computer-based monitoring on grounds that it invades employees' privacy, causes stress, and can be used unfairly by some employers.

"Computer-based monitoring" or "electronic monitoring" systems automatically record statistics about the work of employees using computer or telecommunication equipment in their jobs. Such statistics might include number of keystrokes made, types of transactions completed, or time spent for each transaction, for example.

Computer work monitoring is affecting a small but growing segment of the office work force. It is estimated that around six million office workers have part or all of their work evaluated based on computer-generated statistics; for many others, such statistics may be collected but are not currently used for evaluation. The number of monitored workers can be expected to grow as computers begin to be used in more jobs, for example retail sales, as computers are introduced in a greater variety of workplaces.

The uses of technology are controversial because they point out a basic tension between an employer's right to control or manage the work process and an employee's right to autonomy, dignity, and privacy. This same tension is also evident in the use of other technologies for surveillance and testing in the workplace, for example, controversy over polygraph testing, drug testing, genetic screening, and emerging brain wave testing.

Source: *The Electronic Supervisor*, Office of Technology Assessment, 1987.

The number of instances in which viruses cause damage is increasing. Once introduced, viruses are hard to detect and remove. For individual users, the best defense is to use only commercial programs and not to exchange files with other users. Especially avoid downloading files from public bulletin boards.

EXERCISE

Exercise 7-2A
LICENSE AGREEMENTS

Ask the person in charge of your computer lab to show you a license agreement covering a software program that you will be using. Read the agreement, list the rights it gives you, and list the things it prohibits.

QUESTIONS

1. What does it mean when a disk is copy protected? Why is copy protection sometimes necessary?
2. Do you think it is legal or ethical to copy disks when a publisher has asked you not to? Why or why not?
3. When you buy a program, do you usually buy all rights to it?
4. What is the purpose of a site license?
5. What is a virus? What is one way to avoid them?
6. What is a password used for on some programs?

7-3 CAREERS IN INFORMATION PROCESSING

The increased computerization of the workplace has led to the development of several new positions and a change in responsibilities for existing positions. One major company divides its employees into two categories—originators and processors. Originators are those people who draft original documents, reports, numeric analysis, and so on. Processors are those people who take this material and polish it for presentation. For example, a typical originator/processor relationship is that of an executive and secretary. The executive writes a letter to a client and her secretary then uses a word processing program to print it and the envelope for mailing.

The originator/processor division is not absolute because each person's work usually combines some of each. If the executive handwrites a memo to a co-worker, she is playing both roles. If the secretary prepares a new log to keep track of projects he is also playing both roles. However, despite its limitations, it does help to organize the types of jobs and careers that are open to people with computer experience.

In addition to originator/processor positions, there are also several specialist positions for those who not only work with computers, but who service, supply, or train computers and users.

ORIGINATOR POSITIONS

In most originator positions, the computer is a tool that is used to speed up tasks. Generally, the computer is not essential—it's just very useful. For example, managers use computers to draft memos, letters, and reports. They also use them to prepare financial plans and forecasts, and to evaluate data stored in the company's computers.

Designers, engineers, and scientists use computers to run experiments, analyze structures and designs, and prepare working drawings from which things can be built.

PROCESSOR POSITIONS

In most processor positions, the computer is used extensively but not exclusively. For example, a secretary uses the computer to prepare correspondence but he also has many other responsibilities. However, there are also positions that are primarily computer-based, like data entry and word processing operator positions. Typical processor positions include the following:

- **Data entry operators** enter data into computers. For example, they enter the prices and stock numbers of items in inventory, sales and shipments, and employee records.

- **Word processing operators** prepare finished documents based on what others prepare. Some of these positions are secretarial. The operator works for a person directly and prepares only his or her work. Others work in centralized departments that prepare work from people in one or more divisions in the company.

- **Editors** edit and proofread reports, advertising materials, articles, and books.

Career paths. A sequence of jobs that leads to advancement through a corporation.

Career ladder. The arrangement of jobs from entry-level workers to senior management.

SPECIALIST POSITIONS

Specialist positions are generally those directly related to the computer business. These positions are usually with computer firms or in computer departments in large corporations. Typical specialist positions include:

- **Computer operators** actually operate large computers. They load programs and data, back up files, run jobs, and print reports.
- **Computer librarians** maintain files and databases of company data, and in some cases, provide employees with access to company and public databases of information. They also maintain corporate data, keep records, and determine which files can be deleted.
- **Programmers** write programs that are used to process the company's information.
- **Systems analysts** analyze, evaluate, and design company information systems. They perform the job of ensuring that an information system meets the needs of both management and employees. Once they determine the needs to be met, they design a system, and consult with the developers who write the programs and design the reports.
- **Information systems managers** manage all of a company's information systems and resources. They generally report to high-level officers and manage a staff of people in the information processing, or data processing, department who perform the tasks required to implement the company's systems.
- **Trainers** teach people how to use computer systems. Some trainers work for companies that use computers. Many others work for firms that provide training to these companies on a contract basis.
- **Microcomputer specialists** train and assist computer users, and answer questions, so users get the most benefit from their computers.
- **Technical support people** answer questions from people who use computers. Many of these people work for companies that supply computer equipment to large firms.
- **Technical writers** write descriptions of programs and computer systems so that others can understand and use them.
- **Consultants** fulfill several roles, from designing systems to installing them and training users on how to operate them.
- **Sales personnel** determine the needs of their clients and recommend specific hardware and software. They work for hardware or software companies and sell to large accounts or to other outlets. Typical outlets are retail stores such as Computerland, and value-added dealers who put systems together for companies. Both retail stores and value added dealers also have salespeople who call on clients to sell them their products or services.

CAREER PATHS

Almost all positions have *career paths* that allow you to move up the *career ladder* to positions with more responsibility and higher pay. Secretaries can become supervisors, programmers can become department managers, and salespeople can become marketing or sales managers. In some cases, employees gain extensive experience within a large firm, and then start their own small business. For example, many word processing operators have started small firms that do word processing for professionals and other self-employed people who do not have their own full-time staffs to do work of this kind.

EXERCISE

Exercise 7-3A
LOCATING JOBS THAT REQUIRE COMPUTER KNOWLEDGE

Look through the want ads for a nearby major metropolitan area, and look for ads for positions that require an understanding of computers.

QUESTIONS

1. Briefly describe what an originator position is and list some examples.
2. Briefly describe a processor position and give some examples.
3. Briefly describe a specialist position and give some examples.
4. What is a career path? Give some examples.

7-4
COMPUTERS IN THE WORKPLACE

As you have seen, computers are very powerful tools. Let's take a look at some of their applications through the eyes of people who use them. In the process, you will learn more about how computers are used, and be introduced to additional programs that are used in business.

PROFESSIONAL WORD PROCESSING

Sheila is the secretary for a group of 8 people whose primary need is for professional-quality word processing. Her personal computer and its word processing software make every part of her correspondence work more efficient.

Right now, she needs to edit a long report. Her personal computer uses menus to list all of the things the computer can do. And there are indexes that list the names of all the documents Sheila has stored on the computer. Sheila could use the menus and the index feature to get to the report, but since she knows the document she wants, she just enters the file's name and retrieves the report immediately.

The first problem with the report is that one of the subsidiary companies has changed its name. The old name appears many times in the 20-page report. To change it, Sheila selects the Global-Search-And-Replace feature and enters the old and new company names. The computer searches the entire document, finds each instance where the old name appears, and replaces it with the new company name. The computer makes these changes to the entire report in seconds.

The first section that needs to be edited begins on page eight. Sheila's word processing software includes a Go-To-Page command that lets her bring this page onto the screen with a few keystrokes. It is easy to edit the document, using the labeled keys and the side keypad. Sheila selects a sentence that needs to be moved to the end of the paragraph. Then she presses a key labeled "Cut." The sentence disappears from the text. Using the directional keys, she moves the cursor to the new location and presses "Paste." The sentence has been moved, and the rest of the text has adjusted itself to the new position.

There is a paragraph on page 15 that needs to be moved to the end of the document to become the summary. Sheila uses the Go-To-Page 15 commands, selects and "cuts" the paragraph from its current position. To get to the end of the document Sheila uses a key labeled "Bottom Document." The bottom of the document appears on the screen and Sheila presses the "Paste" key, to complete this edit. The summary paragraph is now in the correct location.

The other minor editing takes only a few minutes with the rapid movement between pages and the labeled function keys on the personal computer. Satisfied with the revised document, Sheila is ready to print the report. She could do this process by following the choices in a series of menus that give her complete control over the look of the finished document. However, Sheila has already stored her standard print format in a User-Defined Key on her personal computer. By using this key, the report is sent automatically to the printer in standard departmental format.

The contents of Topic 7-4 are copyright, Digital Equipment Corporation, 1991. All rights reserved. Reprinted by permission.

The letter-quality printer will take a few minutes to print the 20-page report. But Sheila doesn't have to wait to begin her next project. Her personal computer can control the printing at the same time that she works on her next job.

Now Sheila is ready to prepare the cover memo that will accompany the report. With a few keystrokes she prompts the computer to retrieve the right memo letterhead and display it on the screen. Sheila only has to type in the name of the person the report is for and the sentences that describe its contents, and this memo is ready to print. She uses the same User-Defined Key to send the memo to the printer. The computer will hold the memo in a "print queue" until the report is finished and then will begin printing the memo.

Specialized mailings are an area where professional-quality word processing improves efficiency. Sheila's next task is to send out personalized invitations to a product demonstration. She needs to send one to every account that does over $30,000 worth of business with her company. And she needs a separate list of all the accounts that do over $75,000 worth of business a year, so someone can follow up the invitation with a personal call. The demonstrations will be in three different locations on different dates, and this information has to be in each invitation.

Altogether, she needs to send nearly one hundred different invitations. Done by hand, they wouldn't get in the mail in time. Even conventional word processing would be tedious and cumbersome. But Sheila's personal computer has two features, Merge-Printing and Sorting, that can take care of the whole job in less than an hour.

Sheila already has a list of all of their customers stored on a diskette. It contains the names and addresses of hundreds of customers, information about their credit ratings, the volume of business they represent, and other key information. By preparing a Selection Specification she can have the computer search the list and generate another list of customers representing over $30,000 worth of business. Another Selection Specification can sort the customers into groups, by ZIP code, so that their invitation will be to a nearby demonstration. And the lists can be made so that customers go in order, with the highest volume of business at the top. In a few minutes, Sheila prepares four customer lists, one for each of the demonstrations, and one for the customers doing over $75,000 worth of business a year.

While the lists are being printed, Sheila begins on the invitation. She types the invitation in a special way, using a merge code for each part of the text that will change from one letter to the next. These code phrases match the labels in the customer lists. When she has finished this primary document, she is ready to print the invitations.

She selects the Merge Print option from the menu and follows the computer's messages to start printing personalized invitations for each company on the first list. Her letter-quality printer ensures that each invitation will be of the same high quality as an individually typed letter. When the invitations from the first list are finished, Sheila edits the invitation primary document to replace the city location and date with the location and date for the next presentation. Then she starts printing the invitations from the second list. For the last set of invitations, she changes the location and date again and sends that list to the printer. That's all it takes for her to print nearly 100 personalized invitation letters.

Before she goes home that afternoon, Sheila puts a special diskette into the drive of her personal computer. This diskette is for sales and prospect information from the branch office on the West Coast. It will be another three hours before their workday is over. At that time, a secretary will send the day's information to the home office over the telephone.

All Sheila has to do is leave her personal computer on and turn on the autoanswer modem that will receive calls and transfer the information to the computer. Sheila doesn't have to be in the office. Another personal computer, just like Sheila's, on the West Coast can send the information directly to Sheila's computer and have it stored on the diskette in her computer. Tomorrow when Sheila arrives at work she can scan the information and transfer it to the collective sales-and-prospects files or print it for the group's information.

INFORMATION MANAGEMENT FOR AN ENTIRE DEPARTMENT

Ellen is a manager within a marketing group that is responsible for writing all of the company's promotional literature. The business also creates a large number of internal documents—memos, studies, competitor analyses, etc. In addition, there are the forms, budgets, and schedules that are necessary for the smooth operation of the department. All of this text and the entire information flow for the department has been placed on computers, and personal computers are the first link in this communications network.

The writers, managers, and secretaries each have a personal computer on their desk. Every personal computer is connected by a communication line to a larger departmental computer that handles the tasks common to everyone—including printing, connection to the company's electronic mail system, and running complex programs that everyone uses.

The writers that work for Ellen find that personal computers add greatly to their productivity. They can compose copy at their own desks on the personal computer and store their work safely on diskettes. When a printed copy of the work is needed, they transfer a whole manuscript to the departmental computer. From there, it is routed to a high-speed printer that makes as many copies as the writer requires.

Getting printed material reviewed is just as fast. A writer sends a "copy" to the departmental computer indicating all of the people who should receive a review copy. The departmental computer forwards copies through the company's electronic mail system to each of the people named. The reviewers can edit the copy or insert comments at their own personal computer, and they can print a copy if needed. When finished with the review, the same mail system returns their comments to the writer. The departmental computer can act as the electronic file cabinet for over a million pages of literature and records. Moving copy electronically has saved an enormous amount of productive time for Ellen's writers. The review process is systematic, and the final copy much more accurate.

When the text is thoroughly reviewed and ready for production, the writers can do all the necessary paperwork in minutes on the personal computer. Each of the necessary forms is available in a special library on the department's computer. This rapid, efficient method of producing and tracking promotional literature has dramatically reduced the cost of the company's entire promotional effort.

Ellen and the other managers make extensive use of their personal computers. They can compose memos and send them anywhere in the company over the electronic mail system. This mail is delivered instantly. Going through an electronic mailbox is an easier way to deal with the paper crunch that typically greets managers and supervisors. Ellen has even instructed her secretary to search through her mail file and put the messages in order by priority. She can also display an index of the names of everyone who has sent her mail and immediately bring important correspondence onto the screen.

There are special programs contained on the managers' personal computers that do long-term and short-term schedule planning. There are programs for budgeting and graphics. The graphics programs can create bar charts, pie charts, and other business graphics.

The budgeting and scheduling programs work like the popular spreadsheet programs for executive planning. When Ellen is creating the schedule for each person in her department, the program automatically takes the writing time and document type/length information and adds it to the department's totals. Ellen can compare these totals with the department's budget and schedule printing and writing to match the deparment's resources.

The graphics programs let Ellen and the other managers take any portion of the planning spreadsheets and create graphic representations of the information. Complete reports, including the graphs, can be sent to the printer through the department's computer. The printer can print the text and the graphs in order, just as they will appear in the report. The final reports for the department are stored on the larger computer. These records are protected and can only be accessed by supervisory personnel using a password. This procedure is easier than trying to store this dynamic data in special restricted file cabinets.

The department's secretaries also share the computer network. Their personal computers have the complete word processing software that they need to do high-volume, fast turn-around correspondence. From their personal computers, they can send internal letters, memos, and announcements over the company's electronic mail system.

The secretaries also have access to a special "calendar" program that lists the appointments and meetings for everyone in the group. They can check anyone's schedule in seconds and can tentatively "pencil in" appointments for people. When people return to their desk, their personal computer will automatically display a message on the computer's message board so that they can check these new appointments.

Personal computers have made taking phone messages faster and more efficient. The secretaries can type the message onto a prepared form. After the message is taken, the computer files it in the person's "message box" on their personal computer.

Since all of these scheduling and message-taking activities have been automated, the secretaries find they have more time for other productive work. Ellen has been able to let her secretary handle several important tracking projects—something that could never have been done before, given the constant stream of interruptions. With the electronic mail system, all of the writers and supervisors can handle more of their own internal correspondence and communications. This has freed up a tremendous amount of secretarial time.

INCREASED PRODUCTIVITY FOR INDEPENDENT PROFESSIONALS

Rodger is a licensed tax consultant and accountant who works independently out of his home. He uses his personal computer to prepare tax returns and as his major tool for analyzing investment and withholding strategies for his clients.

One of Rodger's clients wants to liquidate some stock from his portfolio to provide the down payment on an investment property. The client needs to have Rodger's advice on which stocks he should sell. He also wants Rodger to consider the long-term question of how the property taxes and the taxes on the rental income will affect his investment strategy.

Before Rodger can provide this advice, he needs to check the recent activity of the stock in his client's portfolio. Setting the personal computer in terminal mode allows Rodger to dial into a New York Stock Exchange database service by telephone. His personal computer can work directly with the computer system at the other end of the line to get the information. He needs yesterday's price and volume, the year's high and low, and other vital information on each stock in his client's portfolio. This information is displayed on the screen of the personal computer and using the "Copy" feature of the computer, Rodger prints a copy of the screen display.

Next Rodger loads a program that will run an analysis on a stock portfolio. This is one of several programs he has that were especially designed for tax consultants. He enters information regarding his client's stocks, and the program does a complete analysis in a few seconds, displaying the results on the screen. The analysis shows which stocks are doing well, which are lagging, and how they all compare to each other. Rodger transfers this information to a diskette that contains his client's other financial records and has the analysis printed.

Now Rodger wants to compare several different plans for liquidating some of his client's stock. He can do this comparision best with the spreadsheet program on the personal computer. This program uses information from another diskette that contains his client's previous tax forms. Rodger set up the tax forms, which he maintains for all of his clients, using the spreadsheet program. The form already contains formulas that will calculate each line item on the return and all of the tax totals. All Rodger has to do is change the input for any given tax item, and the spreadsheet program will create a new tax return.

To do the analysis his client wants, Rodger enters the mortgage payments and the interest percentage. The program calculates the tax-deductible interest. Next he moves to the line of the return that records the capital gains. To see how each combination of stock sold will affect his client's final tax payment, he uses the split-screen capability of his personal computer to display both the capital gains portion of the form and the totals that appear at the end.

Rodger now enters the figures for the sale of various amounts of his client's stock. The spreadsheet program will compute the net gain or loss and enter the amount under capital gains. The program then follows through and recomputes the entire tax return. In just a few minutes, Rodger can do a complete analysis of how various stock sales will affect his client's bottom line — the amount of his tax. He decides upon three or four combinations of stock to sell that give reasonable results and has the personal computer print the tax return that would be associated with each one.

For the next part of the analysis Rodger copies his client's tax column several times and places them next to the current one on the spreadsheet. The computer program can make these copies without his having to retype all the labels and formulas. He will use these new columns in the spreadsheet to represent his client's returns for the next several years. Now Rodger fills in these columns with figures for the rental income, mortgage interest deductions, rough estimates of deductible business expenses, and the rest of the information that will change with his client's purchase. The spreadsheet program can compute the new tax returns as fast as Rodger can enter the changes. When he is done, he has a complete set of tax returns for the next several years. All are lined up side-by-side on the spreadsheet for easy comparison. Rodger prints these and is ready to meet with his client.

Index

* (asterisk), as wildcard, 83, 159
$. *See* Dollar signs
? (question mark), as wildcard, 83, 159

Absolute references, 237, 237(fig.), 239(fig.)
Access, 91
Access levels, 295. *See also* Security
Access points, 300
Accidents, and saving files, 142
Acoustic coupler modems, 303, 303(fig.)
Active cell, 206
Add-on boards, 23–24, 313
Addressing, 83
Administrators
  information systems managers, 323
  of networks, 295
Alignment, paragraph, 153
Alignment, text, 136–37, 137(fig.), 164, 168–69, 169(fig.)
Alphabetic keys, 28, 29(fig.)
Alt (Alternative) key, 29(fig.), 30
American National Standards Institute (ANSI) code, 14
American Standard Code for Information Interchange. *See* ASCII
ANSI (American National Standards Institute) code, 14
Answer mode, 297
Applications, 8
Applications programs, 8, 8(tab.)
  basic types of, 59
  communications programs, 58–59, 305–6, 307–8(fig.)
  database management, 57–58, 252–56, 258–61 (*see also* Database management programs)
  desktop publishing, 32, 55–56, 183–84 (*see also* Desktop publishing)
  and DOS commands, 96–97
  and drivers, 52–53
  files for, 142
  graphics, 4, 5(fig.), 58–59, 188–89 (*see also* Graphics)
  integrated, 59, 59(fig.)
  loading, 123
  and operating system, 72(fig.)
  program updates for, 60
  quitting, 124
  spreadsheets, 56–57, 197–203 (*see also* Spreadsheet programs)
  word processing, 5, 6, 55–56, 111–17 (*see also* Word processing)
ARC program, 310
Argument, 227
Arithmetical operators, 222, 222(tab.), 273
Ascending order, 278, 279(fig.)
ASCII (American Standard Code for Information Interchange), 14, 14(tab.)
  and file exchange, 146
  for special characters, 190
  and text scanners, 31
ASCII text file, 144
  displaying, 88(tab.), 95–96, 309–10
  printing, 88(tab.), 96
  transferring, 309
  uploading and downloading, 310
Asterisk (*), as wildcard, 83, 159
Audit trail, 295
Authorized user, 295
Auto-answer, 297
AUTOEXEC files, 106–7
AUTOEXEC.BAT file, 106, 107(fig.), 108, 123
Automated attendant, 313
Automatically generated lists, 193
Automatic paragraph reforming, 153, 154(fig.)
Auto-redial feature, 305
Autorepeat feature, 28
Auxiliary storage, 63. *See also* External storage

Background, 76
Backspace key, 29(fig.), 30, 136
Backtab key, 31
Backup copies, 69
  through copying and renaming, 108
Bar codes, 31
Bar graph, 245(fig.)
BASIC program, and booting, 78
Batch file, 82
Batch file commands, 88(tab.)
Beeping
  error messages, 132
  modifier key use, 31
  validity check, 267
Binary digit, 13
Binary file, 144
  transferring, 309
  uploading and downloading, 310
Binary system, 10, 10(fig.)
Binding (gutter) margin, 171, 172(fig.)
Bins, 48–49
Bin selection, 51
Bit, 13, 13(fig.)
Bit-mapped displays, 39
Bit-mapped fonts, 187
Block, 149, 155–58
Boldfaced text, 171
Boolean fields, 266
Booting the system, 77–78
Border (spreadsheet), 205
Boundary, 206
Boxes, 190–92
Broadcasting, 293
Buffers, 49, 152, 157
Bulletin boards, 297
  and viruses, 321
Bulletin board system (BBS), 299–300
Business, computers in, 7–8, 325–29. *See also* Applications programs
Business graphics, 241–45
Business graphics programs, 58, 58(fig.)
Bytes, 13–14

Calculating fields, 266
Calculation, through mathematical functions, 229, 229(fig.)
"Calendar" program, 328
Calling bulletin boards, 299–300
Calling electronic mail services, 298–99
Calling information services, 298
Caps lock key, 28
Capture program, 188

INDEX   **331**

Cards (add-on boards), 23–24, 313
Careers in information processing, 322–23
Carriage return, 135
   hard, 135–36, 152–53
   soft, 135
Cathode ray tubes (CRTs), 37, 37(fig.)
CD-ROM disk, 68
Cell address, 205–6
Cell references, absolute/relative/mixed, 236–39
Cells (spreadsheets), 199
   editing and erasing contents of, 219
   entries in, 206(tab.)
   protecting, 214
Cells (tables), 138
Centered text, 169
Centralized information processing, 291–92
   and security, 318
Central processing unit (CPU), 19–20
Centronics interfaces, 22
Character(s)
   legal, 82
   special, 39, 190, 191, 191(fig.)
Character displays, 39, 39(fig.)
Character fields, 266
Character set, 39
Character spacing, 186
Chat mode, 299
Checks, validity, 267
Chips, 13, 13(fig.)
   IBM microprocessor, 20
CHKDSK command, 88(tab.), 94–95
   /F parameter, 88(tab.), 95
   /V parameter, 88(tab.), 95
Christianson, Ward, 310
Clearing the screen, 88(tab.), 116, 203
Clip-art files, 188
Clipboard, 49. *See* Buffer
Clock, 78, 79
   and header/footer date and time, 175
Closed (paired) codes, 165–66
Cluster, 94
Code, 11
   digital, 11–13
Codes (computer language), 144, 165
   control, 151, 156
   hidden, 144(fig.), 151, 152(fig.)
   merge, 179
   open, 165, 165(fig.)
   paired, 165–66
   stop, 186, 187
Cold boot, 77
Collation, 51–52
Color displays, 38
Color graphics adapter (CGA), 40
Column (spreadsheet), 198
Column mode, 155–56
Columns
   inserting and deleting, 220
   newspaper-style, 192, 192(fig.)
   parallel-style, 192, 193(fig.)
Command, 62
   executing, 126–32
   external, 87
   global, 216
   internal, 87
   range, 216–17
Command processor, 73
Command prompt, 74, 74(fig.), 78
   changing, 88(tab.)
Comment fields, 267
Communication, 7, 7(fig.)
Communications applications

communications programs, 305–6, 307–8(fig.)
   facsimile machines, 312–13
   local area networks, 290, 291–96
   telecommunications equipment, 302–4
   transferring files, 309–10
   voice mail, 313
   wide area networks, 290, 297–300
Communications network, departmental, 327
Communications programs, 58–59, 305–6, 307–8(fig.)
Communications protocol, 310
Comparing disks, 88(tab.), 93
Compound statements, 275
Compressing, 310
CompuServe, 297, 298
CompuServe B, 310
CompuServe Information Manager, 59(fig.), 306, 308(fig.)
Computer(s)
   caring for, 24–25
   development of, 24
   as hardware, 2, 2(fig.)
   and health, 315–16
   software for, 3, 3(fig.) (*see also* Applications programs; Operating system; Programs)
   turning off, 25
   types of, 17–19
   in workplace, 325–29
Computer mail, 4. *See also* Electronic mail
Computer viruses, 319, 320(fig.), 321
Conditional page break, 167
CONFIG.SYS files, 106, 106(tab.), 108
Configuration file, 106
Constants, 224–25
Consultants, 323
Context sensitive system, 126
Continuous data, 243–44, 244(fig.)
Continuous form paper, 48, 49(fig.)
Control area, 208(fig.)
Control code, 151, 156
Control (modifier) keys, 30–31, 118, 127
Conversion of files, 144, 146–47
COPY command, 91
   vs. DISKCOPY, 92
COPY CON command, 108
Copying, 234
   block, 156–57
   data (spreadsheet), 234, 234(fig.), 235(fig.)
   files, 88(tab.), 91, 92
Copy protection, 319
Correcting mistakes
   deleting characters, 136
   Undo command, 152
CPU (central processing unit), 19–20
Crash, head, 66. *See also* Park program
Criteria, 273–74
   and operators, 274–76
Crosstalk, 306, 307(fig.)
CRTs (cathode ray tubes), 37, 37(fig.)
Ctrl (Control) key, 29(fig.), 30
Cursor, 30, 113, 117, 117(fig.)
   pointing, 225, 225–26(fig.)
   positioning, 134
Cursor movement, 149
   spreadsheet, 206–7
Cursor movement keys, 30
Customizing, expansion slots for, 23–24
Cutting, 76

Daisy wheel printer, 43, 44, 44(fig.)
Data, 5, 5(fig.)
Database, 57, 253
   defining, 253–54, 265–67
   organization of, 264–65
Database files, 142
Database management, 252–56
   defining database, 253–54, 264–67
   displaying records, 273–76
   entering and updating records, 254–55, 255(fig.), 269–72
   making new databases, 287, 287(fig.)
   printing reports, 256, 256(fig.), 284–85
   sorting and indexing records, 278–82
Database management programs, 57–58, 253, 258–61
   dBASE, 261, 261(fig.)
   Microsoft Works, 262, 263(fig.)
   spreadsheets, 261, 262(fig.)
   WordPerfect, 262, 263(fig.)
Data file, 142
Data processing (DP), 5, 6
Data processing departments, 291, 291(fig.)
Data range, 241
Data set, 241
DATE command, 88(tab.)
Date fields, 267
Date functions, 229–30, 230(fig.)
Dates, entering, 79
Da Vinci eMAIL, 294(fig.)
dBASE, 261, 261(fig.)
   screen, 254(fig.)
DBMS, 259. *See also* Database management programs
Decentralized information processing, 292
Decimal system, 10, 10(tab.)
Decimal tabs, 137–38
   with hanging indents, 139(fig.)
Default directories
   changing, 100–101
   indicating, 101
Default drive, 83
   changing, 83, 84(fig.), 88(tab.)
Default format settings, 114, 164–65
DELETE command, 93
Deleting. *See also* Erasing
   block, 157
   characters, 113, 136, 152
   files (unneeded), 145
   records, 272
   rows and columns, 220
Delimiter, 180
Density(ies) of disk, 89
Descending order, 278, 279(fig.)
Desktop computers, 17, 18(fig.)
Desktop publishing, 32, 55–56, 183–84
   fonts, 184–87
   graphic images, 188–89
   Word for Windows, 120–21
Destination range, 234
Destructive backspace, 30, 136
Dialing directories, 305
Dialog boxes, 130, 131(fig.)
Dictionary, spelling checker, 160
Digital processing, 10
Digital revolution, 10–13
Digital signal, 11
DIR commands, 90
   /P parameter, 90
   /W parameter, 90
Direct access, 281
Direct-connect modems, 303–4

Directional arrow keys, 28, 29(fig.), 30
Directories, 99, 100(fig.), 101(fig.)
 listing, 104
 making and changing, 88(tab.), 103–4
 organizing work in, 104
 and paths, 102–3
 removing, 104
Discrete data, 243, 244(fig.)
Disk-based data files, 269
DISKCOMP command, 92–93
DISKCOPY command, 92
Disk drives, 2(fig.)
Disk operating system. *See* DOS
Disks, 62
 checking, 88(tab.), 94–95
 comparing, 88(tab.), 93
 duplicating, 88(tab.), 92
 floppy, 63–66 (*see also* Floppy disks)
 formatting, 87, 88(tab.), 90, 146
 hard disk drives, 66, 99 (*see also* Hard disk drives)
 protecting and caring for, 68–70
Displaying
 ASCII files, 88(tab.), 95–96, 309–10
 file lists, 88(tab.)
 hidden characters and codes, 144(fig.), 151, 152(fig.)
 records, 273–76
Display screen. *See* Screen, display
Distribution, 7, 7(fig.)
Distribution devices, 2(fig.)
Document(s), 111
 editing, 113, 114(fig.), 149–61
 entering, 113, 113(fig.), 134
 formatting, 114, 114(fig.), 164–75
 naming, 112
 opening, 112
 printing, 115, 115(fig.)
 retrieving, 113
 saving, 115
Document compare feature, 160–61
Document files, 142
Document-oriented program, 151
Document preview, 51, 52(fig.)
Document screen, 112(fig.), 117, 117(fig.)
Dollar signs ($)
 for absolute references, 237, 238
 aligning, 137
DOS (disk operating system), 72, 74
 quitting, 80
 use of from applications programs, 96–97
DOS command prompt commands, 88(tab.)
DOS files, special, 106–8
DOS 4 Shell, 74(fig.), 78, 79–80
DOS version number, displaying of, 88(tab.)
Dot-matrix impact printers, 45, 46(fig.)
Dot-matrix printers, 44–45
 character formation, 43(fig.)
 and font change, 186
Double-density disk, 89
Double-sided disk, 89
Downloadable font, 186, 187
Downloading, 309, 310
Drive
 default, 83, 84(fig.), 88(tab.)
 specifying, 84(fig.), 85
Driver, 52–53
Dumb terminals, 291–92
Duplex printing, 47
Duplicating, of disks, 88(tab.), 92
Dvorak keyboard, 28
Dynamic page display, 167

EBDIC (Extended Binary Coded Decimal Interchange Code), 14
Editing
 document, 113, 114(fig.), 149–61
 models, 219–20
Editing checks, 267
Edit (document) screen, 112(fig.), 117, 117(fig.)
Electrical circuits, logical operators compared to, 276, 276(fig.)
Electronic mail (E-mail), 59, 59(fig.), 292–94
Electronic mail services, 297, 298–99
Electronic supervisor, 320
Electrostatic printers, 47
Embedded numbers, 225
Emphasis, text, 170–71
Emulation, 53
Encrypted messages, 294
Encryption program, 319
Endnotes, 175, 175(fig.)
Enhanced color graphics adapter (EGA), 40–41
ENIAC, 24
Enter (Return) key, 29(fig.), 29–30
Entering
 dates and times, 79
 document, 113, 113(fig.), 134
 formulas, 225, 226(fig.)
 labels (spreadsheet), 213–14
 text to left of left margin, 171, 173, 173(fig.)
Enumerations, 139
ERASE command, 93
Erasing. *See also* Deleting
 cell contents, 219
 files, 88(tab.), 93
Ergonomics, 315–16
Error messages, 77–78, 132
Esc (Escape) key, 29(fig.), 30
Ethical issues, 318–21
Excel. *See* Microsoft Excel
Exchange of files, 144, 146–47
Expansion slot, 23–24
Extended Binary Coded Decimal Interchange Code (EBCDIC), 14
Extensions, filename, 82, 144
 .ASC, 144
 .BAT, 82
 .COM, 82, 309
 .DOC, 144
 .EXE, 82, 309
 .PCX, 189
 .PRN, 146
 .PRT, 146
 .TIF, 189
 .TXT, 144
External commands, 87
External storage devices, 2(fig.), 63, 63(fig.)
 floppy disks and disk drives, 63–66 (*see also* Floppy disks)
 hard disk drives, 66 (*see also* Hard disk drives)
 optical disks, 66–68

Facsimile (fax) machines, 312–13
Fanfold paper, 48
Field, 179–80, 254, 254(fig.), 264
 lengths, 267
 names, 265, 266(fig.)
 types, 266–67

File(s), 63, 142
 checking, 94–95
 copying, 88(tab.), 91, 92
 displaying lists of, 88(tab.)
 erasing, 88(tab.), 93
 indexing, 280–82
 listing of, 90, 104
 naming, 88(tab.)
 protecting and caring for, 68–70
 renaming, 88(tab.), 94
 retrieving, 142–43, 143(fig.)
 saving, 112, 142, 143(fig.), 203
 scattered storage of, 94–95
 sharing, 294–95
 sorting, 252, 278–80
 temporary, 123, 124
 transferring, 309–10
File compression, 33
File conversion, 144, 146–47
File drawer, hard disk compared to, 99(fig.), 100(fig.)
File exchange, 144, 146–47
File locking, 295
File management, 145, 258
Filenames, 82–83
 system for, 145
File recovery program, 93
File types, 143–44, 146
Financial analysis, and spreadsheets, 56–57. *See also* Spreadsheet programs
Financial functions, 228, 228(fig.)
Fixed disks, 66. *See also* Hard disk drives
Fixed pitch, 186, 186(fig.)
Flagged record, 272
Flat file programs, 258
Flat-panel displays, 37, 38(fig.)
Floppy disk drives, 64, 65(fig.)
 care of, 70
Floppy disks, 63–66. *See also* Disks
 backing up, 69
 caring for, 69, 70, 124
 formatting, 87, 88(tab.), 90
 inserting, 65–66
 labeling, 68
 loading programs from, 123
 selecting, 89
Flush left alignment, 169
Flush right alignment, 169
Font cartridge, 186, 187, 187(fig.)
Fonts, 48, 48(fig.), 184–87
 printer settings for, 50
Footers, 173–75
Footnotes, 175, 175(fig.)
Foreground, 76
Format (report), 285
Format (spreadsheets), 199
 as cell entry, 206(tab.)
 changing, 232, 233(fig.)
 global, 216, 232, 233(fig.)
Format (word processing), 111
 and style sheets, 189–90
Format codes, 151. *See also* Control code
FORMAT command, 87
 FORMAT/S, 87
Format line, 165
Formatted disk, 89
Formatting
 of blocks, 157–58
 codes for, 144 (*see also* Codes)
 of disks, 87, 88(tab.), 90, 146
 of documents, 114, 114(fig.), 164–75
Form documents, 111
Formulas, 200, 200(fig.), 222–26
 as cell entries, 206(tab.)

INDEX   333

Form view, 269–70, 270(fig.)
Full-page displays, 37, 38(fig.)
Fully formed character printer, 43, 45
Function keys, 29(fig.), 30, 126–28
Function name, 227
Functions, 200–201, 201(fig.), 227–30
　as cell entries, 206(tab.)

Gigabyte, 15, 15(tab.)
Global command, 216
Global format, 216, 232, 233(fig.)
Global Search and Replace, 159
Glossaries, 139–40. *See also* Macros
Graphical operating system environments
　(graphical user interfaces, GUIs),
　75–76
Graphic displays, 39–41
Graphics, 4, 5(fig.), 188–89
　with character displays, 39
　combined with text, 188(fig.)
　by dot-matrix printers, 44
　Quattro Pro, 210(fig.)
　standards, 189
Graphics processing, 6, 6(fig.)
Graphics programs, 58–59
Graphics scanners, 32–33
Graphic user interface (GUI), 40
Graphs, 197, 241, 243(fig.)
　business, 58(fig.)
　creating, 241–43
　types of, 243–44, 244–45(fig.)
Gray scale, 32, 33(fig.)
Gutter margins, 171, 172(fig.)

Handheld computers, 17, 19(fig.)
Hanging indent, 139, 139(fig.)
Hard carriage return, 135–36
　deleting, 152–53
Hard disk drives (fixed disks; Winchester
　disk drives), 66, 66(fig.), 99. *See also*
　Disks
　care of, 69
　directories, 88(tab.), 99–104
　formatting, 87, 90
　loading programs on, 123–24
　tolerances of, 66, 67(fig.)
Hard page break, 167
Hardware, 2, 2(fig.)
Hard-wired computers, 297
Hayes compatible modems, 305
Head crash, 66. *See also* Park program
Headers, 173–75
Health, and computer use, 315–16
Help key, 126
Help screen, 126(fig.)
Hidden codes, 144(fig.)
　displaying, 144(fig.), 151, 152(fig.)
High-density disks, 89
Horizontal layout, 171–72
Host computer, 297
Hyphen, soft, 170
Hyphenation, 170
Hyphenation zone, 170, 170(fig.)

IBM character set, 39, 191, 191(fig.)
IBM microprocessor chips, 20
Image digitizers, 32
Impact printers, 45
Indent, 114, 139, 139(fig.)
　hanging, 139, 139(fig.)
Indexes, 193
Indexing files, 280–82
Information management, for entire
　department, 327–28

Information processing, 4–6, 6(fig.)
　careers in, 322–23
　cycle of, 7, 7(fig.)
Information services, 297
Information systems (IS) department, 291
Information systems managers, 323
Ink-jet printers, 47
Input devices, 28–34
Input/output (I/O) manager, 73
Insert mode, 151
Insert-off, 151. *See also* Typeover mode
Installation program, 52
Installing, 52
Integrated circuit (IC), 13
Integrated programs, 59, 59(fig.)
　database management programs in,
　57–58
Integrated Services Digital Network
　(ISDN), 303
Interactive graphics programs, 58
Interface, 62
　shells, 74, 74(fig.), 78, 79–80
Internal commands, 87
Internal fonts, 186, 187
Internal memory, 20
Interpolation, 244
Interpreter, operating system as, 73,
　73(fig.)
Italics, 129

Joining
　databases, 287, 287(fig.)
　lines of text, 152–53
Justified text, 169

Kermit, 310
Kerning, 186
Keyboard, 2(fig.), 28–31
Keyboarding, 134
Keyboard template, 127–28
Key field, 265
　primary, 278, 278(fig.)
　secondary, 279, 279(fig.)
Keyword, 248
Kilobyte, 15, 15(tab.)

Label (disks), 145
Label (spreadsheet), 198, 199, 199(fig.),
　206(tab.)
　entering, 213–14
Labeling disks, 68
Label prefix, 213
Landscape mode, 186, 187, 187(fig.)
Laptop computers, 17, 19(fig.)
Laser printer, 46–47, 47(fig.), 111
　and boldfacing, 171
　and font change, 186
　and typestyles, 185
Layout, horizontal, 171–72
Layout, vertical, 172–73, 174
Leading, 184
Learn mode, 248
LED printers, 47
Left alignment, 137, 137(fig.), 169
Left margin. *See* Margin, left
Legal characters, 82
Levels of access, 295
Levels of data organization, 264, 264(fig.)
Library, 139
License, 319
Line(s), ruled, 138
Line blocks, 155, 155(fig.)
Line drawing, 58(fig.), 190–92
Line graph, 244(fig.)

Line length, 164
Line spacing, 173, 173(fig.)
Lines per page, 173
Linking, 287
Link protocols, 310
Listing
　of directories, 104
　of files, 90, 104
Lists, automatically-generated, 193
List view, of database, 269, 269(fig.)
Loading program, 112, 123–24
Local area network (LAN), 290, 291–96
Logging on, 295
Logical fields, 266
Logical operators, 275–76, 276(fig.)
Losing data, and warm boot, 77
Lotus 1-2-3, 207–8
　date functions, 229
　editing, 219
　entering formulas, 225–26(fig.)
　formula conversion in, 220
　pause command, 249
　and Quattro Pro, 210(fig.)
　range selection, 217

Macro language, 248
Macros, 207, 248–49. *See also* Glossaries
Magnets, and floppy disks, 70
Main document, 178
Mainframe computers, 17, 17(fig.)
Main memory, 21
Main menu, 112, 129, 130(fig.)
Management information systems (MIS),
　291
Margin, bottom and top, 164
Margin, left, 164, 171, 172(fig.)
　entering text to left of, 171, 173(fig.)
Margin, right, 164, 171, 172(fig.)
Master document, 178. *See also* Primary
　document
Mathematical functions, 229, 229(fig.)
MCI Mail, 297, 298–99
MD command, 103
Megabyte, 15, 15(tab.)
Memo fields, 267
Memory
　internal, 20
　nonvolatile, 20
　of printer, 48
　random-access (RAM), 21, 21(fig.)
　read-only (ROM), 20–21
　volatile, 21
Memory-based data files, 269
Menu(s), 117, 128–29
　main, 112, 129, 130(fig.)
　multilevel, 128, 128(fig.)
　pull-down, 118–19
　sticky, 129
　user-defined, 249, 249(fig.)
Menu bar, 118
Menu pointer, 128, 208
Menu tree, 129, 129(fig.)
Merge document, 178. *See also* Primary
　document
Merge printing, 178–80, 181(fig.)
Message, 117
Message Handling Service (MHS), 294
Microcomputer, 2(fig.)
　local area networks, 290, 291–96
　wide area networks, 290, 297–300
Microcomputer specialists, 323
Microprocessor, 19, 20(fig.)
Microsoft Excel, 208, 209(fig.)
　editing, 219

334　INDEX

Microsoft Excel *(cont.)*
  range selection, 217
  typing in formulas, 225
Microsoft's Bookshelf CD-ROM Reference Library, 68
Microsoft Windows, 75(fig.)
Microsoft Word, 39(fig.), 119–20
  codes, 144(fig.)
Microsoft Works, 59(fig.), 121, 121(fig.), 211, 211(fig.), 262, 263(fig.)
  main menu of, 130(fig.)
  telecommunications program, 306, 307(fig.)
Minicomputers, 17, 18(fig.)
Misspelling
  and Search/Replace, 158–59
  and Spelling checker, 160
Mistakes, correcting, 152
  character deletion, 136, 152
  file recovery programs, 93
  Undo command, 152
Mixed references, 238, 238(fig.)
MKDIR (MD) command, 103
Mode, 117
Model, 198
  editing, 219–20
  printout of, 225
Modems, 2(fig.), 302
  acoustic coupler, 303, 303(fig.)
  auto-answer, 297
  communications program with, 305–6, 307–8(fig.)
  direct-connect, 303–4
  and serial ports, 22, 22(fig.), 23(fig.)
Modifier (control) keys, 30–31, 118, 127
Monitor. *See* Screen, display
Monitoring, electronic, 320
Monochrome screens, 38
Moral issues, 318–21
Mouse, 131–32
  clicking, 132
  and cursor movement, 149–50
  double-clicking, 132
  dragging, 132, 132(fig.)
  pointing, 132
  selecting with, 156
Mouse pointer, 131
Moving, 234
  block, 157, 157(fig.)
  data (spreadsheet), 234–36
MS-DOS, 74. *See also* DOS
Multitasking, 76

Naming documents, 112
Navigation programs, 306, 308(fig.)
Network(s), 2(fig.)
  and loading, 123
  local area, 290, 291–96
  wide area, 290, 297–300
Network manager, 295
Network operating system, 58–59
Newspaper-style columns, 192, 192(fig.)
Nodes, 300
Nonimpact printers, 46
Nonvolatile memory, 20
Notebook computers, 17, 19(fig.)
Null-modem cable, 297
Number of lines, 164
Numbers, alignment of, 137–38
Numeric fields, 266
Numeric keypad, 28–29
Numeric and mathematical functions, 229, 229(fig.)

Num Lock key, 29, 29(fig.)

Open codes, 165, 165(fig.)
Opening document, 112
Operating system, 72–73. *See also* DOS
  booting, 77–78
  and file exchange, 146
Operator
  arithmetical, 222, 222(tab.), 273
  logical, 275–76, 276(fig.)
  relational, 274, 274–75(tab.)
Operators (personnel)
  computer, 323
  data entry, 322
  word processing, 322
Optical character recognition (OCR) devices, 31, 32(fig.)
Optical disks, 66–68
Order of operations, 223, 223(fig.)
Originator positions, 322
Orphan, 167–68
Outdent, 139
Outdial (service), 300
Output, 7
Output devices, 2(fig.), 37
  display, 37–41
  printer, 43–53
Overtype, 151. *See also* Typeover mode
Overwriting, 82

Packet-switching networks, 300
Packing, 272
Page breaks, 166–67
  conditional, 167
  hard, 167
  soft, 167
Page length, 164, 173
Page numbers, 164, 168–69
Page-oriented program, 151
Page printer, 46
Paint programs, 58
Paired (closed) codes, 165–66
Paper, for printers, 48
Paper clips, and floppy disks, 70
Paradox (program), 260
Paragraph aligning, 153
Paragraph reforming, automatic, 153, 154(fig.)
Parallel port, 22, 23(fig.)
Parallel-style columns, 192, 193(fig.)
Parameter, 87
Park program, 69
Passwords, 295, 318
  and auto-answer modem, 297
  and saved sequences, 305
Pasting, 157
Path, 102, 102(fig.)
  specifying, 102–3
PATH command, 106–7, 124
PC-DOS, 74. *See also* DOS
PC PaintBrush files, 189
PC Pursuit, 300
Peripherals, 2, 2(fig.)
  and local area network, 292
  ports for, 22, 23(fig.)
PgDn key, 29(fig.), 30
PgUp key, 29(fig.), 30
Phone messages, 313, 328
Photographic images, and dot-matrix printers, 44
Phrase storage area, 139
Picture files, 142
Pie chart, 245(fig.)
Pin feed, 48

Piracy, 319
Pitch, 38, 185, 185(fig.)
Pixels, 32, 40, 40(fig.)
Points (type), 185–86
Portable computers, 17, 19(fig.)
  and flat-panel displays, 37
Portrait mode, 186, 187(fig.)
Ports, 22, 23(fig.)
Ports (access points), 300
Precedence, 223
Primary document, 178, 179(fig.)
Primary keys, 278, 278(fig.)
Primary memory, 21
PRINT command, 96
Printer control codes, 151. *See also* Control code
Printers, 2(fig.), 43–53
  accessories, 48–49
  speed, 48
Print file, 144, 146
Printing, 7, 49–50
  ASCII file, 88(tab.), 96
  in columns, 192–93
  document, 115, 115(fig.)
  font change, 186
  options, 51–52
  page numbers, 164
  of print files, 96
  print queue, 50–51
  and proportional spacing, 136–37
  reports, 256, 257(fig.), 284–85
  of screen display, 80
Print queue, 50–51
Print wheel, 43
Private wide area networks, 297
Processor positions, 322
PROCOMM PLUS, 306
Prodigy service, 298
Productivity, and independent professionals, 328
Professional word processing, 325–27
Programmers, 28, 323
Programming, 3
Programs, 3, 3(fig.)
  applications, 8, 8(tab.) (*see also* Applications programs)
  loading, 112, 123–24
  sharing, 294–95
Program updates, 60
Prompt, 117
  command, 74, 74(fig.), 78, 88(tab.)
  in word processing, 129–30
PROMPT PG command, 101, 107
Proportional spacing, 136–37, 186, 186(fig.)
Protecting cells, 214
Protocol, communications, 310
Public Brand Software, 299, 299(fig.)
Public Switched Telephone Network (PSTN), 297
Pull-down menus, 118–19

Quattro Pro, 209–11
Query, 256, 256(fig.)
Query by example (QBE), 273
Query languages, 273
Question mark (?), as wildcard, 83, 159
Quick reference card, 126
Quitting
  DOS, 80
  program, 78, 115, 116, 124
QWERTY keyboard, 28

INDEX **335**

Ragged left alignment, 169
Ragged right alignment, 169
Random-access memory (RAM), 21, 21(fig.)
Range, 216
　copying, 234, 234(fig.), 235(fig.)
　and deletion, 220
　moving, 234–36
　selecting, 217
Range commands, 216–17
Range name, 217
Read-only file, 295
Read-only memory (ROM), 20–21
Read/write slot, 64
Record(s), 180, 254, 254(fig.), 264–65
　displaying, 273–76
　entering, 269–70
　updating, 270–72
Record files, 142
Record locking, 295
Record management programs, 258, 258(fig.)
Record mode, 248
Recovering erased files, 93
Redlining, 161
Reference card, 126
Relational database, 259, 260(fig.)
Relational operators, 274, 274–75(tab.)
Relative references, 236–37, 237(fig.), 239(fig.)
RENAME command, 94
Renaming files, 88(tab.), 94
Repagination, 153, 154(fig.)
Repeating label, 214
Replacing text, 151. *See also* Search and replace
Report, 256, 257(fig.)
Report format, 285
Resolution, 40, 41(fig.)
Retrieving files, 142–43, 143(fig.)
　ASCII text files, 147
　documents, 113
　in information processing cycle, 7, 7(fig.)
　spreadsheet, 203
Return. *See* Carriage return
Return key, 29(fig.), 29–30
Revere, Paul, digital message to, 11, 12(fig.)
Reverse indent, 139
Reverse video, 30, 113
Revisable-form-text (RFT), 146
Ribbons, 48
Right alignment, 137, 137(fig.), 169
Right margin, 164, 171, 172(fig.)
Root directory, 99, 101
Row, 198
　inserting and deleting, 220
RS-232-C ports, 22
Ruler line, 117
Running feet, 174
Running heads, 174

Sales personnel, 323
Saving files, 112, 142, 143(fig.)
　ASCII text files, 147
　and clearing, 203
　document, 115
　and name assignment, 82
　and quitting, 116
　and spreadsheet deletions, 220
Scalable fonts, 187

Scanners
　graphics, 32–33, 188
　text, 31–32
Scrabble, computer memory compared to, 21(fig.)
Scrapbook (scrap), 49. *See also* Buffers
Screen, display, 2(fig.), 37–41
　caring for, 24
　clearing, 88(tab.), 116, 203
　and computer strain, 315, 316
　printing of display from, 80
　spreadsheet display, 205–6, 207(fig.)
Script languages, 305–6
Scrolling, 134, 134(fig.), 149–51
　stopping, 95
Scroll Lock, 207
Search and replace, 158–59
　global, 159
Secondary document, 178, 179–80
Secondary keys, 279, 279(fig.)
Secondary storage, 63. *See also* External storage devices
Sector, 89, 95(fig.)
Security, 295, 318–19
Selecting, 156
　block, 156
Sequential files, 280–81
Serial numbers, 229, 230(fig.)
Serial port, 22, 23(fig.)
Setup program, 52
Sharing files and programs, 294–95
Sheet feeder, 48–49
Shell, 74
　DOS 4, 74(fig.), 78, 79–80
Shell document, 178
Shift key, 28
Shorthand, for number of bytes, 15
Shutter, 64
Signal, digital, 11
Single-density disk, 89
Single-sided disk, 89
Site license, 319
Sneaker net, 296
Soft carriage return, 135
Soft fonts, 186
Soft hyphen, 170
Soft page break, 167
Software, 3, 3(fig.). *See also* Programs
　applications programs, 8, 8(tab.) (*see also* Applications programs)
　theft of, 319
Sorting, 252, 278–80
Source disk, 91
Source range, 234
Spacebar, 29(fig.), 30
　and text alignment, 136
　in typeover mode, 151
Spacing, character, 186
Spacing, line, 173, 173(fig.)
Special characters, 39, 190, 191, 191(fig.)
Specialist positions, 323
Spelling checkers, 160
Spreadsheet, 56–57, 198
Spreadsheet programs, 56–57, 197–203
　business graphics, 241–45
　changing model appearance, 232, 233(fig.)
　copying and moving data, 234–39
　cursor movement, 206–7
　database management, 261, 262(fig.)
　editing models, 219–20
　entering labels and numbers, 213–14
　formulas, 222–26
　functions, 227–30

　Lotus 1-2-3, 207–8 (*see also* Lotus 1-2-3)
　and macros, 248–49
　Microsoft Excel, 208, 209(fig.) (*see also* Microsoft Excel)
　Microsoft Works, 211, 211 (fig.), 262 (*see also* Microsoft Works)
　protecting cells, 214
　Quattro Pro, 209–11
　ranges, 216–17
　screen display, 205–6, 207(fig.)
　tax consultant's use of, 329
Stacked-bar graph, 245(fig.)
Standalone microcomputer, 292
Standalone programs, 59
Startup drive, 77
Static electricity, and floppy disks, 70
Statistical functions, 228, 229(fig.)
Status line, 117
Sticky menu, 129
Stop codes, 186, 187
Storage, 7, 7(fig.)
Storage devices, external, 2(fig.), 63–68
Store and forward ability, 293–94
Storing of files, in scattered sectors, 94–95
Strikeout, 161
Strikeover mode, 151. *See also* Typeover mode
String, 158
Style sheets, 189–90
Subdirectory, 99, 100, 101
Submenus, 128
Subscript, 171, 171(fig.)
Superscript, 171(fig.)
Supervisor, electronic, 320
Surge protector, 24–25
Switches, 293(fig.)
Syntax, 227
System, 2
System disk, 87
System operator (SYSOP), 299
Systems analysts, 323

Tab key, 31
Table of contents, 193, 194(fig.)
Tables, 138–39
　and page breaks, 166
Tab ruler, 117
Tab stops, 136–37
　decimal, 137–38
　indents, 139
Tagged-image-file-format (TIFF), 189
Tags, 189
TAPCIS, 306, 308(fig.)
Target disk/drive, 91
Target range, 234
Tax consultant, and computers, 328–29
Technical support people, 323
Technical writers, 323
Telecommunication, 304
Telecommunications equipment, 302–4
Teleconference, 298
Telegraph, as digital code, 11–12
TeleNet, 300
Telephone messages, 313, 328
Template (keyboard), 127–28
Template (spreadsheets), 198
Temporary files, 123, 124
Text alignment, 136–37, 137(fig.), 164, 168–69, 169(fig.)
Text area, 117
Text capture, 309

Text emphasis, 170–71
Text fields, 266
Text scanners, 31
Theft of software, 319
Thermal printers, 47–48
Thesaurus, 160
Thimbles, 43, 44, 44(fig.)
Time, entering, 79
TIME command, 88(tab.)
Time fields, 267
Time functions, 229–30, 230(fig.)
Time-series graphs, 243
Toggling, 28, 29
Toner, 48
Tracks, 89
Tracks per inch (TPI), 89
Tractor feed, 48
Trainers, 323
Transferring files, 309–10
Transistor, 13, 13(fig.)
Transpose command, 235(fig.)
Tree, menu, 129, 129(fig.)
TREE command, 104
Trends, graphing of, 242(fig.)
Trojan horse, 319
Tymnet, 300
TYPE command, 95
Typefaces, 184–85
Typeover mode, 151
Type size, 185–86
Typestyles, 185

Uncompressing, 310
Underlining (underscoring), 171
Undo command, 152
Updates (upgrades), 60
Updating records, 270–72
Uploading, 309, 310
User-defined menus, 249, 249(fig.)
User memory, 21
Utility programs, 87

Validity checks, 267
Value(s), 198
  formatting, 232, 233(fig.)
  vs. labels, 213
Variables (merge printing), 178
Variables (spreadsheets), 224–25
VER command, 88(tab.)
Vertical layout, 172–73, 174(fig.)
Video display, 37. *See also* Screen, display
Video graphics array (VGA), 41
Viruses, 319, 320(fig.), 321
Voice input devices, 33–34, 34(fig.)
Voice mail, 313
Voice template, 34
Volatile memory, 21

Warm boot, 77
What-ifs, 197, 200, 200–201(fig.), 224
Wide area network, 290, 297–300
Widow, 167–68
Wildcard, 83
  with ERASE command, 93
  and Search and Replace command, 158, 159
Winchester disk drives, 66. *See also* Hard disk drives
Windows, 76
  in Microsoft Word, 119(fig.)
Word (Microsoft), 39(fig.), 119–20, 144(fig.)
WordPerfect, 118–19, 262, 263(fig.)
  keyboard template, 127(fig.)
  releases, 60
  tables, 138(fig.)
Word processing, 5, 5(fig.), 6, 111–17
  carriage returns, 135–36
  correcting mistakes, 136
  and desktop publishing, 183
  editing documents, 113, 114(fig.), 149–61
  entering documents, 113, 113(fig.), 134
  executing commands, 126–32
  file exchange, 144, 146–47

file exchange, 144, 146–47
file management, 145
file types, 143–44, 146
fonts, 184–87
formatting documents, 114, 164–75
glossaries, 139–40
loading programs, 112, 123–24
menus, 128–29
merge printing, 178–81
printing, 115, 115(fig.) (*see also* Printers; Printing)
professional, 325–27
quitting programs, 124
retrieving files, 113, 142–43, 143(fig.), 147
saving files, 115, 142, 143(fig.) (*see also* Saving files)
tables, 138–39
tab stops, 136–38
word wrap, 135, 135(fig.)
Word processing programs, 55–56
  document- vs. page-oriented, 151
  Microsoft Word, 39(fig.), 119–20, 144(fig.)
  Microsoft Works, 121, 121(fig.), 262 (*see also* Microsoft Works)
  WordPerfect, 118–19, 262 (*see also* WordPerfect)
  Word for Windows, 120–21
Word for Windows, 120–21
Word wrap, 135, 135(fig.)
Working area, 205, 205(fig.), 208(fig.)
Workplace, computers in, 315–16, 325–29
Worksheet files, 142
Write-protecting of disks, 64, 68, 69(fig.)
Write-protect notch, 64
Write-protect window, 64
WYSIWYG (what you see is what you get), 120, 120(fig.), 183

XMODEM, 310

YMODEM, 310

Company Trademarks
Adobe Illustrator and PageMaker are trademarks of Aldus Corporation. Apple and Apple II are registered trademarks of Apple Computer, Inc. AT&T Bell Laboratories is a registered trademark of AT&T. CompuServe is a registered trademark of CompuServe, Inc. dBASE is a registered trademark of Ashton-Tate Corp. Crosstalk is an original trademark of DCA, Inc. DaVinci eMAIL is a copyright of DaVinci Systems Corp. Epson LQ-1000 is a registered trademark of Epson America. Fujitsu is a registered trademark. The Genius is a registered trademark of Genius Technologies, Inc. Hewlett-Packard is a registered trademark. IBM PC, XT, AT, PS/2, and PC-DOS are registered trademarks of International Business Machines Corporation. IntroVoice III is a registered trademark of the Voice Connection. Lotus 1-2-3 is a registered trademark of Lotus Development Corp. MCI Mail is a registered trademark of MCI Telecommunications Corp. Microsoft Word, MS-DOS, Windows, and Excel are registered trademarks of Microsoft Corp. Word for Windows and Works are trademarks of Microsoft Corp. PC Scan and PC Scan PLUS are registered trademarks of Dest. PFC is a registered trademark of Software Publishers. ProComm PLUS is a trademark of Datastorm Technologies, Inc. Prodigy is a registered service mark and trademark of Prodigy Services Co. Public Brand Software and PBS-BBS are trademarks of Public Brand Software Inc. Quattro Pro is a registered trademark of Borland International. Qume is a registered trademark. Spinwriter is produced by NEC Technologies. ST225 is a registered trademark of Seagate Technology. Tandy Acoustic Coupler Modem is a registered trademark of Radio Shack, a division of Tandy Corp. The Twin is a registered trademark of Mosaic Software. U.S. Robotics is a registered trademark. Ventura Publisher is a registered trademark of Xerox Corporation. VP Planner is a registered trademark of Paperback Software. WordPerfect is a registered trademark of WordPerfect, Inc. WordStar is a registered trademark of MicroPro International Corp.